The Lakes of Pontchartrain

The Lakes of

Robert W. Hastings

Pontchartrain

THEIR HISTORY AND ENVIRONMENTS

UNIVERSITY PRESS OF MISSISSIPPI / JACKSON

www.upress.state.ms.us

The University Press of Mississippi is a member of
the Association of American University Presses.

Copyright © 2009 by University Press of Mississippi
All rights reserved
Manufactured in the United States of America

First printing 2009

∞

Library of Congress Cataloging-in-Publication Data

Hastings, Robert W.
 The lakes of Pontchartrain : their history and environments /
Robert W. Hastings.
     p. cm.
 Includes bibliographical references and index.
 ISBN 978-1-60473-271-9 (cloth : alk. paper) 1. Pontchartrain,
Lake (La.)—Environmental conditions. 2. Pontchartrain, Lake,
Watershed (La.)—Environmental conditions. 3. Pontchartrain,
Lake (La.)—History. 4. Pontchartrain, Lake, Watershed (La.)—
History. I. Title.
 GE155.L8H37 2009
 508.763'34—dc22   2009008875

British Library Cataloging-in-Publication Data available

Contents

vii	Tables
ix	Figures
xi	Preface
xv	Acknowledgments
xvii	The Lake's Own Folk Song
xix	The Lake's Own Poem

Part 1
ENVIRONMENTAL HISTORY OF THE LAKE PONTCHARTRAIN BASIN

3	Introduction
6	1. Formation and Geology of the Pontchartrain Basin
11	2. Pre-European History
21	3. Initial European Exploration
37	4. European Colonization, Occupation, and Conflict
49	5. Louisiana Statehood
62	6. Civil War
67	7. Post-War Development
77	8. The Twentieth Century: Rapid Population Growth and Urban Expansion

Part 2
ENVIRONMENTAL MODIFICATION AND ABUSE OF THE LAKE PONTCHARTRAIN BASIN AND ITS RESTORATION

101	Introduction
104	9. Loss of Natural Habitats and Biodiversity
129	10. Water Quality Degradation
151	11. Environmental Recovery and Restoration

Part 3
CHARACTERISTICS OF THE LAKE PONTCHARTRAIN ESTUARINE SYSTEM TODAY

161	Introduction
162	12. Physical Description
182	13. Water Chemistry
189	14. Biota of the Pontchartrain Basin
196	15. The Estuarine Communities
217	16. The Marsh Communities
231	17. Estuarine Food Webs
240	18. The Palustrine Communities
247	19. The Riverine and Lacustrine Communities
250	20. The Terrestrial Communities

257	Postscript: Success?
261	References Cited
295	General Index
308	Taxonomic Index

Tables

Table 1 Major delta lobes of the Mississippi River
Table 2 Total population estimates of major Native American tribes occurring in the Pontchartrain basin between 1650 and 1908
Table 3 Population figures (and percentage change) for parishes bordering Lake Pontchartrain
Table 4 The natural communities of the Pontchartrain basin
Table 5 Historic vegetation types of the Florida parishes in the Pontchartrain basin
Table 6 Federally listed threatened and endangered species occurring in the Pontchartrain basin
Table 7 Land loss rates for the Pontchartrain basin
Table 8 Annual rates of shoreline change in the Pontchartrain basin
Table 9 Causes of land loss in the Pontchartrain basin
Table 10 Areal distribution of submersed aquatic vegetation in Lake Pontchartrain
Table 11 Openings of the Bonnet Carré Spillway and discharge amounts into Lake Pontchartrain
Table 12 Dimensions of Lake Pontchartrain and adjacent water bodies
Table 13 Shoreline types in the Pontchartrain basin
Table 14 Lake Pontchartrain place names from selected U.S. Coastal Survey nautical charts
Table 15 River inputs to Lake Pontchartrain
Table 16 Monthly average precipitation and rain days for New Orleans, Slidell, and Covington
Table 17 Natural and ecological communities of the Pontchartrain basin
Table 18 Plant species recorded at Delta Primate Center, St. Tammany Parish, Louisiana

Figures

Figure 1.1 Satellite photo of Lake Pontchartrain
Figure 1.2 Map of the Lake Pontchartrain basin
Figure 1.3 Delta lobes of the Mississippi River
Figure 3.1 The Cortes map of the Gulf of Mexico (c. 1520)
Figure 3.2 The Bisente map of the Gulf of Mexico (1696), Rio de Palisada, and Lago de Lodo
Figure 5.1 Manchac lighthouse
Figure 6.1 "Coffee grounds" on the western shore of Lake Pontchartrain
Figure 7.1 Logging ditches in the Manchac marshes
Figure 7.2 Water hyacinth (*Eichhornia crassipes*)
Figure 8.1 Population changes in the Pontchartrain basin, 1900–2000
Figure 8.2 Former camps and ruins at Milneburg (c. 1920) and Little Woods (2001)
Figure 8.3 Mandeville bulkhead and park
Figure 8.4 New Orleans lakeshore stepped seawall
Figure 8.5 The Bonnet Carré Spillway at the Mississippi River and at Lake Pontchartrain
Figure 8.6 The Pontchartrain Causeway
Figure 9.1 Shoreline erosion in Lake Pontchartrain
Figure 10.1 Tangipahoa River posted sign at Highway 443
Figure 10.2 Turbidity plume at mouth of the Tickfaw River
Figure 10.3 Algal bloom on north shore of Lake Pontchartrain
Figure 12.1 Lake Maurepas cypress shoreline near mouth of the Tickfaw River
Figure 12.2 Lake Pontchartrain cypress shoreline near mouth of the Tangipahoa River
Figure 12.3 Brackish marsh of marshhay cordgrass (*Spartina patens*)
Figure 12.4 Sand beach near Point Platte and Point aux Herbes
Figure 12.5 Rangia shell hash beach in Metairie

Figure 12.6 Metairie Linear Park
Figure 12.7 Riprap shoreline in Metairie
Figure 12.8 Riprap shoreline and old bulkhead at the Washout near Frenier
Figure 12.9 Bonnabel Canal pumping station in Metairie
Figure 14.1 *Rangia cuneata* shells near the mouth of Tangipahoa River
Figure 14.2 Harris's mud crab (*Rhithropanopeus harrisii*)
Figure 14.3 The copepod *Acartia tonsa*
Figure 14.4 Bay anchovy (*Anchoa mitchilli*)
Figure 15.1 Cypress stump with *Sphaeroma* damage
Figure 16.1 Wildflowers of the Manchac marshes
Figure 18.1 Ancient cypress tree along the lower Tangipahoa River

Preface

The Lakes of Pontchartrain are three bodies of water, Lakes Borgne, Pontchartrain, and Maurepas, making up the Pontchartrain estuary in southeastern Louisiana. The lakes have a rich history, correlated with the exploration and settlement of the lower Mississippi River valley and the development and expansion of the New Orleans metropolitan area. In fact, New Orleans was located where it is on the Mississippi River primarily because of Lake Pontchartrain, and the Indian portage (by way of Bayou St. John) between river and lake. The Lakes of Pontchartrain have also been significantly modified by human impacts on the lakes, their tributary streams, and surrounding lands, which have resulted in major environmental problems. As New Orleans and other communities of southeastern Louisiana grew and developed, the quality of the lakes suffered. There is a tremendous assemblage of historical information regarding the lower Mississippi River and New Orleans, but the lakes have been largely neglected and overshadowed by the river and city. However, Lake Pontchartrain gained special prominence when in 2005 it was the source of flood waters that decimated the city of New Orleans in the aftermath of Hurricane Katrina.

This book describes the environmental history, biology, and characteristics of the lakes and their surrounding lands with regard to their modification, degradation, and restoration. By better understanding their environmental history, we can better understand how to protect and restore the lakes for future generations. Much has been written about Lake Pontchartrain, but no comprehensive description of its natural history has ever been published.

Many books provide excellent histories of New Orleans and Louisiana and include much information on Lake Pontchartrain. An intriguing book *Lake Pontchartrain*, written in 1946 by W. Adolphe Roberts, is primarily a history of the area and especially New Orleans, but it has much to say about the lake and its relationship to the city. Edna B. Freiberg's *Bayou St. John in Colonial Louisiana, 1699–1803* (1980) describes in detail the history of the bayou and its relationship to New Orleans and the lake. Frederick S. Ellis's *St. Tammany Parish: L'Autre Coté du Lac* (1981) gives the north-shore perspective of the lake. *Images of America: Lake Pontchartrain* (2007) by Catherine Campanella is a photographic essay and memoir of life on the New Orleans lakeshore. Several somewhat comprehensive reviews of Lake Pontchartrain environments have been produced in recent years as efforts were initiated to restore the lake. These include "Environmental Analysis of Lake Pontchartrain, Louisiana, Its Surrounding Wetlands, and Selected Land Uses" (Stone 1980), "Environmental Characteristics of the Pontchartrain-Maurepas Basin and Identification of Management Issues" (Coastal Environments, Inc. 1984a), and "To Restore Lake Pontchartrain: A Report to the Greater New Orleans Expressway Commission on the Sources, Remedies, and Economic Impacts of Pollution in the Lake Pontchartrain Basin" (Houck et al. 1989). Other important references include the various environmental impact statements relative to shell dredging in the lake, the Bonnet Carré Spillway and diversion, hurricane protection projects, and other major construction affecting the lake (most done by or for the U.S. Army Corps of Engineers). Although very useful and providing a tremendous amount of valuable information, all of these reports are unpublished "gray literature" not readily available. The report by Tarver and Savoie (1976) is useful but somewhat limited in scope. The Lake Pontchartrain Basin Foundation (LPBF) prepared a comprehensive bibliography of literature on the lake (updated and made available at http://pubs.usgs.gov/of/1996/of96-527/). In 2001 the foundation, in partnership with the Environmental Protection Agency, U.S. Geological Survey, and the University of New Orleans, published its "Environmental Atlas of the Lake Pontchartrain Basin" (Penland et al. 2001a). John A. Lopez (2003) completed a doctoral dissertation at the University of New Orleans entitled "Chronology and Analysis of Environmental Impacts within the Pontchartrain Basin of the Mississippi Delta Plain, 1718–2002." Most recently, The Nature Conservancy (2004) prepared a Conservation Area Plan for the Lake Pontchartrain estuary. These and other references on the lake provide a wealth of information regarding Lake Pontchartrain and its environments. Another source of information for those wishing to know more about Lake Pontchartrain is the Lake Pontchartrain Basin Maritime Museum and Research Center located on the Tchefuncte River in Madisonville.

One problem encountered when attempting a book of this nature is the dilemma of setting arbitrary boundaries for the area to be discussed. In the case of Lake Pontchartrain, its realm of influence includes the adjacent rivers, lakes, and sounds, as well as the marine waters of the northern Gulf of Mexico. To the north, it is greatly influenced by runoff from the numerous rivers and streams that make up its drainage basin, some of which extend some 70 mi. (113 km) north and into Mississippi. It is also significantly affected by flood waters diverted from the Mississippi River to the west and from the Pearl River to the east. On the terrestrial side, its adjacent wetlands give way to upland forest communities and urban developments that also impact the lake. My approach has been to focus on Lake Pontchartrain, with somewhat less attention given to Lakes Maurepas and Borgne, while providing somewhat arbitrary references to adjacent freshwater and marine areas. Terrestrial wetland areas are discussed as part of the lake system, but adjacent upland areas are included or neglected at my discretion.

The concept of this book began with a series of teacher workshops conducted at the Turtle Cove Environmental Research Station in Manchac, where I served as director for fifteen years. These workshops presented a survey of the history, geology, biology, and environmental issues of the Lake Pontchartrain estuary and its surrounding swamps and marshes, with the goal of providing teachers with local resource information to enhance their own classes in environmental education, biology, and earth science. Our rationale was that students learn best when presented with local examples to illustrate classroom principles, and students can even enhance discussions of some topics from their personal experiences. The Louisiana student may have no interest at all in the environmental protection of remote places such as Lake Erie or the Nile River, whereas students who have boated, fished, or bathed in Lake Pontchartrain or its tributary rivers can relate to the need for environmental protection of these local waters. Hopefully this account of the natural history and environments of the Lake Pontchartrain basin will provide any resident of the area, including teachers and students, with information to better understand this great natural resource.

Therefore, the book is dedicated to the many teachers who have instilled in their students a love for the natural history, environments, and culture of Louisiana and the Lake Pontchartrain basin. Included are my wife, Diana, and two daughters, Kimberly and Rachel, who have taught and supported me in all my endeavors.

"In the end we will conserve only what we love;
We will love only what we understand;
And we will understand only what we are taught."

—SENEGALESE ECOLOGIST BABA DIOUM

Acknowledgments

I thank Dinah Maygarden, Diana Hastings, and several anonymous reviewers who read and suggested improvements to early drafts of this book. In addition Sue Ellen Lyons and Sharon Flanagan (the Bwanettes) were faithful assistants and coinstructors for the teacher workshops that stimulated thoughts regarding the need for this book. Hayden Reno, station manager at the Turtle Cove Environmental Research Station, shared with me much of his first-hand knowledge of the Manchac swamps and their fauna. Robert Moreau and Mars Stouder, Turtle Cove employees, supported all of my endeavors while I served as research station director. Staff of the Lake Pontchartrain Basin Foundation, including Executive Director Carlton Dufrechou, former Environmental Director Neil Armingeon, Deputy Director Anne Rheams, and Director of the Coastal Sustainability Program John Lopez, were also especially helpful in supporting and encouraging my various activities on Lake Pontchartrain and guiding the restoration process for the lake. Bryan Rogers, formerly of the Lake Pontchartrain Basin Foundation, prepared the map included as Figure 1.2. I thank these and all others who have had a part in helping to restore the lake and its tributaries.

The Lake's Own Folk Song

"The Lakes of Pontchartrain"

'Twas on one bright March morning I bid New Orleans adieu.
And I took the road to Jackson town, my fortune to renew,
I cursed all foreign money, no credit could I gain,
Which filled my heart with longing for
The lakes of Pontchartrain.

I stepped on board a railroad car, beneath the morning sun,
I rode the roads till evening, and I laid me down again,
All strangers there no friends to me, till a dark girl towards me came,
And I fell in love with a Creole girl,
By the lakes of Pontchartrain.

I said, "My pretty Creole girl, my money here's no good,
But if it weren't for the alligators, I'd sleep out in the wood."
"You're welcome here kind stranger, our house is very plain.
But we never turn a stranger out,
From the lakes of Pontchartrain."

She took me into her mammy's house, and treated me quite well,
The hair upon her shoulder, in jet black ringlets fell.
To try and paint her beauty, I'm sure 'twould be in vain,

THE LAKE'S OWN FOLK SONG

So handsome was my Creole girl,
By the lakes of Pontchartrain.

I asked her if she'd marry me, she said it could never be,
For she had got another, and he was far at sea.
She said that she would wait for him, and true she would remain.
Till he returned for his Creole girl,
By the lakes of Pontchartrain.

So fare thee well my Creole girl, I never will see you no more,
But I'll ne'er forget your kindness, in the cottage by the shore.
And at each social gathering, a flowing glass I'll raise,
And I'll drink a health to my Creole girl,
And the lakes of Pontchartrain.

—BARRY TAYLOR

(see http://www.geocities.com/sinker.geo/lakesofpontchartrain.html)

The Lake's Own Poem

"Lake Pontchartrain"

Into thy sapphire wave, fair Pontchartrain,
Slow sinks the setting sun; the distant sail,
On far horizon's edge, glides hushed and pale,
Like some escaping spirit o'er the main.
The sea-gull soars, then tastes thy waves again;
The bearded forests on thy sandy shore
In silence stand, e'en as they stood of yore
While yet the red man held his savage reign,
And daring Iberville's adventurous prow
As yet had never cut thy purple wave,
Nor swung the shadow of his shining sail
Across the bark of the Biloxi brave.
Ah, placid lake! Where are thy warriors now?
Where their abiding places—where their grave?

—MARY ASHLEY TOWNSEND (1881)

Part 1
ENVIRONMENTAL HISTORY OF
THE LAKE PONTCHARTRAIN BASIN

Introduction

In the southeastern corner of Louisiana and just east of the Mississippi River delta is a chain of "lakes" forming the Pontchartrain estuary, or the Lakes of Pontchartrain (Figure 1.1). The most significant of these is Lake Pontchartrain, a magnificent body of water closely tied to New Orleans and the Mississippi River delta by its environments, history, culture, and economics. With Lake Borgne (and Lake St. Catherine) on the southeast and Lake Maurepas on the west, these Lakes of Pontchartrain are located at longitude 89°30' to 90°45'W and latitude 29°50' to 30°30' N (Figure 1.2). Lakes Pontchartrain and Maurepas were named by the French explorer Pierre le Moyne, Sieur d'Iberville, in honor of the two French dignitaries who had helped organize his expedition, Louis Phelypeaux, Comte de Pontchartrain, Minister of Marine for King Louis XIV, and his son Jerome Phelypeaux de Maurepas, the latter being the principal supporter of the expedition, who in 1699 succeeded his father as Minister of Marine (and later assumed the title of Comte de Pontchartrain). Antoine Simon Le Page du Pratz (1774), a historian who first visited Louisiana in 1718, stated that Lake Pontchartrain was called Lake St. Louis. Lake Borgne, which is actually an embayment of Mississippi Sound, was also named by the French (*borgne* meaning "one-eyed" or "blind in one eye") because it is incomplete or defective without a complete shoreline, but instead a large opening to Mississippi Sound (Gayarre 1854). It has also been called Blind Lake (Freiberg 1980).

Narrow and deep natural passes connect the three lakes, and Lake Borgne opens into Mississippi Sound, which opens into the Gulf of Mexico, making the entire system an estuary where fresh water mixes with salt water. The major pass connecting Lake Pontchartrain and Lake Borgne is called the Rigolets, after the

4   ENVIRONMENTAL HISTORY OF THE BASIN

Figure 1.1 Satellite photo of Lake Pontchartrain (Used with permission of the Image Science and Analysis Laboratory, NASA Johnson Space Center, http://eol.jsc.nasa.gov; photo no. ISS013-E-84678)

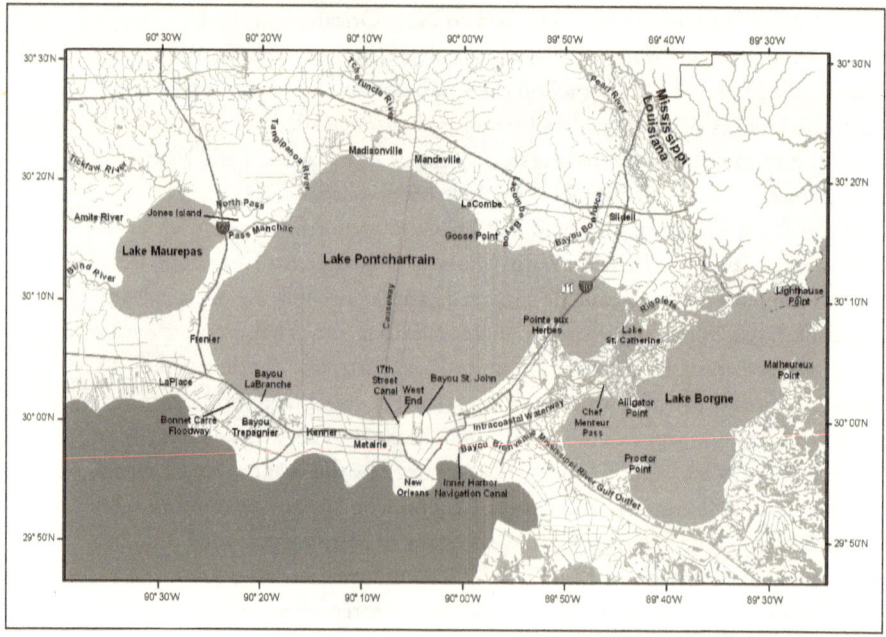

Figure 1.2 Map of the Lake Pontchartrain basin (Map prepared by Bryan E. Rogers)

French word *rigole* (meaning "channel, gutter, or drain" and possibly signifying a stream flowing both ways, or tidal; Castellanos 1895; Darby 1816). The smaller Chef Menteur Pass just to the west also connects the two lakes. Several tales have been offered to explain the curious name of Chef Menteur Pass, which means "lying chief." According to Gayarre (1854), the area and pass were named for a Choctaw chief who settled there after being exiled from Choctaw territory because of his habit of lying. According to Castellanos (1895), old people used to say that the Indians gave it the name of "Big Liar," because it "talked deceivingly." The adjacent Lake St. Catherine was once called Lake Chef Menteur (Romans 1774, in Phillips 1975) and Bay of Pines (1814 map by B. Lafon reproduced by Casey 1983, pl. 124, p. 422). Lakes Pontchartrain and Maurepas are also connected by two passes, Pass Manchac (also known locally as South Pass) and North Pass.

The history of these lakes began long before the coming of the French, with their initial formation by geological events within the Mississippi River delta and their subsequent settlement by Native Americans, who depended upon the lakes as a source of food as well as for transportation routes. European colonization of the area was primarily correlated with use of the lakes, their passes, and their tributaries, as well as the Mississippi River, as transportation routes for commerce along the Gulf coast. With urbanization and increased population expansion, the lakes became the focus of major recreational activities but eventually were to be severely impacted by environmental abuse and modification of the surrounding natural areas. Environmental degradation finally stimulated a call for restoration that is still continuing today. The following chapters will trace the history of this environmental alteration (Parts 1 and 2) and conclude with a detailed description of the lake environment today (Part 3).

1.

Formation and Geology of the Pontchartrain Basin

The geomorphic history of the Pontchartrain basin begins some 5000 years ago (Saucier 1963, 1994), with its separation from the Gulf of Mexico by delta formation of the Mississippi River. Most of the following discussion of geology is taken primarily from Saucier (1963) and Darnell (1962), who provided a good overview of the lake's origin and history. Saucier described the basin as a former embayment of the Gulf of Mexico modified by sedimentation from the shifting Mississippi River and its distributaries. From the time of its formation until the present, the Lake Pontchartrain system has been affected by the land-building forces of deposition and accretion more or less in balance with the destructive forces of faulting, subsidence, erosion, and redistribution of sediments. As described by Darnell, the geology of the basin is related primarily to fluctuations in sea level, migration and alternate delta formation by the Mississippi River, and continual subsidence of coastal deposits.

The higher lands to the north of Lake Pontchartrain, referred to as the Pleistocene Terrace or Prairie Terrace Complex, are much older than the lake. They were formed by deltaic deposition of material during interglacial stages of the Pleistocene epoch of the Late Quaternary period, which occurred some 60,000 to 100,000 years ago. These deposits also extend deep below the younger alluvial sediments of the Pontchartrain basin, all of which have been deposited by rivers in Recent (or Holocene) times (the last 15,000 to 35,000 years). The dividing line (referred to as the Baton Rouge Fault; Flowers and Isphording 1990) is marked by a distinct rise in elevation up to 2 ft. (60 cm) above mean sea level, with a continuous increase in elevation to the north. At one time this boundary was the shoreline of the Gulf of Mexico.

The southern boundary of the Pleistocene Terrace is also marked by a distinct change in sediment type. The Prairie Terrace sediments are largely well-oxidized silty to sandy clays, which may be red, yellowish brown, buff, or light gray, with little organic content. In contrast, the wet swamp and marsh sediments of the Pontchartrain basin proper have a very high organic content. There is also a marked contrast in vegetation types correlated with this sediment difference. The Prairie Terrace has been described as being covered originally by an almost homogeneous forest of longleaf pine (*Pinus palustris*) and slash pine (*Pinus elliotti*), with mixed hardwoods along the streams. This contrasts to the low marshy and swampy Recent sediments of the Mississippi River delta deposits (which have always been virtually devoid of pines; Saucier 1963). Although certainly oversimplified, such a description does demonstrate the dominance of longleaf pine in the upland areas north of Lake Pontchartrain.

The sediments in the Pontchartrain basin were formed by a combination of marine and riverine, or alluvial, influences. Those of marine origin are largely sand (0.0625–2 mm grain size), while those of alluvial origin are mostly silts and silty clays (less than 0.0625 mm). Rivers of the coastal plain produce their own natural levees (as well as deltas near their mouths) by the periodic flooding of their banks with sediment-rich water. The natural Mississippi River levees are about 2–3 mi. (3–5 km) wide and 20 ft. (6 m) above sea level at Donaldsonville and 1.5 mi. (2.4 km) wide and 12 ft. (3.7 m) above sea level at New Orleans. These levees are composed primarily of silt and clay, whereas the lower swampy areas are composed largely of organic matter such as wood fragments, or detritus. There is also a comparable though slight natural levee evident around the perimeter of Lake Pontchartrain and Lake Maurepas, where wave action has pushed up a ridge of flotsam bordering the lake shoreline. In some places, such as along the western side of Lake Pontchartrain, a remnant band of cypress trees remains on this slightly higher ground before receding into the lower marshes, where the trees were removed by logging in the early 1900s.

Lake Pontchartrain was formed some 3000 years ago, when sediment buildup from a former distributary of the Mississippi River separated the former Pontchartrain Embayment from the adjacent Gulf of Mexico. The river is known to have switched course east and west at intervals of about 1000 years, with at least five major delta complexes and sixteen delta lobes evident (Figure 1.3). There is some disagreement among experts regarding the number of delta lobes and their ages (Table 1). Regardless of how many deltas have formed, there is no doubt that active sedimentation from the Mississippi River was the major

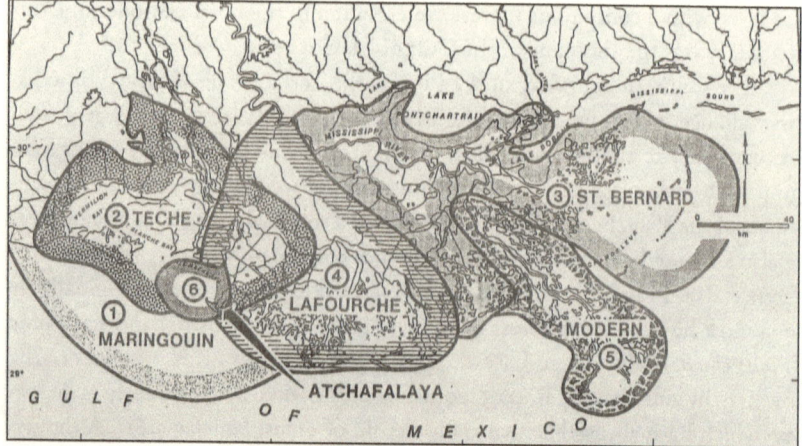

Figure 1.3 Delta lobes of the Mississippi River (From Coastal Environments, Inc. 1984a based on original in Frazier 1967)

factor in the formation of Lake Pontchartrain. According to Saucier (1963), sedimentation rates have decreased during Recent times, but the sediment load of the river still averages about 500 million tons/year. Most of that sediment load is now carried into deep Gulf waters (because of the confining levees on the river), rather than building coastal lands in the delta.

The location of an original shoreline or beach of the Pontchartrain Embayment is identified by the presence of a prominent sand ridge, the Milton's Island Beach Trend, extending from the mouth of the Pearl River near Slidell to Ponchatoula (Saucier 1963). However, it is mostly buried beneath marsh, swamp, or lake-bottom deposits and is exposed only as Milton's Island, a ridge of sandy soil covered with pine and hardwoods in the swamps and marshes near Port Louis just west of Madisonville. On the southern side of the Pontchartrain Embayment, another extensive beach deposit has been identified buried beneath Orleans Parish, the Pine Island Beach Trend (Saucier 1963) or New Orleans Barrier Island (Corbeille 1962; Stapor and Stone 2004). This formation is believed to represent a former barrier spit or series of barrier islands extending from near the present mouth of the Pearl River, which formed about 4500–6000 years ago from sand emanating from the Pearl River. Mollusk fossils indicate a shallow continental shelf habitat with higher salinities, suggesting the spit (or series of islands) was the open Gulf coast some 4000–5000 years ago (Rowett 1957; Saucier 1963; Otvos 1978b). These barrier islands began forming about 4000–7000 years ago by Pearl River deposits in the area now

Table 1 Major delta lobes of the Mississippi River

Delta	Position	Estimated Age in Years B.P.*		
		Frazier (1967)	Saucier (1994)	Törnqvist et al. (1996)
Outer Shoal	west		9200–8200	
Maringouin	west	7000–6000	7240–6150	
Teche	west	6000–4000	6000–3000	
St. Bernard	east	4000–1000	4000–1000	3569 ± 24
Lafourche	west	3000–0	3500–1000	1491 ± 13
Plaquemines (Balize or Modern)	east	1000–0	1000–400	1322 ± 22
Atchafalaya	west	current	50–0	

*B.P., before present

represented by eastern Orleans Parish (that is, the Pine Island Beach Trend). By 4500 years ago, the Mississippi River began influencing the area by adding fresh water and sediments to begin building the western portion of the Pontchartrain basin, or the St. Bernard delta (Saucier 1963). Fossil evidence shows that as salinity levels in the system decreased, the dominant mollusk species became more characteristic of lower salinities (10–30 parts per thousand [ppt]; Darnell 1962; Otvos 1978a). Approximately 3000 years ago, the existing Mississippi River course was established with one of its distributaries flowing to the east along the southern edge of the Pine Island Beach Trend. Formation of this Metairie Bayou–Bayou Sauvage distributary occurred about 1000–2000 years ago. This distributary would have built natural levees to form the land that is now known as Metairie-Gentilly Ridge (a part of the St. Bernard delta) and eventually creating the southern boundary of Lake Pontchartrain. By this stage the salinity of Lake Pontchartrain had become equivalent to what it is today, and the mollusk fauna was dominated by the brackish water rangia clam (*Rangia cuneata*) and dark false mussel (*Mytilopsis leucophaeta*), as well as two small hydrobiid snails (*Texadina sphinctostoma* and *Probythinella protera*; Darnell 1962; also see Solem 1961).

Saucier (1963) postulated that much of what we now know as Lake Borgne would have been filled with sediments of the St. Bernard delta at the time of the delta's maximum extent (2000–2400 years ago), and its subsequent development and enlargement resulted from subsidence and shoreline retreat. He also suggested that there was no open water representing Lake Maurepas when Lake Pontchartrain first formed, Pass Manchac was an old Amite River channel, and North Pass was the Tickfaw-Natalbany River channel. Lake Maurepas possibly formed later in a large depression between natural levees of Mississippi River distributaries and the Prairie Terrace. However, Saucier also recognized the possibility that Lake Maurepas represents a remnant of the Pontchartrain Embayment that was never filled by river sediment.

At present, the Mississippi River is again trying to switch back to the west and has begun to form a new Atchafalaya delta. This latest delta switch, exacerbated by the levees restricting the river flow to a relatively narrow channel, is now robbing the Pontchartrain basin, as well as the rest of the Modern delta, of the annual floods of nutrient and sediment-rich waters that have built and nourished the delta and its wetlands. Much of coastal Louisiana, including parts of the Pontchartrain basin, are "inactive deltas" (Louisiana Coastal Wetlands Conservation and Restoration Task Force 1997) and are being lost to subsidence and sea level rise. Estimated rates of land loss in coastal Louisiana of 35 sq. mi. (90 km^2) per year are largely due to the combined effects of these natural processes plus the unnatural control of the Mississippi River. Considerable effort and expense has been dedicated to the conservation and restoration of coastal Louisiana, but most experts agree that the most effective way to accomplish this would be to restore the Mississippi River to a natural cycle of annual flooding of coastal marshes. Although some attempts have been made to do this, human developments in the delta now prevent a complete return to the natural system. Hopefully continued concern and research on this extremely complex problem will result in some degree of conservation and restoration.

2.

Pre-European History

Prehistory

When Lake Pontchartrain was visited by French explorers in 1699, the area had been inhabited by Native Americans for several thousand years. There have been 143 Indian sites recognized in the Pontchartrain basin (Saucier 1963). We have very little information regarding these earliest residents prior to 1700. Their impact on the lakes would have been minimal, except for the creation of large shell mounds, or middens, composed mostly of the discarded shells of rangia clams (*Rangia cuneata*) that were a major food item. However, Kidder (1998) suggested that there was significant selective burning of some areas to clear forest undergrowth, and later, as agriculture became more important, some land clearing for agriculture or construction of lodges. Of course, Native Americans were also gathering natural foods from the lakes, including clams, fish, turtles, and alligators, as well as game from the surrounding upland areas, but their relatively low population numbers assured a relatively minor impact compared to the much larger human population after 1700.

The earliest human occupation of Louisiana (the Paleo-Indian Period) dates back to about 10,000 B.C. (Neuman and Hawkins 1993), and people were present in the Lake Pontchartrain basin by about 1800 B.C. (Saucier 1963). Only a few scattered artifacts and sites provide evidence of their presence in the area up through about 600 B.C. These are identified with the Archaic, or Meso-Indian, Period (6000–2000 B.C.), and the Poverty Point Period, the first of the Neo-Indian Periods (2000 B.C. to 1600 A.D.; Gagliano 1963; Springer 1973; Cummins 1980; Coastal Environments, Inc. 1983; Neuman and Hawkins 1993).

These include the Bayou Jasmine site (Shell Bank Bayou) on the western side of Lake Pontchartrain just north of Frenier, the Linsley site between New Orleans and Lake Borgne near the junction of the Mississippi River Gulf Outlet and the Intracoastal Waterway, and the Garcia site on the shore of Lake Pontchartrain near the Rigolets (Gagliano 1963; Gagliano and Saucier 1963). Such sites are rare because of the relatively young age of the Pontchartrain basin, and any older sites would have been destroyed by the shifting channels of the Mississippi River delta (Haag 1978).

The Bayou Jasmine site is a midden mostly below sea level (16 ft. of a total 18-ft. thickness, 4.9 m of a total 5.5-m thickness) that rests on a submerged natural levee (Neuman 1976). Apparently the Bayou Jasmine community was a seasonal settlement, centered around fishing and gathering during the warmer months (Duhe 1976). The dominant foods were several species of fish (catfish, *Ictalurus* sp.; bowfin, *Amia calva*; alligator gar, *Atractosteus spatula*; longnose gar, *Lepisosteus osseus*; freshwater drum, *Aplodinotus grunniens*; freshwater bass, *Micropterus* sp.; crappie, *Pomoxis* sp.; and sunfish, *Lepomis* sp.), turtles (the snapping turtle, *Chelydra serpentina*, was most common), and alligators (*Alligator mississippiensis*). Clams (*Rangia cuneata*) were a basic food, although apparently not as nutritionally important as other foods (Byrd 1976). The dependence upon rangia clams was apparently related to their ease of capture and reliability, despite the low nutritional value (Neuman 1984). Numerous mammal remains included beaver (*Castor canadensis*), raccoon (*Procyon lotor*), rabbit (*Sylvilagus floridanus* and *S. aquaticus*), otter (*Lutra canadensis*), muskrat (*Ondatra zibethicus*), opossum (*Didelphis virginiana*), squirrel (*Sciurus carolinensis* and *S. niger*), dog (*Canis familiaris*), and deer (*Odocoileus virginianus*).

The subsequent period beginning in about 600 B.C. and marked by the presence of significant amounts of pottery (Cummins 1980) is referred to as the Tchefuncte (or Tchula) Period based upon shell midden sites excavated in the marshes on the north shore of Lake Pontchartrain in Fontainebleau State Park near the Tchefuncte River (Ford and Quimby 1945; Coastal Environments, Inc. 1983; Shenkel 1984). Others are the Big Oak Island and Little Oak Island sites in the New Orleans East area just south of Lake Pontchartrain, dated at about 600 to 100 B.C. (Gagliano 1969; Shenkel and Gibson 1974; Shenkel 1974, 1981, 1984). These people, living in groups of about twenty-five to fifty, were primarily a hunting, fishing, and gathering culture dependent to a large extent upon the rangia clams (37% by meat weight) and the clam-eating freshwater drum (40%), which were abundant in the lake (Shenkel 1984). Other important foods were deer (8%), other species of fish (catfish; bowfin; buffalo fish, *Ictiobus* sp.; gar; saltwater drum, *Pogonius cromis*; sheepshead,

Archosargus probatocephalus; sea catfish, *Ariopsis felis*; and shark; combined weight of 8%), and alligator (2%). Other mammals included muskrat, raccoon, and opossum. Locations may have been abandoned as they became unsuitable as a dependable source of rangia clams because of shifts in the Mississippi River delta (Shenkel 1984).

During later periods (the Marksville Period from 0 to 400 A.D., Baytown from 400 to 700 A.D., Coles Creek from 700 to 1000 A.D., and Mississippian or Plaquemine from 1000 to 1700 A.D.; Coastal Environments, Inc. 1983), there was increased dependence upon agriculture with maize, beans, and squash being the principal crops (Haag 1978). Several middens in the Pass Manchac area (Dranguet and Heleniak 1985) and in the Bayou LaBranche–Bayou Trepagnier area (Pearson et al. 1993) have been dated as Tchula and early Marksville Period sites (ca. 500 B.C. to 400 A.D.). The Hoover site, located just east of Ponchatoula, has been described as the largest prehistoric Indian site known in the area on the north shore of Lake Pontchartrain (Coastal Environments, Inc. 1983). Its major period of occupancy was during the Baytown and Coles Creek Periods, but could have been first occupied as early as 1000 B.C. Scattered shell middens near the Tangipahoa River contain pottery fragments and other artifacts dated to 600–800 A.D. (Coastal Environments, Inc. 1983; Beavers et al. 1985).

The early settlement sites were chosen for relatively high ground, a source of fresh water, and a supply of food (Saucier 1963). In the Pontchartrain basin, these were on the Prairie Terrace margins, relict beaches, and natural levees of streams. The association of the settlements with Lake Pontchartrain was obviously because of the abundance of shellfish for food, especially rangia clams. Few settlements existed along the Mississippi River, possibly because food was more easily obtained along the lakes. There was definitely a preference for the lake region as opposed to the river, especially during the summer. Kidder (1996) noted that large and permanent communities were never found on the banks of active river channels along the lower Mississippi, but almost always away from the active levees and on the banks of relict channels or oxbows. This was probably due in large part to the seasonal overbank flooding that would have made sites along the river uninhabitable. There was also a pattern of frequent movement and relocation of villages that predates the arrival of Europeans, a characteristic reflected in their being referred to as "wandering tribes" (Davis 1984). These movements were possibly related to intertribal warfare and alliances, as well as the precarious environment of the ever-changing Mississippi River delta with its limited ridges or other high ground suitable as sites for human habitation (Giardino 1984).

Native American History

In the Historic Period beginning in 1700, the margins of the area north of Lake Pontchartrain were occupied by seven tribes known collectively as the Muskogeans (Kniffen et al. 1987). These residents of the lower Mississippi valley have been referred to as "the small tribes" in contrast to the larger Choctaw, Cherokee, and Creek nations (Fabel 2000), although Bushnell (1909) suggested that one of these (the Acolapissa) was closely connected with the Choctaw proper and not clearly distinguished from them. They referred to Lake Pontchartrain as Okwa'ta, the "large" or "wide water," a term which could also apply to any large expanse of water (Bushnell 1909). Bayou Manchac (Ascanthia), Bayou LaBranche-Trepagnier, and Bayou St. John (Choupicatcha), as well as Lakes Pontchartrain and Maurepas, were well-established travel and trading routes prior to the arrival of the first Europeans (Pearson et al. 1989).

The seven tribes of the Pontchartrain area included the Bayogoula, Mugulasha, Quinipissa, Houma, and Okelousa along the Mississippi River and the Acolapissa (Colapissa) and Tangipahoa along the lower Pearl River and north shore of Lake Pontchartrain (Swanton 1911, 1946, 1952). One village occupied by both Bayogoulas and Mugulashas on the Mississippi upriver from New Orleans was reported to be more than 600 years old (Butler 1934). Giardino (1984) suggested that many of these tribal names were actually generic, descriptive terms. Mugulasha, meaning "opposite phratry," or clan group, could have designated membership in a distinctive clan. Colapissa or Acolapissa, and possibly also Quinipissa, translated as "men who see and hear," could have identified sentinels or spies. Giardino concluded that the Bayogoula, Mugulasha, and Quinipissa were identical or at least closely similar groups and were referred to after 1700 only as the Bayogoula. The Acolapissa (and their branch referred to as Tangipahoa) may have also been a part of the Quinipissa. Other tribes, such as the Chickasaw from northern Mississippi and northern Alabama, occasionally entered the Lake Pontchartrain area on slave-hunting raids (LaHarpe c.1723; Kniffen et al. 1987).

The explorer Iberville, on his first visit to the northern Gulf coast in 1699, was searching for a village of Quinipissa that the explorer René-Robert Cavelier de La Salle had visited in 1682. He met a hunting party of Bayogoula and Mugulasha Indians near Ship Island, Mississippi, and concluded that these Bayogoula and Mugulasha, whose home was on the banks of the Mississippi River, were the Quinipissa (McWilliams 1981). He also had contact with Annocchy or Biloxi (Bylocchy) Indians along the lower Mississippi, but these mostly lived along the Pascagoula River. On his second visit to the Gulf coast in 1700,

Iberville examined the site of a former Quinipissa village and abandoned fields, with trees up to 2 ft. (60 cm) in circumference, near a portage in the Bayou LaBranche area. An abandoned Acolapissa (or Quinipissa) village also existed on Bayou St. John prior to the coming of the French (Freiberg 1980). This village was referred to by some as Tchoutchouma or "the city of the red sun," but was reportedly occupied in 1700 by a group of Biloxi Indians. The village was again deserted in 1718, when Le Page du Pratz (1774) lodged in one of the cabins owned at that time by a Canadian settler. Iberville noted that in 1699 the Quinipissa (or Acolapissa) occupied six villages along the lower Mississippi, along streams flowing into Lake Pontchartrain, or along the lower Pearl River (McWilliams 1981). The Tangipahoa were said to be a seventh Quinipissa village that had been destroyed (see also Swanton 1952). In 1682 La Salle had arrived shortly after a "Tangibao" village on the eastern side of the Mississippi River just above the future site of New Orleans (near present-day Goodhope) had been destroyed. In 1650 the Acolapissa and Tangipahoa were estimated to number 1500 (Swanton 1952). According to the journal of *Le Marin*, sister ship to Iberville's *La Badine* (French 1875; Sinclair 1974), tribes referred to as Ananis (Biloxi, according to Swanton 1952) and Mouloubis (?, not referred to elsewhere) were settled along Bayou Manchac when Iberville first explored it.

Some time around 1702 or 1705, the Acolapissa from along the Pearl River moved close to Lake Pontchartrain along Bayou Castine, where they were joined by a small group of Natchitoches Indians from along the Red River (Swanton 1952; McWilliams 1953). Many of these Natchitoches were killed by the Acolapissa several years later, when they were leaving to return to their home on the Red River. Remnants of the Tangipahoa established a village on the Tangipahoa River between 1702 and 1705. Other Acolapissa moved to the Mississippi River about 39 mi. (63 km) above New Orleans in 1718, and other groups of Indians also moved to the banks of the river near New Orleans at this time. After 1718, the Acolapissa were located in the area of LaPlace (Giardino 1984), and shortly thereafter they ceased to exist as a separate tribe but merged with the Houmas (Swanton 1952; Kniffen et al. 1987). The Houmas (or Ouma) mostly occupied the area north of Baton Rouge near the Red River, but some of them relocated to the vicinity of New Orleans after an attack by Tunicas (Giardino 1984). A settlement of Houmas existed near the upper end of Bayou St. John between 1706 and 1720 (Freiberg 1980). There was a group of Biloxi Indians living at an abandoned Acolapissa village on the West Pearl River between 1722 and 1761 (Ellis 1981). In the late 1700s, a group of Pascagoula Indians had established a village on the Amite River, and tribes who had relocated west of the Mississippi River (Biloxis, Chatots, Mobilians, and

Houmas) or to the north (Tunicas) still claimed hunting grounds along Bayou Manchac, the Amite River, Lake Maurepas, and Lake Pontchartrain (Fabel 2000). Swanton (1952) stated that the Choctaw began moving into Louisiana after the settlement of New Orleans.

Relations between the French at New Orleans and the various Native Americans living nearby were relatively good, although some Indians were held as slaves until the transfer of New Orleans to Spanish rule in 1766, when Spanish law prohibited their enslavement (Usner 1989). Free Indians provided important services to the town, including paddling or rowing boats and supplying game, pelts, bear oil, baskets, herbs, and firewood. The Native Americans also gained trade and defensive benefits by relocating near European settlements such as New Orleans (Davis 1984).

By 1768 there were six Indian villages in the area north of Lakes Pontchartrain and Maurepas, which had become British West Florida (in 1763). Their relationship with the English settlers was poor, as was that of the French settlers who remained in the area under British rule (Usner 1989). Indians repeatedly attacked British soldiers moving up the Mississippi River to build a new fort at Bayou Manchac in 1765 (Fabel 2000). The Native Americans seemed to prefer both the French and the Spanish, who were accused by the British of encouraging Indians to harass white settlers on the northern side of the lake (Fabel 2000). Abbadie (in Brasseaux 1979) noted that Biloxi Indians and other small tribes that lived along Lake Pontchartrain in 1764 might attack travelers on the lake, but would also sometimes visit New Orleans to play ball (lacrosse).

Lieutenant Alexander Fraser, a British army engineer involved with clearing operations on Bayou Manchac, en route from New Orleans to Manchac in 1768, encountered a group of Indians (possibly Biloxis) on the lakeshore at the entrance to Pass Manchac (Fabel 2000). The Indians claimed to be starving, having left their settlements for fear of Creek raiders. Fraser befriended the group by giving them food. The approximate site of this encounter is now the location of a fishing camp referred to as "Starvation Landing."

The Tangipahoa people (referred to as Taensapoa) were no longer present along the Tangipahoa River when William Bartram (1791) traveled through in 1777, but Dranguet and Heleniak (1985) suggested that their absence could have been temporary in view of their somewhat nomadic life. According to a report in 1773, there were no Indian villages along the northern side of Lake Maurepas and Lake Pontchartrain, which was then the British side of the Mississippi River, the tribes having moved to the Spanish side as a result of war by the Creeks against the Choctaws and their allies (Fabel 1983).

By the 1800s Choctaw Indians from southern Mississippi had moved into areas on the north shore of Lake Pontchartrain. Usner (1998) mentioned a Choctaw village of Boukfouka (Bonfouca) in 1732, and there was a Choctaw camp at Bayou St. John in 1835 (Power 1836). According to some Civil War era maps, there was a Choctaw settlement on Lake Pontchartrain at Pass Manchac (Dranguet and Heleniak 1985; Irion et al. 1994).

The Lake Pontchartrain area was involved with the transport of Creek Indians to the west during the Seminole War of 1835–1858 in Florida, with some temporarily housed at Fort Pike on the Rigolets. On October 31, 1836, an accident involving two ships (the *Monmouth* and the *Tremont*) on Lake Pontchartrain resulted in the death of more than 300 Creek Indians being transported on one of the boats (Usner 1998).

Penicaut, a ship carpenter and Indian interpreter for Iberville (McWilliams 1953), spent several summers living with the Acolapissa on the north shore of Lake Pontchartrain. King (1893) described Penicaut's account of these sojourns as "the staple of Native American romance and poetry—long boating expeditions, days of hunting, nights of dancing and frolicking with the young folks, around the campfire, under the green leaves." While among the Acolapissa, Penicaut reported hunting deer, buffalo, bear, turkeys, ducks, Canada geese, and snow or blue goose (McWilliams 1953). The ducks and geese were said to be present in "unbelievable numbers" in winter along the shores of Lake Pontchartrain. The Indians served the first French explorers fish cooked in bear fat, sagamité bread made from cornmeal mixed with bean flour, and wild strawberries. Their fishing gear was described as a line about 36 ft. (11 m) long, to which small lines with fish hooks were tied 1 ft. (30 cm) apart. The lines were baited with sagamité dough or meat and caught many fish weighing more than 15–20 lb. (7–9 kg). They also grew peaches, strawberries, plums, and grapes and used nuts to make flour.

Penicaut described the Indian method of making dugout canoes, which could measure up to 25 ft. (7.6 m) long. A large cypress tree was felled by burning its base, and fire was then used to burn out the interior. When the sides and bottom were the proper thickness, the fire was extinguished with mud, and the interior of the canoe was smoothed by scraping with cockle shells (mussels). Pearson et al. (1989) noted that some of the dugout canoes could be as large as 50 ft. (15 m) long.

The Acolapissa and other Indians were said to have regularly supplied the residents of New Orleans with meat from wild game, as well as other items such as corn, cornmeal, fish, bear oil, and persimmon bread (Usner 1998). The early French settlers apparently depended heavily on trade with neighboring Indian villages for their survival. However, by 1749 the supply of wild game in the New Orleans area was severely depleted and no longer a dependable supply of food (Surrey 1916; Kniffen 1990).

Rouquette (1938) described the lives of the Choctaw in and around New Orleans and stated that they planted corn, pumpkins, and potatoes and raised chickens, the latter having been introduced along with pigs (Kniffen 1990) to North America by early European explorers. They made baskets from cane and gathered medicinal plants for sale, including "Virginia snake-root, sage, plantain, tarragon, wild fruit, *pommetes* (medlar tree), blue bottle, persimmons, and Scuppernongs, also, roots of seguiena, sarsparilla, and sassafras." Although the identity of several of these is quite clear, others are unidentifiable with any certainty. Rouquette also stated that the Choctaw sold "ground turtles, which they find on the prairies" (apparently either box turtles, *Terrapene carolina*, or gopher tortoises, *Gopherus polyphemus*).

After the coming of Europeans, Native Americans suffered greatly from disease, war, displacement, and enslavement. By 1700 many had already died from diseases introduced by Europeans, including smallpox, typhus, influenza, measles, yellow fever, dysentery, and cholera (Usner 1998). Iberville stated that one-fourth of the people in the Mugulasha village along the Mississippi River had been killed by smallpox (McWilliams 1981). Most of the small tribes were virtually eliminated soon after European contact and were almost extinct in the Lake Pontchartrain area by the end of the nineteenth century. Some estimates of their declining numbers are given in Table 2.

Two Choctaw settlements with few residents remained in the Pontchartrain area in 1909, one on Bayou Lacombe and one on the Pearl River 12 mi. (19 km) from its mouth (Bushnell 1909). The village on the Pearl River was in 1936 represented only by burial mounds (Hall and Penfound 1939). A few Choctaw remained on the northern side of Lake Pontchartrain into the 1920s and 1930s and continued selling wares such as baskets, filé powder (made from sassafras leaves, *Sassafras albidum*), and various roots and herbs in the New Orleans French Market (Widmer 1989). They would travel by pirogue across Lake Pontchartrain and into the city by way of Bayou St. John (Usner 1998).

The Choctaw at Bayou Lacombe called their village Butchu'wa, which was also their name for Bayou Lacombe (Bushnell 1909). Their primitive dwellings were constructed of a sapling frame covered with palmetto thatch (*Serenoa repens*, and possibly also *Sabal minor*). They ate many local plants, including greenbriar (*Smilax laurifolia*; pounded roots made into cakes and fried), wild bean (*Phaseolus diversifolius*; roots boiled and mashed), acorns of "*Quercus aquatica*" (*Q. nigra?*; pounded, boiled, and used as meal), nuts of hickory ("*Juglans*

Table 2 Total population estimates of major Native American tribes occurring in the Pontchartrain basin between 1650 and 1908

Year	Quinipissa	Bayogoula	Acolapissa	Houma	Biloxi
1650			1500		
1698	merged with Bayogoulas	825	1050	1225	420
1700				700	
1702		350			
1715		140			
1718				450	
1720					175
1722			700		
1739		merged with Houma	merged with Houma	300	
1758				180	
1784				75	
1804				60	
1805					105
1829					65
1908					6–8?

Data from Kunkel (1951) and Swanton (1952)

squamosa" = *Carya* spp.; pounded and made into a soup), and leaves of sassafras (fall leaves dried and pounded into a powder to flavor foods, known as *filé*). They also gathered wild fruits such as berries, haws, and crabapples and grew crops including corn, rice, beans, and potatoes.

According to Bushnell (1909), game such as deer (*Odocoileus virginianus*), bear (*Ursus americanus*), rabbits (*Sylvilagus floridanus* and *S. aquaticus*), and squirrels (*Sciurus carolinensis* and *S. niger*) were hunted with blowguns constructed from cane (as *Arundinaria gigantea*). Cane and palmetto were also used to make baskets. Dyes were made from the roots of yellow dock (*Rumex crispus*; yellow dye), ashes from the bark of red oak and "black gum" (*Quercus falcata*, as *Q. texana*, and water tupelo, *Nyssa aquatica* or possibly also *N.*

sylvatica; red when applied to yellow fabric), and bark from walnut trees (*Juglans nigra*) brought from the north (black or dark brown). Strips of cypress bark (*Taxodium distichum*) were used as cords. At Bushnell's time, the Choctaw seldom ate fish or clams, even though both were abundant and had been eaten by their ancestors.

Many of the place names associated with Lake Pontchartrain are derived from Indian terms, primarily from the Choctaw language. These include *bayou* or *bogue* (river), *amite* (young), *ponchatoula* or *ponchitoawa* (singing hair or Spanish moss), *tangipahoa* or *tanzipao* (corn cob), *tchefuncte* (chinquapin, *Castanea pumila*), *falaya* (long), and *chinchuba* (alligator; Bushnell 1909; Parkerson 1969).

3.

Initial European Exploration

In spite of the centuries of occupation of the area by Native Americans, who were quite familiar with Okwa'ta, Lake Pontchartrain is said to have been "discovered" (and named) by the French Canadian Pierre le Moyne, Sieur d'Iberville, in 1699. Europeans had been in the New World almost 200 years, and the geography of many areas was relatively well known. The Mississippi River delta was a notable exception. In the late 1600s, three European powers were vying for control of eastern North America. Although there was considerable interaction and competition, and at times war, in general the powers eventually developed three primary regions of major activity. The British were focused on the mid-Atlantic coast from New England to the Carolinas. The French were well established in Canada and beginning to move into the upper Mississippi valley. The Spanish were most active in the Caribbean, Central America, Mexico, and Florida. Spanish explorers had claimed the north-central Gulf coast, which they called northern New Spain (Benavides 1630), but they had failed to recognize its value compared to the treasured gold and silver of Mexico. They established no settlements along the northern Gulf coast, and there is no clear evidence that they entered the mouth of the Mississippi, nor Lake Pontchartrain.

Spanish Exploration and Mapping

The Spanish exploration of the northern Gulf had begun in the early 1500s. According to French (1852), the Mississippi River was completely examined by Francisco de Garay (in 1518), but this now is clearly doubtful. As governor of Jamaica, Garay (who had come to the New World with Columbus on his second voyage in 1493) sent four ships to probe the Gulf coast in 1519 with Alvarez de Pineda in charge (Weddle 1985). This expedition resulted in a crude map, now known as the "Pineda map" (attributed to either Pineda or the expedition's pilots; Jackson 1995), which is significant as one of the first maps to show the features of the Gulf of Mexico. On the northern Gulf coast, the Pineda map shows a prominent river and bay labeled as "Rio del Espiritu Santo" (or River of the Holy Ghost), one of the few sites identified on the map.

Many historians have identified the Rio del Espiritu Santo with the Mississippi and have concluded that Pineda discovered and named the mouth of the Mississippi River in 1519 (Thomas 1939; Weber 1992; Kemp 1997). However, his description of a "very large and fluent river" where he entered and stayed for forty days while careening his ships has also been identified with the Rio del Espiritu Santo. A large Indian village at its mouth and more than forty Indian towns upstream within a distance of 6 leagues (about 20 mi. or 30 km), as well as a pear-shaped bay at its mouth, prove that this could not have been the Mississippi. Weddle (1985) concluded that Pineda did indeed map the mouth of the Mississippi in June 1519, but that his description of the pear-shaped bay was based upon a later visit in July or August 1519 to the Panuco River in Mexico. Numerous studies have attempted to determine the true identity of the Rio del Espiritu Santo (as well as its Bahia del Espiritu Santo) and have generated numerous discussions of this historical mystery. Many have concluded that it was most likely Mobile River and Mobile Bay (Hamilton 1904; Ogg 1904; Dunn 1917; Thomas 1939). Other theories have included the Colorado River and Matagorda Bay (Hallenbeck 1940), the Trinity River and Galveston Bay (Delanglez 1945), as well as the Mississippi River and Lake Pontchartrain–Lake Borgne (Upham 1902; Russell 1936). The theories of Upham (1902), although largely discredited, will be discussed below in view of their application to the Pontchartrain system.

The mystery of Rio del Espiritu Santo is further clouded by the habit of early explorers naming numerous sites "Espiritu Santo." It was common practice among the Spanish explorers to name sites based upon special days on which they were discovered (such as Pascua del Espiritu Santo, Whitsunday, Pentecost, or Festival of the Holy Spirit). These included the Bay of Espiritu Santo on the Florida coast where Hernando de Soto landed in May 1538 (now thought to be Tampa Bay [French 1875; Ogg 1904] or Charlotte Harbor [Weddle 1985]). Membre (an associate of La Salle) identified Espiritu Santo Bay as being to the northeast of the Mississippi River mouth (possibly Apalachee Bay according to Shea 1903). Coxe (1722, in French 1850) referred to the Apalachicola River as "river of Spirito Santo," and LaHarpe (c. 1723) used the name "Saint-Esprit River" in reference to the St. John's River in Florida.

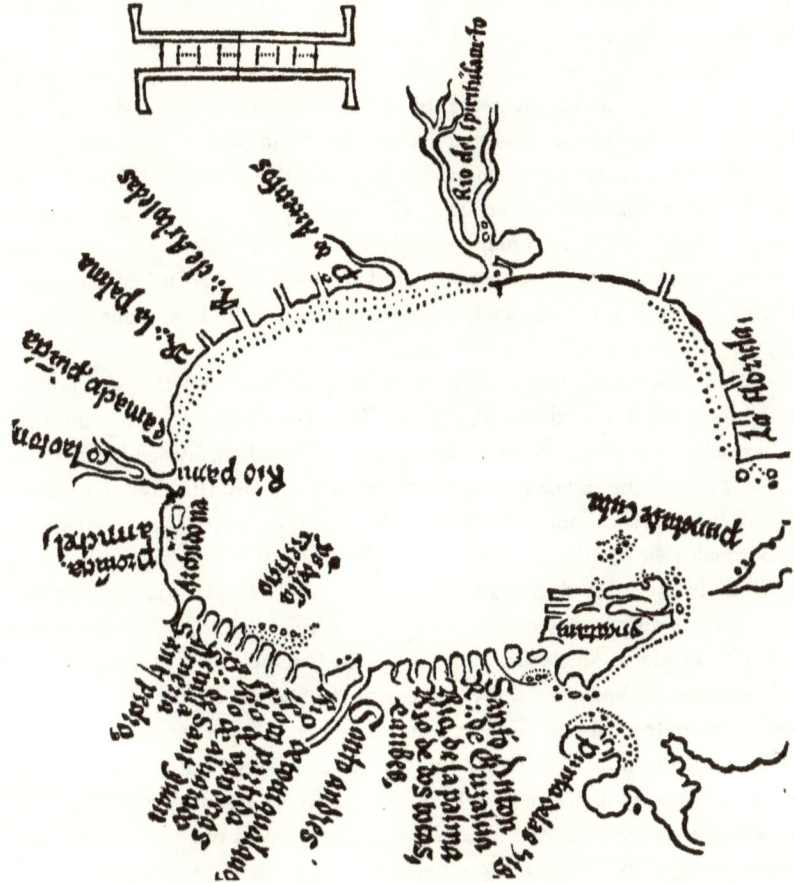

Figure 3.1 The Cortes map of the Gulf of Mexico, c. 1520 (Reprinted from Weddle, *Spanish Sea*, 1985; used with permission of Texas A&M University Press)

To add to the confusion, several names had been given to the Mississippi River by the early explorers. In addition to Rio del Espiritu Santo, the Spanish called it Rio de la Palizada, Rio Grande de la Florida, and Rio de Escondido (French 1852, 1875; Caruso 1966). The French gave their own names to the great river, first the Colbert River (a name given by La Salle) and then the St. Louis, the Conception, and the Baude (although the latter three never seemed to be commonly used; Caruso 1966). Several Native American names had been assigned to different parts of the river, such as Malbanchia, Chacaqua, Tamalisieu, Taputu, Mico, and Oquechiton (Lowery 1959; Caruso 1966). Coxe (1722) also listed the Native American name Sassagoula and the Spanish Rio Grande del Norte. The Algonquin name of Mechesebe for the upper Mississippi (meaning "big river") has stood the test of time.

In spite of this confusion, there was definitely a tendency among early explorers to associate the great river of mid-America with the Rio del Espiritu Santo of Pineda. Several other maps of the 1500s and 1600s (apparently based upon the Pineda map) show a large river and bay labeled Espiritu Santo in the central Gulf coast with connections to New France, or Canada (Dunn 1917). One of these is the "Cortes map" published in the 1520s, which shows Rio del Espiritu Santo with two large branches and a prominent circular bay to the east near its mouth that is remarkably similar in appearance to Lake Pontchartrain (Figure 3.1).

Panfilo de Narvaez skirted the northern Gulf coast in 1528 and reported fresh water far at sea off the Mississippi River (Kniffen 1990). Hernando de Soto reached the river, in what is now northern Mississippi, overland from Florida in 1543, and the remnants of his expedition descended the river en route to Mexico. One of these survivors (Luis de Moscoso) identified this *rio grande* of de Soto with the Rio del Espiritu Santo (Weddle 1985). Subsequently, the "Soto map," made by Alonso de Santa Cruz prior to 1559 (Delanglez 1945), shows Rio del Espiritu Santo emptying into a large bay named Bahia del Espiritu Santo and Mar Pequena ("little sea"; Weddle 1985). Doctor Pedro de Santander, a royal overseer at Veracruz in 1557, described the Rio del Espiritu Santo based upon reports from the de Soto expedition as having "eight leagues [24 mi. or 38 km] of mouth. . . . It is fertile and luxuriant, and its banks twenty leagues [60 mi. or 96 km] upstream are well populated. There are many mulberry trees for silk, walnuts, grapes, and various other fruits. Down this river come many canoes manned by Indian archers" (Weddle 1985). Survivors of the disastrous Don Tristan de Luna y Arellano expedition to establish a settlement at Pensacola Bay in 1559 were aware of the Rio del Espiritu Santo west of Mobile Bay (which they called Bahia Filipina; Weddle 1985). In spite of these early explorations, the Spanish neglected the northern Gulf for the next 100 years or so, and much of this earlier Spanish knowledge of northern Gulf geography was mostly forgotten.

Based upon incomplete knowledge of the reports of these early expeditions and maps, Upham (1902) proposed a theory that "the course of navigation entering the Mississippi from the Gulf of Mexico, or going out from the river, in all instances definitely identifiable previous to 1699, was by way of the Bayou Manchac" and thus through Lakes Maurepas, Pontchartrain, and Borgne. He suggested that the Indian town described by Pineda at the mouth of the river may have been at the mouth of Bayou Manchac, either at the Mississippi River or near Lake Maurepas. He was also convinced that remnants of de Soto's expedition "did not pass down the Mississippi to its delta, but went out to the Gulf of Mexico by way of the Bayou Manchac, lakes Maurepas, Pontchartrain, and Borgne, and Mississippi sound." Also according to Upham, the large freshwater bay they entered and sailed through for three days must have been "the Vaya (Bay) del Espiritu Santo, which is also called Mar Pequena (Little Sea), taking the place of the lakes north of New Orleans," or Lakes Pontchartrain and Borgne. Russell (1936) cited Upham (1902) regarding Pineda and de Soto's followers possibly passing through Lake Pontchartrain. There is no clear evidence that any Europeans entered Lake Pontchartrain prior to Iberville, so Upham's intriguing theory relative to the history of Lake Pontchartrain is obviously incorrect.

Renewed Spanish interest in the northern Gulf was sparked by the shocking news in 1685 that the French had established a colony along the coast. In 1682 the French explorer René-Robert Cavelier de La Salle journeyed by birchbark canoe down the Mississippi (or Colbert) River from the Great Lakes to its mouth and claimed its entire drainage for France, naming the land Louisiana in honor of King Louis XIV. He returned in 1684 intending to explore the river by way of the Gulf of Mexico and establish a colony there, but this expedition resulted in disaster and his death. He missed the river and continued along the coast to the west 435 mi. (700 km), where he established his settlement on Matagorda Bay, which he named Saint Louis Bay. Some scholars have suggested that La Salle may have intentionally bypassed the Mississippi River to be closer to the coveted silver mines of Spanish Mexico (de Vorsey 1982). Because the Spanish had claimed the Gulf coast area since 1493, when a Papal Bull had divided the New World between Spain and Portugal (Caruso 1966; Rule 1969), they felt threatened by this French invasion and began looking for the settlement in order to drive the French out of their territory. The Spanish attempt to find La Salle's colony, beginning in 1686, resulted in eleven expeditions to explore and map the northern Gulf coast and establish Spanish settlements to defend their claim (Leonard 1936).

Not knowing the location of La Salle's settlement, the Spanish assumed that it must be on the great bay or river that they called Espiritu Santo, poorly known but supposedly the best harbor on the Gulf of Mexico (Dunn 1917). Thus, when the Spanish began looking for La Salle's colony, they were looking for Espiritu Santo Bay, but did not know its location. The first of these expeditions, led by Juan Enriques Barroto and Antonio Romero in 1686 (diary kept by Juan Jordan de Reina 1686; see Leonard 1936), reached the large river and named it Rio de la Palizada because of the large quantity of trees and driftwood that choked its mouth. The point of land associated with this mouth they named Cabo de Lodo (Mud Cape), and the adjacent waters to the east they apparently named Lago de Lodo (the Mississippi Sound–Lake Borgne area). But they did not recognize the river as the Mississippi or Espiritu Santo, because it was supposed to empty into the excellent harbor of Espiritu Santo Bay (Dunn 1917). Another expedition in 1687, under the command of Captains Martin de Rivas and Antonio de Iriarte (with Barroto and Romero as pilots), found evidence of the French colony at a large bay, which they named San Bernardo Bay (now known as Matagorda Bay), but the remnants of the colony just 5 mi. (8 km) up the Garcitas River were not found (Thomas 1939). This expedition followed the coast to the Rio de la Palizada, explored and mapped many of its distributaries (Weddle 1987), and then continued to Mobile Bay, which they concluded must be the bay shown on the maps as Espiritu Santo, since no other body of water fit so closely its general description (Dunn 1917). Subsequent Spanish expeditions were instructed to explore "Espiritu Santo or Mobile bay" (Leonard 1939). Another expedition in 1687, led by Don Andres de Pez and Francisco de Gamarra, arrived at the Mississippi River delta on August 2 and explored four channels of the river mouth (Holmes 1982).

The ruins of La Salle's colony were finally found at Matagorda Bay in 1689. According to Bolton (1916), the Spanish applied the name Bahia del Espiritu Santo to the mouth of the Mississippi until La Salle's landing at Matagorda Bay; because he was reported to have sailed for Bahia del Espiritu Santo, they transferred the name to that location, and many references continued to refer to Matagorda Bay as Espiritu Santo Bay. In the words of LaHarpe (c. 1723), La Salle "arrived at the bay which he named for Saint Louis, and which the Spaniards now call Bay Saint-Esprit."

The Spanish continued their explorations in the northern Gulf with special attention given to Pensacola Bay (their Bahia de Santa Maria de Galve). In 1693 Don Carlos de Siguenza y Gongora, professor emeritus of the University of Mexico, was sent with Don Andres de Pez to further explore and map the Gulf coast from Pensacola to "Espiritu Santo or Mobile bay" and then continue on to map the entire coast, including "the Colbert, which is called the Palizada, river" (Siguenza 1693, in Leonard 1939). They were instructed to "enter this stream at its mouth and sail up and examine it as far as circumstances permit; a map and plan must be drawn with very great care and the utmost accuracy, indicating whatever is seen and noted on this river, its harbors, island, and coves; he will likewise endeavor to find out about the Indian tribes living on its banks, the quality of the fruits produced in the length and breadth of that region, and its limits and boundaries." In the report of this expedition, they referred to

"Mosquito island sound" (Breton Sound), "the San Diego islets" (Chandeleur Islands), and "cape Lodo" at the mouth of the "Palizada river," but failed to enter the river because of the violent current and the numerous trees that blocked their way. de Siguenza y Gongora and de Pez apparently also labeled the Chandeleur Sound or Lake Borgne area "Laguna de Pez" (Dunn 1917). Returning to their ship, they marveled "that the fame and celebrity of such a great river had come to this." Unfortunately for the future of Spanish interests in the Mississippi valley, their description of the river was summarized in the brief report: "as it was impossible to get into the Palizada river as set forth in my entry of Wednesday, May 6, it is also impossible to satisfy in whole or in part what was ordered under this heading."

There is no evidence that any of these Spanish expeditions ever entered Lake Pontchartrain. However, Iberville noted the Spanish application of "baye du S. Esprit" to Lake Pontchartrain or Lake Borgne, although apparently erroneously. In a letter to the French Minister of Marine, Louis Phelypeaux, Comte de Pontchartrain, written on December 19, 1698, Iberville wrote "I shall follow my first intention which is to search for it [the Mississippi] in the vicinity of the *baye de Lago de Lodo.*" In a 1699 narrative of his first expedition to Louisiana, Iberville (in French 1869) referred to "Lago de Lodo (Muddy Lake), which is the name the Spaniards give to the Bay of St. Esprit," and apparently named because of its association with the Cabo de Lodo (Mud Cape) of Barroto and Romero at the mouth of the river (Dunn 1917). Iberville reported that his route from the Mississippi River through Bayou Manchac, Lake Maurepas, and Lake Pontchartrain "terminates by emptying at the extremity of the Bay of Lago de Lodo" (also see Hamilton 1904).

Delanglez (1945) argued that "Lago de Lodo" was a mistaken reading on the part of Iberville for Cabo de Lodo. Delanglez also included a list of questions submitted to Iberville by French geographer Claude Delisle: "What is *Lago de Lodo?* Is it Lake Pontchartrain? Does it include St. Louis and Biloxi bays? Is its entrance very far from the sea? Is it what the other maps call baye du St. Esprit?" Apparently Iberville's answers, if he did respond to these questions, are not available to us. On one of the anonymous maps examined by Delanglez (Archives du Service Hydrographique, Paris, 138bis-1-5), the legend "Lac du pontchartrain" of the original is crossed out and is replaced by "baye du S. Esprit."

Jackson (1995) attempted to correct Delanglez' error regarding Iberville's perceived "mistake." One of the Spanish charts apparently in Iberville's possession during his 1699 expedition was a map drawn in 1696 by Juan Bisente (that is, Juan Vicente a Spanish pilot who accompanied Iberville; Delanglez 1945) as a faithful copy of the lost map of Juan Enriquez Barroto drawn in 1687 (Figure

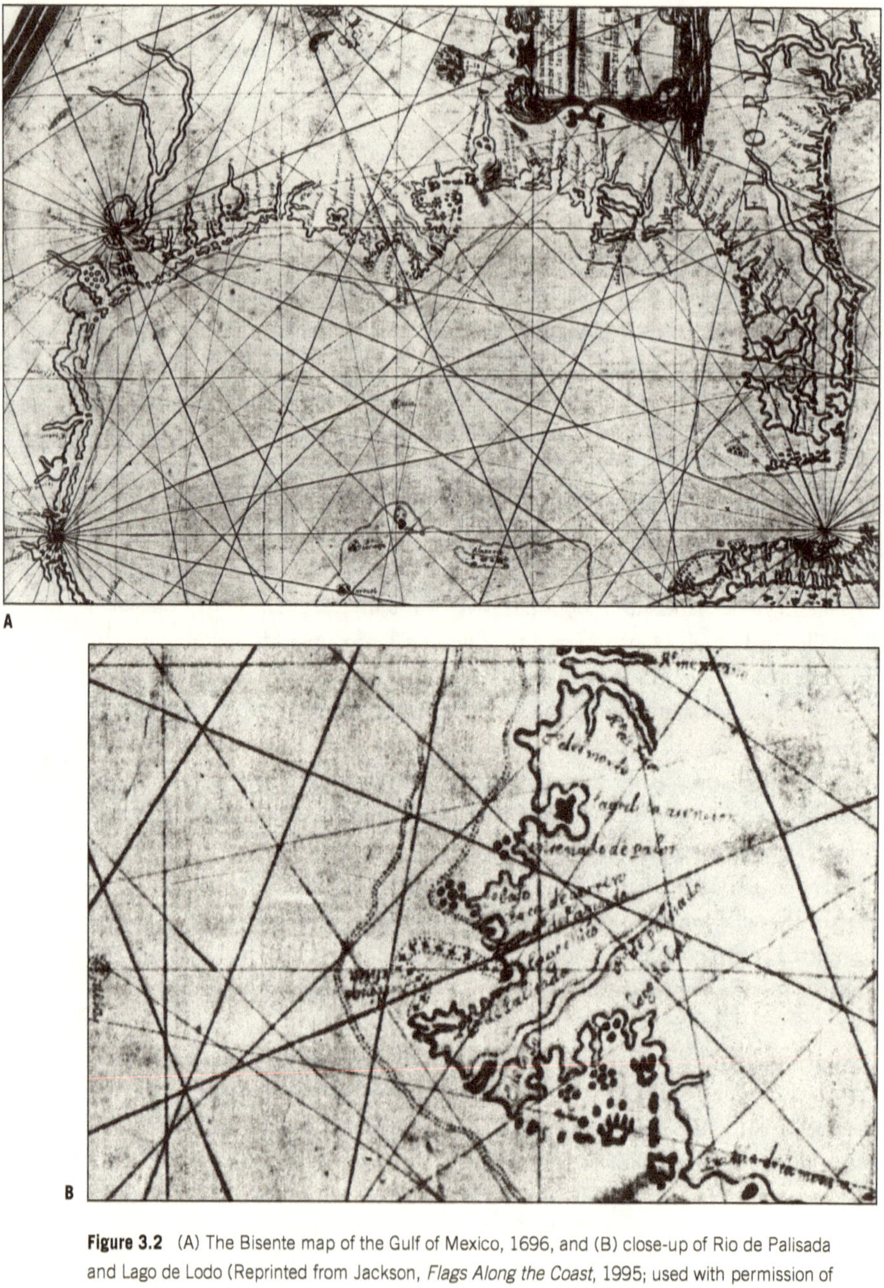

Figure 3.2 (A) The Bisente map of the Gulf of Mexico, 1696, and (B) close-up of Rio de Palisada and Lago de Lodo (Reprinted from Jackson, *Flags Along the Coast*, 1995; used with permission of the author)

3.2). Delanglez was not aware of Bisente's map. This map had been obtained in 1697 from the Spanish ship *Santo Cristo de Maracaibo*, along with Bisente who was taken prisoner, by the French ship *Bon* (Captain M. de Patoulet). The label Lago de Lodo, as well as Cabo de Lodo, does appear on Bisente's map. Lago de Lodo (the Mississippi Sound–Lake Borgne area) must have been named during the 1686 Barroto and Romero expedition, although it is not mentioned in the Juan Jordan de Reina log (Jackson 1995; also see Leonard 1936) nor in Barroto's 1686 diary (Weddle 1987). It probably was labeled on the Enriquez Barroto maps, the source for Bisente's copy. Another Bisente map drawn in 1700 also included a label for Lago de Lodo (Jackson 1995).

Lake Pontchartrain was again referred to as Spiritu Santo Bay by Dr. John Sibley, a visitor to New Orleans in 1802, which Whittington (1927) noted incorrectly was the "first time we have seen this name applied to Lake Pontchartrain." However, Sibley also mentioned "very large Oysters" as plentiful in this bay, so his application of the name could have extended into Lake Borgne, Chandeleur Sound, and Breton Sound, where oysters are more common than in Lake Pontchartrain.

Initial French Exploration

Fourteen years after La Salle's ill-fated expedition, the French renewed their efforts to establish a permanent settlement near the mouth of the Mississippi River to protect their interests in Louisiana and the Mississippi valley. Iberville, a French naval hero from Canada, was sent by the French government to establish this settlement and to assure French control of the Mississippi valley (McWilliams 1981). Fortunately for the historical record, Iberville and others with him kept detailed journals of their activities in exploring and colonizing the lower Mississippi valley. These include Iberville's Gulf journals (Iberville 1699a, 1699b, 1700, 1702; McWilliams 1981), the journal of Sauvole, who was placed in command when Iberville returned to France (Higginbotham 1969), the journal of "Le Marin" (Sinclair 1974; anonymous but attributed to Sauvole by Brasseaux 1979 and Weddle 1991), the journal of Paul du Ru, a priest traveling with Iberville on his second expedition (Butler 1934), *The History of Louisiana* by Le Page du Pratz (1774), *The Historical Journal of the Establishment of the French in Louisiana* (LaHarpe c. 1723), and the *Penicaut Narrative*, written by a ship carpenter and Indian interpreter for Iberville (Penicaut 1722; McWilliams 1953). The last two must be referred to with caution, however, because of obvious errors in chronology and misstatements (McCann 1941; Conrad 1971).

On the first of three visits to the northern Gulf coast (from December 31, 1698, through May 31, 1699), Iberville learned from a hunting party of Bayogoula and Mugulasha Indians near Ship Island, Mississippi, of a great river to the west where their village was located. Iberville correctly assumed that this river, called the Malbanchia, must be the Mississippi (McWilliams 1969, 1981).

Iberville entered the Mississippi River for the first time on March 2, 1699, and camped among the reeds about 5 mi. (8 km) above the mouth. He noted that the river water was muddy and "white" and did not blend with the salt water for about three-quarters of a league (2.25 mi. or 3 km) seaward. He described the land adjacent to the river as very low with reeds and brambles and very tall grass, with clumps of "alder" (probably willow, *Salix nigra*) short and as wide as a leg or thigh, then upstream 6 leagues (18 mi. or 29 km) alders 30–40 ft. (9–12 m) high and as wide as a man's body (McWilliams 1981). He described abundant canes along the river as large as 6 in. (15 cm) in circumference. The canes were more than 25 ft. (7.6 m) high and 1.5 in. (3.8 cm) thick (Sinclair 1974). They saw several Indian boats, including several composed of "three sections of canes bundled together" and a "canoe made from the trunk of a tree that had been hollowed out by fire." The crew of *Le Marin* saw abundant game including "ducks, bustards [turkeys or rails?], sarcelles [teal?], and sarrigue, the latter being an animal that carries its offspring in a bag in its stomach [opossum]," as well as "stags, roebucks and buffaloes." There were numerous "crocodiles" and a rattlesnake 6 ft. (1.8 m) long. The group was given smoked buffalo and bear meat to eat by the Indians, as well as "millet" or "Indian wheat" (maize or corn).

On March 9, Iberville reached the site of a portage (said to be about 50 leagues [150 mi. or 240 km] from the sea, apparently near the current location of the Bonnet Carré Spillway; Weddle 1991), through which the Indians often traveled from the Mississippi River by way of Lake Pontchartrain to the bay where the French ships were anchored (in Mississippi Sound). Farther upstream (at about 70 leagues [210 mi. or 338 km] from the sea), the Indians pointed out a waterway they called Ascanthia into which the Mississippi flowed and through which they could go to the land of the Biloxis, or into this same bay where Iberville had left his ships (McWilliams 1981). Surprisingly, no mention is made on this trip up the river of the portage to Bayou St. John, even though Iberville camped on the night of March 7 at a nearby site where there were ten thatch huts and a few additional huts surrounded by a redoubt of canes.

In continuing his explorations upriver to the site of Natchez, Iberville confirmed that this was indeed the river that La Salle had explored in 1682. On their return downstream, Iberville's group divided, with most continuing down the Mississippi in their longboats (including his second in command, M. de

Sauvole, and Iberville's younger brother, Jean Baptiste le Moyne, Sieur de Bienville). Iberville with a small crew in two birchbark canoes explored the shortcut described by the Indians as Ascanthia, which Iberville named for himself, the Iberville River (McWilliams 1981). This waterway eventually became known as Bayou Manchac. Read (1927) suggested that the Indian name "Ascantia" [sic] meant "cane is there," an appropriate name in view of the immense canebrakes described by Darby (1816) as occurring along the banks.

Penicaut (writing prior to 1723) applied the name *manchacq* to both Bayou Manchac and Pass Manchac and noted that this word "in French means a channel" (McWilliams 1953). In France, the term *la manche* literally means "the sleeve," but has also been applied at least since the 1600s to narrow, elongated bodies of water such as the English Channel (Joseph Garreau, personal communication). However, Read (1927, 1928, 1931) held that the name Manchac was derived from the Mobilian or Choctaw word *imashaka* or *mashake*, meaning "rear entrance," and local tradition has held that this passageway was the "back door to the Gulf" (Dranguet and Heleniak 1985). Read (1928) further supported his theory by noting the label of a small tributary stream on Captain Philip Pittman's 1770 map of the Iberville River (McDermott 1976) as "Mashake," which seems to correspond in location to Bayou Barbary in Livingston Parish, Louisiana. Pittman stated that the French referred to Pass Manchac as Grand Massiac (McDermott 1976), but there seems to be no other reference to this name being applied to the pass. The name could have been in recognition of the French Minister of Marine for 1758, Claude Louis d'Espinchal, marquis de Massiac, who died in 1770. The true derivation of the name Manchac for the bayou and pass may not be determined with certainty, although Penicaut seems to have been the first to apply the name in writing and indicated a French origin for the term. McCann (1941) suggested that Penicaut must have been using a name for this waterway assigned at a much later date than Iberville's explorations. However, the "back-door" theory of Read has become well-established folklore relative to the Lake Pontchartrain system.

After about 13 leagues (39 mi. or 63 km) of repeated portages over fallen trees and dense vegetation, Iberville's group reached the clear, relatively fast-flowing Amite River, which carried them into Lake Maurepas, then Pass Manchac, and finally into Lake Pontchartrain. Iberville described one of the spots where they rested along Bayou Manchac as "one of the prettiest spots I have seen, fine level woods, clear and bare of canes; but ... inundated to a depth of 5 to 6 ft. [1.5–1.8 m] during high water" (McWilliams 1981). He reported seeing many turkey, fish, and "crocodiles," the last being "very good to eat." One was reportedly 18 ft. (5.5 m) long. Near the mouth of the Amite River, a herd of 200 buffalo (*Bison bison*) was seen. Upon reaching Lake Pontchartrain on March 27,

1699, the group camped on the northern side of the pass near the current site of the Manchac lighthouse.

Iberville's group continued around the southern perimeter of the lake to exit through the Rigolets. In his narrative of the expedition, Iberville (1699a; in French 1869) stated that the system "terminates by emptying at the extremity of the Bay of Lago de Lodo," apparently a reference to Mississippi Sound, Chandeleur Sound, and Breton Sound. Le Page du Pratz (1774) noted two passes into Lake Pontchartrain named the Great and the Little Channel, with the Great Channel to the south. These names could have applied to the Rigolets and Chef Menteur Pass, but since the Rigolets is much larger than Chef Menteur Pass (which lies to the south), the Little Channel of Le Page du Pratz was most likely one of the channels leading from the Rigolets into the Pearl River. On some early charts the Rigolets is labeled "Pass á Guyon," and "les Rigolets ou passant les chaloupes" (channels for ships' boats) designates a waterway off the mouth of the Pearl River (Cipra 1997).

On this first expedition, Iberville considered erecting a fort on the shore of Lake Pontchartrain, but instead erected Fort Maurepas (or Fort Biloxi) on Biloxi Bay near the mouth of the Pascagoula River (at the current site of Ocean Springs, Mississippi; McWilliams 1981). After Iberville left to return to France on May 3, 1699, M. de Sauvole was placed in command of the fort. On May 22 he sent out a party to sound out Lakes Pontchartrain and Maurepas, led by Bienville (only twenty years old at the time), who concluded that it would be impossible to "make establishments at their edges" because the land was so low and wet (Higginbotham 1969). In August another party of six men under the command of Bienville was sent to explore the Mississippi River, which they entered by way of Lakes Pontchartrain and Maurepas and the Manchac portage (LaHarpe c. 1723; Caruso 1966). After visiting Indian villages along the river, they descended to the mouth and en route encountered an English frigate at the now-famous "English Turn," where Bienville successfully defended French possession of the river by convincing the English to depart. After returning upriver, Bienville crossed into Lake Pontchartrain by way of the portage near the Bonnet Carré Spillway site (eventually known as the Tigonillou portage, by way of Bayou LaBranche-Trepagnier) on October 11, and then proceeded across the lake en route to Biloxi (LaHarpe c. 1723).

On his second visit to the northern Gulf of Mexico (from December 22, 1699, through May 28, 1700), Iberville returned to Lake Pontchartrain, this time by way of the Rigolets. On January 17–19 he explored the portage from the lake to the river, apparently also the Tigonillou portage by way of Bayou LaBranche "at the far end of the lake" (although incorrectly identified as Bayou

St. John by McWilliams 1981, p. III, fn. 16). Many references have perpetuated McWilliams' misidentification of this portage as Bayou St. John, and considerable confusion has been generated regarding the identity of the several portages between the southern side of Lake Pontchartrain and the Mississippi River (Weddle 1991). The first portage used by Iberville to enter Lake Pontchartrain was the Manchac portage (or Iberville River) by way of Bayou Manchac, Amite River, Lake Maurepas, and Pass Manchac. Three other portages in the New Orleans area were also mentioned, but have been the source of confusion. The earliest of these, found first by Bienville, and later by Iberville as noted in his journal for January 17, 1700, was apparently in the Bayou Trepagnier/LaBranche or Bayou Piquant area (described as 22 leagues [66 mi. or 106 km] above Fort Boulaye [or about 115 mi. or 186 km above the mouth of the river] and 4 leagues [12 mi. or 19 km] from the Manchac portage). It was given several names, including Tigonillou (or Tigouyn) portage or Ravine du Sueur, having been named after French explorer Pierre-Charles LeSueur. In February 1700, both Iberville and Bienville were visiting Bayogoula villages on the river and met LeSueur (who was traveling up the river to establish a settlement in what is now Minnesota) at the Tigonillou portage (Conrad 1971). He was having his supplies transported across the portage from the lake, and henceforth the portage was known as "Ravine du Sueur." Because two of LeSueur's men became lost during this portage, it has also been referred to as "Portage des egarez" or "portage of the lost" (Butler 1934; Pearson et al. 1993). On March 1 and again on March 29, Iberville described his initial exploration of another "portage," located only 2 leagues (6 mi. or 10 km) above the fort, but found this one so bad that he was forced to turn back. Sometime later, Bayou St. John was to become an important shortcut between the lake and the river, but apparently Iberville did not mention using this portage, even though he had camped nearby on the night of March 7, 1699, and mentioned the presence of several Indian huts there. Eventually with the development of New Orleans in 1718 (at a location about 12 leagues [36 mi. or 58 km] above the fort and about 1.25 mi. or 2 km from the upper end of Bayou St. John), the St. John portage became the most important connection between the lake and the river.

Iberville described the stream leading to the Tigonillou portage, as "20 yards wide, 10 feet deep, and 1 league long" (18 m wide, 3 m deep, and 4.8 km long), but only 1–2 ft. (0.3–0.6 m) deep at the lake (McWilliams 1981). The portage was also 1 league long (3 mi. or 4.8 km), the first half "full of water and mud up to the knee," the other half fairly good, "being a country of canes and fine woods, suitable to live in." The southern side of the lake was bordered by a wide "prairie" before the tall trees. On January 20, Iberville's group crossed the lake and spent the night near a small freshwater stream 3 leagues (9 mi. or 14 km) from the Rigolets at a site probably near Goose Point or Cane Bayou.

On February 5, 1700, Iberville returned to the Mississippi River and began clearing land to build the first French post in what is now Louisiana, Fort Boulaye (also known as Fort Mississippi), at the first high spot (about 50 mi. or 80 km) above the mouth of the river (McWilliams 1981), thought to be located at the present location of the community of Phoenix. Blackberry bushes were abundant here, and there was a border of hardwood trees 600 yd. (550 m) wide along the river. Upstream about 6 mi. (10 km) they found "cedar trees, called cedars of Lebanon," which they used to make wooden dugout canoes. These were most likely cypress (King 1893), although Butler (1934) suggested that they could have been either red cedar (*Juniperus virginiana*) or white cedar (*Chaemaecyparis thyoides*). Pearson et al. (1989) reported that the wooden dugout canoes, or pirogues, of the Indians and the French were usually made of cypress logs. Du Ru reported parakeets (*Conuropsis carolinensis*) by the thousands at the bayou portage, 66 mi. (106 km) upriver from the fort (Butler 1934).

Penicaut reported his observations of Lake Pontchartrain while exploring with Bienville (McWilliams 1953). He described both sides of the entrance to the Rigolets as being elevated by masses of shells, and thus called Pointe-aux-Coquilles. Within the lake he noted the projection to the left called Pointe aux Herbes (Grass Point). A short distance to the west they identified a small river called Choupicatcha by the Indians, which the French named Riviere d'Orleans (but ultimately became known as Bayou St. Jean, and later St. John, supposedly in honor of Bienville, or Jean Baptiste le Moyne, Sieur de Bienville; Giraud 1974). According to Le Page du Pratz (1774), the bayou, or probably the upper branch of it extending west along what is now Metairie Road, was named "Bayouc Choupic, so designated from a fish of that name" (bowfin, *Amia calva*).

According to Penicaut (McWilliams 1953), they bypassed Bayou St. John and proceeded along the southern shore to the other portage (5 leagues [15 mi. or 24 km], and thus in the vicinity of Bayou LaBranche), where their Indian guides explained that they could reach the Mississippi River. They camped there for the night and the next morning made their way across to the river, which was described as "light-colored, very good to drink, and quite clear." There were large cypress trees and reeds with seeds like oats (possibly *Phragmites* or *Arundinaria*) that were used by the Natives to make bread and sagamité, as well as abundant wild turkeys. Bienville and Penicaut continued their explorations by circling the lake and camped for the night at Pass Manchac. The following day they came to "another river that the savages guiding us called Tandgepao, which in savage signifies white corn; the water in it is very good to drink." They spent the night at

Bayou Castine, then left Lake Pontchartrain to enter the Pearl River, where they collected "cockles," or mussels, from which they removed pearls. Prior to this discovery, the Pearl River had been known as "Talcatcha," which meant Rock River in the Acolapissa language, and as "River of the Acolapissa" to the first European visitors (Hall and Penfound 1939).

Almost immediately after its construction, Fort Boulaye (Fort Mississippi) became a center of activity, with all sorts of visitors present, including French Canadian voyageurs, soldiers, and Canadians from the Illinois (McWilliams 1981). Because the strong currents and many bends in the Mississippi River made sailing ship travel slow and dependent upon favorable winds, the route from Fort Biloxi by way of Lake Pontchartrain and the portages was commonly used to reach Fort Boulaye.

Also during the early to mid-1700s, the first fortification was built by Bienville on Lake Pontchartrain at the mouth of Bayou St. John, a log house with artillery to guard the entrance to the bayou from the lake (Kelly 1975; Freiberg 1980; Casey 1983). At about the same time, a small fortification was built on the lakeshore at the mouth of Bayou Tigouyou (that is, Bayou Trepagnier). Thus, the two primary portages between the lake and river could be defended.

Iberville's third voyage to the Mississippi occurred from December 15, 1701, to April 27, 1702 (McWilliams 1981), and a new fort was built on the Mobile River. Transport of goods such as buffalo hides, deer skins, and beaver pelts from the upper Mississippi continued through Lake Pontchartrain. Penicaut reported numerous trips up and down the river in subsequent years, including many fur traders from the north. One shipment included more than 12,000 buffalo hides. The French center of activity was to become Mobile and Biloxi, however, and Fort Boulaye was abandoned in 1705 (Penicaut, in McWilliams 1953). Iberville died of yellow fever contracted in Havana in 1706, and Bienville became acting governor of the Louisiana Territory (Kemp 1997).

English Intrusions

The English had also begun to show signs of invading the Mississippi valley in the late 1600s (Rule 1969). Two Englishmen led 200 Chickasaw slave hunters in attacking an Acolapissa village on Pearl River near Lake Pontchartrain in 1699 (LaHarpe c. 1723). Later that year, the English frigate *Carolina Galley*, under Captain Lewis Bond, appeared in the Mississippi River apparently in the service of Daniel Coxe (1722, in French 1850), an English landowner in the colony of "Carolana." At the major bend in the river now known as "English Turn," they met the party of French explorers led by Bienville, who convinced the English to depart back down the river. Subsequently the English were to have little influence in the area until about 1750 with the beginning of the French and Indian War. However, an English map produced by Richard Mount and Thomas Page in 1700 shows substantial detail of the "Entrance of the River Mefafhebe or Mifchifipi" and shows a branch of the river going east from the vicinity of Bayou Manchac to Chandeleur Sound (which is labeled "Nassau Bay"), but with no lakes indicated (Jackson 1995). Coxe (1722, in French 1850), described what is apparently Mississippi Sound, Chandeleur Sound, and Breton Sound as "the Bay of Nassau or Spirito Santo," and noted that the Mississippi River branch through Lake Pontchartrain "empties itself into the N.E. end of the great Bay of Spirito Santo."

4.

European Colonization, Occupation, and Conflict

French Colonization

Even before New Orleans was developed, Lake Pontchartrain, Bayou Manchac, and Bayou St. John had become important waterways for the transport of goods to the French colony at Mobile. The voyageurs were active in the upper Mississippi valley and would transport to Mobile by way of Lake Pontchartrain pelts, lead, bear's oil, slaves, smoked meat, wheat, and flour (Giraud 1974), even though Bayou Manchac was almost dry for nine months of the year and choked up with dead wood (Le Page du Pratz 1774). In 1712 Martin D'Artaguiette, a French Commissary of Marine, made plans for diverting the Mississippi River into Bayou Manchac to improve its use as a transportation route, but these plans apparently never materialized (Giraud 1974). Marc-Antoine Hubert, commissary-general from 1716–1720, suggested that storehouses be built at "Biloxy on the Mississippi," the future site of New Orleans, to shorten the journey of French Canadian voyageurs traveling down the river from the "Illinois country" (Giraud 1993). Penicaut (McWilliams 1953) reported that plans for the settlement began in 1717, with some living quarters and two large warehouses built.

Major land clearing began the following year for the settlement that was to become the city of New Orleans, on a site supposedly safe from floods, but it had to be postponed because the river rose and flooded the site 6–12 in. (15–30 cm) deep (Roberts 1946). Bienville chose this site because of its elevation (10 ft. [3 m] above sea level) on the natural levee built up by the annual overflows and deposition of sediments carried by the river (Barry 1997) and because of its proximity to the portage to Lake Pontchartrain through Bayou St. John. An Indian trail led from the site to the bayou, where French settlers had been located since 1708 (Kemp 1997). The first palmetto hut dwellings were all destroyed by another flood in 1719, but they were immediately rebuilt. Subsequently each square block of the town was ditched, and the first levee was built along the river three years later (Association of Levee Boards of Louisiana 1990).

John Law, a Scottish banker in France, had much to do with the early development and settlement of Europeans in Louisiana. He convinced the Duc d'Orleans that Louisiana had potential for great wealth (Kemp 1997) and then began a publicity campaign, dubbed the Mississippi Bubble, to encourage emigrants from Europe to come to the Louisiana colony. Numerous concessions of land near New Orleans were given to settlers moving into the area, including more than 3000 given in 1720 (McWilliams 1953). Some of these extended from the river to Lake Pontchartrain. New Orleans was recognized as the capital of Louisiana in 1722.

According to Conrad (1971), the site chosen for New Orleans was little understood by Bienville's contemporaries but was clearly of strategic importance. With this site the French could control the major portage between Lake Pontchartrain and the Mississippi River and thus effectively prevent any English intrusion into French territory either upriver or through the lake. At the time this was the "inevitable" place to locate a settlement (Lewis 1976; Kidder 2001), the "Impossible but Inevitable City." There had to be a city at the mouth of the Mississippi River, and its importance has been clearly demonstrated by the development of New Orleans into a major port for Mississippi River commerce. However, the test of time has also revealed the negative aspects of this location. Floods from the river or hurricanes were to be a major and perpetual concern for the Pontchartrain basin. The first tax to help expand and maintain the levees was passed in 1732, but a flood in 1735 destroyed most of the levees (Association of Levee Boards of Louisiana 1990). As early as 1722, Pierre-François-Xavier de Charlevoix had wisely predicted such problems and suggested that the "best place for settlements is not on the banks of the river, but at least a quarter if not half a league back in the country" (O'Neill 1977). In what is now considered standard logic for the Mississippi River delta (although unfortunately too late), he stated his opinion that "it would be very advantageous to leave free room to the annual overflowing of the river." The river was always a potential threat, and has continued to be so, in spite of the levees. Another idea presented long before its time was that of Darby (in 1816), who apparently was the first to propose a diversion of Mississippi River flood water through an artificial channel at "Bonnet Quarré" to reduce the incidence of damaging floods along the lower Mississippi River (a project that was not to become reality until 1931). Cline (1945) listed more than ten major floods from the Mississippi River affecting New Orleans in the 1800s.

Le Page du Pratz (1774), who arrived in the Louisiana colony the year New Orleans was founded, described the plant and animal life of the Louisiana Territory, which included most of the Mississippi valley. He noted that Lake Pontchartrain contained an abundance of both marine and freshwater fish, "some of which, particularly carp, would appear to be of monstrous size in France." Since Eurasian carp (*Cyprinus carpio*) were not introduced to North America until 1877 (Lee et al. 1980), Le Page du Pratz referred to another large carp-like fish, possibly tarpon (*Megalops atlanticus*) or drum (*Aplodinotus grunniens*, *Pogonias cromis*, or *Sciaenops ocellata*). Le Page du Pratz also told of the killing of alligators 19 ft. (5.8 m) and 22 ft. (6.7 m) long. Significant crops at the time were indigo, tobacco, cotton, and mulberry (for growing silkworms). He also noted the use of berries from the "wax tree" (wax myrtle, *Morella cerifera*) for making wax for candles (the process was described by Charlevoix 1722). Le Page du Pratz expressed surprising concern for the cypress trees, which he said were formerly very common in Louisiana but were "wasted so imprudently, that they are now somewhat rare," and the price of cypress wood was three times what it had been. In addition to being used for making lumber for local use and export, the cypress bark was used to "cover their houses." He must have been referring to cypress conveniently located near the villages and along the river, because cypress remained abundant and difficult to harvest from the swamps until the beginning of the twentieth century (Colten 2003).

Although larger ships arrived at New Orleans from the river, the Lake Pontchartrain route by way of Bayou St. John continued to be important for smaller vessels in the early 1700s. The trip upstream from the mouth of the river to New Orleans could take as much as thirty days because of the strong currents and dependence upon favorable winds, while the lake route through Mississippi Sound and the Rigolets took only a day or two (Freiberg 1980). Ships were sometimes forced to anchor at bends of the river for periods up to a month while awaiting favorable winds. The continuing importance of the bayou as a transportation route resulted in the hiring of Jean-Baptiste Boudreau, known as Graveline, to maintain the bayou by clearing away tree trunks and driftwood that clogged it (Giraud 1993). By 1726 there were twenty-one Europeans living along Bayou St. John, but there was still no main road to New Orleans (Giraud 1993). A canal between "St. Jean Bay" and Lake Pontchartrain was begun in 1728 (Surrey 1916).

Pitch and tar production became an important business on the north shore as early as 1708 (Holmes 1968). By 1734 there were at least three commercial operations for the production of tar, located at Bayou Lacombe, on the Tchefuncte River, and at Bonfouca on the western bank of Bayou Liberty (Ellis 1981). The pine forests of the north shore provided an important source of these economically important products, as well as resin and turpentine. The resin, or sap, collected from the pine trees was heated to melting and thus converted to tar. Further burning of the tar to remove its moisture resulted in pitch (Le Page du Pratz 1774). Cypress and pine timber were also important products. Crops such as tobacco, indigo, rice, cotton, and sugar became significant. Cattle grazing also became important in the area (Ellis 1981). Furs from the upper Mississippi were largely transported through the lakes to New Orleans and Mobile (Roberts 1946).

The French and Indian War (in Europe known as the Seven Years War) began in the early 1750s and resulted in English privateers becoming active in the lower Mississippi and Lake Borgne (Roberts 1946). Eventually France was to lose the war and most of its control over Louisiana. With the Treaty of Paris in 1763, French territory in North America, including Louisiana east of the Mississippi River, was ceded to Great Britain. New Orleans and lands west of the Mississippi were not included. The "Isle of Orleans," bordered to the south by the Mississippi River and to the north by Lakes Pontchartrain and Maurepas, had been ceded to Spain the previous year. Thus the two lakes, Bayou Manchac, the Amite River, and Pass Manchac became the boundary between Spanish territory to the south and British territory to the north. The Rigolets, Lake Borgne, and the open Gulf formed the island's eastern border (Kemp 1997).

Spanish and British Occupation and Conflict

British settlers began entering the British colony of West Florida, which extended from the Mississippi River to the Perdido River between Mobile and Pensacola and included the "Florida Parishes" area north of Lake Pontchartrain. Settlers of this area primarily occupied lands adjacent to Bayou Castine, the Tchefuncte River, and the Pearl River. There were already French settlements in the north-shore area, and the British Lieutenant Governor Montfort Browne, on a survey of the area in 1768, reported administering the oath of allegiance to several French families at the mouth of the Tangipahoa River (Johnson 1942). The town of Tangipahou was inhabited by Frenchmen and Choctaws, who delivered deer skins, pitch, tar, lumber, charcoal, lime, and cattle to New Orleans (Ellis 1981). According to Hickman (1966), the early settlers on the north shore would drive their cattle to the Rigolets and then swim them across en route to New Orleans.

Recognizing the strategic importance of the Lake Pontchartrain water route through West Florida, British Lieutenant Philip Pittman (Pittman 1770; McDermott 1976) surveyed the area in the 1760s and published a remarkably accurate map of Bayou Manchac (or Ibbeville River [sic]), the Amite (or Amit [sic]) River, Pass Manchac (SW Massiac, which the French called Grand Massiac), and North Pass (NW Massiac, or Le Petit Massiac). The West Florida governor, George Johnstone, with another British officer Captain James Campbell, organized a project to clear Bayou Manchac to make it navigable and contracted with two French residents of Bayou St. John to do the work (Abbadie, in Brasseaux 1979). On their first attempt in September 1764, they were unable to find the waterway, supposedly because of high water on the Amite River. Returning in October and November, Campbell was able to pass through and cleared the bayou for a distance of 4 leagues (12 mi. or 19 km) from the river. The project was never successfully completed, although a road from the Mississippi to the Amite was built, providing a more convenient portage (Roberts 1946). Lieutenant Alexander Fraser was in charge of clearing operations along the waterway in 1768 (Dalrymple 1978).

Pittman (1770; McDermott 1976) described the two passes between Lakes Pontchartrain and Maurepas as having depths of 4–5 fathoms (19.5–32.5 ft. or 6–10 m), whereas Pass Manchac is considerably deeper today (26–56 ft. or 8–17 m deep, with at least one hole of 98-ft. or 30-m depth; average center-of-channel depth is 36 ft. or 11 m; U.S. Army Corps of Engineers 1992). Pittman referred to Jones Island between North Pass and Pass Manchac as Sand Island (Irion et al. 1994), an erroneous name since virtually no sand is to be seen on the island, but did not label it on his map. It has also been labeled Gage Island (Romans 1774; Phillips 1975; also see Fabel 1983).

In the spring of 1765, the British Fort Bute was built on the Mississippi River on the northern side of Bayou Manchac, abandoned just a few months later, and then reoccupied in December 1766 (Pittman 1770; McDermott 1976). In 1767 the Spanish built a small stockade called Fort San Gabriel de Manchac about 800 yd. (730 m) away on the southern side of the bayou (Fabel 2000). Both forts were abandoned in 1768, but then reoccupied with the beginning of the American Revolution in 1776 (Dranguet and Heleniak 1985).

A small English settlement called Manchac developed near Fort Bute, and for a short time it became a rather significant commercial center for goods transported on the Mississippi and through Bayou Manchac and Lakes Maurepas, Pontchartrain, and Borgne to Mobile and Pensacola (Dalrymple 1978; Fabel 2000). There was even some consideration given to moving the capital of West Florida to Manchac (Johnson 1942). The voyage from Pensacola to Manchac by way of Lakes Pontchartrain and Maurepas took about eight to ten days, whereas the Mississippi River route required about seven to eight weeks because of the strong currents and sandbars on the river (Dalrymple 1978). The return trip from Manchac to Pensacola took four days by either route.

Hutchins (1784) reported that the Iberville River flowed only two to three months (May, June, and July) every year, but quickly dried up when the Mississippi River ceased to overflow, and that one could then walk on dry ground from the English to the Spanish fort. On the other hand, there was a good road for carriages the 10 mi. (16 km) between the Mississippi and the navigable waters of the Iberville. He described the Amite River as clear, with a gravelly bottom. The river banks were described as being covered with canes, oaks, ash, mulberry, hickory, poplar, cedar, and cypress. Settlers along the river raised indigo, cotton, rice, hemp, tobacco, and Indian corn, as well as horses, cows, hogs, and poultry. Indigo was the most important agricultural export of the region (Dalrymple 1978).

With deteriorating relations with the Spanish, who controlled New Orleans and the lower Mississippi River, the Lake Pontchartrain route became even more important to the British. Boats would travel from Mobile and Pensacola through Lakes Pontchartrain and Maurepas, then up the Amite River to "the forks," and then up Bayou Manchac about 12 mi. (19 km; Dalrymple 1978). Cargoes would be unloaded and stored there in large warehouses or transported by horse the remaining 10 mi. (16 km) to Manchac, where stores and additional large warehouses were constructed. Large numbers of furs from the upper Mississippi were transported the opposite direction through Manchac and Lake Pontchartrain. According to Johnson (1942), 700,000 skins were transported annually down the Mississippi to New Orleans. Pittman (1770; McDermott 1976) noted that tobacco, tallow, and bear's oil, as well as furs, were traded at Manchac for "spirituous liquors, grocery, dry goods of all kinds, and all the articles necessary for their commerce with the savages." The settlement also became an important center for illegal trade between West Florida and Spanish Louisiana. Harry Gordon (1766), British chief engineer of the Western Department in North America, in his diary of a reconnaissance trip down the Mississippi to New Orleans, reported that there were three schooners employed in smuggling tar from the eastern side of Lake Pontchartrain to Bayou St. John. He suggested that a small post "between the Lakes Maurepas & Pontchartrain would put a stop to this Smugling."

Fort St. John on the Pontchartrain lakeshore near the mouth of Bayou St. John was described at this time as a "Block House" and was manned by both French and Spaniards and armed with some small cannons (Gordon 1766). There was a small community beginning to develop in the vicinity of the fort and a fishermen's village on the eastern bank of the bayou just south of the fort (Freiberg 1980). Lime cement was being made in this area using the rangia clam shells abundant along the edge of the lake. The bayou was also popular for swimming, and the initial interest in developing Lake Pontchartrain as a recreational resort began at this time.

Relations between the British and other nationalities in the area were not especially good, and British residents of New Orleans were expelled in 1769. The British Engineer Thomas Hutchins, who had accompanied Harry Gordon, secretly inspected Fort St. John and others in the Spanish territory in 1771–1772 for a possible takeover (Hutchins 1784; Freiberg 1980). Hutchins had arrived at Fort Bute in September 1766 and again revived the concept of creating a year-round connection from the Mississippi River through the Iberville River. The transportation route through Lake Pontchartrain continued to be especially important for the British, who could travel from their colonies on the Mississippi River to their Gulf ports at Mobile and Pensacola and bypass Spanish-controlled New Orleans (Pearson et al. 1989).

With the beginning of the American Revolution in 1776, Spanish-British relations continued to deteriorate, and the Spanish in New Orleans sided with the Americans. While the British were strengthening their fortifications along the waterways between Bayou Manchac and Lake Maurepas, the Spanish village and fort of Galveztown (named for the Spanish Governor Bernardo de Galvez) was established at the confluence of the Amite River and Bayou Manchac in 1778 to protect Spanish interests in the area (Dalrymple 1978; Casey 1983; Din 1988). A British town to be called Dartmouth had been laid out at this junction in 1775, but it was never erected (Johnson 1942). Galveztown had a population of about 400 in 1779, mostly Spanish immigrants from the Canary Islands. The community suffered from frequent flooding and disease and would eventually disappear by about 1810.

Fort St. John was badly damaged by a hurricane in October 1778 (Freiberg 1980), but it was rebuilt by the Spanish the following year and eventually became known as Spanish Fort. The fort was rebuilt again in 1793 by Governor Don Francisco Luis Hector, Baron de Carondelet, who had a large garrison stationed there (Kelly 1975). Apparently never very substantial, it was described as being a redoubt of earth "dressed with wood," with masonry consisting of a barracks with walls of colombage (a timber frame with stone or brick between the posts).

There was also a brick powder magazine (Favrot 1943). Only a small remnant of the fort is now visible as brickwork between the bayou and Beauregard Avenue (just north of Robert E. Lee Boulevard). Another fort on Lake Pontchartrain, a small redoubt at "Bayou Tigouyou" (Bayou Trepagnier) on the western side of the lake, was also destroyed in the hurricane of 1778 (Freiberg 1980). On his 1774 map of Lake Pontchartrain, however, Romans (in Phillips 1975) labeled a site just to the east of Ravine du Sueur (that is, Bayou Trepagnier) as "Petit Gojou an abandoned post."

An important visitor to the area in August 1777 was the naturalist William Bartram (1791), who kept a journal of his travels, including his passage through Lake Pontchartrain to the Mississippi River. Bartram's party skirted the northern shore of the lake for about 20 mi. (32 km) to a "little bay," then camped for the night on "clean sand banks," probably on the shore between Goose Point and Green Point. He noted that "crocodiles" were there in great numbers and of "enormous bulk and strength." Most of the northern shore he described as being low, reedy marshes separating the lake from the higher forested lands. However, to the west they arrived at a stretch where the forests approached the shore and found "houses, plantations, and new settlements," apparently the precursors of Lewisburg and Mandeville. At the "Taensapaoa" (Tangipahoa) River, "which takes that name from a nation of Indians, who formerly possessed the territories lying on its banks," there were several dwellings and cultivated fields, apparently of European settlers, but the inhabitants mostly were employed in hunting and fishing. From there Bartram continued through North Pass into Lake Maurepas and then across to the Amite River. He described the waters of the Amite as being "dark, deep, turgid and stagnate" and covered with a scum of "green and purplish cast," suggesting that the waters were "a strong extract of the leaves of the trees, herbs and reeds, arising from the shore," or the tannins characteristic of swamp waters. About 30 mi. (48 km) up the Amite they arrived at a large plantation of a "Scotch gentleman." Entering the Iberville River (Bayou Manchac) a little way, they came to "the landing, where are warehouses for depositing merchandize, this being the extremity of navigation up this canal." They continued by land 9 mi. (14 km) to the community of Manchac on the Mississippi River, by way of a "road straight, spacious, and perfectly level, under the shadow of a great forest" of *Magnolia grandiflora* [magnolia], *Liriodendron tulipifera* [yellow poplar], *Platanus* [*occidentalis*, sycamore], *Juglans nigra* [black walnut], *Fraxinus excelsior* [*Fraxinus* spp., ash], *Morus rubra*, red mulberry], *Laurus sassafras* [*Sassafras albidum*, sassafras], *Laurus borboia* [*Persea borbonia*, red-bay], *Tilea* [*americana*, basswood], *Liquidamber styraciflua* [sweetgum], &c." At the river, Bartram observed the remnants of a levee, or "high artificial bank," built by the

French in a vain attempt to prevent flooding from the river. He stated that the "Iberville in the summer season is dry, and its bed twelve or fifteen feet [3.6–4.6 m] above the surface of the Mississippi; but in the winter and spring has a great depth of water, and a very rapid stream which flows into the Amite." He noted that the "Spanish have a small fortress and garrison on the point of land below the Iberville," but did not mention a British fort. Upriver from Manchac about 2 mi. (3 km) was a village of Alabama Indians, a group that had moved into the area from their native lands along the Mobile River. Hutchins (1784) stated that they had followed the French there in 1762.

Both the Spanish and the French came to the aid of the American cause during the American Revolution. Spain declared war against the British in June 1779 and blocked the Amite River at Galveztown. Fort Bute was almost immediately captured by Bernardo de Galvez, governor of Spanish Louisiana, who went on to capture Baton Rouge and then Mobile in 1780 and Pensacola in 1781, when the British surrendered all of West Florida to the Spanish (Kemp 1997).

During the war, Spanish gunboats from Bayou St. John were active in the upper Pontchartrain basin, attacking British boats and posts along the Iberville Passage at Galveztown and along the Amite River (Roberts 1946). In 1779 Captain William Pickles captured the British sloop *West Florida*, which had controlled Lake Pontchartrain during the early part of the war (Nichols 1990). Pickles went on to accept the surrender of British settlers living on the north shore between "the Bayou Lacombe and the River Tanchipaho" (Ellis 1981).

With the end of the war in 1783, the north-shore area, as well as New Orleans, became part of Spanish West Florida, with Galvez as governor (Roberts 1946). At this time citizens from New Orleans began buying land on the northern side of Lake Pontchartrain. One of these was Antonio (or Antoine) Bonnabel, who acquired some 4000 acres (16 km^2) of land east of Bayou Castine in 1799 (Roberts 1946). There were also many British and American settlers who had moved into the north-shore area after 1763 (Dranguet and Heleniak 1985). Several Choctaw villages were located on the north shore at this time (Ellis 1981). The population of New Orleans was about 5000, with another 700 or so living in the small communities of St. John and Gentilly at the upper end of Bayou St. John (Freiberg 1980). In 1785 the population of Manchac was 77, Galveztown 242, and Baton Rouge 270 (Dalrymple 1978).

Lake Pontchartrain, by way of Bayou St. John, continued to be a significant port for New Orleans, although the nearest access at the upper end of the bayou was about 1.5 mi. (2.4 km) from the city. Better access to the bayou and its port was to be provided by the Carondelet Canal. Governor Carondelet, who became the Spanish governor in 1791, had the canal dug to drain water from the northern side of the city into Bayou St. John (Kemp 1997). It was completed in 1794, but originally was only 6 ft. (2 m) wide and 3 ft. (1 m) deep, enough to provide drainage but not navigation. It was widened to 15 ft. (4.6 m) and 4 ft. (1.2 m) deep with a "basin" at the upper end the following year. The Carondelet Canal ran from the upper end of the bayou to the rear central gate of the city (to Basin Street along a route that is now Lafitte Avenue) and thus provided a navigable waterway from the city to Bayou St. John and Lake Pontchartrain (Freiberg 1980). The canal was not properly maintained, however, and by 1801 it was described as "daily filling up by the filth of the city to which it serves as a common sewer" (John Pintard, in Sterling 1951). In later years the canal was to be enlarged even further so that in 1907 it was 60 ft. (18 m) wide and 9 ft. (2.7 m) deep. It was eventually filled in between 1927 and 1938 (Widmer 1993).

Even with the new canal and basin, the port was not ideal. At low tide, water over the bar at the entrance to the bayou was only 8–18 in. (20–45 cm) deep, and it was dry on occasions (Freiberg 1980). Ships often had to wait for days before high water allowed passage into the bayou, which was choked with debris and fallen trees. The canal rapidly filled with sediment. Chalans, or shallow draft flatboats, were employed to unload cargo from larger vessels and carry it across the bar. In spite of these inconveniences, about 500 vessels entered Bayou St. John in 1802 (Freiberg 1980). In 1803, 314 boats crossed the lake from the bayou to north-shore locations such as Bayou Lacombe and Bayou Bonfouca (Ellis 1981). In 1816, 937 vessels were said to have embarked from Bayou St. John, carrying cargo of "barks, coals, cotton, corn, furs, hides, pitch, planks, rosin, skins, tar, timber, turpentine, sand, shells, lime, &c." (Brown 1817).

Spanish domination of the area lasted until 1800, when the Treaty of Ildefonso nominally returned Louisiana to the French (Roberts 1946). However, the French did not take actual control until November 30, 1803. Less than a month later, on December 20, 1803, the Louisiana Purchase made New Orleans and most of the Mississippi drainage a U.S. territory. Under American rule, Fort St. John was again enlarged and strengthened; any ships entering the bayou were subject to search and passports of passengers were checked (Kelly 1975). In 1803 the population of New Orleans was more than 10,000, and by 1810 it was more than 24,000, making it the largest city in the south (and fifth largest in the nation; Kemp 1997).

A visitor to New Orleans in 1803, Mr. C. C. Robin (1807) described Lake Pontchartrain as "passably clear," with well-built houses at intervals along its shore. He reported about thirty to fifty flat-bottomed schooners and smaller vessels operating into and out of Bayou St. John, which was stagnant, "brownish and thick with sediment." At this time the Carondelet Canal was so choked with mud that it was used only by small pirogues. About ten of the vessels in the bayou operated from the north shore with cargoes of lumber, pitch, tar, turpentine, brick, charcoal, bark, lime, vegetables, fish, and fowl. In addition there were five or six oyster boats and several hunters' pirogues. The bayou was shaded with moss-covered cypress trees and was "swarming with reptiles and alligators." According to Robin, the most lucrative industry of the region was manufacture of pitch from pine resin.

Darby (1816) described most of Orleans Parish as "morass, covered with grasses of different kinds" and wood found only on the banks of the Mississippi, Bayou St. John, Bayou Sauvage, and the sources of Bayou Bienvenue. Darby also provided lists of the common trees in New Orleans and the "Indigenous forest trees and shrubs" for Ascension Parish, which he described as possessing "an extraordinary richness of natural production" and "possessing almost every forest tree and shrub in the state of Louisiana." Cypress (as *Cupressa disticha* = *Taxodium distichum*) was the desired wood for buildings, and "red ash" (as *Fraxinus tomentosa* = *F. profunda*, pumpkin ash), box elder (*Acer negundo*), "swamp white oak" (*Quercus lyrata*, overcup oak), black willow (*Salix nigra*), and "blackberry" (as *Celtis crassifolia* = *C. laevigata*, sugarberry) were used for fuel. An 1849 map of New Orleans (in Lewis 1976) describes Metairie Ridge as "covered with live oak [*Quercus virginiana*], persimmon [*Diospyros virginiana*], Liriodendron [*Liriodendron tulipifera*], pecan [*Carya illinoensis*], wild cherry [*Prunus serotina*], interspersed with acacia trees [*Acacia farnesiana*]."

In the upland areas north of Lake Pontchartrain between the Mississippi and Pearl Rivers, Darby (1816) recognized two distinctive portions: a flat plain in the southern section and the more elevated and diverse lands to the north. The southern section was described as thickly forested, with sweetgum (*Liquidamber styraciflua*) and "black oak" (probably *Quercus nigra* or water oak, Darby's "*Q. tinctoria*" and "*Q. aquatica*") the most abundant trees. Darby described the northern section as mostly "covered with pine (pinus rigida) [*Pinus palustris*, longleaf pine] and sterile".

Giant cane (*Arundinaria gigantea*) covered the banks of water courses, including the Amite and Comite Rivers. Darby (1816) noted that giant cane grew in immense brakes in parts of the parish not liable to submersion, but that much of it had been destroyed by land clearing. One area where such brakes still existed was along the banks of New River. Lands too low for giant cane but not flooded annually nor to a depth greater than 15–20 in. (38–50 cm) were said to be "palmetto land" (as *Chamaerops louisiana* = *Sabal minor*). According to Darby, tupelo and cypress were not "so commonly met with on palmetto land, as might be expected," but were either sometimes intermingled (cypress) or growing on land adjacent to (tupelo) the palmetto lands. The trees in these areas were said to be usually covered with "immense quantities of vines, of many different species," especially *Smilax* (greenbriar). Darby also noted that loblolly pines (*Pinus taeda*) were first observed in the Amite River area (and not to the southeast on the "island of Orleans").

The north-shore area, still under the control of the Spanish in 1803, began to develop as a trade and transportation center, with Indian trails and other roads converging in the Covington-Madisonville area to supply vessels crossing the lake to the port at Bayou St. John (Ellis 1981). Boat building also became an important industry in the Tchefuncte River, Bayou Lacombe, and Bayou Bonfouca. Other towns were beginning to form, such as Springfield, where the Old Spanish Trail crossed the Natalbany River north of Lake Maurepas (Dranguet and Heleniak 1985).

In 1810 a revolt in West Florida resulted in the creation of the short-lived West Florida Republic, with its capital at St. Francisville (Roberts 1946). It survived only seventy-four days, from September until December 1810, when all of West Florida was retroactively claimed by the United States (apparently illegally) as part of the Louisiana Purchase. It then became part of the U.S. territory of Louisiana (Nichols 1990).

Prior to 1810, Lake Pontchartrain (with Pass Manchac, Lake Maurepas, Amite River, and Bayou Manchac) had repeatedly been an important international boundary. Between 1763 and 1783, it was part of the northern border of the Spanish Isle of Orleans, which it separated from British West Florida to the north. It was the boundary between Spanish West Florida and French Louisiana from 1783 to 1803, and it was the boundary between Spanish West Florida and U.S. territory from 1803 to 1810.

5.

Louisiana Statehood

Louisiana became the eighteenth state in 1812, and with the coming of statehood, more and more American settlers moved into the area. Louisiana's population doubled between 1810 (76,556) and 1820 (153,407), with most of this growth in the southeast. The nineteenth century was to be a period of rapid population increase for the Pontchartrain basin, with the state's population surpassing 1 million by 1890 and New Orleans exceeding 240,000. This population expansion brought major environmental impacts as the natural areas became modified by human activities, including development of new towns, roads, and railroads, increased clearing of land for farming, extensive timber cutting, development of steamship traffic on the lakes, increased hunting and fishing, and increased recreational activity on the lake, as well as the pumping of sewage and other pollutants into the lake and its tributaries.

In 1813 Wharton (renamed Covington in 1816) was established on the Bogue Falaya River, a tributary of the Tchefuncte (Ellis 1981), and was described as being at the head of navigation on the Bogue Falaya, with schooners and sloops traveling between there and Bayou St. John (Tatum's journal; Bassett and Bradshaw 1922; quoted by Ellis 1981). Madisonville, surveyed and dedicated in 1814, was said to be important only "as a depot for country produce destined for New Orleans," and for travelers from New Orleans going north. However, Darby (1816) called it a "thriving town" and "remarkable, from standing on the best harbour for vessels in lake Pontchartrain." Brown (1817) suggested that Madisonville was destined to become "a great commercial city" because of its location on the "Chefuncti" River.

A new war with England had begun in 1812. With a British invasion imminent, Fort Petite Coquilles was constructed on the lakeshore just south of the entrance to the Rigolets (Casey 1983). This strategic location was described by Darby (1816) as "one of the most important posts in Louisiana" and the "key to West Florida," and, along with Fort St. Philip on the lower Mississippi River, one of "the great outposts" defending New Orleans. Although British vessels entered the Rigolets, they never advanced "within cannon shot of the fort."

General Andrew Jackson came to the defense of New Orleans in 1814. He entered the state from the east, proceeding initially to Wharton (Covington) and Madisonville (Ellis 1981) and then crossing the lake to arrive on December 2, 1814, by way of Bayou St. John at Spanish Fort (Roberts 1946). He fortified the fort with two new batteries (Kelly 1975) and had a battery constructed to defend Pass Manchac, apparently located at the eastern end of Jones Island (Casey 1983). Jackson was also to have a significant and long-term effect upon the Pontchartrain basin by ordering the closing of Bayou Manchac to prevent a possible British attack from the north. In 1826 the State of Louisiana authorized the permanent closing of the waterway (Marchand 1931; Pearson et al. 1989). This "Iberville Passage," with its annual flow of Mississippi River water into the lakes, has never been reopened, although there was an unsuccessful movement to reopen it for navigation in the early 1930s (Kniffen 1935).

Several additional fortifications were constructed in the Lake Borgne area in response to the British threat, including the battery at Bayou Bienvenue, a redoubt at Chef Menteur Pass, and a redoubt at Bayou Dupre (Casey 1983). These initial attempts to adequately protect New Orleans from attack by way of Lake Pontchartrain were complemented a few years later with more substantial forts. Between 1819 and 1827, Fort Pike, named for explorer and soldier Zebulon Pike, was built at the upper end of the Rigolets to replace Fort Petit Coquilles, which was considered too far away to adequately guard this important passage into Lake Pontchartrain. An almost identical fortification was built concurrently on Chef Menteur Pass at its junction with Bayou Sauvage. Initially referred to as the Fort at Chef Menteur, it was named Fort Wood in 1827 (in honor of Eleazer Derby Wood), but then renamed Fort Macomb in 1851, in honor of Major General Alexander Macomb, a noted officer during the War of 1812. Tower Dupre (or Tower Philippon) was a three-story structure built in 1830 as a "Martello tower" (a circular, tower-like fort with guns on the top) on the shores of Lake Borgne at the mouth of Bayou Dupre (Bayou Philippon). Its ruins are now commonly referred to as Martello Castle.

Although their strategic locations were important to the defense of New Orleans, none of these fortifications was ever to see significant military action.

Most were subsequently occupied during the Civil War by Confederate and then Union forces and abandoned not long after that war ended. The forts were officially abandoned in 1890, but Fort Pike is now a state and national historic site. Most have suffered the ravages of time and frequent storms, as well as coastal erosion. Martello Castle is now surrounded by water, and the remnants of Fort Petite Coquilles are submerged beneath the waters of Lake Pontchartrain.

One of the first recreational resorts to develop on Lake Pontchartrain was at the community of Milneburg developed by Alexander Milne. He owned much of the lakeshore from the Rigolets to Jefferson Parish, which at that time was cypress swamps, marshes, and sand. In 1831 the Pontchartrain Railroad was built along the route now known as Elysian Fields Avenue from New Orleans to the lakeshore at Milneburg. Soon the area became a major resort with parks, bathing beaches, restaurants, and the Washington Hotel. Steamships from across the lake and from the Gulf coast began docking at this terminal known as Port Pontchartrain. In the mid-1850s, more than half a million tons of cargo passed across the wharves at Port Pontchartrain each year, even though the port was mostly inactive during the winter because of stormy weather on the lake (Cipra 1997). In 1853 a wooden breakwater to provide safe anchorage was constructed about 4800 ft. (1465 m) from shore directly north of the terminus of the Pontchartrain Railroad, which extended into the lake some 1600 ft. (488 m), with a lighthouse at the end (Senate Ex. Doc. No. 1, 1st Sess. 33 Cong 1853, Louisiana State University Hill Memorial Library).

Harriet Martineau, an English visitor to New Orleans in 1835, gave an account of the train ride from the lake by which they were "whirled away to the city, five miles in a quarter of an hour" (Roberts 1946). She also noted long piers extending out into the lake, baths, and the large Washington Hotel. On a carriage ride along the shell road through the swamps to the lake, which was "thronged with carriages," she observed "cypress, flowering reeds, fleur-de-lis of every color, palmetto, and a hundred aquatic shrubs" as well as Spanish moss and many snakes.

Another railroad was constructed a few years later from New Orleans to Proctor's Landing and the small town of Proctorsville, on the southern shore of Lake Borgne (near the current location of Yscloskey and Shell Beach). A fortification to defend this route into New Orleans was constructed between 1856 and 1859 (Casey 1983). The structure was officially referred to as "the tower at Proctor's Landing" but has also been called Fort Proctor and Fort Beauregard, in reference to Major P. G. T. Beauregard, the supervising engineer when it was built. The fort was severely damaged by a storm in 1860, which also destroyed the town of Proctorville. The ruins of the fort still stand but are now completely surrounded by water.

In the early 1800s voodoo (or hoodoo) made its appearance in New Orleans, and it generated significant activity on the lakeshore at least through the nineteenth century. The mysterious Marie Laveau was said to have built a house called the Maison Blanche (reported by some to be a bordello) on Lake Pontchartrain between Bayou St. John and Milneburg, where voodoo gatherings were held in the swamps along the lakeshore (Roberts 1946). A major celebration occurred there each June 23, or St. John's Eve, and Lake Pontchartrain was called St. John's Lake. According to Luke Turner (Hurston 1935), who claimed to be Marie Laveau's nephew, no one saw Marie Laveau "for nine days before the feast. But when the great crowd of people at the feast calls upon her, she would rise out of the waters of the lake with a great communion candle burning upon her head and another in each one of her hands. She walked upon the waters to the shore. As a little boy I saw her myself when the feast was over, she went back into the lake, and nobody saw her for nine days again." However, noted New Orleans writer Lafcadio Hearn (Starr 2001) claimed that Marie Laveau's supposed connection with "voudouism" was very mythical, and due wholly to "her marvellous skill in the use of native herb medicines." Regardless of Marie Laveau's involvement, the secretive celebrations, which involved bonfires, music, drums, and dancing, would attract thousands of curious visitors from the city. Hearn described observing one of these events in a small hut along the lakeshore "about three-quarters of a mile below Milneburg." On a 50-ft. (15-m) wide strip of land between the lake and the swamps, pine-knot fires were lit at 300-yd. (274-m) intervals from Milneburg to Spanish Fort.

Between 1832 and 1835, the New Orleans Canal and Banking Company dug the New Basin Canal, or New Canal, a toll canal 5.5 mi. (9 km) long (Cipra 1997) connecting the Faubourg Ste. Marie, or "American Sector" of the city upriver from the Vieux Carré, with Lake Pontchartrain at West End (Kemp 1997). The canal was dug primarily by Irish and German immigrants, some 8000 of whom lost their lives to cholera and yellow fever while digging through the mosquito-infested swamps (Bezou 1973; Kemp 1997). During its early years the canal became an important route for ships transporting cargo such as lumber, sand, gravel, shells, and charcoal into the city from across the lake (Huber 1970).

A second railroad to Lake Pontchartrain was built just west of the New Canal in 1837, initially called the New Orleans and Carrollton Railroad and later the Jefferson and Lake Pontchartrain Railway (Groene 1986). The Lakeview subdivision was to develop along the canal in the early 1900s, on swamp land that was drained and filled between the canal and City Park (Huber 1970;

Widmer 1989). The canal became a popular waterway for fishing, crabbing, and swimming by neighborhood children, as well as for rowing contests. In contrast to its popularity for such recreational activities, its commercial value decreased during the early 1900s as fewer ships used it. It was eventually filled in during the early 1950s and now forms the bed for the wide grassy "neutral ground" between West End and Pontchartrain Boulevards, on which a monument to the laborers who lost their lives digging the canal has been erected, and for Interstate 10 to the Superdome region, where the "New Basin" was located (Bezou 1973).

The old Fort St. John site at the mouth of Bayou St. John had been sold as surplus military property in 1823 to developer Harvey Elkins, who built the Pontchartrain Hotel there and renamed it Elkinsburg (Widmer 1993). However, it continued to be known as Spanish Fort and became another popular resort and eventually an amusement park (Roberts 1946). The resort reached its peak in popularity after the Civil War, and another railroad was built to connect Spanish Fort with New Orleans (Huber 1970). At the time of its construction, the hotel had been recently rebuilt and a theater and casino were added. A trestle pier was built out into the lake, where steamers could pick up passengers bound for the north shore (Kelly 1975).

West End at the New Basin Canal was also to become a major recreational site, and the Southern Yacht Club was established there in 1849 (Nichols 1990), originally built on pilings in the lake (Huber 1970). At this time there were also jetties extending into the lake 1600 ft. (488 m) at New Canal and Bayou St. John, with lighthouses at their ends. In 1850 the land along Bayou St. John that was to become City Park was willed to the city by John McDonough. Another Jefferson and Lake Pontchartrain Railway from New Orleans to the lakeshore was built in 1851 from Carrollton to the wharves at Bucktown (or East End for Jefferson Parish; Bezou 1973).

The first steamboat to enter Lake Pontchartrain was the *Maid of Orleans* in 1819, providing regular passage from New Orleans (through Lake Pontchartrain) to Mobile (Roberts 1946). In 1821 the *Neptune* was the first steamboat to cross Lake Pontchartrain from New Orleans to Madisonville, and by 1850 regular Sunday and summer outings to the north-shore communities were available (Nichols 1990). On July 5, 1852, the 207-ft. (63-m) *St. James* exploded while entering Lake Pontchartrain en route from Mississippi, killing thirty people including Louisiana Supreme Court Justice J. M. Wolfe. A race with the vessel *California* preceded the explosion, the worst steamboat accident in Lake Pontchartrain history.

Ship building became an important industry on the north shore, with shipyards at French Settlement, Pass Manchac, Bonfouca, and Madisonville

(Pearson et al. 1989). The *Pontchartrain* was the first steamboat to be built on the north shore, in 1836 (Ellis 1981). Several letters written by Sailing Master J. D. Ferris of the "United States Shipyard Tchifoncte" reported on relatively unsuccessful searches for quality live oak timber stands along the north shore of Lake Pontchartrain (published in the journal of James Leander Cathcart 1819; Prichard et al. 1945), the trees being described as mostly hollow and wind-shaken, yielding "trifling quantities of good timber." Saltus (1987, 1988, 1991) reported the location of 104 historic wooden watercraft sunken in Lake Pontchartrain, and suggested that there should be many more, possibly as many as 800 and another 800 in adjacent waterways. The Lake Pontchartrain Basin Maritime Museum and Research Center located on the Tchefuncte River in Madisonville opened in 2001 to further document the history of boating on the lake, and it now sponsors the annual Wooden Boat Festival held on the Tchefuncte at Madisonville.

In 1829 Bernard Xavier de Marigny de Mandeville, the wealthy developer of Faubourg Marigny downriver from the Vieux Carré and owner of about one-third of New Orleans, bought the Antoine Bonnabel and the Lewis Davis land on the north shore at Green Point. This land became the site of his Fontainebleau Plantation, including a sugar mill and brick factory (Ellis 1981; Nichols 1990; Gathright 1992). He eventually acquired additional land to the west and, in 1834, subdivided the area to form the town of Mandeville. An important provision of his plan for this town was that the land along the lakefront would be held in common and never fenced. This land remains today as the public park along the Mandeville lakeshore. Conditions on the sale of lots in Mandeville were as follows (Nichols 1990): "That the space situated between Lake Street, and the Lake will always remain free and for the common use; that no individual nor corporation shall raise any edifice whatsoever, nor change its destination, and that the banks of the Lake facing the said space will also remain forever free and for common usage."

Marigny also provided ferry service across the lake to Port Pontchartrain at Milneburg (Roberts 1946), and hotels, fine restaurants, and a gambling casino were established at Mandeville, which became a popular resort. An outing to the north shore in August 1855 was described as including a two and a half hour steamboat ride from the dock at Milneburg to the beach at Mandeville, with a fresh and cool morning breeze, providing a respite from the heat of the city; meals of croaker, trout, redfish, oysters, shrimp, and chicken; and "lounging with coats, vests, and cravats off, reading, bathing, fishing, sailing, eating and drinking" (Ellis 1981). A special treat was the unusual meal of boiled and broiled sturgeon (*Acipenser oxyrinchus desotoi*), from a large specimen taken from the lake.

Just west of Mandeville was another lakeshore community called Lewisburg (or Louisburg), also laid out in 1834 (Ellis 1981). Beyond that, on the Tchefuncte River, was the port of Madisonville, and further upriver was the town of Covington. The remainder of the northern lakeshore, both east and west, was mostly undeveloped.

Another wealthy family of New Orleanians to own land on the north shore were the Rouquettes, who had a country estate on Bayou Lacombe northeast of Fontainebleau (Roberts 1946). Dominique Rouquette (1938) wrote an account of the Choctaw peoples living in and around New Orleans. Adrien Rouquette, a priest and younger brother of Dominique, devoted his life to missionary work among the Choctaw people on the north shore, where he built several small, wooden chapels at places such as Lacombe, Chinchuba, and Bonfouca. He knew the Choctaw language, usually dressed as an Indian, and often crossed the lake in a rowboat. The Choctaw gave him the name of Chata-Ima, meaning "like a Choctaw."

The lumber and brick-making industries continued to expand on the north shore, and in 1850 there were fifteen brickyards and fourteen sawmills (Ellis 1981). Their products were mostly shipped across the lake to New Orleans or other destinations. Springfield, which reached a population peak of about 2000 in 1860, continued to develop as the shipping center between New Orleans and the western part of the basin, especially for pine lumber, turpentine, and cotton (Dranguet and Heleniak 1985).

Groene (1986) documented some ninety steamboats operating out of the New Orleans lake ports between 1850 and 1900 and identified five primary destinations. A few traveled up the lake to Lake Maurepas and the Amite and Tickfaw Rivers for lumber. Most traveled across the lake to Mandeville, Madisonville, and Covington. Others traveled out of the lake bound for Biloxi, Mobile, or Pensacola. Shipping statistics for the year 1881 indicate that both Bayou St. John and the New Basin Canal were important ports for incoming cargo, but that the latter had surpassed the former in total amounts shipped (Pearson et al. 1989). The major commodities entering the ports were lumber, timber and logs, charcoal, bricks, staves, sand, oysters, firewood, shells, rosin, and hides.

By 1852 a European settlement had been established on Bayou Bonfouca, at a site known as Robert's Landing. This boat landing was involved with the shipping of lumber, cattle, and wild game to New Orleans. The community was eventually to become the city of Slidell, incorporated in 1888.

The New Orleans, Jackson, and Great Northern Railroad was completed from New Orleans to Canton, Mississippi, in 1854 and to Ohio by 1860. It became part of the Illinois Central Railroad system in 1867. The railroad passed through the marshes and swamps along the western shore of Lake Pontchartrain, elevated for much of the way on cribwork of cypress logs, with stations at Kennerville, LaBranche, Manchac, and Ponchatoula (Dranguet and Heleniak 1985).

Several communities of mostly German immigrants such as Frenier, Wagram (later known as Napton), DeSair, and Ruddock developed along the railroad on the western shore of Lake Pontchartrain. The first German settlers to this area arrived in 1836 and developed the community of Frenier (Dranguet and Heleniak 1987). Eventually the area became well known as a producer of cabbage and other crops such as beets, lettuce, and potatoes. Initially the crops were delivered to markets in New Orleans by boat across the lake. They also helped feed the crews working on the new railroad, and eventually the railroad provided the transportation to deliver the crops to New Orleans, as well as cities to the north such as Chicago. Another important occupation of residents on the western side of the lake was the gathering of Spanish moss (*Tillandsia usneoides*) for use as padding in furniture.

Levees were also built in this area to help protect from flooding, a perpetual problem in this low-lying landscape. In 1859 a crevasse at the Bonnet Carré bend on the Mississippi River caused flooding of the tracks near Frenier for three months. During that period, passengers from New Orleans were transported by rail to the New Orleans lakefront, where they boarded chartered steamers to be carried across the lake to catch the train at Pass Manchac (Pearson et al. 1993). In 1874 another crevasse covered the railroad tracks and left river sand sediment that elevated low areas several inches. This crevasse began in 1872 and lasted eleven years, cutting a wide channel from the river to the lake through which steamboats navigated to give sightseers a view of the crevasse (Laurent 1982). These Bonnet Carré crevasses flowed at rates of 70,000 to 225,000 cfs (1982 to 6372 m^3/sec; Saucier 1963) between 1849 and 1882. The Nita Plantation crevasse that occurred in the Convent area in 1890 flowed at rates of 385,000 to 402,000 cfs (10,903 to 11,385 m^3/sec) for several weeks and flooded most of the area between LaPlace and Ponchatoula. Storm-tides from the lake also often caused floods. In spite of these difficulties, there were some 4000 acres (1619 ha) under cultivation in the area by 1900.

With increased boat traffic on the lakes during the nineteenth century, lighthouses were built at strategic locations to guide mariners into and across the lakes. As many as ten lighthouses (not counting replacements) have existed around the periphery of Lake Pontchartrain, although none is operational today. The first, constructed in 1811, was an octagonal wooden tower on an artificial shell island off the mouth of Bayou St. John (Cipra 1997). It was replaced by a "real lighthouse" in 1838, another wooden tower on pilings in the lake. This structure was poorly built and severely damaged within a few years, and it was replaced in 1856 by a square dwelling with a light centered on its top. This structure was also damaged by a hurricane in 1860 and replaced by another tower with no dwelling in 1869. The structure no longer exists.

At Port Pontchartrain, an unusual lighthouse was built in 1832 that was said to resemble a guillotine, a square lantern hoisted between two channels (Cipra 1997). It was replaced in 1839 by an octagonal tower identical to the one at Bayou St. John. A more substantial brick tower was built there in 1855, and the wooden structure was removed. Although the lighthouse was built 2100 ft. (640 m) offshore, it is now on land because of landfill projects (at the site to later become Pontchartrain Beach). It was deactivated in 1929, but still stands at the Research and Technology Park of the University of New Orleans.

To the west of Bayou St. John and Port Pontchartrain, a third identical octagonal tower lighthouse was built in 1839, off the mouth of the recently completed New Canal (Cipra 1997). It was replaced by a square dwelling structure in 1855, which was replaced by a similar but taller, two-story structure in 1890. Originally built some 1000 ft. (305 m) offshore, landfill around the site eventually placed it on shore by 1936. It was restored in 1976 to become the Coast Guard Station at the end of West End Boulevard. The station was severely damaged by Hurricane Katrina in 2005, and a year later it was leased to the Lake Pontchartrain Basin Foundation to be rebuilt as the Lake Pontchartrain Basin Foundation New Canal Lighthouse Education Center.

Two lighthouses were built on the Rigolets. In 1833–1834, a brick tower was constructed at the eastern end on Rabbit Island across from the western mouth of the Pearl River (Cipra 1997). It was decommissioned in 1874 and apparently no longer exists. The West Rigolets Lighthouse was built in 1855 just west of Fort Pike at the junction of the Rigolets with Lake Pontchartrain. It was a square dwelling built on pilings, with the light centered on its roof. It was raised and repaired in 1917 but then deactivated in 1945. It was destroyed by Hurricane Katrina.

The Tchefuncte River Lighthouse, just to the west of that river, was built in 1838, badly damaged during the Civil War, and completely rebuilt on its old foundation in 1868 (Cipra 1997). It is now owned and maintained by the city of Madisonville and the Lake Pontchartrain Maritime Museum.

The Pass Manchac Lighthouse (Figure 5.1), located at the entrance of Pass Manchac into Lake Pontchartrain, was first built in 1839, but was almost immediately damaged by rain and wave action. A second lighthouse was completed in 1842, about 50 ft. (15 m) to the northwest, but it too was soon threatened by

58 ENVIRONMENTAL HISTORY OF THE BASIN

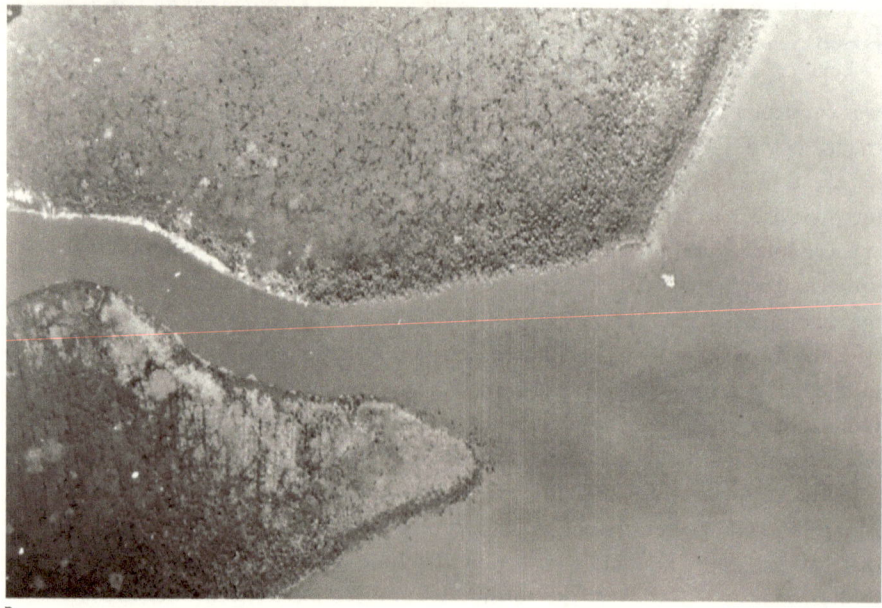

Figure 5.1 Manchac lighthouse in (A) 1940, (B) 1954, (C) 1994, and (D) 1985. (Photographs A and B from the National Archives, aerial photos CQB-1A-73 and CQB-2K-41, respectively; photographs C and D by the author)

C

D

shoreline erosion. The third lighthouse, just east of the second, was completed in 1846, with the light on a cupola on top of a two-story Victorian dwelling of cypress. Even before construction was completed, this new lighthouse was damaged and leaning toward the lake. In 1857 a fourth (and final) lighthouse, with an attached two-story dwelling of brick, was built about 200 ft. (60 m) northwest of the previous lighthouses, on a site "seldom overflowed." This lighthouse was extensively damaged by "military" activity during the Civil War, with major repairs completed in 1867. Photographs taken at that time show several structures, including a lighthouse keeper's residence, several outbuildings, and a dock and boat shed surrounded on the west by large cypress trees. A photograph from 1918 shows extensive flooding and erosion of the surrounding land and a wooden bulkhead constructed to protect the remaining land. By 1940 only a narrow spit of land outlined by the wooden bulkhead connected the lighthouse to the adjacent shoreline. In 1941 the lighthouse was automated, and in 1952 the abandoned lighthouse keeper's house was razed. The spit of land had been broken by 1954, and the lighthouse tower and brick foundation of the keeper's house were left surrounded by water on a small island of low land. The light was deactivated in 1987. The remaining lighthouse tower and a jumble of broken brickwork at its base about 1000 ft. (300 m) from shore were transferred to state ownership in 1999 and an effort begun to preserve and restore the structure. The tower was stabilized with wooden pilings around its base, and the metal lantern room removed for restoration.

At the mouth of Bayou Bonfouca a wooden lighthouse was built in 1848, a wooden dwelling with a light tower on top (Cipra 1997). It was burned by Confederate soldiers in 1862 and never rebuilt. Instead it was replaced by a light across the lake at Pointe aux Herbes in 1875. The latter structure was a square dwelling with the light centered on top, placed on a concrete and timber slab resting on 8-ft. (2.4-m) brick piers. It was threatened by storm-caused shoreline erosion in 1888 and 1890 and subsequently protected by breakwaters and tons of rocks. Most of the surrounding land was sold to the New Orleans Pontchartrain Bridge Company in 1928, and the lighthouse was decommissioned just after World War II. The wooden structure was burned in the 1950s, and only the damaged foundation remains today at the southern end of the Interstate 10 bridge.

A structure said to just barely be considered a lighthouse once stood at the mouth of the Amite River in Lake Maurepas (Cipra 1997). A minimal station was built in 1882, but almost immediately began to settle into the mud. It was raised and its pile foundation improved. The lighthouse consisted of a "house," with a light raised on a mast above the dwelling. The structure no longer exists today.

With the decline in commercial maritime traffic on the lakes, most of the lighthouses were decommissioned and abandoned. None is in service today, and the few that survive are in danger of further deterioration.

6.

Civil War

Union forces controlled Lake Pontchartrain, as well as New Orleans, for most of the Civil War (Nichols 1990). At the beginning of the war in 1861, New Orleans and other Gulf coast ports were blockaded, and Confederate blockade runners became common, traveling across the lake or to Mobile and other ports to provide New Orleans with supplies (Roberts 1946). Forts at the Rigolets (Fort Pike) and Chef Menteur Pass (Fort Macombe) guarded the entrance into Lake Pontchartrain but saw little action during the war. On April 24, 1862, New Orleans fell to the Union forces invading from the Mississippi River, and the two forts were abandoned by the Confederates, who moved across the lake to Madisonville. They subsequently moved up the Tchefuncte River into the Bogue Falaya, where they deliberately sunk their three steamers (*Oregon*, *Carondelet*, and *Bienville*) in the vicinity of Covington (Groene 1985). Many Confederate sympathizers in New Orleans were allowed to cross the lake to Madisonville. For the remainder of the war, New Orleans was occupied by the Union army under General Benjamin F. Butler, and the adjacent north-shore areas remained under Confederate control. Subsequently Lake Pontchartrain played a relatively minor role in the war, although legal trade across the lake ended and smuggling became common. Much of this traffic involved transport of supplies needed by the Rebel army, such as salt, blankets, and shoes, from New Orleans to the train depot at Ponchatoula (Groene 1985). Union forces would occasionally cross the lake to seize cotton, lumber, timber, tar, turpentine, and bricks at Madisonville or other north-shore communities (Nichols 1990).

The most significant military presence on Lake Pontchartrain was provided by the Union gunboat *New London*, under the command of Captain Abner Read

(Groene 1985). During the summer of 1862, the *New London* landed troops at Manchac to attack Confederate forces who had established batteries there. As the Confederates retreated, they set fire to the railroad drawbridge over Pass Manchac. The docks and landings at Lewisburg and Mandeville were also burned by the Confederates (Ellis 1981).

A Union officer from Michigan, Lieutenant-Colonel Edward Bacon, wrote of his experiences during the war while at New Orleans, Manchac, and Ponchatoula (Bacon 1867). He described New Orleans as a "filthy city, where drainage is almost impossible, and during all the spring months the river has been more than six feet higher than the streets, and liable at any time to make the city the bottom of a lake, as nature intended?" Of Camp Williams on Metairie Ridge, Bacon wrote, "The dense forest of tall cypress and live oak, their boughs hung with long festoons of Spanish moss, shut out every breeze.... The ground is called a ridge, because it is dry enough for human habitations, but no perceptible elevation is ever found in the low lands of Louisiana, where there is not a pebble or stone, and where every particle of earth appears to be made of decayed vegetation, and alligators and crawfishes appear to be the rightful owners of the land, as swarms of musquitoes [sic] are proprietors of the air."

Bacon seems to have had a more positive attitude toward the waters of Louisiana, stating that "Among the curious lakes, bayous and inlets, seen in the Louisiana lowlands, the most remarkable are the Lakes Pontchartrain and Maurepas, with their passes" and "great marshes covered with reeds and canes." He considered Pontchartrain as a "lake without a shore" because when vessels approach "most parts of the ragged line of cypress trees supposed to designate a shore, it is perceived that the color of the water becomes uniformly like that seen in vats of a tan yard, and that this color is given by particles of rotten vegetation, which thickens the sluggish waters that lose themselves among the cypresses and water plants of a dismal swamp." Bacon was obviously describing the "coffee grounds" or detritus so characteristic of Louisiana coastal lakes (Figure 6.1). This particulate material looks very much like coarse coffee grounds when piled along the shore or like a thick slurry of mud when washed by wave action. Bacon also described time spent on "cypress-covered" Jones Island between North Manchac Pass and South Manchac Pass, an island today almost completed devoid of cypress trees.

Bacon was participating in an assault on Ponchatoula in 1863, under the command of Colonel Thomas Clark, involving both troop transport by boat across the lake, as well as forces who marched up the railroad from New Orleans (Groene 1985). Bacon led the troops who marched along the railroad "from the sugar plantations near Kennerville into the cypress swamp" (Bacon 1867). Five

Figure 6.1 "Coffee grounds" on the western shore of Lake Pontchartrain (Photograph by the author)

miles (8 km) from Kenner, there was "an opening in the timber, made by a great marsh flooded from the lake." Bacon reported many alligators on floating wood, and then more cypress at "La Branch station." They spent the night at a small settlement along the lakeshore, near a railroad station called De Sair occupied by Union troops. It was described as being 1.5 mi. (2.4 km) north of Shellbank Bayou and 1 mi. (1.6 km) south of Bayou De Sair (letter of April 8, 1864, from Captain M. Hawke to Lieutenant R. Skinner, Official Records of the Civil War, vol. 34, ch. 46). There was concern that enemy troops could approach "within about half a mile of that station" by way of a bayou from Lake Maurepas. This seems to be the location designated on current maps as Desert Bayou (or Bayou deSert; Laurent 1982), which now flows into Ruddock Canal. Just to the north on the southern side of Pass Manchac was Fort Stevens, also occupied by Federal forces (Groene 1985).

According to Bacon (1867), from Manchac the advance on "Pontchitoula" [sic] was made from two directions. One group was to proceed up the railroad track, while the other crossed Lake Maurepas to enter the Tickfaw River and mount a flank attack by way of "Wadesborough" [sic]. There was not much Confederate resistance at Ponchatoula, so the Union forces proceeded to loot the town, an action that Bacon condemned. He described Ponchatoula as "a little village of neatness and thriftiness uncommon in the South." Just south of Ponchatoula, Bacon described the "great open, flooded marsh, covered with reeds and grass...eight or ten miles [13–16 km] long, and from one mile to three miles [1.6–4.8 km] wide," which "divides the pine woods from the cypress swamp." This marsh, or "prairie," is still present today much as it was then.

One of the most significant historical occurrences involving Lake Pontchartrain during the Civil War was the testing of some of the first submarines. An original submarine has been on exhibit at various locations in New Orleans, but incorrectly identified by some as the C.S.S. *Pioneer* (Kloeppel 1987; Ragan 1999). It was supposedly built in 1861 and is probably the oldest known Civil War submarine still in existence. It is said to have been built by Frances Joseph Wehner, a New Orleans machinist and later Confederate soldier ("History Detectives," a Public Broadcasting Service television program 2004). It was salvaged from the lake in 1878, when a young boy swimming near the mouth of Bayou St. John pointed it out to the crew of the dredge boat *Valentine* (Lambousy 1999). The submarine was placed on display at Spanish Fort in 1895 (where it was photographed by Mugnier; Kemp and King 1975), moved to the Camp Nicholls Confederate Home on Bayou St. John in 1909 (Ragan 1999), and then to the State Museum at Jackson Square in 1942 (for photographs, see Roberts 1946; Ragan 1999). Subsequently it was moved inside the Lower Pontalba Building adjacent to Jackson Square and then to the arcade of the Presbytere in 1957. The submarine was again removed in 2000 for extensive conservation work (Lambousy 1999) and is now on display in the Louisiana State Museum in Baton Rouge. Although most likely black originally, the submarine was painted yellow during the 1960s by Tulane University students who were obviously greater fans of the Beatles than of Civil War history (MacCash 2001).

James McClintock and Baxter Watson made another submarine in New Orleans in 1861 (Kloeppel 1987; Ragan 1999), which was launched in the New Basin Canal on March 12, 1862, christened the *Pioneer*, and towed down the canal into Lake Pontchartrain for testing. McClintock and Watson were joined in their venture by Captain Horace Lawson Hunley, a lawyer and assistant customs agent at the New Orleans Customs House. Their initial testing included several apparently successful descents in the vessel and the destruction of a small schooner and several rafts. They were given authorization by the Confederate government to "privateer," or destroy Union ships. Their main quarry was the Union gun boat *New London*, which controlled the lake, but their unsuccessful attempt to sink it resulted in the smothering of two men in the submarine. With the fall of New Orleans to Union troops in April 1862, the vessel was scuttled in New Basin Canal and McClintock, Watson, and Hunley moved their operation to Mobile. Shortly thereafter, Union sailors found the *Pioneer* and dragged it ashore, where it was thoroughly examined and diagramed by Union engineers.

It was lying on the banks of the canal near Claiborne Street in February 1868, when it was sold for scrap for $43 (*The Daily Picayune*, February 15, 1868). Its subsequent fate is unknown (M. K. Ragan, personal communication).

McClintock, Watson, and Hunley went on to construct another three (or possibly more) man-powered, iron-hulled vessels in Mobile, the C.S.S. *Pioneer II*, the *American Diver*, and the *Hunley*. The *Hunley* was transported by railroad to Charleston in August 1863, where it made many successful test dives, in spite of being lost twice and causing the deaths of thirteen men, including Captain Hunley. It made maritime history in 1864, however, by sinking the Union warship *Housatonic* in Charleston Harbor; when the vessel itself sank, its twelve-man crew was lost (Ragan 1999).

7.

Post-War Development

After the Civil War, the lakeshore at Milneburg, Spanish Fort, and West End, as well as Mandeville on the north shore, again became popular recreational sites for residents wanting to escape the city and the fear of yellow fever. The wealthier residents fled to summer cottages in Mandeville or to the Mississippi Gulf coast. The north shore became known as the "Ozone Belt," because of the erroneous perception of the medicinal quality of its air (Stall 1997). Paddlewheelers to carry visitors from Milneburg to Mandeville became popular (Roberts 1946). One of these was the *Zephyr*, launched in 1847 in New York but made famous after the Civil War as the *Camelia* and later the *New Camelia*. After being decommissioned, it sank in the Tchefuncte River in 1920 (Roberts 1946). Kemp and Colvin (1981) included a photograph of the *New Camelia* moored on the Tchefuncte, apparently taken shortly before it sank. In July 1879, six steamships were making regular trips across Lake Pontchartrain on Wednesdays and Sundays (Ellis 1981).

Yellow fever had first appeared in New Orleans in 1767, apparently brought into North America from Central or South America (Roberts 1946). Iberville himself had died of yellow fever contracted in Havana in 1706. The first epidemic in New Orleans occurred in 1796, and between that year and 1905, 38,771 people died in New Orleans as a result of yellow fever, an average of 359 per year (Fossier 1951). After mosquitoes (*Aedes aegypti*) were identified as the transmitting agents for the disease, mosquito-control measures eventually reduced its incidence. Yellow fever was finally eliminated as a serious threat to New Orleans in the early 1900s, with the city's last epidemic in 1905. Malaria, another mosquito-borne illness, although carried by a different group of mosquitoes (*Anopheles* sp.), was also a significant concern in early Louisiana.

Drainage and sewerage disposal continued to be a major problem for the city through the nineteenth century. In 1879–1880 Ernst von Hesse-Wartegg observed that the sewer system was inadequate, but noted that sewers could be made to empty far out into Lake Pontchartrain (Trautmann 1990). Ironically, he described the lake as a blessing to the city, "with its seawater ever renewed by tides, its beautiful beaches, and the fresh sea breezes that sweep across it from Gulf to city!"

Initial dredging and filling activities began on the New Orleans lakeshore in 1871, extending from the New Basin Canal west to the Jefferson Parish line. An embankment was built about 800 ft. (240 m) offshore in the lake to form a harbor that was completed in 1876 (Huber 1970; Bezou 1973). Eventually this area was to be known as West End and would replace other sites as the most popular lakeshore resort. A short distance to the west, the Metairie Relief Outfall, or Upper Line Tail Race (now known as the 17th Street Canal), was dug in 1896 (Maygarden et al. 1999). The Bucktown area just to the west became popular with fishermen and crabbers, and many "squatters' camps" were built on pilings over the lake. Undoubtedly, none of these camps had any type of sewage treatment system.

Nathaniel H. Bishop (1879), a visitor to Lake Pontchartrain in 1876–1877, recounted his experiences in rowing and sailing a 12-ft. (3.7-m) Barnegat Bay sneak-box, or duck-boat, on a voyage from Pittsburgh to the Gulf of Mexico. Bishop arrived at Bayou Manchac intending to pass through en route to New Orleans. However, he found the bayou dry and about 15 ft. (4.6 m) above the water level in the Mississippi River, and so proceeded downriver to New Orleans. From New Orleans, Bishop entered Lake Pontchartrain by way of the New Basin Canal, where he found "a small lighthouse, two or three hotels, and a few houses, making a little village." He spent the night there, observing the evening merriment, as city people drove out in their carriages to have a "lark" with card-playing, dancing, drinking, and swearing. He noted that the water of the canal was made foul, "dark and heavy by the city's drainage." On January 24, Bishop rowed out of the canal in heavy fog, passed the Pontchartrain Railroad pier at Milneburg, and described the coast as low and swampy, with occasional short, sandy beaches, and the bottom covered with stumps of trees. He spent the night along the "prairie shore," with swarms of mosquitoes, then proceeded to the Point aux Herbes lighthouse and across the lake to the Rigolets. He described the marshes around the lake as extensive, with coarse grass 4–5 ft. (1.2–1.5 m) in height, and home to "coon, wildcats, minks, hogs, and even rabbits," and abundant alligators and "moccasin-snakes." Bishop reported the region as a favorite one with hunters and fishermen. Rowing past the picturesque Fort Pike, he entered Lake Borgne, "the shores of which were desolate."

Another visitor who explored this route in 1883 was Lafcadio Hearn (Starr 2001), who wrote of his visit to the settlement of Saint Malo, a fishing station occupied by Tagalas from the Philippine Islands. Departing from Spanish Fort, his group observed the sinking shoreline with rushes and marsh grasses waving in the wind. The water became "deeply cluded [sic] with sap green—the myriad floating seeds of swamp vegetation" (probably the floating leaves of duckweed). They passed the "reedy waste" of Point aux Herbes, with its picturesque lighthouse rising above the wilderness of swamp grass and bulrushes. Passing through the Rigolets, Hearn's party observed the walls of Fort Pike, and then the U.S. Customs House rising "on stilts out of the sedge-grass." Finally passing the enormous skeleton of the Rigolets railroad bridge, they moved into Lake Borgne and headed due south to find the entrance to "Saint Malo Pass" (or Bayou St. Malo). About thirteen or fourteen structures built on piles above the marsh in "true Manila style" composed this village of Philippine fishermen and alligator hunters. About thirty residents supplied dried fish and shrimp to New Orleans markets (Condrey and Fuller 1992).

During the late 1800s, railroads were becoming increasingly important around Lake Pontchartrain, many of which developed in conjunction with the expanding lumber industry in the area. Even before the end of the Civil War, the damaged railroad from New Orleans to Ponchatoula was being repaired and put back into service (Dranguet and Heleniak 1985). Soon after the war, plans for a railroad line from New Orleans to Mobile were initiated and completed in 1869 with the opening of the New Orleans, Mobile, and Texas Railroad (Roberts 1946), which eventually became part of the Louisville and Nashville Railroad system. With the coming of the railroads, waterborne shipping from Port Pontchartrain through Lake Pontchartrain to other Gulf coast ports became unimportant. Waterborne transport across the lake was still significant, with considerable commercial freight traffic to ports such as Madisonville, Springfield, and Port Vincent for lumber and farm produce, but continued to decrease with the increasing importance of the railroads. Rail service on the Pontchartrain Railroad, which also was taken over by the Louisville and Nashville system, continued to be used by New Orleans residents heading to the lakeshore for picnics, swimming, and fishing, as well as to the amusement parks, restaurants, and clubs. In addition, there was the usual transport of vacationers to the north-shore resort of Mandeville.

The first proposal to construct a bridge to the north shore across the middle of Lake Pontchartrain was developed in 1880, with the New Orleans and Northeastern Railway Company proposal for a railroad trestle. Instead the shorter route to the east (and Robert's Landing or Slidell Station and Jackson, Mississippi) was chosen (Nichols 1990).

Most of the swamps in the Manchac area, as well as in other parts of the Pontchartrain basin, were still covered with cypress and tupelo gum trees in the late 1800s. Although considered extremely valuable, most of the cypress trees were relatively inaccessible in the dense swamps. However, the construction of the railroads on pilings involved the use of large numbers of trees cut from the railroad right-of-way, and then the railroads provided an efficient means for large-scale harvesting of cypress and transport of logs to mills (Dranguet and Heleniak 1987). At the end of the nineteenth century, the pullboat method of harvesting cypress trees was developed, allowing relatively inaccessible swamps to be logged (Mancil 1972, 1980). Within about forty years, the massive virgin cypress forests of the Pontchartrain basin were gone.

In 1889 William Burton purchased 3100 acres (12.5 km^2) of land near the railroad north of Frenier, and three years later in partnership with C. H. Ruddock he formed the Ruddock Cypress Company. Eventually the company would own about 16,000 acres (65 km^2) extending from Pass Manchac to Frenier and west to Blind River south of Lake Maurepas (Dranguet and Heleniak 1987). A sawmill and company town called Ruddock were constructed in the swamps and began operation in 1892. By 1910 Ruddock's population had grown to 700. Also in 1892, the Strader Cypress Company began cutting trees north of Pass Manchac and operated a sawmill at Owl Bayou (Heleniak and Dranguet 1987). The Lotham Cypress Company and St. Bernard Cypress Company cut large stands of cypress in the St. Charles Parish area in the early 1900s and had depleted most of the cypress in that area by 1918 (Poplin et al. 1988).

A series of catastrophes, including fire and storms, contributed to the demise of Ruddock, as well as the nearby town of Frenier. The Ruddock mill was destroyed by fire in 1902 but was subsequently rebuilt. Hurricanes were to bring the final end to these communities. An "extreme" storm hit the state in September 1909, with 15-ft. (4.5-m) storm tides, and caused 350 deaths. Eight people died in Frenier, and many homes were destroyed. Over 4 mi. (6 km) of the railroad track was washed out. The towns were again rebuilt, only to face another disaster six years later. In September 1915, another "extreme" hurricane hit the Louisiana coast and passed west of New Orleans and up the western side of Lake Pontchartrain, right over Frenier and Ruddock. The storm totally destroyed both towns, and 58 people died (of a total of 275 deaths in

Louisiana). Today nothing remains of Ruddock except rotting timbers overgrown by swamp trees. Frenier, or more properly Frenier Beach, was to be partially rebuilt about 0.5 mi. (0.8 km) to the north at the lake end of Peavine Road. It was described by Laurent (1982) as the pleasure resort of St. John the Baptist Parish, offering visitors fishing and bathing in Lake Pontchartrain and hunting in the surrounding scenic woods. Theriot (1991) noted that a bathhouse and pier were built there in 1931. Laurent also predicted that with the completion of the Hammond–New Orleans Highway, Frenier would soon become one of the important towns of St. John Parish. Today, however, it is a community of only about twenty-five to thirty houses or camps. In 1995 the public boat launch at the end of Peavine Road was rebuilt, providing public access to the lake.

Logging of cypress in the western basin of Lake Pontchartrain was continued by other sawmills, such as the Louisiana Cypress Lumber Company in Ponchatoula, until 1956 when the supply of trees was depleted (Heleniak and Dranguet 1987). The virgin cypress-tupelo swamps were gone, leaving behind a scarred landscape of open marshes dissected by numerous logging canals, pullboat ditches, and abandoned railroad lines (Figure 7.1). These left a landscape open to increased flooding, with reduced cover and food for wildlife, and more susceptible to erosion and subsidence. Much of the Manchac area has still not recovered almost 100 years later.

Because the railroad lines included wooden trestles across Lake Pontchartrain and Chef Menteur Pass and the Rigolets, as well as other coastal waters to the east, wood-boring marine organisms soon became a significant concern (as they had been for wooden boats in the past). These invertebrates damaged the supporting pilings placed in salt water. The most important was the unusual mollusk called the teredo, or shipworm (*Teredo navalis*). This pest was also recognized by Hesse-Wartegg in 1879–1880 (Trautmann 1990) as preventing the use of wooden pilings or jetties along the lower Mississippi River, (although his reference to these organisms as "tenedoes" misled Trautmann [fn. on p. 233] into interpreting this reference as the insect *Tenebrio*). The wood-borer problem was to be solved by the use of creosote, a coal tar distillate, impregnated into the pilings. Soon creosoted timber companies became common all along the Gulf coast, including in the Lake Pontchartrain area at Bayou Bonfouca (in Slidell), Madisonville, and Hammond. Creosoted pilings became a standard feature in coastal waters thereafter. The 52-acre (0.2 km^2) site on Bayou Bonfouca, first built by the Alabama Great Southern Railroad Company in 1882 and operated by American Creosote Works and Gulf States Creosoting Company until a fire in 1972, was found to be severely contaminated by creosote spills that also

Figure 7.1 Logging ditches in the Manchac marshes (Photographs by the author)

affected the adjacent bayou (and certainly also Lake Pontchartrain; www.epa.gov/region6/superfund).

Additional railroads were constructed inland on the north shore in the late 1880s, running from Pearl River to Abita Springs and then to Covington (Ellis 1981). A branch to Mandeville was completed in 1892 and to Slidell in 1905. From 1909 to 1918, an electric railroad line operated from Covington to Abita Springs and then to Mandeville, where the line ended on a long pier built out into the lake (Ellis 1981). Passengers would then transfer to or from steamships crossing the lake to New Orleans.

Figure 7.2 Water hyacinth (*Eichhornia crassipes*) (Photograph by the author)

In the 1880s an event in New Orleans, though not directly involving the lake, was to have a profound effect on Lake Pontchartrain and other aquatic areas throughout the state and Gulf coast. The World's Industrial and Cotton Centennial Exposition was held on the site that eventually became Audubon Park (Roberts 1946). Water hyacinths (*Eichhornia crassipes*) from Venezuela were on display and were bought by many visitors to the exposition. Eventually water hyacinths escaped from cultivation to become a menace to Louisiana waterways, which they choked by their prodigious growth. Although very attractive, with bright green foliage and lavender blooms, the water hyacinth has become one of Louisiana's most hated invasive exotic species (Figure 7.2).

In the "Official Exposition Guide," Zacharie (1885) described the various railroad routes that a tourist could take upon arriving at New Orleans and had much to say about the lake and its environs. He noted the ruins of a "redoubt" built by Federal troops on the southern side of Pass Manchac, just east of the railroad bridge (this was the fortification named Fort Stevens; Casey 1983; Groene 1985). Zacharie stated that the swamps south of Manchac contained gigantic cypress trees "festooned with moss." The German farmers at Frenier raised "fine cabbages." After crossing Bayou LaBranche, the railroad entered "a large, trembling prairie." At Kennerville, there were sugar plantations, "shell roads, as white as snow, and drainage canals, as black as ink." From the east, Zacharie described the railroad bridge over the Rigolets as being "a fine iron bridge (recently built at a great cost)." At the end of the bridge was the East Rigolets lighthouse and the Custom House Station. "Lake Catherine" and Miller's Bayou were said to be a great resort for hunters and fishermen from the city.

From the north one took the Queen and Crescent Route, named for the queen city of Cincinnati and the crescent city of New Orleans. The railroad passed through the "small place" called Slidell, then over the Pontchartrain Bridge, "the longest bridge in the world, being over 26 mi. [42 km] long" (if one includes the entire trestle work built of creosoted timbers). The bridge proper, from shore to shore, was only 7 mi. (11.3 km) long. Zacharie pointed out that the lake was "navigated by schooners and other small craft" that carried cargoes of lumber, sand, bricks, and rosin from Mobile and from north-shore "streams" that flow into the lake.

Zacharie (1885) also described the lakeshore resorts within the city, where there were "excellent restaurants." At West End were the St. John's Rowing Club and other clubs and boathouses, where annual rowing regattas were held. Also here was the Southern Yacht Club, "a large and fine building," a music plaza for summer concerts, theaters, saloons, and restaurants. A promenade along the lakeshore featured gardens, flowers, fountains, kiosks, and an "intricate maze puzzle of shrubbery . . . a source of great amusement to visitors." With reference to yachting, Zacharie stated that the "proximity of the lake permits great indulgence in this favorite sport." For excursions across the lake, one could take a train that ran along New Canal to West End and then a boat to Mandeville, Madisonville, and up the Tchefuncte River to Covington, "a pleasant and cheap excursion." A train also ran to Spanish Fort, described as a "small village with pleasure gardens, situated at the mouth of Bayou St. John." Behind the fort were four equally spaced cypress trees planted to mark the grave of a young Spanish soldier killed in a duel there. Nearby were gardens, a concert hall, a summer theater, and an alligator pond. Also mentioned was the "old torpedo boat, fished up out of the Canal a few years ago, a relic of the civil war." At the end of the Pontchartrain Railroad was the "Old Lake End" at Milneburg, a small village composed of a series of restaurants and bathing houses and a long pier with a lighthouse. At all of the Lake End bathhouses, the charge for use was 15 cents.

Mark Twain (1883) recounted a visit to West End "along a raised shell road, with a canal on one hand and a dense wood on the other." He described West

End as a "collection of hotels of the usual light summer-resort pattern, with broad verandas all around, and the waves of the wide and blue Lake Pontchartrain lapping the thresholds." He noted that "thousands of people come by rail and carriage to West End and to Spanish Fort every evening, and dine, listen to the bands, take strolls in the open air under the electric lights, go sailing on the lake, and entertain themselves in various and sundry other ways."

By 1900 West End had replaced Spanish Fort as the "chief lake resort" for New Orleans (Forman 1900), even though it was considered less attractive. It offered large wharves, a hotel, a restaurant, amusements, and gardens. Originally called New Lake End, it was renamed West End in 1880 (Widmer 1993). It was closer to the city and had a new rail line (the New Orleans City and Lake Railway) that provided more dependable train service. The train, or streetcar, was electrified in 1898 and towed open-sided trailers for tourists to ride. The scenic ride paralleled the New Basin Canal, where riders could watch schooners loaded with lumber, sand, gravel, shells, and charcoal from across the lake moving into the city (Widmer 1989). Unfortunately, racial prejudice was also a factor in the demise of Spanish Fort as it was described as becoming "a favorite place for negro picnics" (Forman 1900). Attempts to revive it continued into the early 1900s with development of the amusement park, a small zoo, and a dance pavilion (Kelly 1975).

With the increased population growth of New Orleans and the continual problems with flooding, the lake increasingly became the place to dump the excess water, as well as the pollutants this urban runoff carried with it. In addition, the city's desire for more developable land made the once-neglected swamps between the city and the lake more attractive for urban expansion. Plans for the complex drainage and pumping system to remove water from New Orleans into Lake Pontchartrain were developed in the late 1800s. Numerous ditches and canals had been dug throughout the city, beginning almost immediately after New Orleans was planned in 1718. Because the Mississippi River side of the city was its highest land, all drainage from this system of canals eventually passed into Lake Pontchartrain, creating major pollution concerns for the lake. The "modern" drainage efforts in New Orleans were initiated in 1893 when the city council passed an ordinance calling for the formulation of a "complete and comprehensive system of drainage" for the city (Maygarden et al. 1999). This ordinance resulted in the development of the New Orleans Drainage Plan of 1895, which called for a system of 95 mi. (153 km) of canals, with a major goal to divert most of the drainage away from Lake Pontchartrain, but instead into Bayou Bienvenue east of the city, and thus into Lake Borgne. Recognizing that it would be impossible to keep all drainage out of Lake Pontchartrain, the plan was to divert the heavily polluted "first flush" after heavy rains toward Lake Borgne, and then the comparatively clean surplus water into Lake Pontchartrain. Unfortunately, these expressed concerns for Lake Pontchartrain were eventually discarded in the face of reality, and urban runoff from the pumping stations and canals continued to be a major source of pollution to the lake.

Construction of the new canals and pumping stations needed for the system was begun in 1896. At this time the major waterways entering Lake Pontchartrain from New Orleans were Metairie Relief Outfall (or the 17th Street Canal), New Orleans Navigation Canal (or New Basin Canal), Orleans Relief Outfall, Bayou St. John, London Avenue Relief Outfall, and Peoples Avenue Relief Outfall (or Lafayette Relief Outfall).

8.

The Twentieth Century
RAPID POPULATION GROWTH AND URBAN EXPANSION

By 1900, the population of New Orleans had reached such a level that significant human impacts on Lake Pontchartrain were becoming more evident, but the population was to continue increasing at an ever higher rate during the twentieth century (Table 3; Figure 8.1). This population growth generated a desire for more developable land as well as additional recreational opportunities, and it increased the sources and volume of pollutants entering Lake Pontchartrain.

The focus on Lake Pontchartrain as a site for recreation reached a peak in the early 1900s. Bayou St. John was populated by numerous boathouses, houseboats, and squatters' shacks (Widmer 1993). Many vacation camps (Figure 8.2) were built on pilings out over the lake with interconnecting piers at West End and Milneburg (Gary and Davis 1978, 1979; Widmer 1993). Camps were also being built all along the lakeshore between West End and Little Woods at Paris Road (Widmer 1989, 1993), as well as in other locations around the lake. Ironically these camps, built to provide recreational opportunities on the lake, were also a major source of untreated sewage entering the lake to pollute the very waters they were built to enjoy. By the middle of the century, these and other pollution sources were to seriously threaten the recreational activities on the lake.

In 1909 the city began constructing a new seawall at West End and then filled in a 30-acre (12-ha) area to form West End Park in 1921 (Huber 1970). In the 1920s pleasure boats departing from West End Park, such as the *Susquehanna*, *Camelia*, and *Southdown*, still took passengers across the lake and on moonlight cruises around the lake (Widmer 1993).

Table 3 Population figures (and percentage change) for parishes bordering Lake Pontchartrain

Year	Jefferson	Livingston	Orleans	St. Bernard	St. Charles	St. John	St. Tammany	Tangipahoa	Total
1900	15,321	8100	287,104	5031	9072	12,330	13,335	17,625	367,918
1910	18,247 (+19%)	10,627 (+31%)	339,075 (+18%)	5277 (+5%)	11,207 (+24%)	14,338 (+16%)	18,917 (+42%)	29,160 (+65%)	446,848 (+22%)
1920	21,563 (+18%)	11,643 (+10%)	387,219 (+14%)	4968 (−6%)	8586 (−23%)	11,896 (−17%)	20,645 (+9%)	31,440 (+8%)	497,960 (+11%)
1930	40,032 (+86%)	18,206 (+56%)	458,762 (+19%)	6512 (+31%)	12,111 (+41%)	14,078 (+18%)	20,929 (+1%)	46,227 (+47%)	616,857 (+24%)
1940	50,427 (+26%)	17,790 (−2%)	494,537 (+8%)	7280 (+12%)	12,321 (+2%)	14,766 (+5%)	23,624 (+13%)	45,519 (−2%)	666,264 (+8%)
1950	103,873 (+106%)	20,054 (+13%)	570,445 (+15%)	11,087 (+52%)	13,363 (+9%)	14,861 (+1%)	26,988 (+14%)	53,218 (+17%)	813,889 (+22%)
1960	208,769 (+101%)	26,974 (+35%)	627,525 (+10%)	32,186 (+190%)	21,219 (+59%)	18,439 (+24%)	38,643 (+43%)	59,434 (+12%)	1,033,189 (+27%)
1970	337,568 (+62%)	36,511 (+35%)	593,471 (−5%)	51,185 (+59%)	29,550 (+39%)	23,813 (+29%)	63,585 (+65%)	65,875 (+11%)	1,201,558 (+16%)
1980	454,592 (+35%)	58,806 (+61%)	557,515 (−6%)	64,097 (+25%)	37,259 (+26%)	31,924 (+34%)	110,869 (+74%)	80,698 (+23%)	1,395,760 (+16%)
1990	448,306 (−1%)	70,526 (+20%)	496,938 (−11%)	66,631 (+4%)	42,437 (+14%)	39,996 (+25%)	144,508 (+30%)	85,709 (+6%)	1,395,051 (−0.1%)
2000	455,466 (+2%)	91,814 (+30%)	484,674 (−3%)	67,229 (+1%)	48,072 (+13%)	43,044 (+8%)	191,268 (+32%)	100,588 (+17%)	1,482,155 (+6%)

Data from U.S. Census Bureau

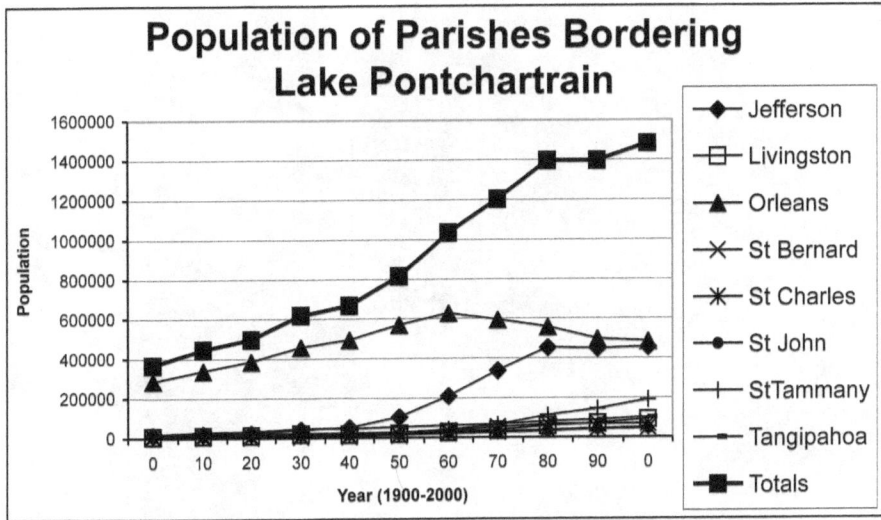

Figure 8.1 Population changes in the Pontchartrain basin, 1900–2000

Piers and bathhouses were also common along the Mandeville lakefront by the early 1900s. However, modesty induced the Mandeville Town Council of 1920 to adopt an ordinance making it unlawful to appear in public in a one-piece "trunk bathing suit" (Nichols 1990). Attempts to improve the beach at Mandeville included a 1925 campaign to remove 6000 stumps. Shoreline erosion had been a continuing problem around the lake, so armoring of many shorelines was attempted. The first seawall to prevent erosion at Mandeville was constructed of wood and was severely damaged by a hurricane in 1893 (Nichols 1990; Tavaszi and Maygarden 1994). A more substantial concrete seawall was begun in 1913, but it too was damaged in the hurricane of 1915, even though Mandeville in general received relatively little damage from this storm, compared to the Rigolets and the western shore of the lake (Roberts 1946). Continued beachfront restoration at Mandeville continued through the late 1930s, when the existing concrete seawall, 7000 ft. (2134 m) long with a series of perpendicular groins extending 150 ft. (46 m) into the lake, was constructed (Figure 8.3). The groins were intended to trap sand and improve the condition of the beach.

In 1900 the low swampy land between higher natural levee land in New Orleans and the lakefront resorts had been mostly undeveloped because of the threat of frequent floods. But with a modern canal and pumping system in operation, new developments could expand toward the lake. This new system to remove water from New Orleans into Lake Pontchartrain was completed in the early 1900s with the installation of the first large screw pumps (12 ft. or 3.6 m

80 ENVIRONMENTAL HISTORY OF THE BASIN

A

B

C

Figure 8.2 Former camps and ruins at (A) Milneburg, c. 1920, and (B, C) Little Woods, 2001 (Photograph A provided by The Historic New Orleans Collection, accession no. 1974.25.39.133, New Orleans, Louisiana; photographs B and C by the author)

Figure 8.3 Mandeville bulkhead and park (Photograph by the author)

in diameter), invented by A. Baldwin Wood, an engineer with the New Orleans Sewerage and Water Board (Thompson 1973; Widmer 1993). Larger 14-ft. (4.3-m) pumps capable of pumping up to 1000 cfs (28 m³/sec) were installed in 1927. Their effectiveness was immediately clear, and some of these original pumps are still in operation today.

The more efficient drainage provided new land for residential development, such as Lakeview between City Park and the New Basin Canal (Widmer 1989), but the drainage system created new problems for the city, as well as the lake. Subsurface drainage caused the water table to sink below the soil surface, and the water level in the drainage canals dropped 8–10 ft. (2–3 m), possibly also modifying the climate of New Orleans (Cline 1945). Prior to 1900, temperatures in the city exceeded 95°F (35°C) on only thirty-five days in fifteen years and were never over 100°F (38°C). After 1900, however, temperatures over 95°F were recorded on seventy-four days in fifteen years (and over 100°F on seven days). Another change was that much of New Orleans immediately began to sink further below sea level, increasing the potential danger of flooding. Houses even at ground level had to be built on 30-ft. (9-m) piles to prevent sinking. Although levees continued to be built higher and higher, the city was still threatened by serious flooding, especially by hurricanes.

Some early attempts at agriculture in the Pontchartrain basin involved construction of levees and draining low-lying wetland sites, such as the LaBranche Wetlands, the Madisonville rice fields, and the Slidell marshes (which eventually became Eden Isles), but such drained or "reclaimed" land along the lakeshore also experienced problems with subsidence and flooding. The low, marshy LaBranche Wetlands, owned by Edward Wisner, was leveed and drained by canals in the early 1900s to be used for truck farming and initially proved fertile (Harrison and Kollmorgen 1947; Dranguet and Heleniak 1987). However, continual problems of subsidence and flooding demonstrated the long-term futility of such reclamation efforts. According to Harrison and Kollmorgen (1947), none of the projects was entirely successful, and most were complete failures. The hurricane of 1915 ended the Wisner project by flooding the subsiding lands. Much of the LaBranche Wetlands has now become open water and continues to be threatened by additional erosion and subsidence.

Bayou Bonfouca in Slidell and Tchefuncte River at Madisonville became significant industrial waterways, especially with the need for ships during World War I. Several ship-building companies still operated in the Madisonville area, and the demand for ships during the war stimulated a population boom in the town that reached 4000 (Ellis 1981). Among the companies were the Jahncke shipyard, which became the St. Tammany Shipbuilding Company, and the Baham shipyard, which became the Gulf Shipbuilding Company (Ellis 1981). World War I ship construction also took place at the Government Shipyard in Slidell (Kemp and Colvin 1981). After the war, the companies lost their government contracts and laid off hundreds of workers, and Madisonville's population declined to its pre-war level. Slidell also lost population, but was eventually to begin growing again because of suburban expansion from New Orleans in the 1950s.

The logging industry continued to expand through the early 1900s with massive cutting of the virgin longleaf or yellow pine forests (*Pinus palustris*) in the uplands, as well as the old growth tidewater cypress (*Taxodium distichum*) in the wetlands. The development of the pulpwood industry in the early 1920s stimulated the replanting of cut-over lands with the faster growing, but less desirable, loblolly pines (*Pinus taeda*; Hickman 1966).

The first complete water connection between the Mississippi River and Lake Pontchartrain was finished in 1921, with the construction of the Inner Harbor Navigation Canal, also known as the Industrial Canal (Widmer 1993). Partial connections had been created years before with the digging of canals from the city to Bayou St. John (Carondelet Canal) or to the lake (New Basin Canal). In addition, the Marigny family had dug a canal from the river into their land along Elysian Fields Avenue prior to 1798. However, all of these were eventually filled in as the city grew.

As its name implies, the Industrial Canal became the major port of New Orleans. It has locks at the river end to control water flow from the river (Roberts 1946), which is about 6 ft. (2 m) above the level of the lake at this point (Widmer 1993). The canal was linked in 1944 with the Intracoastal Waterway, which had been completed to the east to open at the mouth of the Rigolets (Alperin 1983). Although there has always been some movement of boating traffic from the Industrial Canal into Lake Pontchartrain, it is necessarily limited by the shallower depths in the lake.

A very ambitious "reclamation and improvement" of the New Orleans lakeshore was begun in 1926 by the Board of Commissioners of the Orleans Levee District (the New Orleans Levee Board). The Lakefront Land Reclamation Project was to create a permanent lakefront levee and more than 2000 acres (8 km^2) of new land by dredging more than 950 million cu. ft. (27 million m^3) of fill from the lake (Huber 1970; Filipich and Taylor 1971; Association of Levee Boards of Louisiana 1990). The original authorization for the project extended from the New Basin Canal (at West End) to Little Woods (Filipich and Taylor 1971). Although the project's primary purpose was to be the protection of New Orleans from flood waters of Lake Pontchartrain through improved levees, a clear objective was "improving this eroded and untidy lakefront area as a source of pride and satisfaction to the people of New Orleans" (Filipich and Taylor 1971). Parts of this shoreline had receded due to erosion as much as 500 ft. (152 m) between 1832 and 1926, and levees previously built were substandard. The lakeshore within the city was marshes and cypress swamps submerged by several feet of water during storms and was described as "seedy and disagreeable," with its numerous fishing shacks and piers extending into the lake (Lewis 1976). A major goal of the levee board was to have the improvements pay for themselves. Areas were to be subdivided and sold, supposedly to rich and poor alike, to create new residential areas, and 30% of the new land was to be dedicated for public use and parks (Association of Levee Boards of Louisiana 1990).

The project involved building a reinforced concrete step-type seawall in the lake 3000 ft. (914 m) from shore and then pumping dredged material from the lake bottom to fill in the area behind the seawall to create land some 5–10 ft. (1.5–3 m) above lake level. Steel locks were to be installed across the mouths of New Basin Canal and Bayou St. John (Jacobs 1936). The project resulted in some of the highest land in the city, both in elevation and price. In spite of good intentions, the poor were not to be afforded housing in the upscale neighborhoods to be built on these lands. The initial housing development, Lake Vista, began in 1938, but additional development was to be delayed by the start of World War II.

An additional effect of the dredging operations was the creation of deep dredge holes in places along the southern shore of Lake Pontchartrain. Because the lake is relatively shallow and mostly quite uniform in depth, averaging less than about 10–15 ft. (3–5 m), these deeper holes have significant ecological impacts. Stratification of water layers can occur with denser, higher salinity water accumulating near the bottom and becoming anoxic (that is, lacking oxygen), an unsuitable habitat for most living organisms. This is especially significant near the Inner Harbor Navigation Canal, a source of denser high-salinity water coming into the lake (Poirrier 1978b; Georgiou and McCorquodale 2001). However, Davis (1988) noted that these dredge holes provided important haunts for large tarpon during the summer months.

Some of the new land became the 5-mi. (8-km) long Lakeshore Park with its concrete seawall (Figure 8.4) and Lakeshore Drive extending from West End to the Inner Harbor Navigation Canal. Spanish Fort Park was moved out to the new lakeshore at the mouth of Bayou St. John and was renamed Pontchartrain Beach Amusement Park (Widmer 1989, 1993), although it continued to be known as "Spanish Fort" by most New Orleanians. There were long piers out into the lake, a boardwalk, various amusement park rides, bathhouses, and picnic pavilions. Land to form the City Park extension to the lake

Figure 8.4 New Orleans lakeshore stepped seawall (Photograph by the author)

was purchased by the city in 1926, and the numerous boat houses and docks along Bayou St. John were removed. During the Great Depression of the 1930s, much of the work on the project was done by the Works Progress Administration (Lewis 1976). The 11-mi. (18-km) long lagoon system in City Park was also dug by WPA workers. Shushan Airport, eventually to be known as the New Orleans Airport and then the New Orleans Lakefront Airport, was built on additional artificial land created on the eastern side of the Inner Harbor Navigation Canal in 1934 (Widmer 1993).

Pontchartrain Beach and the Pontchartrain Beach Amusement Park were moved again in 1939 to the old Milneburg site at the end of Elysian Fields Avenue, and the Zephyr roller coaster became their symbol (Widmer 1989). Pontchartrain Beach remained the major recreational site for the city until it closed in 1983. The Spanish Fort area became known as "The Old Beach."

Also in 1939, construction of groins and filling of the inshore area along the lakeshore near Little Woods resulted in the creation of the original "New Negro Beach," about 7 mi. (11 km) east of Pontchartrain Beach at a location then described as remote, with poor water quality, and humble rides and attractions (1999 Louisiana House Concurrent Resolution no. 220). Further improvement and construction at the site in the 1950s resulted in the opening of Lincoln Beach on June 29, 1955, as an "amusement and playground resort for the Negro community of New Orleans," with swimming pools, bathhouse, picnic shelters, a roller coaster and other rides, and a restaurant (Burk-Kleinpeter, Inc. 1997). Lincoln Beach closed in 1964 with the opening of other beaches to all citizens of the city as a result of the Civil Rights Act, although increased pollution levels in the lake were also becoming a major concern at all lake beaches.

Flooding from the Mississippi River continued to be a serious threat to New Orleans, even though the levees were being strengthened and increased in height. Prior to construction of any artificial levees, the river would overflow its banks when the river reached a stage of 11 ft. (3.4 m) above sea level at New Orleans (Lopez 2003). As the levees grew higher and higher, the potential for catastrophic flooding from a crevasse or break in the levees grew greater because the water level of the Mississippi River at flood stage was being held at an artificially higher level (Poplin et al. 1988). Higher levees, as well as other modifications upriver, only increased the danger of massive floods along the lower river (Gunter 1979), and the problem was exacerbated by the blocking of major distributaries such as Bayou Manchac, Bayou Lafourche, and Bayou Plaquemine. A record flood on the Mississippi River in 1927 threatened New Orleans before the danger was averted by dynamiting the levee below the city (and flooding much of St. Bernard Parish; Barry 1997). As a direct result of this flood, the Bonnet Carré Spillway was constructed between 1929 and 1931 at the site of the Bonnet Carré crevasse between New Orleans and LaPlace (Roberts 1946; Cowdrey 1977). The spillway was intended to provide flood relief by diverting river water into Lake Pontchartrain when the Mississippi River reached flood stage (defined as 20 ft. or 6.1 m above sea level on the Carrollton gauge) and threatened New Orleans and other communities downriver.

The Bonnet Carré Spillway structure is a dam-like barrier composed of 350 bays, each with twenty creosoted timber pins, which can be removed by a small crane running on a track on top of the spillway (Figure 8.5). Guide levees border the spillway from the river to the lake, a distance of 5.7 mi. (9.2 km). The spillway was first opened in 1937 and several times since then. In addition to providing flood protection, the spillway has also become a popular recreational area during low-water periods and is open to fishing, hunting, and crawfishing. River

Figure 8.5 The Bonnet Carré Spillway at (A) the Mississippi River and (B) Lake Pontchartrain (Photographs by the author)

sand deposited in the spillway has become an important source of fill material for local construction projects.

Plans to build a causeway across the 24-mi. (39-km) wide lake, between Mandeville and West End, were resurrected in 1924, with a proposal to include eighteen man-made islands connected by a series of bridges (Nichols 1990). However, a competing proposal for a bridge at the narrow neck of Lake Pontchartrain at Point aux Herbes (only 5 mi., 8.3 km across) was approved instead. The New Orleans Pontchartrain Bridge Company bought land surrounding the Point aux Herbes lighthouse in 1928 as the starting point for the southern end of the bridge (Cipra 1997). This bridge for U.S. Highway 11, called the Watson-Williams Bridge, was privately owned and charged exorbitant tolls (Roberts 1946). Shortly thereafter, the new governor, Huey P. Long, had a free bridge built not far away (at U.S. Highway 90, or Chef Menteur Highway) and put the toll collectors out of business. Eventually the state bought the Watson-Williams Bridge and renamed it the Robert S. Maestri Bridge (after a mayor of New Orleans) and made it toll-free (Roberts 1946). The bridge is known locally as the "Five-Mile Bridge."

Governor Long also had Airline Highway built through the swamps to the west in the 1930s, and the New Orleans to Hammond Highway had been completed in 1926 (Dranguet and Heleniak 1985), stimulating suburban expansion into Jefferson Parish (Lewis 1976). The Hammond Highway was originally envisioned as a scenic, lakeside roadway skirting the southern and western shorelines of the lake (Bordenave 1940). The road followed the lakeshore out of New Orleans and Jefferson Parish as Route 33, then a borrow pit canal was dug through the LaBranche Wetlands of St. Charles Parish and into St. John Parish along the proposed highway right-of-way near the lakeshore. Spoil from the canal was to provide a road embankment 4 ft. (1.2 m) above lake level and paralleling the Illinois Central Railroad for most of the way. The lakeshore highway was never completed west of Jefferson Parish, apparently because engineers feared that the roadway could not be adequately protected without a seawall on the lakeshore. Viosca (1933) described access to LaBranche hunting and fishing areas as limited to rail or boat pending completion of Highway 51 (which was "under construction," but never completed). Instead maps of the 1930s show this highway as Route 51/33 along the lakeshore west through Kenner to Williams Boulevard and Airline Highway (Route 61) and on the western side from Frenier to LaPlace and Airline Highway. Most of the canal in the LaBranche area has been lost to lakeshore erosion or was eliminated by the Bonnet Carré Spillway construction. The western portion remains as the Old Hammond Road Ditch, which is now the site of a commercial swamp tour near LaPlace. Remnants of the roadway remain on the lakeshore as the four-block Hammond Highway at Bucktown and asphalt pavement between the levee and the lakeshore in Linear Park at Kenner and Metairie (now used as a bike trail). Between LaPlace and Ponchatoula the old Hammond Highway is still visible adjacent to the newer Highway 51 (and still newer Interstate 55, completed in 1979).

With the improved road access into this area, new recreational sites developed along the western side of the lake. Viosca (1933) noted the presence of a lakeshore beach at Frenier, as well as lake fishing and crabbing there and at Ruddock and Manchac. There were also many private camps and gun-and-rod clubs in this area, and Viosca described the deer hunting as "unexcelled" and "one of the best deer hunting grounds in the state." Ponchatoula Beach on the lower Tangipahoa River was described as having a "fine river bathing beach, picnic and camping sites," and a summer resort hotel.

As the popularity of automobiles and the quality of roadways improved, automobile travel became the method of choice and rail and boat traffic became less significant on the lake. The Pontchartrain Railroad was finally closed in 1932, and the tracks removed a few years later (Roberts 1946). Waterborne commerce on the lake continued to decline during the early 1900s and had practically ceased by the 1940s, except for the transport of shell, sand, and gravel (Pearson et al. 1989). The last of the excursion boats to the north shore ceased operation in the 1930s (Ellis 1981). On the other hand, recreational boating increased dramatically during this period.

In 1938 the former Marigny estate between Bayous Castine and Cane was bought by the state to create the 1000-acre (405-ha) Tchefuncte State Park (eventually named Fontainebleau after the original estate name) and a 5000-acre (2023-ha) game preserve or wildlife management area (Nichols 1990). The latter was to include 1000 acres (405 ha) for reforestation; 1000 acres for a quail hatchery; 2000 acres (809 ha) for a game preserve to be stocked with deer, wild turkey, and other game; and 1000 acres of marshland (between Cane Bayou and Bayou Lacombe) as a refuge for muskrat, migratory water fowl, and other wildlife. The project also was to include a 50-acre (20-ha) golf course. The land was cleared and landscaped and a club house constructed, but the course was never completed. Its key supporters, including Governor Richard W. Leche, went to jail as a result of the political scandals of 1939–1940. The now reforested site, with a crumbling clubhouse ruin, is the location of the Northlake Nature Center. Fontainebleau State Park now encompasses 2800 acres (1133 ha), including about 3 mi. (4.8 km) of Lake Pontchartrain shoreline.

With the beginning of World War II, much of the new land created by the dredging and filling project along the New Orleans lakeshore was used for military purposes, rather than the residential subdivisions, parks, and beaches for which it had been planned (Filipich and Taylor 1971; Widmer 1990, 1993). However, the nearby Pontchartrain Beach was said to be especially popular with servicemen during the war.

The Industrial Canal became a site of active ship building and testing during World War II (Roberts 1946). Higgins Industries, initially located at City Park, built a new plant on the Industrial Canal after the attack on Pearl Harbor. Their Higgins landing barges, invented by Andrew Jackson Higgins, were initially tested at Pontchartrain Beach. The design was initially conceived for trappers and oilmen to use in marshes and other shallow-water areas choked with aquatic vegetation (Strahan 1994). The Eureka boat with a spoonbill bow was tested and demonstrated in Lake Pontchartrain by jumping logs, running through masses of water hyacinths and over sandbars, and by running up the concrete seawall along the lakeshore. In addition to the landing barges (or personnel and vehicle landing craft), the company also constructed PT boats. After construction, the boats were launched and tested in Bayou St. John, and photos taken during the early 1940s show more than 100 boats anchored in the bayou awaiting shipment (Strahan 1994). The Higgins Boat Operators and Marine Engine Maintenance School for operating and landing Higgins boats was established on the New Basin Canal opposite the Southern Yacht Club.

Delta Shipbuilding Company, also on the Industrial Canal, built 155 Liberty ships during the war. At the Slidell Shipbuilding Company, tugboats and net tenders were built (Roberts 1946). The Michoud facility on Chef Menteur Highway was first planned as a site to build Liberty ships, but was never used for that purpose, instead opening in October 1943 for aircraft construction (Strahan 1994).

With the end of World War II, most of the military facilities along the New Orleans lakefront were closed, but the industrial development and prosperity stimulated by the war effort continued. The Levee Board resumed its plan to have the lakefront reclamation project pay for itself by selling much of the land for residential development. Eventually most of the new land was sold to private developers who created additional subdivisions such as West Lakeshore (1951), Lake Terrace (1953), East Lakeshore (1955), and Lake Oaks (1964; Filipich and Taylor 1971).

The Pontchartrain Causeway across the lake finally became a reality when planning and construction began in 1946, with the filling of land for Causeway Boulevard, using sand from the Bonnet Carré Spillway (Bezou 1973). The causeway (Figure 8.6), a 24-mi. (38 km) long bridge built at a cost of $51 million, was opened on August 30, 1956 (Nichols 1990). This convenient access

Figure 8.6 The Pontchartrain Causeway (Photograph by the author)

route from New Orleans to the north shore stimulated population growth in St. Tammany Parish, which eventually became the fastest growing parish in the state, growth that has continued until the present (Table 3). A second parallel causeway span was completed in May 1969. An estimated 30,000 automobiles crossed the causeway each weekday during year 2000 (http://www.thecauseway.com). By 1965 Interstate 10 connected New Orleans with Causeway Boulevard (Widmer 2000) and extended east across Lake Pontchartrain on the bridges known locally as the Twin Spans, further contributing to the population growth of Slidell.

One of the most significant biological effects that structures such as the Pontchartrain Causeway and other bridges have had on the lake was to increase significantly the amount of hard substrate available to aquatic organisms. Southeastern Louisiana is devoid of natural rock, so the only hard substrate naturally available prior to such construction was wood from river-borne logs carried into the lake by flood waters. Shoreline protection structures of concrete or rock, as well as concrete power-line stanchions erected in the lake beginning in 1956, also provided artificial hard substrate. Such surfaces are soon colonized by assorted benthic organisms, such as algae, sponges, hydroids, ectoprocts (or bryozoans), mussels, and barnacles (Poirrier et al. 1975; Poirrier and Mulino 1975, 1977; Poirrier 1978a).

With continued population growth in the 1950s, Metairie became New Orleans's first suburb, with large numbers of middle-class families moving out of the city. The population of Jefferson Parish increased from 50,427 in 1940 to 103,873 in 1950 to 207,301 in 1960, more than a 100% increase in each decade (Table 3; Figure 8.1). This urban flight and growth of Metairie, as well as Kenner, was to continue through the 1970s, while New Orleans began a decline that has continued until the present. The increased population brought increased traffic between Orleans and Jefferson Parishes and pressure for better roads. In the 1950s the New Basin Canal was filled in to provide land for the Pontchartrain Expressway, and later Interstate 10 (Widmer 1991). At the lake end of the filled-in canal, on Robert E. Lee Boulevard between West End and Pontchartrain, a Civil Defense bomb shelter was built in the 1950s. At the basin end, the Superdome was completed in 1975 (Widmer 2000).

In 1961 the Michoud aircraft factory became the Michoud Assembly Facility, which built the Saturn S-1 booster rockets for the Apollo space program and was responsible for the rapid development of eastern New Orleans, as well as nearby communities in neighboring St. Tammany and St. Bernard Parishes. Much of the marshland of eastern New Orleans was replaced by residential subdivisions, shopping centers, motels, gas stations, and restaurants (Kemp 1997). The proposed "New Orleans East" development of 32,000 acres (13,000 ha) of low wetlands along Interstate 10 was supposed to provide additional housing for some 250,000 people (Lewis 1976). Fortunately the houses were never built, as the area was flooded by Hurricane Betsy in 1965, despite being surrounded by levees. Instead much of the area became the 23,000-acre (9308-ha) Bayou Sauvage National Wildlife Refuge in 1990.

Another major dredging project to have a significant impact on Lake Pontchartrain was completed in 1963, with the opening of the Mississippi River Gulf Outlet (MRGO), providing a 76-mi. (122-km) long direct connection between the Intracoastal Waterway and Breton Sound. Thus, the Inner Harbor Navigation Canal became another saltwater connection to the Pontchartrain Estuary. The MRGO provided ships a much straighter and more direct route from the open Gulf into the New Orleans port, reducing the distance traveled by about 40 mi. (64 km). It has also provided a direct route for high-salinity Gulf water to move into the lake and caused significant marsh erosion along its margins. The levees of the MRGO, along with those of the Intracoastal Waterway, create a funnel effect that can significantly increase the storm surge entering the Inner Harbor Navigation Canal, which apparently occurred during Hurricane Katrina (Van Heerden and Bryan 2006). In reality the MRGO has been used much less than anticipated, because many ships must wait several days for passage through the locks from the Inner Harbor Navigation Canal into the river (Lewis 1976). Consequently, most still prefer the longer river route rather than risk a long delay at the locks.

A major land reclamation project just south of Slidell that had begun in 1927 received a renewed life in the 1960s. A levee and pumping system had been constructed in 1927 to drain more than 5300 acres (2000 ha) of wetlands along the eastern shore of the lake between Highways 11 and 90. The drained land was used for agriculture until the 1930s, when the drainage district abandoned the area and it again flooded as the levees deteriorated. The St. Tammany Parish Police Jury renovated the levees between 1962 and 1966 and again pumped the wetlands dry. In 1969 the land was sold to developers (Leisure, Inc.), who built the Eden Isles West community on 3000 acres (1200 ha) to the west of the recently completed Interstate 10, eventually to provide more than 1000 residences on a network of canals entering the lake. The Oak Harbor development adjacent to Eden Isles was begun in 1988. Across the interstate the newer Lakeshore Estates was begun in 2000 on land that was formerly referred to as Eden Isles East. The similar Venetian Isles development was built on filled wetlands along Chef Menteur Pass at Highway 90 between about 1975 and 1985. Numerous older lakeshore communities in this area include, North Shore, Northshore Beach, Howze Beach, and Treasure Island. Carr Drive, the main lakefront road at Northshore Beach, was built at public expense in 1953, in exchange for donated land to provide a public beach.

Such developments promised a life of leisure and recreation in waterfront living, but also contributed to the degradation of the lake environment that people found so appealing. The wetlands that help feed the estuary are diminished. Dead-end canals have poor water circulation, resulting in low dissolved oxygen levels. Surface runoff adds contaminants such as lawn fertilizers, pesticides, and motor oil to the canals and eventually the lake, further reducing water quality. And the developments also result in increased demands for hurricane protection.

A new era of cargo shipping on Lake Pontchartrain was begun in 1984, with the construction of Port Manchac on North Pass in Tangipahoa Parish (U.S. Army Corps of Engineers 1992). The facility was a shallow draft barge terminal where cargo from truck or rail transport was transferred to barge and thus shipped by way of North Pass and Lake Pontchartrain to the Port of New Orleans. During the first six years of operation, the port averaged about 35,000 tons (38,580 metric tons) of cargo, consisting primarily of plywood, grain, and gravel.

With the continued expansion of housing developments into lakeshore and other low-elevation areas of the Pontchartrain basin, there was increased concern for potential flooding from Lake Pontchartrain and thus pressure to provide flood protection in the form of more substantial levees. As much of New Orleans subsided below sea level, the threat of flooding and destruction by hurricanes became even greater (Fischetti 2001). The city has only survived because of the monumental effort and expense of maintaining hurricane protection levees, as well as the massive drainage canal system and pumping stations throughout the city, but there have still been many catastrophic floods that have impacted New Orleans and surrounding areas.

Hurricanes have always been a serious problem for coastal Louisiana and the New Orleans area and caused numerous significant floods. A total of thirty-eight hurricanes reportedly damaged New Orleans between 1718 and 2000 (Shallat 2001). The most deadly of these was in 1893, when 1500 people were killed. The "extreme" storm in September 1909 caused 350 deaths. Another devastating hurricane in September 1915 that passed between Lakes Pontchartrain and Maurepas destroyed Frenier and Ruddock and damaged New Orleans (Cline 1945; U.S. Army Corps of Engineers 1992). A 13-ft. (4-m) storm surge hit the western side of Lake Pontchartrain, then came back across the lake and over the levees at New Orleans (Roberts 1946). The community of Bucktown was destroyed. Many people were killed in the Rigolets area (Nichols 1990), and the reported loss of life was 275 (Zumwalt 1963). Yamazaki and Penland (2001) described four hurricanes of the twentieth century that caused devastating damage to the Pontchartrain basin: an unnamed hurricane on September 19, 1947, Hurricane Betsy on September 10, 1965, Hurricane Camille on August 17, 1969, and Hurricane Georges on September 28, 1998. To this list could be added the storms of 1909 and 1915 and certainly Hurricane Katrina in 2005.

Hurricane Betsy in 1965 was to result in major changes in the New Orleans attitude toward such storms, and Katrina in 2005 was a grim reminder that the problem had not yet been solved. Betsy came ashore at Grand Isle and devastated the Pontchartrain basin, flooding much of New Orleans, including 164,000 homes. The storm killed 75 and injured more than 17,000 people. Property damage was estimated to be about $1.4 billion, making it the most costly storm on record at the time (National Hurricane Center, http://www.nhc.noaa.gov/gifs/table3a.gif). Shortly thereafter, Congress enacted the Flood Control Act of October 1965 that included plans for the U.S. Army Corps of Engineers Lake Pontchartrain and Vicinity Protection Project (Cowdrey 1977; Shallat 2001). This plan called for improved levees along the southern shore of Lake Pontchartrain from the Bonnet Carré Spillway to South Point (U.S. Army Corps of Engineers 1988). The plan also called for barrier structures across the Rigolets, Chef Menteur Pass, and the Inner Harbor Navigation Canal, but these were challenged under the National Environmental Policy Act and eventually excluded from the project because of environmental concerns, as well as excessive costs (Kysar and McGarity 2006).

Despite the improvements in the levee system, flooding continued. Hurricane Camille went ashore 50 mi. (80 km) east of Lake Pontchartrain in August 1969, but the storm still significantly affected the area. Tidal surges recorded in the lake were 9 ft. (2.7 m) at the Rigolets, 5.2 ft. (1.6 m) at the New Orleans lakefront, and 4.6 ft. (1.4 m) at Mandeville and Frenier (Lewis 1976). Montz and Cherubini (1973) noted that the LaBranche Wetlands area was flooded with 2 ft. (0.6 m) of saline water (18 ppt) for several days following Hurricane Camille. The relatively weak but significant Hurricane Juan, which remained off the mouth of the Mississippi River for several days in October 1985, caused severe flooding around the lake with maximum stages of 7.6 ft. (2.3 m) at Frenier and at Mandeville (U.S. Army Corps of Engineers 1992).

Continued concern for potential flooding resulted in the adoption of the Lake Pontchartrain and Vicinity Hurricane Protection Project and High Level Plan in 1985, with the majority of the system of higher levees and floodwalls completed by 1990 (Association of Levee Boards of Louisiana 1990). Construction on various phases of this project continued into the twenty-first century with the levees and floodwalls on the southern shore of the lake ranging in height up to 18 ft. (5.5 m) above lake level. A hurricane protection levee was also proposed for the north shore at Mandeville, but was never built (Williams et al. 1996). The levees protecting New Orleans from floods can also function in reverse by holding water in during severe rainstorms, such as occurred on May 8, 1995, with up to 20 in. (50 cm) of rain falling in the New Orleans area and causing seven deaths and more than $1 billion in damages (U.S. Army Corps of Engineers 1998b). Thus, the canal and pumping system of the city has required continual updating and expansion since its creation.

During each annual hurricane season, especially when storms have threatened the northern Gulf coast, concerns for New Orleans and its potential for serious flooding have been revived. Predictions were that "when" (not "if") the big storm finally hit New Orleans directly, storm surge from Lake Pontchartrain would top the levees and result in catastrophic flooding of the city, most of which is below sea level. In 1998 Hurricane Georges came close and had a major impact on the Lake Pontchartrain area, destroying many of the remaining camps along the southern shore of the lake (Yamazaki and Penland 2001). Tropical storm Isidore in 2002, a relatively minor storm, still flooded Lake Pontchartrain and parts of Interstate 10. Some people attempting to evacuate New Orleans were stranded on the flooded highways. Over 12 in. (30 cm) of rain fell in some areas of New Orleans, so much so that the city pumping system was overwhelmed and parts of the city were flooded. Hurricane Ivan in 2004 was an even greater concern, but eventually spared New Orleans by going ashore to the east near Pensacola, Florida, with widespread coastal destruction.

The unthinkable finally happened on August 29, 2005, when Hurricane Katrina, a Category 5 storm with winds over 160 mph, threatened New Orleans with a direct hit. Some had predicted that such a storm hitting New Orleans directly or passing just to the west could be the death knell of the city (McQuaid and Schleifstein 2002). On August 28, there was ample warning from the National Hurricane Center and the Louisiana State University Hurricane Center that Katrina could be that "perfect storm" and flood much of New Orleans. Shortly before making landfall, the storm weakened slightly (to Category 4) and veered to the east, sparing the city a direct hit and the worst case scenario. Winds over Lake Pontchartrain and in New Orleans were estimated to be below Category 3 strength, with sustained winds less that about 70 mph (Knabb et al. 2006a).

However, the extremely high storm surge in Lake Pontchartrain on August 29, estimated to be about 15 ft. (4.6 m) in the eastern part of the lake and 5–10 ft. (1.5–3.0 m) on the western shore, broke the levees and flooded most of New Orleans and surrounding parishes, causing what has been described as "one of the most devastating natural disasters in United States history" (Knabb et al. 2006a). Flood walls constructed to raise the level of the levees broke in the Inner Harbor Navigation Canal, 17th Street Canal, and London Avenue Canal, resulting in water from Lake Pontchartrain flooding 80% of the city up to 20 ft. (6 m) deep in some places, with some 250,000 homes flooded. More than 1200 people died in the New Orleans area. Structural damage and flooding was a catastrophic problem for New Orleans and the surrounding Pontchartrain basin, as well as coastal Mississippi and Alabama. Many houses and camps in towns and communities surrounding Lake Pontchartrain were destroyed or severely damaged, and numerous trees throughout the basin were felled by the powerful storm winds. Bridges crossing Lake Pontchartrain were severely damaged. Just four weeks later, on September 24, Hurricane Rita made landfall on the Louisiana-Texas state line and generated a storm surge on Lake Pontchartrain of about 6.5 ft. (2 m), which caused new breaks in the partially repaired levees and additional flooding around Lake Pontchartrain (Knabb et al. 2006b). Low wetlands surrounding the lakes were completely inundated by floods of Katrina and Rita, including the LaBranche Wetlands, the Manchac land bridge, Goose Point, Fritchie Marsh, and most of St. Bernard Parish.

The subsequent overwhelming tragedy now commonly referred to as the "aftermath of Katrina" is a story told many times and in many formats (CNN

News 2005; Gannett News 2006; Van Heerden and Bryan 2006), and need not be repeated here. But efforts to restore Lake Pontchartrain became secondary to the incredible needs to restore New Orleans.

A major effect of Hurricane Katrina was an extraordinary amount of land loss in the Pontchartrain basin, with preliminary estimates of more than 60 sq. mi. (155 km^2) of marsh lost throughout the basin and 9–14 sq. mi. (23–36 km^2) in the middle sub-basin. This land loss is greater than that occurring during the previous decade (LPBF 2006a). There was also much wildlife mortality and wildlife habitat destruction. Presley et al. (2006) reported numerous dead animals during their sampling in canals and along the lakeshore following Katrina, including fish, snakes, alligators, nutria, armadillos, raccoons, hogs, and deer.

The ultimate effects of Katrina and Rita on the city and the lake environment will probably never be completely determined. This generation will remember Katrina as the worst natural disaster to hit the United States, and in monetary losses that may be true. A preliminary cost estimate of the total damage of Katrina was about $81 billion, roughly double that of Hurricane Andrew, now the second most costly hurricane (Knabb et al. 2006a). But there have been equally destructive storms to affect the northern Gulf coast in the past when coastal construction, property values, and the human population were less. Katrina has been ranked as the fourth or fifth deadliest hurricane on record for the United States by the National Hurricane Center (Knabb et al. 2006a). Two of the worst to hit the northern Gulf coast are the Cheniere Caminada hurricane of 1893 and the Galveston hurricane of 1900, both of which killed more people (more than 2000 and 8000, respectively) than Katrina. Other violent hurricanes have occurred in the past, and they will occur in the future. There have been many floods of New Orleans in the past, and floods can be expected in the future. The extensive expansion of the city and other coastal communities into low-lying areas where construction should be avoided has set the stage for such disasters.

As described by Lewis (1976), New Orleans was an inevitable city, built to provide the major port for shipping into and out of the Mississippi River basin. But nature should have dictated limits to its size and restricted construction to the higher ground of the natural river levees and other ridges. Instead, low swampy areas were leveed and drained and developed for urban expansion (Colten 2005). Today, many of those areas have sunk below sea level, making them even more susceptible to devastating storms. If such areas are to be protected from future floods, the levees must be constructed accordingly to withstand Category 5 hurricanes (Van Heerden and Bryan 2006). Any new construction, or reconstruction, should be regulated to require storm protection.

Low-elevation areas that cannot be protected should be off-limits to further development. Instead such areas and other coastal marsh lands and swamps should be restored and maintained to provide increased buffers to help protect inland areas from storm damage. Ironically, nature has to some extent acted to reduce the size of New Orleans. In 2005, before Katrina, the population of Orleans Parish was approximately 450,000, but a year later it was only about 190,000. Many of those former residents will never return, and their communities may never be rebuilt. However, the devastation of New Orleans by Hurricane Katrina increased the incidence of families relocating to the north shore of Lake Pontchartrain. While the population of Orleans Parish dropped by about 260,000 during the year following Katrina, the population of St. Tammany Parish grew from about 220,000 to about 260,000, an increase of 18%.

The natural environment of Lake Pontchartrain and its surrounding wetlands were damaged by Hurricane Katrina, but less so than the artificial human environment. The lake will cleanse itself in time by the flushing of fresh water (if it is not overloaded with additional human pollution), and the cypress swamps and other coastal environments have adapted to and recovered from many past devastating hurricanes. But can they recover from continued human abuses, such as increased pollution, wetland destruction, forest clearing, global warming, and sea level rise? The value of these natural environments and the protection they can provide in future storms must be recognized. And they must be protected.

Part 2

ENVIRONMENTAL MODIFICATION AND ABUSE OF THE LAKE PONTCHARTRAIN BASIN AND ITS RESTORATION

Introduction

The story of Lake Pontchartrain during the latter part of the twentieth century has primarily revolved around its abuse and increased pollution, its potential loss as a valuable recreational resource, and its attempted restoration. Of course, environmental modification of the Pontchartrain basin and pollution problems began much earlier. Some were even evident on a local scale when New Orleans was first settled and began to experience sewage and drainage problems almost immediately. Lopez (2003) identified periods when human activities resulted in significant environmental degradation or alteration of the natural environment in the Pontchartrain basin:

1718–1844	Clearing and development of natural levees and ridges and mining of shell middens
1812–1895	Separation of the Mississippi River from its natural delta plain, including the Pontchartrain basin, via artificial levees
1890–1938	Deforestation through commercial logging of cypress swamps and pine savannahs
1932–1990	Dredging of canals and dredging the lake for clam shells and armoring of the shorelines
1950–2002	Water pollution

These problems were to become more serious as the city and the surrounding metropolitan area grew. New Orleans was still the largest city in the south in 1940, with a population of 494,537, and the city was expanding into new subdivisions and suburbs. The eight parishes bordering Lake Pontchartrain all experienced growth following World War II, and their populations exceeded 1 million in 1960 (Table 3). With this major population growth in the mid-1900s, many perpetual problems became more severe and new problems began to affect the lake.

With the growing human population, however, Lake Pontchartrain was also becoming ever more popular for recreational activities, including swimming, sailing, and fishing. Numerous new camps were built around the lake and on its tributary rivers. Many camps in the West End and Bayou St. John areas had been removed as part of the lakefront reclamation project, but there were still reported to be ninety-eight camps along the lakeshore off Hayne Boulevard in 1989 (Houck et al. 1989). Chef Menteur (with 900 camps) and the north shore (with 400) were included in a list of five main camp clusters built in Louisiana coastal marshes (Gary and Davis 1978). Larger, more elaborate homes were also being built in many of these lakefront locations. Numerous camps and homes were built along most of the waterways entering the lakes, and especially the Tchefuncte, Tangipahoa, Tickfaw, and Amite Rivers. Tubing and canoeing in rivers such as the Tangipahoa had become popular. The lake continued to be a popular site for fishing, crabbing, and shrimping (Davis 1978, 1988). In fact, water quality in the offshore areas of the lake (away from the south shore and the mouths of rivers) has always been relatively good (Coastal Environments, Inc. 1984a), because the major sources of pollution are the urban areas of the south shore and the rivers and streams of the north shore. Lake Pontchartrain is large enough that dilution of pollutants occurs with distance away from these major sources.

But the continually expanding human population and urbanization of the metropolitan region, along with the modification and abuse of the natural environment, caused the lake's degradation, with loss of many recreational benefits. The especially dramatic population growth after 1940 brought significant environmental modifications that greatly affected the lake both directly and indirectly, such as by increasing surface runoff and forest and wetland destruction. The increased population also brought increased water pollution in the form of sewage and urban runoff. Most of the sewage treatment systems were soon overloaded and releasing untreated or only partially treated sewage into local waterways.

Although nothing new, environmental abuse became much more obvious and visible to the average citizen, who now recognized that there were potential dangers in swimming in a lake that had begun to resemble a sewer. More and more sewage was entering the lake or its tributaries, and water quality in most of the rivers and streams was degraded. Other environmental problems were also beginning to affect the lake. Wetlands were being drained and filled to provide additional lakefront construction sites. Forests of cypress and pine were disappearing at rates exceeding their rate of regrowth, and many sites were becoming severely eroded. Overfishing and water pollution reduced the populations of many aquatic organisms. Oyster beds were being closed because of potential health risks. The effects of the degradation of the lake environment began to be most apparent and publicized when conditions became so bad that water recreation activities were discouraged or prohibited. However, many citizens developed an attitude of indifference and apathy that such a natural treasure could ever be lost, followed by a sense of helplessness and acceptance that nothing could be done about such environmental abuse. Such abuse was considered an inevitable price to pay for "progress." To many, Lake Pontchartrain became a lost resource, with no hope of ever restoring its former status. Such attitudes then contributed to the lake's continued deterioration.

Fortunately a small group of concerned citizens still recognized the value of a clean lake environment and began discussing the potential for restoration. Efforts to restore Lake Pontchartrain beginning in the late 1980s brought it increased attention and have been partially successful, but they must be continued. The major study that stimulated the environmental restoration effort, "To Restore Lake Pontchartrain" (Houck et al. 1989), identified five major sources of pollution to the lake: shell dredging, urban runoff, sewage, agricultural runoff, and freshwater diversion from the Bonnet Carré Spillway. Other environmental concerns addressed but considered of lesser significance were industrial discharges, canal and sand dredging, saltwater intrusion, discharges from vessels and camps, release of produced waters from oil and gas drilling, atmospheric deposition, upstream flood control and diversion, additional urban development, and shoreline erosion. In its Conservation Area Plan for the Lake Pontchartrain Estuary, the Nature Conservancy (2004) recognized eight "highly-ranked threats to the long-term viability of the Lake Pontchartrain Estuary": Mississippi River levees and flood control; incompatible urban development (indirect effects, nonpoint source pollution); drainage and development (direct effects of conversion of wetlands to urban landscape); Mississippi River Gulf Outlet; channelization of rivers and streams; invasive/alien species; construction of ditches, dikes, drainage and diversion systems; and development of roads, utilities, and levee rights of way. Two other significant environmental concerns not considered in these reviews are solid waste and litter and endangered species.

In general this complex mix of environmental concerns may be grouped into two broad categories to simplify their discussion: loss of natural habitats and biodiversity and water quality degradation. These, as well as the attempted restoration effort, will be described in more detail in the chapters that follow.

9.

Loss of Natural Habitats and Biodiversity

Land Clearing and Urban Development

Most if not all environmental problems begin with human modification of the natural environment, such as clearing of land, changing water flow characteristics, introduction of new species, and release of wastes. As long as the human population is small and functioning in harmony with the natural environment, the environmental problems will be minimal. Such was apparently the case with the indigenous peoples who occupied the Pontchartrain basin. Although there was some land clearing for agriculture or construction of lodges and setting fires to clear forest undergrowth, their activities were mostly in harmony with nature and relatively minimal compared to modern human impacts. However, Kidder (1998) considered the concept that the Native Americans lived in harmony with the land a "myth" and their alteration of the Mississippi River delta area as substantial. In any case, European settlement brought with it a change in philosophy and an increased incentive to modify the environment. The change from a subsistence existence to a market-based economy meant increased harvesting of natural resources, such as timber and fur, and introduction of new crop species for commercial production. Export of resources or profits back to the mother country (initially France) meant greater pressure on residents to cut more trees, kill more game, and plant more crops. As the human population grew, so did these modifications of the environment. One tragic result of European settlement of the region was the almost total extinction of the indigenous peoples within about 200 years. The natural environment was to suffer as well.

Even in the late 1700s, cypress trees were considered rare in the immediate vicinity of New Orleans and were said to have been "wasted so imprudently" (Le Page du Pratz 1774). In addition, the supply of wild game near the city was severely depleted (Surrey 1916; Kniffen 1990). Throughout the basin, loss of natural habitat was a significant and continuing concern, and with the loss of natural habitat, there was also a loss of wildlife and biodiversity. Such waste with little regard for conservation of natural areas continued until the present, when only a small remnant of these natural areas remains.

Cypress Logging and Canal Dredging

Extensive logging of cypress (*Taxodium distichum*) goes back to the 1700s, but continued to increase to reach a peak in the early to mid 1900s. In the late 1800s, the "industrial cypress logging" period began and virtually all of the virgin cypress forests were destroyed within about fifty years. The logging of swamp trees has had a profound effect on the Pontchartrain basin wetlands, with its cypress and tupelo swamps changed dramatically in the past 100 years. Forests of massive cypress trees typically 400–600 years old (Sharitz and Mitsch 1993), but thousands of years old in some cases, have been destroyed, in many places never recovering but converting to open marsh habitat or even open water. Where regeneration did occur, only small, relatively young trees of only about a hundred years of age are now present. Those few large ancient trees that do survive are virtually all hollow, having been spared the saw because of their limited potential for board-feet of lumber. According to Conner et al. (1986), four requirements are necessary for successful regeneration and reestablishment of cypress forests: an abundant supply of seeds, abundant moisture during germination, lack of flooding for a period sufficient for the seedlings to grow tall enough to stay above subsequent flooding, and lack of predators. Cypress seeds will not germinate if submerged, and seedlings must grow above flood levels to survive their first year (Demaree 1932). The abundance of nutria (*Myocastor coypus*) now creates excessive predation on any cypress that do germinate. Increased flooding and predation appear to be the major factors preventing regeneration of cypress in these areas, although saltwater intrusion may also be significant.

To gain access to the dense swamps, the loggers dug canals and ditches, and additional canals have been dug to facilitate boating activity or provide access to wetlands areas for oil and gas exploration drilling. The canals expedited boating activity into once remote areas, but they also contributed to wetland loss and erosion. Some canals have increased in size through shoreline erosion and subsidence and have become conduits for increased flooding of the interior swamps.

Such hydrological changes often involve waters of increased salinity, which can have additional detrimental impacts on the cypress and other swamp vegetation. Another new threat to cypress in recent years has been the cutting of second-growth cypress to be shredded for garden mulch, a tragic waste of hundred-year-old trees and wildlife habitat.

The loss of virgin cypress swamps with numerous large mature trees must have eliminated important habitat for many animals and greatly reduced their numbers. The classic examples are the ivory-billed woodpecker (*Campephilus principalis*), Bachman's warbler (*Vermivora bachmanii*), Louisiana black bear (*Ursus americanus luteolus*), and cougar (*Puma concolor*), all of which are now extirpated from the Pontchartrain basin.

Pine Forest Logging

Hickman (1966) estimated that originally more than 75% of the upland terrace area in the Florida Parishes was covered by pure longleaf pine (*Pinus palustris*) forests, with almost no shrubbery or undergrowth. These open pine savannas were important habitats for many wild species and were used for grazing cattle and sheep, harvesting resin for naval stores, and for lumbering. By the early 1920s, the upland longleaf pine forests had been virtually eliminated, either from lumbering or clearing for agriculture and residential development (Ellis 1981). Forest lands that were replanted mostly became monoculture loblolly pine (*Pinus taeda*) plantations to supply the pulpwood industry (Hickman 1966). The southern pine beetle (*Dendroctonus frontalis*) became a more serious pest because loblolly pines are more susceptible to their attack than are longleaf pines, and this insect has been the cause of much forest mortality in recent years. Exclusion of fire from the region has also contributed to a replacement of the former fire-maintained longleaf pine forests with a southern mixed hardwood forest (Ware et al. 1993). Today the upland terrace area is a mix of urban and suburban development, cleared agricultural lands, and a few remnant reforested areas.

Imperiled Species and Ecological Communities

Major changes of many natural areas occurred with human development of the Pontchartrain basin, and today they are quite different from what was present when European explorers first entered the area. Undisturbed natural areas are unfortunately rare in the Pontchartrain basin. Those that do remain in most cases now support species assemblages quite different from those originally present.

The estuarine communities of the lake have been impacted by water quality changes, including increased turbidity and nutrients. Substrates have been disturbed by dredging, trawling, and other human activities, and shorelines have been modified by filling and armoring projects. Most wetland areas have been modified by the digging of canals and ditches, and many have been drained and leveed or filled to create new land for development. Almost the entire south shore of Lake Pontchartrain is now occupied by the metropolitan area of New Orleans, Metairie, and Kenner, and urban sprawl is rampant on the north shore in Slidell and Mandeville on the east and Baton Rouge and Denham Springs on the west, as well as other communities in between. Most forested lands have been logged at least once, and many of the upland areas have been permanently cleared for agriculture or construction.

Correlated with this natural habitat destruction and environmental abuse, as well as overhunting and overfishing of some species, many species and ecological communities have become imperiled. Of fifty ecological communities identified by the Louisiana Natural Heritage Program (1988) as occurring in the Pontchartrain basin, at least twenty are regarded as being of conservation concern (Table 4). Smith (1999) listed twenty-two historic vegetation types occurring in the Florida parishes of the basin and noted that eleven had become rare or extirpated from the area (Table 5). These included the dominant forest types of longleaf pine flatwoods/savannahs and upland longleaf pine forests (dominated by longleaf pine). In recent years there has been increased concern for protecting the few remaining stands of longleaf pine, as well as increased restoration of some sites with this species.

Some species have become extinct or extirpated from the area, and many others are stressed and could be in danger of extinction if not properly protected. Some 141 species of plants and sixty-six species of animals occurring in the Pontchartrain basin are listed as being of conservation concern by the Louisiana Natural Heritage Program (www.wlf.louisiana.gov/experience/naturalheritage). Fourteen species officially listed as threatened or endangered by the U.S. Fish and Wildlife Service occur in the Pontchartrain basin (Table 6). Extinct species include the once abundant passenger pigeon (*Ectopistes migratorius*), which was last recorded in Louisiana in about 1903 (Lowery 1974b). The Carolina parakeet (*Conuropsis carolinensis*), described by Du Ru in the 1700s as being present by the thousands at the bayou portage near New Orleans (Butler 1934), had not been seen in the area for many years prior to 1900 (Kopman 1900). It was last recorded in Louisiana in 1880 (Lowery 1974b). The ivory-billed woodpecker (*Campephilus principalis*) was also virtually extirpated, having been dependent upon the large expanses of mature bottomland swamp forests for its

Table 4 The natural communities of the Pontchartrain basin

Community System	Community Type	Natural Community
Estuarine	A. Intertidal emergent vegetation	1. Salt marsh
		2. Brackish marsh
		3. Intermediate marsh
	B. Subtidal aquatic bed	4. Submergent algal vegetation
		5. Submergent vascular vegetation
	C. Intertidal flat	6. Intertidal sand/shell flat
		7. Intertidal mud/organic flat
		8. Intertidal mollusk reef
	D. Subtidal open water	9. Bay
		10. Tidal channel/creek
		11. Tidal pass
Lacustrine	A. Limnetic open water	12. Upland lake
	B. Littoral open water	13. Marsh lake
		14. Swamp lake
Palustrine	A. Aquatic bed	15. Submergent algal bed
		16. Submerged/floating vascular vegetation
	B. Emergent vegetation	17. Freshwater marsh
		18. Hillside bog
	C. Scrub/shrub wetland vegetation	19. Scrub/shrub swamp
		20. Shrub swamp
	D. Forested wetland	21. Bald cypress-tupelo swamp
		22. Bald cypress swamp
		23. Tupelo–black gum swamp
		24. Batture
		25–29. Bottomland forest
		25. Overcup oak–water hickory
		26. Sugarberry–American elm–green ash
		27. Sycamore-sweetgum–American elm
		28. Sweetgum–water oak
		29. Live oak forest

Community System	Community Type	Natural Community
		30. Wooded seep
		31. Bayhead swamp
		32. Slash pine–cypress/hardwood forest
		33. Pine flatwoods
		34. Wet hardwood flatwoods
		35. Wet/mesic spruce pine/hardwood flatwoods
		36. Pine savannah
		37. Riparian forest
Riverine	A. Riverine subtidal channel	38. Tidal mud flat
		39. Subtidal open water
	B. Riverine lower perennial channel	40. Sand/gravel beach/bar
		41. Mud bar
		42. Lower perennial open water
	C. Aquatic bed	43. Submerged/floating vascular vegetation
Terrestrial	A. Deciduous forests	44. Hardwood slope forest
	B. Mixed evergreen/deciduous forests	45. Shortleaf pine/oak-hickory forest
		46. Mixed hardwood-loblolly forest
		47. Slash pine/post oak forest
		48. Live oak–pine–magnolia forest
	C. Evergreen forests	49. Upland longleaf pine forest
	D. Woodland	50. Sandy woodland

Modified from Louisiana Natural Heritage Program (1988)

habitat. Recent reports of its possible occurrence in the Pearl River swamps of the Pontchartrain basin have yet to be verified, although it was reliably sighted in the Big Woods of Arkansas in 2004 (Fitzpatrick et al. 2005; Gallagher 2005) and in the mature swamp forests of the Choctawhatchee River in western Florida in 2005 (Hill et al. 2006), more than sixty years after its previous confirmed sighting. Bachman's warbler (*Vermivora bachmanii*) is apparently extinct, as a result of destruction of its old-growth bottomland forest habitat.

Other species once common but now extirpated from the basin include American bison (*Bison bison*), cougar (*Puma concolor*), and black bear (*Ursus americanus luteolus*). Those that have become rare include Gulf sturgeon

Table 5 Historic vegetation types of the Florida parishes in the Pontchartrain basin

Vegetation Type	EBR	EF	Liv	SH	ST	Tang	Wash
Brackish/intermediate marsh					S		
Submergent estuarine grass beds (r)					ss*		
Fresh marsh					S	S	
Hillside seepage bog (r)					ss*	ss*	ss*
Bald cypress swamp	S	ss	P	ss	S	P	S
Pond cypress/black gum swamp					S	S	
Gum swamp		ss	ss	ss	ss	ss	ss
Bottomland hardwood forest	S	ss	S	ss	S	S	S
Live oak forest (r)	ss*						
Forested (wooded) seep					ss	ss	ss
Bayhead swamp		ss*	ss*	ss*	S	S	S
Slash pine–pond cypress/ hardwood forest (r)					S*		
Longleaf pine flatwoods/ savannahs (r)		(ss)	(P)	(ss)	P*	P*	S*
Wet hardwood flatwoods	P						
Spruce pine/ Hardwood flatwoods (r)	P*		P*				
Small stream (riparian) forest	S	S	S	S	S	S	S
Hardwood slope forest (r)	ss	ss*	ss*	ss*	ss*	ss*	ss*
Shortleaf pine/oak-hickory forest (r)	ss*	P*	ss*	ss*	ss*	ss*	ss*
Mixed hardwood-loblolly pine forest	ss	S	S	S	S	S	S
Upland longleaf pine forest (r)	(S)	(P)	(S)	P*	P*	P*	P*
Prairie terrace loess forest (r)	P*						
Saline prairie (extirpated from Pontchartrain basin)	(ss)	(ss)	(ss)				

Modified from Smith (1999)

EBR, East Baton Rouge Parish; EF, East Feliciana Parish; Liv, Livingston Parish; SH, St. Helena Parish; ST, St. Tammany Parish; Tang, Tangipahoa Parish; Wash, Washington Parish; r, now rare in the Pontchartrain basin; P, primary vegetation type; S, secondary vegetation type; ss, historic small-scale vegetation type; ( ), now extirpated from parish; *, now rare in parish

Table 6 Federally listed threatened and endangered species occurring in the Pontchartrain basin

Species	Status	Notes
Plants		
Louisiana quillwort, *Isoetes louisianensis*	endangered	Occurs on sand and gravel beach bars in the Bogue Chitto River drainage and the Bogue Falaya and Abita Rivers
Animals		
Inflated heelsplitter mussel, *Potamilus inflatus*	threatened	Currently found in the Amite River; once also occurred in the Pearl and Tangipahoa Rivers
Gulf sturgeon, *Acipenser oxyrinchus desotoi*	threatened	An anadromous marine species that moves up into coastal rivers to spawn, including the Pearl and Tchefuncte Rivers
Gopher tortoise, *Gopherus polyphemus*	threatened	Occurs in upland pine forests with sandy soils, including Tangipahoa, Washington, and St. Tammany Parishes
Ringed map turtle, *Graptemys oculifera*	threatened	Occurs only in the Pearl River drainage, including the Bogue Chitto River
Loggerhead sea turtle, *Caretta caretta*	threatened	A marine turtle usually found along the Gulf coast but may occasionally stray into Lake Pontchartrain
Bald eagle, *Haliaeetus leucocephalus*	threatened	Once rare in the state, but now becoming more common; several nests occur in the Pontchartrain basin
Louisiana black bear, *Ursus americanus luteolus*	threatened	Once common in the basin but now mostly characteristic of heavily wooded bottomland hardwood forests of the Tensas and Atchafalaya River basins; apparent strays may occasionally be seen in the Pearl River swamp
Mississippi gopher frog, *Rana sevosa*	endangered	Now known to survive only in a few isolated ponds in southern Mississippi
Kemp's ridley sea turtle, *Lepidochelys kempii*	endangered	A marine turtle usually found along the Gulf coast but may occasionally stray into Lake Pontchartrain
Brown pelican, *Pelecanus occidentalis*	endangered	A shore bird extirpated from Louisiana by the early 1960s, but reintroduced and now common on Lake Pontchartrain
Red-cockaded woodpecker, *Picoides borealis*	endangered	Nests only in mature pine forests
Ivory-billed woodpecker, *Campephilus principalis*	endangered	Possibly extirpated but supposedly sighted in the Pearl River swamp in 1999; sighted in Arkansas in 2004
West Indian manatee, *Trichechus manatus*	endangered	Primarily a resident of more southern coastal waters but occasionally sighted in Louisiana waters, apparently becoming more frequent in recent years

(*Acipenser oxyrinchus desotoi*), striped bass (*Morone saxatilis*), Alabama shad (*Alosa alabamae*), gopher frog (*Rana sevosa*), and red-cockaded woodpecker (*Picoides borealis*). Gulf sturgeon, striped bass, and Alabama shad are anadromous species once common in the Pontchartrain basin, spending most of the year and feeding in the estuary and coastal Gulf waters and then migrating up tributary rivers to spawn in early spring (March through May). Critical habitat was designated for Gulf sturgeon in 2003 and included the eastern half of Lake Pontchartrain and all of Lake Borgne, although the species has also been recorded in lesser numbers in the upper parts of the system, including several of the rivers (U.S. Fish and Wildlife Service 2003). Ross (2001) reported that the species may be fairly common in the lower Pearl River.

Striped bass abundance in the Gulf of Mexico was never as great as on the Atlantic coast, and the Pontchartrain basin was apparently the western limit of its natural range in the Gulf. However, large schools were once recorded in the Tangipahoa River near Osyka, Mississippi (Bean 1884; McIlwain 1968; Ross 2001). Most Gulf coast populations were extirpated in the early 1900s as a result of dam building and water quality degradation, and individuals seen today in the Pontchartrain area are most likely the Atlantic coast strain present as a result of restocking efforts. There does not appear to have been any natural spawning of striped bass in the Pontchartrain basin in recent years.

Alabama shad was once abundant in the Mississippi River and other rivers of the northern Gulf coast, and it occurred in rivers of the Pontchartrain basin. This species has experienced a significant decline since the 1960s, apparently as a result of dams that block migration and increased siltation (Gunning and Suttkus 1990).

Several species have been nearly extirpated in the past but with proper management and protection have once again become common. Among these are the American alligator (*Alligator mississippiensis*), brown pelican (*Pelecanus occidentalis*), osprey (*Pandion haliaetus*), bald eagle (*Haliaeetus leucocephalus*), wild turkey (*Meleagris gallopavo*), and beaver (*Castor canadensis*).

Recovery of the alligator populations in Louisiana and other states is a true success story in wildlife conservation. The species was hunted almost to extinction in the late 1800s and early 1900s. There are numerous reports of alligator hunters who had killed thousands of individuals (Walker 1885). According to McIlhenny (1935), an estimated 3.0–3.5 million alligators were killed in southern Louisiana between 1880 and 1933. Populations reached a low point about 1960, and the species was placed on the federal endangered species list in 1967 (Newsom et al. 1987). By 1972 with protection and proper management, alligator populations in Louisiana had recovered sufficiently that the state implemented a controlled harvest program. Alligators are now common throughout the Pontchartrain basin in appropriate habitats.

The restoration of Louisiana's state bird, the brown pelican, is another impressive conservation success story (Norman and Purrington 1970). The species was abundant in coastal Louisiana prior to the late 1950s, but then suffered a precipitous decline in numbers until there were no brown pelicans in Louisiana by the mid-1960s. The cause of this dramatic loss was unknown initially, but was later attributed to the poisonous effects of DDT and other chlorinated hydrocarbon pesticides. Nesting colonies were subsequently reestablished in coastal Louisiana beginning in 1968, with birds imported from Florida, and the populations have steadily increased since then (McNease et al. 1992). Brown pelicans began reappearing on Lake Pontchartrain in 1987 and have since become quite common (Brantley 1998). Ospreys, bald eagles, and double-crested cormorants (*Phalacrocorax auritus*) experienced a similar decline and subsequent increase during the same period, apparently associated with the same causes. Their recovery in the Pontchartrain basin, however, has occurred without the benefit of human reintroductions.

The recovery and restoration of such species demonstrates what can be done with a reasonable measure of environmental protection, proper wildlife management, and species protection. The ultimate concern in protecting any species must be adequate protection for its habitat. Fortunately large areas of natural habitat for some species still remain within the Pontchartrain basin, although these are continually threatened by human impacts. Hopefully sufficient natural environments can be protected and restored in perpetuity so that future generations can experience and enjoy such natural biodiversity.

Invasive Exotic Species

Many introduced exotic species have become established in the Pontchartrain basin, and in some cases these have become among the most abundant species, usually with detrimental effects on native biota. In their atlas of vascular plants in Louisiana, Thomas and Allen (1993, 1996, 1998) listed 2423 native species and 826 exotic species (25%) statewide. Not all of these exotic species are established in the Pontchartrain basin and not all are invasive, but the number certainly reflects the enormity of the problem. The number of nonnative animals established in the state is unknown (especially among the invertebrates), but their numbers are substantial. Exotic species usually compete with native species and can cause serious environmental problems by displacing native species or by becoming significant pests. Among the most serious pests are various aquatic plants, such as water lettuce (*Pistia stratiotes*), water hyacinth (*Eichhornia crassipes*; see Figure 7.2), alligatorweed (*Alternanthera philoxeroides*), Eurasian watermilfoil (*Myriophyllum spicatum*), and water spangle (*Salvinia minima*). Many of these exotic plant species have become so abundant in basin waterways that they impede or prevent boat traffic. Their abundance also inhibits the growth of native aquatic plants and can reduce aquatic habitat or dissolved oxygen levels and thus reduce the populations of aquatic animals.

Water lettuce, thought to be native to South America or Africa, was first reported in Florida in 1765 and has been established so long that it is sometimes listed as a native species. Water hyacinths from Venezuela were on display at the World's Industrial and Cotton Centennial Exposition held in New Orleans in the 1880s (Roberts 1946). After being released into local waterways, it became one of the most abundant aquatic plants in much of southeastern North America. Alligatorweed, another native of South America, was introduced to Louisiana in the early 1900s. Montz and Cherubini (1973) noted that a dense undergrowth of alligatorweed covered most of the soil surface in a cypress swamp of the LaBranche Wetlands area. Eurasian watermilfoil was introduced to North America in the 1880s, but the plant was first recorded in Louisiana in 1966 (in False River, Pointe Coupe Parish; Reed 1977). It probably soon spread to other waterways. Water spangle is a fairly recent invader, having been first reported from southeastern Louisiana and the Pontchartrain basin in the 1980s. It has spread rapidly and now occurs in most enclosed waterways tributary to Lakes Pontchartrain and Maurepas. Several terrestrial exotic plant species have also become invasive in the Pontchartrain basin, including Chinese tallow tree (*Triadica* or *Sapium sebiferum*), Chinese privet (*Ligustrum sinense*), Japanese privet (*Ligustrum japonicum*), Japanese honeysuckle (*Lonicera japonica*), kudzu (*Pueraria montana*), cogon grass (*Imperata cylindrica*), and Japanese climbing fern (*Lygodium japonicum*). These also tend to compete with and displace native vegetation.

The introduced nutria (*Myocastor coypus*) has greatly affected the wetlands of coastal Louisiana (Kidder 1998). This South American rodent's consumption of wetlands vegetation, and especially seedling cypress trees, has contributed to the changed nature of many wetland sites. In some areas, such as the Manchac Wildlife Management Area, there is virtually no survival of seedling cypress because they are quickly destroyed by nutria. Nutria also appear to have caused a decline in muskrat (*Ondatra zibethicus*) populations in coastal Louisiana. They were first introduced to Louisiana in the 1930s, but quickly spread throughout the state. Tradition has blamed Edward Avery McIlhenny of Avery Island, Iberia Parish, for introducing nutria to Louisiana (Lowery 1974a), but this has been challenged by Bernard (2002). However, McIlhenny certainly was instrumental in the propagation and release of large numbers of nutria in Louisiana. The first importation of nutria to the United States (in California) was in 1899. The first recorded occurrence in Louisiana was in 1933, when Susan and Conrad Brote established a nutria farm in Abita Springs, which closed after only four years, having sold some nutria and "turned the rest out." Another nutria farm in St. Bernard Parish provided McIlhenny with his first nutria in 1938. Subsequently McIlhenny's captive population increased to more than 500, and many were deliberately released into the wild. All of his remaining nutria were released in late 1945. During the 1945–1946 trapping season, at least 8784 nutria were captured statewide and during the following season 18,015. By 1970 nutria numbers had reached such a level that more than 1.5 million were trapped for fur (Lowery 1974a).

This introduction of an exotic fur-bearing animal was encouraged and promoted by then-director of Louisiana Department of Conservation's Fur and Wildlife Division Armand P. Daspit, in spite of warnings from the U.S. Bureau of Biological Survey: "It may be highly objectionable to turn them loose.... Numerous examples exist in this and foreign countries of the introduction of species from one part of the world to another with very disastrous results" (Bernard 2002). Those disastrous results were to become clearly evident within about forty years. Soon after its initial introduction to Louisiana in the 1930s, nutria had replaced muskrat as the dominant fur-bearer being trapped. By 1962–1963, the statewide harvest of nutria was more than 1.3 million skins valued at $1.35 per skin (compared to 300,000 muskrat skins valued at $1.60 per skin; Davis, Donald W. 1978). By 1976–1977, the 1.9 million nutria harvested in the state were valued at about $8.00 per skin, for a total of over $14 million. However, with declining markets for furs in the 1980s, the price of furs became too low to provide a profit, and trapping of nutria declined dramatically and remained low through the 1990s. With the decrease in trapping, the population of nutria in the marshes increased to a level that nutria damage to the marsh vegetation became apparent in many areas. In recent years, cash incentives paid to nutria trappers to increase their profit margin have been attempted as a means of controlling the nutria population. In addition, human consumption of nutria meat has been encouraged, but with only limited success. In Metairie, sheriff's department sharpshooters were employed to reduce nutria populations along the urban canals, where they have also become an abundant nuisance.

The common carp (*Cyprinus carpio*) is another exotic species present in the Pontchartrain basin, although it is not especially common. Very large individuals are occasionally seen in the lakes. The species was first introduced to North

America in 1831 and subsequently widely distributed, but its first occurrence in Louisiana is unknown. Fuentes and Cashner (2002) documented the establishment of the Rio Grande cichlid (*Cichlasoma cyanoguttatum*) in the canals of New Orleans and along the southern shore of Lake Pontchartrain near canal pumping stations. It was first reported in 1996, but now seems to be well established in most of the urban canals of Orleans and Jefferson Parishes and may be expected to spread to other areas. It will potentially compete with native sunfishes (Centrarchids) and other species. Two other nonnative fish species, the goldfish (*Carassius auratus*) and the fathead minnow (*Pimephales promelas*), have been reported from the Pearl River (Ross 2001), but are not known to occur elsewhere in the Pontchartrain basin.

Large numbers of the Florida strain (subspecies) of largemouth bass (*Micropterus salmoides floridanus*) have been released into waters of Louisiana, including the Pontchartrain basin, in recent years. Initial reports of trophy-sized bass being caught have encouraged additional introductions. The potential impacts of this exotic genetic strain on the native subspecies (*M. s. salmoides*) are unknown, but hybridization could result in an inferior strain not well adapted to this environment (Ross 2001).

The exotic Asian clam *Corbicula fluminea* was introduced to North America in 1938 and has occurred in Louisiana at least since 1961 (Counts 1986, 1991). It is now present in all freshwater tributaries of the Pontchartrain basin. *Corbicula fluminea* is the most common species of bivalve mollusk in the upper Tangipahoa River, where it represents almost 88% of the total bivalve fauna (Miller et al. 1986).

Another mollusk of special concern is the zebra mussel (*Dreissena polymorpha*), a native of western Asia, which has become established in the Mississippi River. It was first recorded in the Great Lakes in 1988, and by 1993 this species had become abundant in the lower Mississippi River. Thus far no records of zebra mussel have been documented from Lake Pontchartrain, although the planktonic veliger larvae have been found in the Bonnet Carré Spillway (Bruce Thompson, personal communication). Research suggests that the species should be able to survive throughout most of the Pontchartrain basin, except possibly the more saline parts of Lake Borgne, so why it has not become established is not known. If it ever does become abundant in Lake Pontchartrain, it could profoundly affect food webs by filtering vast quantities of phytoplankton and outcompeting native species of filter-feeders.

The South American fire ant (*Solenopsis invicta*), introduced to North America in 1918, is now one of the most abundant, and hated, species in southeastern Louisiana, as well as throughout the southeastern United States. It is common in both upland and wetland habitats, including the swamps and marshes surrounding Lake Pontchartrain, where the nests occupy any slight elevation, including mounds, cypress stumps and logs, canal spoil banks, and alligator nests. In addition to being a dangerous pest to humans, fire ants are thought to be detrimental to numerous ground-nesting species, including other insects, reptiles, birds, and mammals. They kill and consume many other animals and displace others with their aggressive and painful stings. An interesting characteristic of the fire ants is their ability to survive flood waters in wetland areas by congregating in floating masses. Thousands of ants will hold on to one another in a writhing mass, apparently alternating those who are submerged with those on top of the mass. This behavior allows the colony to survive flood waters of hurricanes and other storms.

Most introduced exotic species can have profound effects on native species and significantly modify the environment. Although any introduction of an exotic species is potentially harmful and should be avoided, some introductions have been considered either beneficial or neutral. The honey bee (*Apis mellifera*), first introduced to North America in about 1638, is often cited as an example of a beneficial introduction, but its impact upon native species of bees is unknown. Other exotic species established in the Pontchartrain basin that are considered beneficial or neutral include Mediterranean gecko (*Hemidactylus turcicus*), greenhouse frog (*Eleutherodactylus recordi*), and Queen Anne's lace (*Daucus carota*; Thomas 1996). Additional exotic wetland plants that do not appear to cause significant harm include wild taro ("elephant ear," *Colocasia esculenta*), which is fairly common along much of the lakeshore, and Timothy canary grass (*Phalaris angusta*), which is also well established in much of the basin, including the Manchac marshes. Such species, however, may have subtle but significant effects upon native species, and they may also introduce exotic parasites and diseases that can be detrimental to native species. Once a nonnative becomes established, it is too late to become concerned about the consequences and virtually impossible to eradicate the invader. The best approach is to be satisfied with our native flora and fauna and not experiment with nature under uncontrolled conditions.

Shoreline Erosion and Wetland Loss

Coastal erosion and wetland loss is a significant environmental problem throughout coastal Louisiana, including the Pontchartrain basin (Templet and Meyer-Arendt 1988; Penland et al. 1990; Boesch et al. 1994; Turner 1997). Louisiana has 40% of the nation's coastal wetlands but experiences 80% of the nation's

Table 7 Land loss rates for the Pontchartrain basin

Quadrangle	Annual Land Loss Rate by Time Period			
	1932–1958	1954–1974	1974–1983	1983–1990
North Shore				
Springfield	0.01 sq. mi. (0.03 km²)	0.01 sq. mi. (0.03 km²)	0.03 sq. mi. (0.08 km²)	0.003 sq. mi. (0.01 km²)
Ponchatoula	0.07 sq. mi. (0.18 km²)	0.09 sq. mi. (0.23 km²)	0.08 sq. mi. (0.21 km²)	0.05 sq. mi. (0.13 km²)
Covington	0.02 sq. mi. (0.05 km²)	0.18 sq. mi. (0.47 km²)	0.02 sq. mi. (0.05 km²)	0.18 sq. mi. (0.47 km²)
Slidell	0.06 sq. mi. (0.16 km²)	0.15 sq. mi. (0.39 km²)	0.05 sq. mi. (0.13 km²)	0.04 sq. mi. (0.10 km²)
South Shore				
Mount Airy	0.05 sq. mi. (0.13 km²)	0.08 sq. mi. (0.21 km²)	0.08 sq. mi. (0.21 km²)	0.12 sq. mi. (0.31 km²)
Bonnet Carré	0.10 sq. mi. (0.26 km²)	0.44 sq. mi. (1.14 km²)	0.19 sq. mi. (0.49 km²)	0.07 sq. mi. (0.18 km²)
Spanish Fort	0.03 sq. mi. (0.08 km²)	0.01 sq. mi. (0.03 km²)	0.003 sq. mi. (0.01 km²)	0.01 sq. mi. (0.03 km²)
Chef Menteur	0.49 sq. mi. (1.27 km²)	0.41 sq. mi. (1.06 km²)	0.28 sq. mi. (0.73 km²)	0.28 sq. mi. (0.73 km²)
Lake Borgne				
Rigolets	0.11 sq. mi. (0.29 km²)	0.24 sq. mi. (0.62 km²)	0.26 sq. mi. (0.67 km²)	0.12 sq. mi. (0.31 km²)
St. Bernard	0.29 sq. mi. (0.75 km²)	1.23 sq. mi. (3.19 km²)	0.70 sq. mi. (1.81 km²)	0.26 sq. mi. (0.67 km²)
Yscloskey	0.12 sq. mi. (0.31 km²)	0.60 sq. mi. (1.55 km²)	0.53 sq. mi. (1.37 km²)	0.14 sq. mi. (0.36 km²)
Total	1.35 sq. mi. (0.94 km²)	3.44 sq. mi. (8.91 km²)	2.22 sq. mi. (5.75 km²)	1.27 sq. mi. (3.29 km²)

Data from Britsch and Dunbar (1993)

coastal wetland loss, at a current estimated rate of about 25–35 sq. mi. (65–90 km²) per year (Louisiana Coastal Wetlands Conservation and Restoration Task Force 1993). The total amount of coastal land in Louisiana in the early 1930s was 8511 sq. mi. (22,043 km²) and in 1990, 6985 sq. mi. (18,091 km²), for a loss of 1526 sq. mi. (3952 km²) or 17.9% (Britsch and Dunbar 1993). The greatest land loss occurred in the period from 1956 to 1974, at a rate of approximately 42 sq. mi. (109 km^2) per year. The rate decreased to about 25 sq. mi. (65 km^2) per year by 1990. The concerted efforts to reduce the rate of land loss and to restore many eroded areas have been only slightly successful. A more realistic explanation of the reduction in land loss rate is that the more sensitive lands were lost prior to the 1980s, and lands remaining were somewhat more resistant to erosion.

Land loss rates within the Pontchartrain basin (Table 7) are generally lower than those along coastal Louisiana, but still are highest for the period of 1954–1974 (Britsch and Dunbar 1993). As might be expected, rates were higher in the areas nearest the open coast (that is, the Lake Borgne area, including the Chef Menteur quadrangle) than within Lakes Pontchartrain and Maurepas. Relatively high rates were recorded for the Bonnet Carré quadrangle, apparently related to land loss in the LaBranche Wetlands.

Penland et al. (1990) identified two major types of coastal land loss: coastal erosion (or retreat of shorelines) and wetland loss (development or expansion of water bodies within wetlands). Shoreline erosion had apparently been a problem for structures built on the unstable soils of the lake shoreline since the early 1700s, but it became an even greater problem in the 1900s. Shoreline armoring had been employed at least since 1852 to reduce this erosion and now covers some 40% of the Lake Pontchartrain shoreline (Lopez 2003). There was significant shoreline erosion on the northern shore near Mandeville in 1895 (Mugnier photograph in Kemp and King 1975). Parts of the lake shoreline in Orleans Parish had eroded as much as 500 ft. (152 m) at the turn of the century, providing justification for the lakeshore reclamation project and seawall between West End and the Industrial Canal. Along many eroded shorelines living cypress trees are now standing in the lake, and other trees once growing on land now lie prostrate along the shore (Figure 9.1).

Steinmayer (1939) reported shoreline recession between 1870 and 1917 at several locations on the eastern side of Lake Pontchartrain, such as between Point aux Herbes and Chef Menteur Pass (annual rate of about 14 ft. or 4.3 m) and between Bayou St. John and New Basin Canal (about 8 ft. or 2.4 m). He noted shorelines on the northeastern side of the lake where some areas had receded while others showed a slight advance into the lake (at Grand Lagoon [now Howze Beach and Eden Isles] and between Big Point and Point Platte).

The western side of the lake also was experiencing significant shoreline erosion during the period from 1930 to 1974 (Britsch and Dunbar 1996). Pearson et al. (1993) estimated that shorelines in the LaBranche area had receded almost 1000 ft. (305 m) during the past 100 years. In the Ruddock area, a wooden seawall was built at some early date along the shoreline at a site known as the

Figure 9.1 Shoreline erosion in Lake Pontchartrain near (A) the mouth of the Tangipahoa River and (B) Ruddock (Photographs by the author)

Table 8 Annual rates of shoreline change in the Pontchartrain basin

Location	1850–1995*	1930–1995	1960–1995
Lake Maurepas	–3.15 ft./year (–0.96 m/year)	–1.97 ft./year (–0.60 m/year)	–2.59 ft./year (–0.79 m/year)
Lake Pontchartrain, northern side	–4.10 ft./year (–1.25 m/year)	–6.23 ft./year (–1.90 m/year)	–3.90 ft./year (–1.19 m/year)
Lake Pontchartrain, southern side	–2.43 ft./year (–0.74 m/year)	–4.07 ft./year (–1.24 m/year)	–3.81 ft./year (–1.16 m/year)
Lake Borgne	–7.87 ft./year (–2.40 m/year)	–8.83 ft./year (–2.69 m/year)	–7.12 ft./year (–2.17 m/year)

Data from Zganjar et al. (2001)
*Rates for 1899–1995 for Lake Maurepas

"washout," which threatened the Illinois-Central Railroad. Erosion apparently continued, and only remnants of this seawall now remain. The shoreline was later reinforced with rocks, many of which contain crinoid fossils, a unique occurrence in the Lake Pontchartrain area where rocks, and thus fossils, do not naturally occur.

The Manchac lighthouse (see Figure 5.1) also illustrates the problems of shoreline erosion and wetland loss affecting coastal Louisiana. The existing lighthouse was built on land in 1857 approximately 1000 ft. (305 m) from the current shoreline. Sea level rise, land subsidence, and storm surges from the lake have combined to erode the land, currently at a rate of 12 ft. (3.7 m) per year in this area, and threaten the future existence of the lighthouse. The lighthouse tower is only a remnant of the once more extensive structure that included a lighthouse keeper's residence, several outbuildings, and a dock and boat shed. Today only the lighthouse tower and a jumble of broken brickwork remain in the lake, about 1000 ft. from shore.

By comparing shorelines on recent topographic maps with those of the 1800s, Zganjar et al. (2001) estimated the rates of shoreline movement in the basin (Table 8). Virtually all areas have experienced some shoreline erosion. Overall rates were highest in Lake Borgne and lowest in Lake Maurepas. In Lake Pontchartrain, erosion rates on the northern shore exceeded those on the southern shore because of the higher level of armoring and land creation along the New Orleans lakefront. The unprotected shorelines on the western side, such as near Pass Manchac, and on the eastern side near Point aux Herbes have experienced the highest rates of erosion.

Table 9 Causes of land loss in the Pontchartrain basin (in order of their significance and percent contribution to total land loss)

Causes of Land Loss	Source	Acres Lost (ha)	Percent Effect
Erosion by natural (wind-generated) waves	N	55,603 (22,502)	29.5%
Submergence due to altered hydrology with multiple causes	H	54,514 (22,061)	28.9%
Submergence due to altered hydrology from oil/gas channels	H	16,715 (6764)	8.9%
Direct removal of land to form oil/gas channels	H	12,781 (5172)	6.8%
Submergence due to natural water-logging or subsidence	N	11,188 (4528)	5.9%
Submergence due to failed land reclamation	H	7091 (2870)	3.8%
Direct removal of land to form navigation channels	H	6787 (2747)	3.6%
Erosion by channel flow	N?	6334 (2563)	3.4%
Submergence due to altered hydrology from roads	H	4767 (1929)	2.5%
Submergence due to altered hydrology from impoundments	H	4480 (1813)	2.4%
Erosion by navigation waves or boat wakes	H	3139 (1270)	1.7%
Direct removal of land to form borrow pits	H	3117 (1261)	1.6%
Direct removal of land to form access channels	H	1280 (518)	0.7%
Submergence due to substrate collapse following excessive herbivory or overgrazing	H?	561 (227)	0.3%
Direct removal to form drainage channels	H	0.13 (0.05)	<0.01%

Data from Penland et al. (2001b)
N, natural; H, human-induced cause

In addition to the loss of land from shoreline erosion, there has also been substantial loss within the wetlands of the Pontchartrain basin. The total land loss within the basin (but including Chandeleur and Breton Sounds) between 1932 and 1990 has been estimated to be 188,356 acres (76,226 ha), of which 127,000 acres (51,396 ha) or 67% was interior loss (Penland et al. 2001b). Marsh areas in the basin between Lake Maurepas and Lake Borgne (excluding the Plaquemines Wetland and Birdfoot Delta Areas) decreased from 303,555 acres (122,847 ha) in 1932 to 231,370 acres (93,634 ha) in 1990, a loss of 72,185 acres (29,213 ha) or 24% (Penland et al. 2001c).

The Louisiana Coastal Wetlands Conservation and Restoration Task Force (1993) identified four critical wetland loss problems facing the Pontchartrain basin: (1) increased salinity and reduced sediment and nutrient input; (2)

erosion along the Mississippi River Gulf Outlet (MRGO); (3) potential loss of the land bridges separating Lakes Pontchartrain and Borgne and Pontchartrain and Maurepas; and (4) potential rapid erosion of especially vulnerable wetlands, such as those separated from the lakes by just a narrow rim of shore (such as the Prairie at the Manchac Wildlife Management Area, the LaBranche marshes, and the shoreline from Goose Point to Green Point).

Land loss in the Pontchartrain basin, as in all of coastal Louisiana, results from a complex mixture of both natural processes and human activities, but the human-induced losses far surpass those caused by natural factors (61.2% vs. 38.8%; Penland et al. 2001b). Human activities in the basin have greatly exacerbated a natural process that would have occurred at a much slower rate in the absence of human influences. Thirteen factors contributing to land loss have been identified, which can be classified in three primary categories (Table 9): erosion (mechanical removal and transport of land by water action, 34.6%), submergence (increase of water level relative to ground surface elevation, 52.7%), and direct removal (physical removal of land by actions other than water, 12.7%).

Hurricane Katrina resulted in major losses of marsh habitat in the Pontchartrain basin, including 9–14 sq. mi. (23–36 km^2) in the middle sub-basin, especially in the north shore marshes between Green Point and North Shore, in the LaBranche Wetlands, and in the East Orleans Land Bridge (LPBF 2006a). Even greater losses (estimated to be 40.9 sq. mi. or 106 km^2) occurred in the lower sub-basin southwest of Lake Borgne. These preliminary estimates of the one day loss from Katrina exceeded the total land lost in the previous decade (1990–2000).

Sea Level Rise and Subsidence

The natural processes contributing to land loss in the Pontchartrain basin, as in all of coastal Louisiana, are in general correlated with sea level rise and subsidence. Mean global sea level has risen about 4.7 in. (12 cm) in the past 100 years or about 0.05 in. (1–2 mm) per year (Gornitz et al. 1982; Gornitz 1995), and the sea level has risen about 0.09 in. (2.3 mm) per year in the Gulf of Mexico. During the next 100 years as global warming continues, the rates of sea level rise are projected to increase four to seven times over current rates, or an additional 19 in. (48 cm) by the year 2100 (Gornitz 1995; Twilley et al. 2001). In coastal Louisiana, relative rates of sea level rise are considerably higher than global sea level rates because of the combined effects of global sea level rise and land subsidence (Ramsey and Penland 1989).

Subsidence, resulting from consolidation and compaction of Holocene (Recent), Pleistocene, and Tertiary sediments of the Mississippi River deltas, is at least partly a natural process in that alluvial sediments tend to become more consolidated and compacted with time, and thus subside. If new sediments are continually or regularly deposited, then the subsidence is not noticeable. Without those new sediments, the land sinks, and low-elevation wetlands may become submerged. Loss of sedimentation from the Mississippi River is partly a natural process in the Pontchartrain basin correlated with Mississippi River delta shifts, which have occurred about every 1000 years. The Pontchartrain area has not been the primary building-delta of the Mississippi River since the formation of the St. Bernard delta (and the lake) some 1000–4000 years ago (Saucier 1994). However, some significant sedimentation and land building probably occurred in the basin during the formation of the Modern (Plaquemines or Balize) delta and even up through relatively modern times before Bayou Manchac was closed (in 1812) and the Mississippi River levees were finally completed (in 1930). Most of the sediments now carried by the river are retained within the river levees and lost to deeper waters of the Gulf of Mexico. With the loss of sedimentation or severe reduction in its amount, the effects of delta subsidence have become evident. The combined effects of subsidence and sea level rise produce a dramatic rate of land loss in coastal Louisiana.

Subsidence rates have been estimated at several sites in the Pontchartrain basin to be about 0.06–0.19 in. (0.15–0.47 cm) per year (Ramsey et al. 2001), based upon a contribution of about 43% to the relative rate of water level rise (Ramsey and Penland 1989). This combined effect of subsidence and global sea level rise resulted in a relative sea level rise for sites in the basin of 0.40 in. (1.01 cm) per year at South Point, 0.43 in. (1.09 cm) per year at Little Woods, 0.16 in. (0.40 cm) per year at West End, 0.14 in. (0.36 cm) per year at Frenier, and 0.18 in. (0.45 cm) per year at Mandeville since 1931.

Storms, and especially hurricanes, can have a much more profound effect in coastal areas because of the continuing subsidence and loss of coastal buffer lands. The storms further contribute to the erosion of coastal areas, resulting in accelerated shoreline retreat, destruction of beaches, destruction or modification of vegetation, and either scouring or filling of channels (Saucier 1963). Although some storm tides can deposit silt in swamp and marsh areas, thus building land, the net effect is not nearly sufficient to offset the loss of sediments from the Mississippi River.

A major continuing threat to New Orleans has been potential flooding, a long-standing problem exacerbated by the subsidence of most of the city below sea level (or lake level). Many had warned that it was just a matter of time before

New Orleans was hit by a devastating hurricane with extensive flooding, property damage, and loss of life (McQuaid and Schleifstein 2002). That devastation finally came in August 2005, with Hurricane Katrina, and flooding of 80% of the city.

Land Reclamation

Another significant factor in the loss of wetlands in some locations is land reclamation projects, where wetlands have been drained for agriculture or drained and filled for residential developments or other construction. Wetlands were once considered almost worthless, and landowners were encouraged to drain or fill them to make more profitable land. The extensive marshes surrounding Lakes Pontchartrain, Maurepas, and Borgne, which early explorers described as a wide "prairie" between the lake and the tall trees on the shore, have been greatly reduced in extent and dissected by numerous canals and ditches. Most of the marshes on the southern shore have been destroyed by the dredging, filling, and bulkheading of the New Orleans lakeshore. Others, such as the lakeshore areas near Slidell, have been filled for construction of housing developments including North Shore, Northshore Beach, Howze Beach, Eden Isles, Oak Harbor, Lakeshore Estates, Treasure Island, and Rigolets Estates, and Venetian Isles on Chef Menteur Pass. Although such developments create high ground and choice waterfront property for residents who desire convenient recreational opportunities on the lake, they also contribute to its demise, by increasing surface runoff, adding pollutants, and destroying wetlands or water bottom habitat. The developments also become prime targets for storm damage and flooding. Most suffered severe damage from Hurricane Katrina, as well as from previous storms.

The wetland reclamation projects for agriculture, such as the LaBranche Wetlands and the Madisonville rice fields, also contributed to wetland loss. Such sites were apparently productive for a few years, but eventually failed because of increased subsidence and flooding. Today they are mostly open-water ponds. The Bayou LaBranche Wetlands Restoration Project in 1994 was an attempt to return one of these areas to a productive marsh wetland. It resulted in the filling of 342 acres (138 ha) of eroded wetlands to create new marsh by dredging sediments from the adjacent lake bottom (Pearson et al. 1993; Louisiana Coastal Wetlands Conservation and Restoration Task Force 1997). Additional information on the LaBranche Wetlands is available in an excellent teacher's guide, "LaBranche: Lessons of a Wetland Paradise" (Maygarden 1996), and in a videotape "Bayou of the Lost: The Legacy of the LaBranche Wetlands" (Tyler 1996).

One marsh type that seems to have been virtually eliminated from the Pontchartrain basin is the immense canebrakes (monotypic stands of giant cane or switch cane, *Arundinaria gigantea*) described by Darby (1816) as once occurring along waterways such as the Amite, Comite, and New Rivers, on lands "not liable to annual submersion." Even at the time of Darby, much of this community type had been destroyed by clearing of the land for cultivation, the presence of cane being a sign of soil fertility (Platt and Brantley 1997). It is difficult to imagine the vast canebrakes and massive sizes of this native bamboo that once occurred along waterways in the Pontchartrain area and reportedly grew as tall as 40 ft. (12 m) and 4 in. (10 cm) in diameter; the canebrakes are now an ecological community type considered critically endangered (Platt and Brantley 1997; Brantley and Platt 2001; Platt et al. 2001). Canebrakes have also been suggested as an important site for feeding of the apparently extinct Bachman's warbler (*Vermivora bachmanii*).

Saltwater Intrusion

Saltwater intrusion continues to be a problem in much of coastal Louisiana, including the Pontchartrain basin. The increased salinity has caused mortality of cypress and other primarily freshwater wetland species, and standing forests of dead cypress can be seen in areas severely stressed by saltwater intrusion. These standing dead trees may remain for years as reminders of the negative impacts that human activities can have even in remote locations. Studies have indicated that salinities in Lake Pontchartrain have continued to increase at least since the 1960s, when the most significant cypress mortality seems to have occurred. The MRGO, which provided a direct route for high-salinity Gulf water to move into the lake, has been cited as the most significant cause of this increase (Overton et al. 1986).

Sikora and Kjerfve (1985) demonstrated a mean annual salinity increase of about 2 ppt in Lake Pontchartrain between 1963 and 1982, thought to be correlated with the opening of the MRGO (in 1963). However, statistical significance of such a correlation was not possible because of the extreme variation in the salinity records.

Salinity stratification has been demonstrated in the lake adjacent to the Inner Harbor Navigation Canal (Poirrier 1978b; Junot et al. 1983), with more dense, high-salinity water flowing into the lake below the lower salinity lake water. Such salt wedges can occur when fresh waters leaving the estuary move along the surface and high-salinity waters entering the estuary remain near the bottom. This is especially true in the MRGO and Inner Harbor

Navigation Canal because of the greater salinity difference between water entering at Breton Sound and water flowing out of Lakes Pontchartrain and Borgne (Swenson 1980b).

Because the dense, saline water from the Inner Harbor Navigation Canal is also low in oxygen, it has caused "dead zones" in the adjacent part of the lake. The saltwater intrusion creates a plume of higher salinity water in the lake adjacent to the canal, and the stratified bottom water in such areas can become hypoxic and devoid of life, with dissolved oxygen levels of 1–4 ppm (Poirrier 1978b; Sikora and Sikora 1982; Junot et al. 1983; Overton et al. 1986; McCorquodale et al. 2001b). The increased salinity has also caused dramatic changes in wetlands vegetation along the course of the MRGO. Its margins have eroded very rapidly so that today it has increased in width from 500 ft. (51 m) to more than 2000 ft. (600 m). This erosion had destroyed 3000 acres (1241 ha) of marsh by the mid-1970s (Shallat 2001).

The MRGO was also blamed for much of the storm surge that entered adjacent wetlands and Lake Pontchartrain as a result of Hurricane Katrina (Van Heerden and Bryan 2006). Subsequently the MRGO was deauthorized as a deep draft ship channel and may eventually be closed (LPBF 2006b).

Several major hurricanes and storms since 1960 have produced significant flooding of the Pontchartrain basin by saline waters (including Betsy, 1965; Camille, 1969; Bob, 1979; Juan, 1985; Tropical Storms Beryl and Florence, 1988; Andrew, 1992; Tropical Storm Frances, 1998; Georges, 1998; and Katrina and Rita, 2005). In addition to the human consequences of hurricanes and other storms, the flood waters generated may contribute additional stresses to adjacent marsh vegetation, and cause rapid coastal erosion, wildlife mortality, and increased pollution levels. Such flooding now has a more significant impact on basin wetlands, because many areas are lower as a result of subsidence and numerous canals and ditches allow flood waters to more rapidly penetrate deep into these wetland areas. Once such saline water enters the swamps and marshes, evaporation may further concentrate the salt in ponds and ditches.

On a positive note, Froomer (1982) suggested that increased salinity can decrease the erodibility of marsh soils in the basin. In addition, the higher salinity water may be clearer and can result in increased biodiversity as more marine species move into the lake. However, these minor benefits cannot compensate for their substantial negative impacts.

Subsidence, increased flooding, and saltwater intrusion have all contributed to additional land loss and vegetational changes in places such as the Prairie, an open grassy area in the Manchac Wildlife Management Area adjacent to Lake Pontchartrain. This area has been popular for many years as a significant duck-hunting site. Aerial photographs taken in 1953 show the Prairie to be almost entirely covered with marsh vegetation, which was most likely fresh floating marsh of maiden cane or paille fine (*Panicum hemitomon*). By 1970 the area was 75% open water, and by 1983, 92% open water. There has been significant concern that eventually the narrow strip of land separating the Prairie from Lake Pontchartrain (at a small shoreline indentation called Turtle Cove) would be eroded away and the Prairie would become part of the lake. Because of this concern, the shoreline along this part of the lake was armored in 1994 with rock-filled gabions. A few years later, additional shoreline protection was added by the U.S. Army Corps of Engineers in the form of rock breakwaters constructed at intervals along 4.5 mi. (7.2 km) of shoreline. Other shoreline stabilization projects around the lake, such as bulkheads and seawalls, have effectively stopped shoreline erosion, but have also usually eliminated the adjacent wetlands.

10.

Water Quality Degradation

By 1962 water quality had become so degraded that Pontchartrain Beach and other bathing beaches were posted with "no swimming" signs. Pollution concerns had been significant years before but any substantive action had mostly been avoided. Rivers and streams of the north shore had also been treated as sewers and contributed to the lake's pollution. People had continued swimming in the lake and rivers during the period when water quality was at its worst, even though health concerns were warranted (Cabelli et al. 1982; Englande et al. 2002). Such actions only emphasize further the tremendous potential value of a clean lake to the local populace.

Initially the New Orleans Health Department monitored the lake for fecal coliform and fecal streptococci densities and closed the beaches when counts were high (Ktsanes et al. 1981). Such bacteria are referred to as "indicator organisms" because they can be used to indicate the presence of sewage or other animal waste materials. Although fecal coliform bacteria can cause some health problems, of greater concern are other bacteria and viruses that often are found in the presence of these bacteria. Because pollution levels could be directly correlated with levels of surface water pumped into the lake from New Orleans and Jefferson Parish drainage canals, and thus varied excessively from day-to-day, permanent warnings were posted indicating the presence of higher pollution levels after heavy rains. Those who continued swimming in the lake in spite of the warnings incurred a significantly higher incidence of gastrointestinal symptoms such as diarrhea (Ktsanes et al. 1981; Cabelli et al. 1982).

Numerous factors contributed to this water quality degradation. Drainage and sewage disposal had always been a problem for the area and was an immediate concern for residents of the new French settlement of New Orleans. Consequently, a system of ditches and canals was dug as the settlement developed. By 1800 the Carondelet Canal, which drained into Bayou St. John, was said to serve as a common sewer for New Orleans. Union officers during the Civil War described the city as filthy with impossible drainage. By the mid-1980s, the drainage system of New Orleans consisted of 83 mi. (133 km) of open canals, 83 mi. (133 km) of covered canals, 57 mi. (92 km) of large pipelines, and 1258 mi. (2024 km) of subsurface drain pipes, plus twenty-one pumping stations (Maygarden et al. 1999).

Because of the natural contour of the land, with the higher land along the Mississippi River, the drainage tended to flow toward Lake Pontchartrain. The continual flooding increased the complexity of the drainage and sewage problem, which became even greater with the growth of the city and surrounding communities. Such drainage problems continued to be a major source of pollution to Lake Pontchartrain even to the present, in spite of modern technology. The major sources of pollutants into Lake Pontchartrain are urban stormwater drainage, discharges of domestic sewage treated at less than acceptable levels, and discharges and spills from marine-related facilities and marine vessels (Overton et al. 1986). These sources have continued to increase because of the burgeoning population and increased surface runoff, and new sources of waterborne pollutants have become apparent.

Urban Runoff

Urban runoff, especially from New Orleans, Metairie, and Kenner, is a very serious concern for Lake Pontchartrain. Water collecting in the drainage canals of urbanized areas is loaded with a broad assortment of pollutants. Sewage can seep from antiquated piping systems. Animal wastes can wash into the canals. Pesticides from yards or other sources can be carried into the canals. Oil and grease or other materials can leak from automobiles and find their way into the canals. Heavy metals from automobile wastes can accumulate. Pumping stations then transfer enormous volumes of this potent cocktail of dangerous materials into Lake Pontchartrain. These urban runoff waters carry excessively high levels of fecal coliform bacteria (indicators of sewage contamination) and harmful substances such as heavy metals and organic chemicals and have excessively high nutrient levels and very low dissolved oxygen levels (Coastal Environments, Inc. 1984a). Because of this, many pollutants present in Lake Pontchartrain occur in greatest concentrations along the southern shore and decrease exponentially with distance offshore, reaching background levels 3–6 mi. (4.8–9.7 km) offshore (Overton et al. 1986). Several studies have demonstrated that pollution levels in the lake increase with storm events and the increased pumping from the urban pumping stations, then gradually decrease several days later (Jin et al. 1999, 2003; Barbé et al. 2001; Englande et al. 2002; Jeng et al. 2005).

Houck et al. (1989) estimated the annual pollutant loadings from the eight Orleans Parish and five Jefferson Parish pumping stations discharging into Lake Pontchartrain to include 134 million lb. (61 million kg) of total suspended solids and 25 million lb. (11 million kg) of biological oxygen-demand (BOD) material. Jefferson Parish input to the lake each year was estimated in 1993 to include about 11 million lb. (5 million kg) of suspended solids, 49 million lb. (22 million kg) of dissolved solids, 300,000 lb. (136,000 kg) of total Kjeldahl nitrogen, 62,000 lb. (28,000 kg) of nitrates and nitrites, 66,000 lb. (30,000 kg) of total phosphorus, 1700 lb. (771 kg) of lead, 33,000 lb. (15,000 kg) of zinc, 27,000 lb. (12,000 kg) of cyanide, and 1.3 million lb. (590,000 kg) of oil and grease (NPDES Storm Water Permit 1993; French 1995).

The catastrophic flooding caused by Hurricane Katrina in 2005 contaminated Lake Pontchartrain with unknown but massive quantities of every possible hazardous material present in the city, including raw sewage, dead animals and plants, oil and gasoline, pesticides, heavy metals, and other toxic chemicals (Pardue et al. 2005; Presley et al. 2006; Van Metre et al. 2006). Although levels of some pollutants, such as lead and fecal coliform bacteria, were especially high and greatly exceeded EPA health standards, initial studies revealed that most pollutants were present at concentrations comparable to typical stormwater runoff from the city. These reports were generally regarded as positive and indicated that the effects of Katrina were not as bad as they could have been. However, they also further emphasized the polluted nature of typical stormwater runoff pumped from New Orleans canals into Lake Pontchartrain. The massive volume of contaminated flood water pumped into the lake over a short time period was certainly an unusual negative impact. Because of the subsequent flooding of the city by Hurricane Rita, the "unwatering" process continued until October 11, a total period of forty-three days. During that time, a volume of water equivalent to about 6–7% of the lake's volume was pumped out of the city into Lake Pontchartrain at a rate of more than 1 million gal. (3.8 million L) per day. Even so, the levels of fecal coliform bacteria (including *Escherichia coli* and *Enterococcus*), although excessively high in New Orleans canals and north-shore rivers, remained within recreational swimming standards in the open waters of Lake Pontchartrain (Stoeckel et al. 2005). Analysis of sediments in the lake along the southern shore indicated that accumulation of hazardous chemicals had not occurred except for a small area near the 17th Street Canal and that effects of

Hurricanes Katrina and Rita were limited both spatially and temporally (Van Metre et al. 2006). By December 2005, the EPA had issued statements that lake levels for most pollutants were at levels comparable to historical pre-Katrina levels and within recreational standards (http://www.epa.gov/cgi-bin/epa-printonly.cgi). One year after Katrina, the NOAA issued a press release stating that Gulf seafood showed no signs of elevated contaminants and no lingering threats to human health (NOAA News Release 2006-R119, August 25, 2006). Although such reports were encouraging and indicated that the rapid dilution of pollutants and flushing of the lake prevented more significant impacts, the overall effects of such pollution on the lake and its biota will probably never be determined, but must have presented a massive jolt to the lake environment.

Nonpoint sources of pollution are generally the most difficult to address and correct because their sources are not always clear—or rather the sources are diverse. There is not a single pipe that the pollution comes from and where it could be treated. In the case of New Orleans and Jefferson Parish, some attention has been given to constructing treatment systems such as man-made wetlands adjacent to canal pumping stations where water could be pumped and treated before it is allowed to enter the lake (Englande et al. 2002). Wetland plants are known to be effective in filtering and absorbing many types of waterborne pollutants. Although considered feasible, such systems have not yet been constructed.

The most effective means to address the nonpoint source pollution problem is reduction. Citizens need to be educated to reduce their own waste stream by properly disposing of yard wastes, limiting the use of pesticides and other chemicals, recycling motor oil, and keeping automobiles properly tuned and running clean, and thus preventing these pollutants from entering the drainage canals and eventually the lake.

Sewage

Houck et al. (1989) reported that more than 500 community sewage treatment facilities discharged into the Lake Pontchartrain basin, plus tens of thousands of individual home sewage systems. Many communities have poor sewage treatment systems, and even good systems can become overloaded by rapid population growth. The individual home treatment systems are rarely maintained in such a way as to keep them functioning properly. Septic systems are notoriously inefficient in southern Louisiana because of the high water table and frequent floods. Technology is available to provide tertiary treatment of sewage so that effluent from treatment systems could be safe to drink, but such treatment is expensive and most communities are unwilling to pay for it. Thus, much of the human waste is released into waterways only partially treated or even untreated. But citizens pay the price anyway. If citizens do not pay to treat waste, they pay in not being able to use the region's waterways for recreational activities, in lost natural food resources such as oysters, or in increased medical costs to treat those who become ill from contact with contaminated waters. Pathogenic bacteria and viruses carried in polluted waters can cause significant illnesses such as hepatitis, typhoid fever, Asiatic cholera, polio, and salmonella. And the health risks will only become more complex as the human population increases.

In addition to the potential health risks of poor water quality, the excessive nutrients characteristic of most polluted waters can cause other problems in the lake, such as algal blooms and subsequent fish kills. Overenrichment or eutrophication of the lake can occur when the naturally high levels of plant nutrients such as nitrates and phosphates reach levels far beyond those normally occurring. Turner (2001) and Turner et al. (2002) estimated that there had been a ten-fold increase in nitrogen loading in the Lake Pontchartrain basin during the past 180 years as a result of anthropogenic influence (agriculture and urbanization). In addition, opening of the Bonnet Carré Spillway can triple the typical annual input of nitrogen to the lake. These excess nutrients stimulate excess algal growth until waters may turn green. Subsequent conditions, such as reduced light penetration, can cause the algae to begin dying, their decomposition can further reduce oxygen levels in the water, and fish and other aquatic organisms may begin dying.

Such excess nutrients can have beneficial effects if directed into wetland areas, where low nutrient levels may be limiting vegetation growth. Brantley et al. (2008) demonstrated that secondarily treated effluent from waste water systems could enhance plant productivity in forested wetlands, as well as also increasing sediment accretion rates.

Camps and Boats

Camps and waterfront residences, as well as boats on the lake, have been a significant source of sewage and other pollutants. As pointed out by Houck et al. (1989), few of the camps located on Lake Pontchartrain or its tributaries had adequate sewage treatment. Ironically, the hundreds of recreational camps built on piers over the lake between Milneburg and Little Woods in the early 1900s (see Figure 8.2) discharged raw human wastes into the very waters they were built to enjoy. Fortunately, most of these camps have since been removed or destroyed. By 2005 virtually all of the camps on Lake Pontchartrain had been removed, many by storms such as Hurricanes Georges in 1998 and Katrina in 2005. Many of their supporting pilings still remain as ghostly reminders of happy times on the lake (Figure 8.2). However, the number has increased in other locations, although these new camps, as well as the remaining older camps, are now required to install individual sewage treatment systems or to tie into available community systems.

In the past, recreational boaters operating on the lake were not restricted from discharging human wastes into the lake, and the number of vessels on the lake and the amount of such wastes has steadily increased with the population increase. Studies cited by Houck et al. (1989) estimated more than 46,000 recreational boaters per day on Lake Pontchartrain in 1975, in addition to commercial vessels (which numbered 4973 vessel-trips in 1985). Discharge of wastes from boats at the New Orleans Municipal Yacht Harbor was considered a significant source of microbial contamination to the lake (Jin et al. 1999). Strict regulations implemented in recent years banning the discharge of wastes from boats into inland waters have helped to reduce this source of pollution. However, the ultimate solution to eliminating such discharges should be the personal responsibility of each boat owner who would prefer to operate in a clean lake.

Most of the boats on Lake Pontchartrain are powered by two-stroke outboard motors, which are notorious polluters, releasing large amounts of unburned oil and gasoline into the water. Estimated amounts of oil and gasoline released from recreational boats on Lake Pontchartrain are 150,000 gal. (568,000 L) per year, not including spillage and bilge discharges (French 1995). Stricter EPA standards for boat motors and the increased popularity (and availability) of four-stroke outboard motors, which are also quieter and more fuel efficient, will help reduce this problem in the future.

A new type of boat, as well as a new type of pollution, came to the lake in 1994, when Treasure Chest Casino opened at Laketown in Kenner, and the Bally's Southshore Harbor Casino soon followed in 1995. These 350-ft. (107-m) long boats were floating casinos, but never sailed, remaining moored to the shore for ready access by their gaming patrons, most of whom probably never realize the significant history and beauty of the lake upon which they float and gamble. Both facilities were damaged by Katrina, but Treasure Chest only minimally and it was reopened after only seven weeks. Bally's casino was heavily damaged and subsequently moved out of Lake Pontchartrain.

Rivers and Bayous

Another source of pollution causing water quality degradation in Lake Pontchartrain is the numerous rivers and bayous that drain into the lake. These rivers have been important recreational waters for local residents, as well as fish and wildlife habitat, and several have been recognized as state natural and scenic streams. But they have also been abused and carry pollutants that reduce their water quality, as well as that of the lake. With the rapid population growth in the Florida Parishes, pollution levels from untreated or inadequately treated sewage, surface runoff, and toxic chemicals such as pesticides have also increased. Runoff from dairy farms and other agricultural operations in the north-shore parishes has also contributed to the pollution load of the rivers draining into the Lake Pontchartrain system.

Of ten pesticides analyzed for occurrence in Lake Pontchartrain and its tributaries between 1943 and 1995 (DDT, diazinon, lindane, chlordane, malathion, endrin, parathion, dieldrin, endosulfan, and 2,4-D), only diazinon and 2,4-D were frequently present at levels above their reporting levels (Garrison 1999). In 949 samples analyzed for diazinon, its reporting level (0.01 µg/L) was exceeded in 403 (42%). In 668 samples analyzed for 2,4-D, its reporting level (0.01 µg/L) was exceeded in 570 (85%). Highest levels recorded were 0.13 µg/L (diazinon) and 0.42 µg/L (2,4-D). Other organic chemicals have at times been present at high levels in Mississippi River waters and may enter the lakes, but such occurrences have been infrequent. There have also been spills in tributaries that have affected the lakes, such as a major spill of pentachlorophenol in the MRGO in 1980 (Sikora and Sikora 1982).

In 1979–1980 most streams in Tangipahoa Parish were found to carry moderate to high levels of total and fecal coliform bacteria, especially in the more densely populated southern part of the parish (Dardis 1980). These high pollution levels would cause further deterioration of water quality in Lakes Pontchartrain and Maurepas. Further microbiological studies of the Tangipahoa River in 1986–1987 demonstrated conclusively the high levels of fecal coliform bacterial contamination (Janes 1987). These data were especially disturbing because of the excessively high levels observed (1000 to 10,000 colonies per 100 ml), far above the primary contact (swimming) standard of 200 colonies per 100 ml and above the secondary (fishing) contact standard of 1000.

Another study conducted during 1989–1990 found high fecal coliform and *Escherichia coli* levels in the Tangipahoa River that exceeded primary contact standards (126 bacterial cells per 100 ml for *E. coli*) in ten of the twelve months

Figure 10.1 Tangipahoa River posted sign at the Dunnington Bridge on Highway 443 (Photograph by the author)

tested (Anderson et al. 1990). *Enterococcus* standards (33 cells per 100 ml of water for human streptococcus bacteria) were exceeded during all months.

Initially agricultural runoff from dairy farms and other agricultural operations was considered the major source of pollution in the Tangipahoa River, because each dairy cow can produce the amount of waste equivalent to fifteen humans. When dispersed in a pasture, cows and other farm animals are not a major pollution concern, because any waste material dropped in a pasture tends to be dried and sterilized by sunlight and provides nutrients to stimulate the growth of pasture grasses. However, when dairy cows are taken into a holding area or barn for milking, their concentrated wastes can become a major problem. The farmer must wash out the wastes, which will flow downhill into a ditch or stream, eventually enter the river, and be carried into the lake. The excess nutrients then contribute to eutrophication of the river or lake, and any pathogens such as bacteria and viruses can produce a health threat to humans. Janes (1987) compared the ratios of fecal coliform to fecal streptococci (an indicator of waste from cattle) to conclude that most of the pollution was of human origin, although dairy farm runoff was still a significant concern in the area. Anderson et al. (1990) also analyzed samples for *Streptococcus bovis* bacteria, a species characteristic of cows and other ruminants, and found levels lower in the main river than in tributaries where dairy farm runoff was more significant.

Figure 10.2 Turbidity plume at mouth of the Tickfaw River, December 1985 (Used with permission of the Stennis Space Center, frame no. 1973, image identification 585003550ROLL)

Much of the concern regarding Lake Pontchartrain tributaries focused on the Tangipahoa River because of its significance as a very important recreational resource for southeastern Louisiana during the 1970s and 1980s (Waldon and Smythe 1994). There were an estimated 200,000 visitors to the river each year, primarily for tubing and swimming and other activities, and this recreational industry contributed significantly to the local economy. After the high pollution levels were publicized in 1987, indicating that the water was not safe for swimming, the river was posted (in March 1988) with warning signs against both primary (swimming) and secondary (fishing) contact (Figure 10.1). This action effectively ended the tubing industry on the river and drew attention to the Tangipahoa River as "the" polluted river. Actually water quality in other rivers of the Florida Parishes was also degraded and an environmental concern. For example, water quality in the Tickfaw River during 1990 was found to exceed primary contact standards 66% of the time for fecal coliform and *E. coli* and 100% of the time for enterococci (Higginbotham et al. 1991). In February 1991, primary contact advisories were issued for the Tchefuncte and Bogue Falaya Rivers. Several grassroots organizations were established to address these pollution problems, with the fight being led primarily by Citizens for a Clean Tangipahoa.

Another significant pollution problem in rivers of the Pontchartrain basin, especially the Amite and Tangipahoa, has been generated by sand and gravel mining. Extraction of the deposits of sand and gravel from beds adjacent to the river releases large quantities of clay and silt into the rivers, resulting in excessive sediment load and turbidity of the river. Aquatic organisms can be smothered by the excess siltation, and the turbid waters can be carried into the lake, where they further degrade water quality (Figure 10.2). The turbid rivers and lake are aesthetically less attractive than clear, pristine waters. Most of the mined areas are never restored, but remain for long periods as barren, unvegetated land or as open borrow pits, which may continue to erode sediments into the river. Although over time the sites might become revegetated, the process could be accelerated by replacing topsoil and replanting. The borrow pits may eventually become colonized by aquatic plants and animals to become productive fishing lakes or ponds, but this process could also be encouraged by proper management practices.

Shell Dredging

An especially significant factor affecting water quality in the lakes came with the initiation of shell dredging for the extensive deposits of rangia clam shells on the bottom of the lakes, which became an important commercial enterprise in the early 1930s (Price and Kuckyr 1974; Bouma 1976; U.S. Army Corps of Engineers 1987). Houck et al. (1989) considered shell dredging the single largest contributor of pollution by volume to Lake Pontchartrain. An estimated average of 5 million cu. yd. (3.8 million m^3) of shells per year were mined from the lake in 1975–1985, with an estimated value of $34 million annually. The shells were an important construction material used to build roads and driveways. Large suction dredges moved across the lake, pumping up the shells that had accumulated for thousands of years. This dredged material was pumped onto a barge where the shells were retained and the sand, silt, and clay were washed overboard. Any living organisms sucked into the dredge were killed, and the bottoms adjacent to the barge were covered with the sand and silt particles washed overboard. The finer clay particles were left in suspension to greatly increase the turbidity of the

Table 10 Areal distribution of submersed aquatic vegetation in Lake Pontchartrain

Year	Area	Change	Percent Change	References
1954	2667–2985 acres* (1079–1208 ha)			Suttkus et al. (1954), Turner et al. (1980)
1973	2000 acres (809 ha)	–667 to 985 acres (–270 to 399 ha)	–25 to 33%	Montz (1978)
1984	927 acres (375 ha)	–1073 acres (–434 ha)	–54%	Mayer (1986)
1992	217 acres (88 ha)	–710 acres (–287 ha)	–77%	Cho and Poirrier (2001)
2000	1112 acres (450 ha)	+895 acres (+362 ha)	+412%	Cho and Poirrier (2001)

*Acreage based upon Turner et al. (1980) estimate of 25–33% decrease between 1954 and 1973

lake. Total suspended solids generated by the shell dredges exceeded 99 million lb. (45 million kg) per day, and increased biological oxygen demand levels were estimated to exceed 81,000 lb. (37,000 kg) per day. Dredging was estimated to contribute 95.6% of the total suspended solids discharged into the lake, causing excessive turbidity levels throughout the lake. The water was nearly always a chocolate brown color, with virtually no underwater visibility. A hand placed just below the water surface could not be seen.

The substrate of the lake became an unconsolidated "fluid mud" or semisolid slurry of suspended materials, which was much more susceptible to resuspension by storm-generated wave action, further increasing the turbidity levels of the lake. And this material never became consolidated and compacted into a firm habitat needed to support most of the benthic organisms.

The pros and cons of shell dredging were hotly debated for many years, and much has been published on the issue (Price and Kuckyr 1974; Bouma 1976; Sikora et al. 1981; U.S. Army Corps of Engineers 1987). Although some areas of the lake were closed to dredging (44% in 1987), the massive amounts of sediment removed from the bottom had a significant impact on the benthic fauna (Sikora et al. 1981) and greatly affected the entire lake ecosystem. The increased turbidity, or decreased water clarity, had a negative impact on submerged grassbeds, which needed light for photosynthesis. There was a drastic decline in the distribution of aquatic vegetation in the lake between 1954 and 1992 (Table 10; Perret et al. 1971; U.S. Army Corps of Engineers 1974; Montz 1978; Turner et al. 1980).

Because of the obvious negative impacts of shell dredging, the Lake Pontchartrain Basin Foundation led an effort to end shell dredging in the late

1980s. The practice had been banned in Lake Maurepas in 1984 and finally in Lake Pontchartrain in 1990. After shell dredging was banned, the water clarity significantly improved (Francis and Poirrier 1999) and the grassbeds began to recover (Cho and Poirrier 2001, 2005).

Channel dredging to provide deeper access channels for boats has many of the same effects as shell dredging, but on a much smaller scale, and therefore it has a relatively minor effect lakewide. However, in the immediate vicinity of any dredge, water clarity can decrease considerably, especially if dredge spoil is released into the lake water. Consequently, terrestrial spoil disposal sites are usually preferred, although in coastal Louisiana, dredge spoil is also used in some areas to reduce the rates of shoreline erosion. For example, maintenance dredging at the mouth of the Tangipahoa River in 1996 was correlated with shoreline protection of a rapidly eroding area along the lakeshore just south of the river.

Effects of the Bonnet Carré Spillway

Prehistorically, the Mississippi River was an annual contributor of fresh water, nutrients, and sediments to Lake Pontchartrain and its surrounding wetlands when the river was at flood stage in the spring (by way of Bayou Manchac and crevasses at Bonnet Carré and other locations). This natural process built the delta lands and the natural levees along the river and nourished the estuary. Leveeing of the river for flood control, however, eliminated (or at least reduced) that annual source of fresh water, nutrients, and sediments, but also increased the danger of potential floods. The river now exceeds the prelevee flood stage of 11 ft. (3.4 m) virtually every year, and with the present height of the levees at New Orleans at 30 ft. (9.1 m) above sea level, the Mississippi routinely reaches much higher levels with much greater flood danger. This increased danger was demonstrated by the catastrophic flood of 1927 (Barry 1997). The Bonnet Carré Spillway was constructed to alleviate some of this increased danger by allowing controlled spillway discharges at rates up to the design capacity of 250,000 cfs (7000 m^3/sec; with average maximum flows of about 219,000 cfs or 6202 m^3/sec). The spillway was completed in 1932 and has been opened in 1937, 1945, 1950, 1973, 1975, 1979, 1983, 1997, and 2008 (and by vandals in 1995). The amounts of water discharged during these openings are shown in Table 11.

When the Bonnet Carré Spillway was first opened in 1937, the total volume of water released into the lake was said to have been sufficient to fill the lake 2.5 times and raised the level of the lake about 20 in. (50 cm) above normal (Viosca 1938). Swenson (1981) estimated that the 1979 opening allowed enough water to

Table 11 Openings of the Bonnet Carré Spillway and discharge amounts into Lake Pontchartrain

Year	Peak River Stage*	Average Discharge	Maximum Discharge	Volume Discharged
1937	19.1 ft. (5.8 m)	155,675 cfs (4409 m³/sec)	211,000 cfs (5976 m³/sec)	12.5 million acre-ft. (15.4 billion m³)
1945	19.8 ft. (6.0 m)	224,416 cfs (6355 m³/sec)	318,000 cfs (9006 m³/sec)	24.5 million acre-ft. (30.2 billion m³)
1950	20.0 ft. (6.1 m)	156,114 cfs (4421 m³/sec)	223,000 cfs (6315 m³/sec)	10.8 million acre-ft. (13.3 billion m³)
1973	18.4 ft. (5.6 m)	131,000 cfs (3710 m³/sec)	195,000 cfs (5522 m³/sec)	19.5 million acre-ft. (24.1 billion m³)
1975	17.8 ft. (5.4 m)	74,000 cfs (2096 m³/sec)	110,000 cfs (3115 m³/sec)	1.9 million acre-ft. (2.3 billion m³)
1979	17.0 ft. (5.2 m)	109,000 cfs (3087 m³/sec)	228,000 cfs (6457 m³/sec)	9.75 million acre-ft. (12.0 billion m³)
1983	17.2 ft. (5.2 m)	227,600 cfs (6446 m³/sec)	268,000 cfs (7590 m³/sec)	15.3 million acre-ft. (18.9 billion m³)
1995†	16.8 ft. (5.1 m)	n.a.	n.a.	n.a.
1997	16.9 ft. (5.2 m)	154,000 cfs (4361 m³/sec)	243,000 cfs (6882 m³/sec)	9.2 million acre-ft. (11.4 billion m³)
2008‡	17.0 ft. (5.2 m)	155,000 cfs (4390 m³/sec)	169,000 cfs (4786 m³/sec)	

Data from Lopez (2003)
*River stage above sea level at Carrolton Gauge
†An unofficial opening
‡Preliminary data from U.S. Geological Survey and U.S. Army Corps of Engineers (August 2008)

enter the lake over a 60-day period to completely replace the entire lake volume, or about six times the normal flushing rate for the lake.

When the river level is above the minimum level of the Bonnet Carré Spillway (above 12.3 ft. or 3.75 m; Turner et al. 2002), there is a significant amount of leakage through the spillway even when it is not opened. This normally occurs only in the spring when the river rises because of snowmelt in the Midwest. During summer, autumn, and winter, the river level is usually below the sill of the spillway and no diversion of water is possible. To some extent this mimics the natural prehistoric condition of the lake, when the Mississippi River would each spring overflow its banks and flood the surrounding floodplain.

Figure 10.3 Algal bloom on the northern shore of Lake Pontchartrain, spring 2008 (Used with permission of the Lake Pontchartrain Basin Foundation)

Each time the spillway is opened, its massive volume of water greatly affects the normal condition of the lake. The large amounts of nutrients (nitrates and phosphates) can stimulate eutrophic algal blooms (Figure 10.3). A major algal bloom on the lake in June and July 1995, possibly the largest to that date, apparently resulted from the unplanned release (by vandals) for several days of approximately 15,000 cfs (425 m^3/sec) of nutrient-rich Mississippi River water into the lake (LPBF 1995b). This bloom covered some 300 sq. mi. (777 km^2) with a thick green scum resembling turquoise paint and caused the death of thousands of fish.

The spillway was opened again in March 1997, the first official opening since 1983, and more than 3 trillion gal (11 trillion L) of river water flowed into Lake Pontchartrain. As feared, but also expected, the lake suffered another severe algal bloom in May and June, apparently the worst in the history of the lake (LPBF 1997b, 1997c; Day et al. 1999). Much of the lake was again covered with a thick scum of blue-green algae (the cyanobacteria *Anabaena circinalis* and *Microcystis aeruginosa*), which remained through September. Toxins and anoxic conditions generated by the decomposing algae resulted in fish kills on the lake, and an advisory against recreational use of the lake (Dortch et al. 1999). These excessive nutrients also stimulated the growth of epiphytic algae (*Cladophora*), causing overgrowth and death of macrophytic plants (Poirrier et al. 1999).

The spillway water changes the lake in other ways, such as lowering temperatures and salinity (Gunter 1953; Swenson 1980a, 1981), increasing turbidity, and carrying industrial wastes, pesticides, and pathogenic organisms into the lake. Temperature of the river water is usually about 10–16°F (6–10°C) lower than the lake in spring when the maximum diversion occurs. Suspended sediments in Mississippi River water greatly increase turbidity of the lake. Swenson (1981) reported average suspended loads of about 15–25 mg/L dry weight in 1978, but a plume of turbid spillway water entering the lake in 1979 had suspended loads up to 160 mg/L.

Fecal coliform bacteria levels are also increased in the lake by the diversion of Mississippi River water, as are organic compounds such as polychlorinated biphenyls (PCBs), dieldrin, and chlorinated hydrocarbons and various metals such as copper, mercury, and zinc (Houck et al. 1989). The effects of such chemicals on the lake biota are unknown, although some can bioaccumulate in living organisms, as well as in the sediments. High levels of PCBs (0.32 µg/g) have been reported for sediments in Lake Pontchartrain (Sikora et al. 1981).

Some benefits to the lake from the entrance of Mississippi River water have been claimed, such as increased fish and shellfish production because of the increased nutrients, sediments to replenish marshland loss, and reduced salinity levels (Tarver 1974). These are benefits that the Bonnet Carré crevasse provided in prehistoric times. In view of these benefits, proposals have been made to modify the spillway so that river water could be diverted throughout the year. Such a diversion project was first proposed in 1976 as a means of providing fresh water into Lake Pontchartrain and Mississippi Sound, primarily to aid oyster fisheries in the sound. The project as proposed was intended to allow freshwater diversion into the lake during all months of the year and not just during river flood stages when the level of the river is above that of the spillway. At the time, Lake Pontchartrain was severely polluted and its use as a conduit for channeling Mississippi River water into Mississippi Sound seemed appropriate. However, in recent years with the improved water quality in Lake Pontchartrain, consideration of impacts of Mississippi River water on the Lake Pontchartrain system has made such diversions a major concern. However, other Mississippi River diversions have been proposed in recent years as a means of restoring subsiding wetlands.

Mississippi River Diversions

Continued subsidence of wetland areas in coastal Louisiana has increased the potential value of suspended sediments carried by the Mississippi River and the need to use such sediments in wetlands restoration. Most wetland experts now recognize river diversions as the only feasible means of significantly restoring substantial areas of coastal Louisiana wetlands. Several such diversions have been proposed and in some cases implemented. However, diversions must be designed in harmony with nature. Natural diversions from the Mississippi River into adjacent wetlands have occurred almost exclusively in the spring, when the river is at flood stage from rain and snowmelt in the Midwest. In addition, to be beneficial diversions should be overland, that is, directed into wetlands and not confined to narrow and/or artificial ditches, such as the Bonnet Carré Spillway. Any diversion projects should be conservative in their nature (that is, preserving as much of the natural environment and scenario as possible), and any suggested benefits to Mississippi Sound should not occur at the expense of Louisiana or Lake Pontchartrain or its adjacent wetlands.

A proposed diversion into Lake Pontchartrain has been proposed for the Garyville area to channel water into the Blind River drainage area and thus into Lake Maurepas. Such a diversion could provide additional fresh water to the lower basin, as well as nutrients and sediment to nourish deteriorating wetlands in the Lake Maurepas/Manchac area. Viosca (1927), in remarkable foresight when the Bonnet Carré Spillway was being proposed, suggested that the spillway would be most beneficial to fisheries if constructed at a proposed site near Burnside (about 20 mi. or 32 km upriver from Garyville), because sheet flow of the water through the extensive swamps southwest of the Lake Maurepas area would promote fisheries production in that area. In contrast, he suggested that the Bonnet Carré site subsequently chosen, with its waters confined within levees and shunted directly into Lake Pontchartrain, could cause harm and would not provide such great fisheries benefits.

Overland flow within the spillway results in a slight reduction in nitrogen entering the lake via the diversion (Lane et al. 2001), but complete overland flow through forested wetlands would result in a major reduction in the amount of nitrogen entering the lake. Such overland flow, although difficult to achieve, could significantly reduce the risk of algal blooms occurring in the lake as a result of the diversion. In addition, the nutrients and sediments added to these wetlands would provide significant benefits and significantly reduce cypress mortality in some areas, such as the Manchac marshes and the marshes south of Lake Maurepas.

Turbidity

Estuaries, because of their high levels of nutrients, suspended sediments, and biological productivity, are generally not especially clear. On the other hand, excessive amounts of suspended sediments can greatly increase turbidity, reducing light penetration and visibility, and causing the death of grassbeds and other biota. Aquatic plants dependent upon sunlight for photosynthesis will die in turbid waters. Animals that depend upon the grassbeds for food or shelter will die from loss of habitat. Fishes and other animals that depend upon vision to find their prey may be eliminated from excessively turbid waters.

As noted previously, shell dredging and Mississippi River diversions have greatly increased turbidity levels in Lake Pontchartrain, but these sources are mostly reduced or eliminated at present. In most estuaries, the main source of suspended sediments is upland soil erosion, which is carried into the estuary in tributary rivers, especially after periods of heavy rain. Such is the case with all of the rivers flowing into Lakes Pontchartrain and Maurepas, and plumes of especially turbid water are often visible at the mouths of these rivers (Figure 10.2). Where extensive land clearing for farming, timbering, or construction removes the natural vegetation cover of the land, soils will erode excessively. Proper soil conservation methods for farming and "best management practices" for forestry operations can greatly reduce soil erosion. Such methods also can and should be implemented around construction sites. Protection of the soil benefits the land owner as well as protecting rivers and lakes.

Oil and Gas Drilling

Oil and gas production, which also contributed to pollution of the lakes, became significant in 1946, with the drilling of the first commercial well (Conatser 1992). Wells were located in several different areas of the Pontchartrain basin, including Lakes Maurepas and Borgne, with the most productive field being the Big Point Field southeast of Goose Point (Louisiana State University Center for Energy Studies, personal communication). Of the 266 wells drilled in the lakes, 86 (or 32%) have been commercially productive, yielding more than 10 million barrels of liquid hydrocarbons and 116 billion cu. ft. (3.3 billion m^3) of natural gas (Conatser 1992). Some production of oil and gas from wells in Lake Maurepas continued through the 1980s, with 49,500 tons (54,564 metric tons) of crude petroleum and 5600 tons (6172 metric tons) of liquefied gases transported by barge through Pass Manchac in 1989 (U.S. Army Corps of Engineers 1992). Houck et al. (1989) reported the presence of 28 active wells in Lake Pontchartrain in 1989.

The drilling results in occasional oil spills and releases of produced waters with high salinity levels, heavy metals, and other pollutants. High barium levels (average, 482 ppm) in lake sediments have been attributed to spillage of oil well drilling muds (Flowers and Isphording 1990). A moratorium on new drilling in the lakes was issued in 1991 and renewed every two years until the present, although existing leases allowed some production to continue.

Industrial Wastes

Because of its location adjacent to the "chemical corridor" between New Orleans and Baton Rouge, one might think that Lake Pontchartrain would be grossly polluted with chemical wastes. However, such is not the case. There is little industrial development on the Pontchartrain shorelines and tributaries. Some of the industrial plants in the area produce large amounts of hazardous wastes, but most that are released go into the Mississippi River. Some, such as dioxin, can be quite hazardous in small quantities, but fortunately the levels released are much less than in years past. Relatively little normally enters Lake Pontchartrain, although substantial amounts may be carried into the lake when the Bonnet Carré Spillway is open.

However, several significant industrial sites in the Lake Pontchartrain basin have directly affected the lake or its tributaries for many years. One of these is the Norco facility, which was first built in 1916 as the Marine Terminal by the Roxana Petroleum Company. Then an adjacent asphalt refinery was built by the New Orleans Refining Company (NORCO), which eventually gave the community its name (Pearson et al. 1993). Roxana Petroleum Company became Shell Petroleum Corporation and took over the Norco refinery in 1929.

For many years after its construction, Norco dumped large amounts of organic wastes and heavy metals into Bayou Trepagnier, a tributary of Lake Pontchartrain just north of the facility. Such massive dumping no longer occurs (Flowers et al. 1998), but sediments at the bottom of the bayou are severely contaminated with a diverse assortment of organic compounds (polycyclic aromatic hydrocarbons) and heavy metals (zinc, chromium, and lead), which negatively impact the macrofaunal and meiofaunal communities (Oberdorster et al. 1999). Tissue samples from western mosquitofish (*Gambusia affinis*) collected in the bayou contain highly elevated levels of lead and zinc (Klerks and Lentz 1998). Devall et al. (2006) and Marcantonio et al. (1998, 2000) demonstrated elevated levels of lead in tree rings of cypress trees growing adjacent to the bayou. It is ironic that this very scenic waterway, designated as one of Louisiana's natural and scenic streams, has been posted with skull-and-crossbones signs warning of hazardous chemicals. A controversy has existed as to whether the contaminated sediments should be pumped out and incinerated or left in place, where they are somewhat immobilized by overlying sediments (DeLaune and Gambrell 1996).

Some fear that removing the sediments will mobilize contaminants and cause more harm to fish and other organisms in the area. In February 2008, however, an agreement was signed by the Louisiana Department of Environmental Quality and Motiva Enterprises (operator of the refinery since 1998) to implement a clean-up project at Bayou Trepagnier (LDEQ press release).

Another heavily polluted industrial site is the Inner Harbor Navigation Canal. Sediments in the canal are known to be heavily contaminated with various polycyclic aromatic hydrocarbons and heavy metals. Houck et al. (1989) reported very high and hazardous concentrations of coliform bacteria, phenol, iron, nickel, zinc, cyanide, DDT, and dieldrin. Significant numbers of organic priority pollutants have been reported in oysters, clams, and sediments from the Inner Harbor Navigation Canal, the Rigolets, and Chef Menteur Pass, with the largest number of pollutants in the Inner Harbor Navigation Canal (Ferrarrio et al. 1985; McFall et al. 1985a, 1985b). There was a significant spill of pentachlorophenol in the canal in 1980 (Sikora and Sikora 1982). Similar spills have probably been a common occurrence during the history of this industrial canal.

The numerous creosote treatment plants that once existed in the basin are another source of industrial wastes into Lake Pontchartrain. In recent years creosote (a complex mixture of at least 300 chemicals and possibly as many as 10,000) has been shown to be a significant health hazard because of the presence of polycyclic aromatic hydrocarbons, phenol, and cresols, probable human carcinogens. Its use has now been severely restricted. However, its legacy has remained in the form of hazardous waste sites that continued to be an environmental problem long after the companies had gone out of business. Some of these have been abandoned and eventually covered by new industries or other construction. A few have been designated as U.S. Environmental Protection Agency Superfund sites, such as those in Madisonville and Slidell. The latter was a site on Bayou Bonfouca, where large amounts of creosote had accumulated in sediments on the bottom of the bayou. When the site was initially inspected for contamination, divers employed to collect sediment samples from the bottom of the bayou surfaced with second degree burns on their skin from contact with the creosote. Rangia clams transplanted from the lake to the bayou were found after four weeks to have accumulated substantial concentrations of polynuclear aromatic hydrocarbons, including benzopyrene at concentrations almost seven times background levels (DeLeon et al. 1988). The Bayou Bonfouca site was designated a Superfund site in 1983, and between 1993 and 1995 about 500 million lb. (226 million kg) of bayou sediment and soil was removed and incinerated on site to reduce this contamination, at a cost of $120 million (EPA, personal communication 2001). Groundwater cleanup began in 1991 and continued for more than ten years, with an average of 500 gal. (1892 L) of creosote removed per month.

Another Superfund site on Bayou Bonfouca was the Southern Shipbuilding Corporation, where industrial wastes including benzopyrene and other polynuclear aromatic hydrocarbons, tributyltin, asbestos, lead, arsenic, and PCBs had been dumped for more than eighty years. Superfund cleanup of this site was completed in 1997 (www.epa.gov/superfund).

The Madisonville Creosote Works, a 29-acre site located just west of Madisonville, operated from 1956 to 1984 and contaminated areas that drained into Black River, which flows into the Madisonville rice fields adjacent to Lake Pontchartrain. The Madisonville site became a Superfund site in 1996, and cleanup was declared complete in July 2000.

Heavy metals are a significant environmental contaminant in Lake Pontchartrain, but their sources are sometimes difficult to identify. Heavy metal pollution to the lake, including lead, copper, barium, zinc, and nickel, is associated with urban stormwater runoff and municipal discharges (Byrne and DeLeon 1987). The highest levels were generally higher on the southern shoreline, although high levels of zinc (161 ppm dry weight) and nickel (18 ppm) were found off Bayou Bonfouca, apparently associated with the ship repair facilities on the bayou. The lowest levels of all five metals occurred on the northern shore off the Tchefuncte River. On the southern shore, highest levels of lead (231 ppm), zinc (169 ppm), and copper (46 ppm) were found off the 17th Street Canal. Highest levels of barium (207 ppm) occurred off the Inner Harbor Navigation Canal, where levels of zinc (160 ppm) and lead (49 ppm) were also high.

In another study, high levels of chromium, zinc, vanadium, lead, and barium were reported at several locations in the Pontchartrain basin, but levels generally compared well with other Gulf of Mexico estuaries, with the exception of lead and barium (Flowers and Isphording 1990). Lead content (average, 81 ppm) was four times the level considered an unpolluted background concentration. Suggested major sources were stormwater discharge and runoff from cities, highways, and bridges; atmospheric fallout; and leaded boat fuels. High barium levels were attributed to spillage of oil well drilling muds.

Mercury contamination is a serious problem in some waterways, where potential food fish become dangerous to eat because of the high levels of mercury accumulated in their flesh. Fish consumption advisories for mercury have been issued for the Amite River (largemouth bass, *Micropterus salmoides*; spotted bass, *Micropterus punctulatus*; bigmouth buffalo, *Ictiobus cyprinellus*; white crappie, *Pomoxis annularis*; freshwater drum, *Aplodinotus grunniens*; and bowfin, *Amia calva*), Tickfaw River and its tributaries (largemouth bass, white crappie, freshwater drum, and bowfin), Tangipahoa River (largemouth bass, spotted bass, freshwater drum, bowfin, and flathead catfish, *Pylodictus olivaris*), Bogue Falaya and Tchefuncte Rivers (largemouth bass; spotted bass; crappie, *Pomoxis* spp.; freshwater drum; and catfish, *Ictalurus* spp.), Bayou Liberty (largemouth bass, crappie, freshwater drum, and redear sunfish, *Lepomis microlophus*), Blind River (bowfin), Bogue Chitto River (bass and bowfin), Pearl River (bowfin, bass, bigmouth buffalo, catfish, and freshwater drum; Louisiana Department of Health and Hospitals Fish Consumption Advisories 2006). The major sources of such mercury contamination are not clearly understood, but are thought to be primarily from atmospheric deposition of materials that become airborne through coal incineration or other industrial activities. However, some local industrial sources can greatly increase the local concentrations. Reducing such contamination is not a simple process and not a local problem, but one that must be addressed on a national level. Atmospheric deposition of other pollutants has also been suggested as a significant concern for the Pontchartrain basin, but it is poorly understood (Houck et al. 1989; Flowers and Isphording 1990; Paerl et al. 2002).

The frequent floods that affect the Pontchartrain area will often cause leaks or spills from industrial sites or leach substances from hazardous waste sites that are normally contained. Hurricane Katrina's massive flooding of New Orleans and the surrounding area included several Superfund hazardous waste sites, active industrial sites, and hospitals. As noted previously, the resulting mixture of these leached materials was pumped back into Lake Pontchartrain along with the flood waters.

Solid Waste and Litter

Another serious problem affecting the aesthetics of Lake Pontchartrain is solid waste and litter. Anyone who has walked the shores of Lake Pontchartrain or other waterways should be appalled at the gross negligence demonstrated by people who dump their trash and garbage into the lake. The same must be said for the area's rivers, which some people tend to consider convenient garbage dumps. Much of this garbage is carried across the lake or down the river to remote shorelines far from any road access. Logjams on area rivers now seem to contain more plastic than wood. Even inaccessible shorelines on the western side of Lakes Pontchartrain and Maurepas, long distances from any development, are littered with flotsam and jetsam discarded miles away by thoughtless and ignorant individuals too lazy to properly dispose of their garbage. The modern paper, plastic, glass, and aluminum junk may remain there for decades. Our throw-away society generates so much garbage that some people seem to think that they can discard their garbage anywhere and everywhere. It then becomes somebody else's problem. Every year litter cleanups around the lake, as well as elsewhere, generate tons and tons of litter removed by concerned volunteers. Hopefully as Lake Pontchartrain becomes cleaner in water quality, we can also find ways to keep it clean in all ways and not use it as a garbage dump.

11.

Environmental Recovery and Restoration

As the Lake Pontchartrain environmental quality continued to degrade through the second half of the twentieth century, more public and official concern was being expressed for the need to remedy the environmental problems and restore the lake. Although there were many studies documenting environmental concerns prior to 1980, the first comprehensive environmental analysis of Lake Pontchartrain and its surrounding wetlands was completed in that year by personnel at Louisiana State University (Stone 1980; also see Stone et al. 1982). This document, known as the "Stone Report," recognized three major environmental trends within Lake Pontchartrain: loss of wetlands, increased nutrients, and decreased water clarity. By 1980 almost half of the wetland area had been destroyed, mostly since 1950; the rate of phosphorus loading into Lake Pontchartrain had almost doubled since 1900; and water clarity had decreased by half since 1953. Also in 1980, the Lake Pontchartrain Basin Water Quality Management Plan was completed for the Louisiana Department of Natural Resources Division of Water Pollution Control (Stanley Consultants, Inc. 1980). This document identified many of the pollution sources to the lake and its tributaries.

In 1984 the governor's Executive Order EWE 84-23 created the Lake Pontchartrain Task Force to "study the feasibility of designating the Lake Pontchartrain–Lake Maurepas basin a special management area" by the Coastal Management Division of the Louisiana Department of Natural Resources. The task force began meeting in October 1984 and continued through 1986. Although a special management area was never designated, the materials prepared and issues discussed, including background documents, provided an excellent basis for future protection efforts (Coastal Environments, Inc. 1984a, 1984b).

During the 1990s, the fate of Lake Pontchartrain was guided by a new organization, the Lake Pontchartrain Basin Foundation, established to "restore and preserve the ecological balance of the Lake Pontchartrain basin" (LPBF 1990). Recognizing the potential economic, aesthetic, and recreational value that a restored lake could have for the citizens of southeastern Louisiana, the Greater New Orleans Expressway (Causeway) Commission financed an interdisciplinary study of the lake that resulted in the report entitled "To Restore Lake Pontchartrain" (Houck et al. 1989, the "Houck Report"). The environmental problems of Lake Pontchartrain were summarized in this report, which served to catalyze the efforts to return the lake to its previous status as a premier estuarine resource.

Shell dredging was considered the pollution source of greatest concern because of excessively high levels of biological oxygen demand and total suspended solids released into the lake during the shell-washing process. Urban runoff carried with it a diverse assortment of contaminants that contributed to the low water quality along the southern shore. Many of the sewage treatment systems in the basin did not provide adequate treatment for the sewage passing through them, and many rural residences in the basin had no treatment system at all. Agricultural runoff, especially from dairy farms, was a major source of pollution to the rivers of the north-shore. The Houck Report also identified the proposed Bonnet Carré freshwater diversion as a significant potential contributor of pollution to the lake, but did not take an official position in opposition to the diversion.

A major contribution of the Houck Report was its economic impact analysis. By estimating and quantifying the diverse values that a clean lake could provide to southeastern Louisiana, the report concluded that restoring the lakes and rivers of the Pontchartrain basin by the year 2000 would provide a total economic benefit of over $756 million dollars. These benefits included recreational swimming ($143 million), public recreational facilities ($65 million), incremental tourism spending ($335 million), real estate increases ($106 million), and tax revenues generated ($105 million).

At the recommendation of this report and at the request of the Greater New Orleans Expressway Commission, State Senator John Hainkel sponsored legislation creating the Lake Pontchartrain Basin Foundation in July 1989 (Act 716). The goal was to restore the lake (within eight years) to the condition it was in when it was the most popular site for swimming, boating, fishing, crabbing, and picnicking in southeastern Louisiana. "Save Our Lake" became the rallying cry for this new movement. Robert J. Lambert initially served as the acting director but was soon replaced by Executive Director Steve Cochran, former chief of staff for Governor Buddy Roemer.

One of the first successful campaigns of the foundation was the termination of shell dredging in June 1990. The following year brought a moratorium on oil and gas leasing in the lake (LPBF 1991a). This was also the year the foundation began its long-term opposition to the proposed Bonnet Carré freshwater diversion project (LPBF 1991b). After a six-year battle, the project, which threatened the lake cleanup effort with turbid, high-nutrient Mississippi River water, was effectively killed when Governor Mike Foster withdrew Louisiana state support for the project (LPBF 1996). In November 1990, the first of annual fundraising "Back to the Beach" festivals was held at the former Pontchartrain Beach. Although successful in helping to fund the activities of the foundation, a more important effect of "Back to the Beach" was to annually focus attention on the goal of lake restoration and the recreational potential that a clean lake could provide.

The foundation also became an important voice for environmental education in the area, and sponsored many important programs and publications focused on the lake. One of these was the "Lessons of the Lake" teacher workshops held at the Turtle Cove Environmental Research Station on Pass Manchac. Initiated in April 1991, this program allowed several groups of teachers each year to spend a weekend at Turtle Cove to learn about the biology and ecology of the lake and its surrounding wetlands and to obtain resource materials for their own classroom activities to teach students about the lake. Many of these teachers then returned to Turtle Cove or other lake sites for field trips with their students for further lessons about the lake. This tradition of educational activities became an important part of the mission of the Lake Pontchartrain Basin Foundation. Educational materials produced by the foundation have included "Lessons on the Lake: An Educator's Guide to the Pontchartrain Basin" (Banbury et al. 1997) and "A Guide to the Wetlands of the Lake Pontchartrain Basin" (Maygarden et al. 2000).

The year 1992 brought new leadership to the foundation, when Carlton Dufrechou replaced Steve Cochran as executive director and Neil Armingeon was appointed as the environmental director (LPBF 1992a, 1992b). This pair was to provide outstanding leadership for the foundation through the next decade.

Another continuing program sponsored by the Lake Pontchartrain Basin Foundation was the "Basics of the Basin" research symposia, held every two years since 1992. These symposia, the brain-child and pet project of foundation board member John Lopez, became an important forum for scientists conducting research on the lake and its surrounding environments to communicate their research results to others.

Probably the most significant contribution of the foundation has been its ability to build coalitions of citizen groups and state agencies working together to improve the Lake Pontchartrain environment. These have included north-shore river groups concerned with water quality in lake tributaries, such as Citizens for a Clean Tangipahoa, Sparkling River Committee, Tickfaw River Basin Group, Three Rivers Basin Foundation, and Lake Maurepas Society. Often competitive groups, such as recreational and commercial fishermen, have worked together for the mutual benefit of the lake. Scientists from various universities around the lake, such as University of New Orleans, Tulane University, Louisiana State University, and Southeastern Louisiana University, have cooperated on research projects. Personnel from various state or federal agencies have often met with volunteers from these grassroots organizations and academic institutions to discuss issues relative to the lake.

In 1991 the foundation held a series of public meetings to begin the process of developing a Comprehensive Management Plan for the Basin (Phase I). Then an interagency working group of state and federal agencies, with substantial input from a diverse advisory working group, began meeting in monthly workshops (Phase II) to formulate a plan in five major issue categories: education/outreach, renewable resources, uses, pollution, and institutional (LPBF 1993c). The Draft Comprehensive Management Plan was issued in April 1993, consisting of sections on improving the basin's water quality, protecting the basin's essential habitat, increasing education and public participation, and promoting plan implementation. For each of these sections, goals were identified and specific objectives outlined to meet the goals. The four goals were: (1) improve basin water quality through a comprehensive program of point and nonpoint pollutant source reduction that targets urban stormwater runoff, sewage, industrial pollution, agricultural runoff, and saltwater intrusion; (2) protect and restore land-based and aquatic essential habitat in the Pontchartrain basin; (3) educate the public on a broad array of issues involving pollution in the basin to encourage active public and private participation in the cleanup and to deter further environmental degradation; and (4) develop an organizational structure for the basinwide cleanup effort that will promote coordination among public and private entities whose actions affect the use, restoration, and/or preservation of the Lake Pontchartrain basin. This Draft Comprehensive Management Plan became the basis for developing strategies for implementing the plan, ranking actions, determining costs and schedules, identifying lead agencies and groups, pinpointing sources of funding, and utilizing existing information and programs

(Phase III). The final official Lake Pontchartrain Basin Foundation Comprehensive Management Plan resulting from Phase III was released in October 1995 (LPBF 1995c), with focus on three major environmental concerns impacting the basin: sewage and agricultural runoff; stormwater runoff; and saltwater intrusion and wetland loss. The plan was intended to serve as a road map to guide the restoration efforts of the foundation during subsequent years. The plan was enhanced in 2004 when a Comprehensive Habitat Management Plan Committee was formed to revise and expand the section on saltwater intrusion and wetland loss to include all habitats, resulting in an addendum to the Comprehensive Management Plan (LPBF 2006a).

The lake cleanup effort received a significant boost in 1993, when Senator J. Bennett Johnston was successful in securing a federal appropriation of $3.8 million through the Environmental Protection Agency to address the problems of untreated dairy farm waste, community sewage, and urban runoff in the basin (LPBF 1993a, 1993b).

Increased environmental awareness has resulted in greater attempts to preserve or restore natural areas in the basin, and fortunately there are many areas of public lands set aside for protection and public access (Maygarden et al. 2000). New national wildlife refuges, state parks, wildlife management areas, and other nature preserves have been created to protect these remnants. Hopefully their size and number will continue to increase. Among these was the Bayou Sauvage National Wildlife Refuge established in 1990 with about 23,000 acres (9308 ha) of mostly marsh habitat within the city limits of New Orleans (in the area once slated to become the New Orleans East development). Another was the Big Branch Marsh National Wildlife Refuge dedicated in October 1994, beginning with a parcel of 3700 acres (1497 ha) of marsh and forest habitat on the north shore of Lake Pontchartrain but projected to eventually encompass some 12,000 acres (4856 ha; LPBF 1995a, 1997a). Subsequent growth has actually resulted in a total of more than 15,000 acres (6070 ha) in the refuge. Another major public land acquisition occurred in 2001, when the Richard King Mellon Foundation donated 62,500 acres (25,300 ha) of mostly cypress-tupelo swamp on the southern side of Lake Maurepas to create the state Maurepas Swamp Wildlife Management Area.

But the restoration effort has been neither easy nor straightforward, and there have been significant setbacks. Algal blooms are still frequent, and major blooms occur following each opening of the Bonnet Carré Spillway, such as in 1995, 1997, and 2008. In spite of these all too frequent setbacks, the coordinated restoration effort spearheaded by the Lake Pontchartrain Basin Foundation has resulted in significant water quality improvements in the lake. With the banning of shell dredging, water clarity increased dramatically (Francis et al. 1994; Francis and Poirrier 1999). Improved control of sewage and dairy farm runoff into rivers of the north shore resulted in reduced fecal coliform levels on the northern side of the lake. Several municipal sewage treatment systems on the north shore were improved. Camps and other residences located on the rivers were required to install individual water treatment systems. Many farmers in the area installed catchment basins or lagoons to collect and retain the runoff from their milking operations. Within these lagoons, solids will settle out and be decomposed by aerobic bacteria. Excess water and eventually the accumulated sludge at the bottom of the lagoon can be pumped out and spread over pasture land. The continuing effort to address these and other pollution problems of the Tangipahoa River and other drainages of the Pontchartrain basin resulted in significant improvement to the water quality in these rivers, as well as that of the lake. Although not considered completely clean, the Tangipahoa River had improved sufficiently that the warning signs were finally removed in 2002. This improvement also contributed to the improvement of Lake Pontchartrain water quality and hopefully will continue.

Significant progress also has been accomplished for the southern shore of Lake Pontchartrain. By the close of the century, public swimming could be once again considered feasible during dry weather conditions (Jin et al. 1999; Englande et al. 2002), and in October 1999 a Lake Pontchartrain Swimming Task Force was named to consider options for reopening south-shore beaches. Microbial levels, however, remain high in the stormwater discharge canals and increase levels in the lake during pumping activity following storm events. Thus, the lake is unsuitable for swimming near the drainage canals for at least two to three days following a storm event with rainfall greater than 0.5 in. (Barbé et al. 2001). But for samples taken during the summers of 1996–2000, with a minimum of three days of dry weather and no pumping activity from the drainage canals, analyses for fecal coliform, *Escherichia coli*, and enterococci were almost all within recommended standards for swimming.

The cleanup effort received another significant boost when the Pontchartrain Restoration Act was passed by the U.S. House of Representatives in May 2000. The foundation began more intensive water quality monitoring in August 2000 at ten sites considered important historical recreation sites (Laketown, Bonnabel Boat Launch, Old Beach at Bayou St. John, Pontchartrain Beach, Lincoln Beach, Bogue Falaya Park, Tchefuncte Boat Launch, Bayou Castine, Fontainebleau Beach, and Northshore Beach) and made their results available to the public on a weekly online report (LPBF 2000b, 2001b, 2001c). Initial efforts were focused on Lincoln Beach as the first site to be redeveloped. In February

2002, the Lake Pontchartrain Basin Foundation declared the lake "recovered" and safe for swimming based upon water quality testing conducted on more than 2000 water samples collected during the previous year (*Baton Rouge Advocate*, February 21, 2002).

Although significant progress has been made in cleaning up the lake and restoring its value as a recreational resource, much is yet to be done. Water quality degradation has been, and continues to be, one of the major environmental concerns in the Pontchartrain basin. Health advisories are still in effect for the lake and several tributaries, and water quality problems will remain for years to come. In 2005 Hurricane Katrina had a profound impact on the lake and its surrounding environments and resulted in a massive influx of all types of pollutants into the lake. The long-term effects of these pollutants are not known, but they could be substantial, although initial reports of minimal effects were encouraging. Hopefully flushing of the system with clean water, time, and continued environmental protection efforts will continue to diminish their long-term effects.

As the human population continues to grow, the threats to water quality will also increase, but so will the potential value of a clean lake. Environmental protection must continue to be a major concern if the lake's true value is to be restored. Constant vigilance and concern must be maintained in the future to continue this progress toward a restored Lake Pontchartrain. If these efforts continue, those who recognize its value will eventually be rewarded with a pristine Lake Pontchartrain that will be a treasure to us all.

Part 3

CHARACTERISTICS OF THE
LAKE PONTCHARTRAIN
ESTUARINE SYSTEM TODAY

Introduction

Lake Pontchartrain and its sister lakes are major Gulf coast estuarine waters supporting an abundance of life and providing significant fisheries and recreational opportunities. Efforts to conserve and restore this ecosystem will hopefully continue and its environmental quality will improve. The following chapters describe the major environmental characteristics of the lakes as they are today.

12.

Physical Description

Definition

Because the Lake Pontchartrain system receives saline water input from its passes (average about 1.5 cu. mi./year, 6.4 km³/year, or about 33% of the total inflow to the lake; Waldon and Bryan 1999), as well as fresh water from its tributary rivers and bayous (1.7 cu. mi./year, 7.2 km³/year, or about 36% of the total inflow), it is defined as an estuary. In the strict sense, this mixing of fresh and salt water means that Lake Pontchartrain is not truly a lake. By definition, a lake is "an inland body of water, usually fresh water, formed by glaciers, river drainage, etc., larger than a pool or pond" (*Webster's New World Dictionary*, College Edition). Although somewhat inland, formed by river drainage, and larger than a pool or pond, Lake Pontchartrain is actually more coastal and brackish water rather than fresh water. Thus, it more closely fits the definition of an estuary, "a semi-enclosed body of water that has a free connection with the open sea and within which the sea water is measurably diluted with fresh water derived from land drainage" (Pritchard 1967). However, Swenson (1980a) noted that Lake Pontchartrain does not fit this definition either because it has a "restricted" connection to Lake Borgne, rather than a free connection with the open sea, and therefore should be considered an "associated water body" to an estuary (Officer 1976). According to this definition, Lake Borgne and Mississippi Sound are the estuary, and Lake Pontchartrain and Lake Maurepas are associated water bodies. However, the two passes connecting Lake Pontchartrain to Lake Borgne, although narrow, are still freely open and allow continuous mixing of fresh and salt water. Thus, the entire Lake Borgne-

Pontchartrain-Maurepas complex may be regarded as an estuarine system. It certainly functions as one continuous unit. In fact virtually all coastal waters of Louisiana, even though they are not semi-enclosed, function as one large estuarine complex because of the dramatic effect of the Mississippi River in the northern Gulf of Mexico. This mixing of fresh and saline waters is the most significant and definitive characteristic of estuaries and gives Lake Pontchartrain its characteristic estuarine nature. Freshwater inflow provides three key functions to an estuary: reduction of salinity, induction of mixing, and delivery of nutrients and sediments (Stickney 1984).

Dimensions

Lake Pontchartrain is one of North America's largest bodies of water, with a surface area of 640 sq. mi. (1660 km^2), about the same size as Lake Okeechobee in Florida (Table 12). Lake Borgne is about 268 sq. mi. (694 km^2) and Lake Maurepas about 91 sq. mi. (235 km^2). The lakes are relatively shallow and mostly quite uniform in depth, averaging less than about 10–15 ft. (3–5 m). However, deep dredge holes have been created in places along the south shore of Lake Pontchartrain (Connor et al. 2001a, 2001b). Two large dredge holes more than 30 ft. (10 m) deep once occurred off the Lakefront Park area where the lake was dredged to provide fill for the Lakefront Land Reclamation Project in 1926–1930, but these have been largely filled in to a depth of about 20 ft. (6 m) by natural accretion of new sediments. Two deeper holes are present at the mouth of the Inner Harbor Navigation Canal, the results of dredging to create land for the Lakefront Airport in 1934, and these have apparently been maintained at a current depth of 39–52 ft. (12–16 m) by tidal scouring from the canal. Just to the east is the Lakefront Airport dredge pit, with depths of 66–72 ft. (20–22 m), created in 1977–1980 for an airport expansion project. Further to the east off of South Point is the South Point dredge pit, with depths of about 56 ft. (17 m), created in the 1970s by dredging to fill the Little Woods Canal prior to construction of the hurricane protection levee. The LaBranche dredge pit off the LaBranche Wetlands is 16 ft. (5 m) deep and was created in 1993–1994 when the lake was dredged to provide fill for the LaBranche Wetlands Marsh Creation Project. These deeper holes can become stratified, with denser, higher salinity water accumulating near the bottom and becoming anoxic, unsuitable habitat for most living organisms.

Deep scour holes maintained by tidal water movement exist at the mouths of rivers and passes entering the lakes, and depths within the passes are also much greater, apparently as a result of scouring from tidal currents. Beyond the

Table 12 Dimensions of Lake Pontchartrain and adjacent water bodies

Lake	Surface Area	Volume	Typical Maximum Depth
Lake Pontchartrain	640 sq. mi. (1660 km²)*	223 billion cu. ft. (6.6 billion m³)*	13–15 ft. (4–5 m)‡
Lake Borgne	268 sq. mi. (694 km²)†	49 billion cu. ft. (1.4 billion m³)†	7–10 ft. (2–3 m)‡
Lake Maurepas	91 sq. mi. (235 km²)†	23 billion cu. ft. (0.6 billion m³)†	10–12 ft. (3–4 m)‡
Lake St. Catherine	8 sq. mi. (20 km²)†	696 million cu. ft. (20 million m³)†	4–5 ft. (1.5 m)‡

Pass	Length	Width	Average Depth	Maximum Depth
The Rigolets	9 mi. (14.5 km)*	875 yd. (800 m)*	26 ft. (8 m)*	93 ft. (28 m)‡
Chef Menteur Pass	7 mi. (11.3 km)*	284 yd. (260 m)*	43 ft. (13 m)*	90 ft. (27 m)‡
Pass Manchac	9 mi. (15 km)*	360 yd. (330 m)*	26 ft. (8 m)*	56 ft. (17 m)‡

*Swenson (1980b)
†Barrett (1970)
‡From NOAA nautical chart no. 11369 (1996)

scour holes in the lakes, shoaling areas occur where sediments settle out of suspension as flow velocities drop when the pass water enters the lake.

The Pass Manchac channel was described as being 7 ft. (2.1 m) deep in 1924 (H.R., 68 Cong. 2 Sess., Doc. 473:11; referenced in Irion et al. 1994), but is considerably deeper today (25–56 ft. or 8–17 m deep, with at least one hole of 98-ft. or 30-m depth; average center-of-channel depth is 36 ft. or 11 m; U.S. Army Corp of Engineers 1992). The pass was apparently never dredged, although a Corps of Engineers project authorized in 1910 called for removal of snags, logs, and other obstructions throughout its length (U.S. Army Corps of Engineers 1998a). Its increase in depth has apparently resulted from natural effects of scouring and subsidence in the absence of sediments from Mississippi River water that previously accumulated in the passes.

Shorelines

The Lake Pontchartrain shoreline is approximately 125 mi. (200 km) long, with about 30% being urban (New Orleans, Metairie, and Kenner on the south;

Figure 12.1 Lake Maurepas cypress shoreline near the mouth of the Tickfaw River (Photograph by the author)

Slidell on the east; and Mandeville on the north). The remaining 70% is relatively natural wetlands of marshes and cypress swamps, with a few scattered groups of lakeshore camps such as along Chef Menteur Highway near Fort Pike, at the mouth of the Tchefuncte River near Madisonville, and at Frenier on the southwestern side of the lake. The original condition of the New Orleans lakeshore is unknown, except that Iberville described the southern side of the lake as bordered by a wide "prairie" (or marsh) before the tall trees (McWilliams 1981). The 42-mi. (68-km) shoreline of Lake Maurepas is almost completely natural cypress swamps (Figure 12.1) or fresh marsh, with the only road access at Manchac. Lake Borgne, arbitrarily bordered on the east by a line from Malheureux Point to Lighthouse Point, has an approximate shoreline length of 78 mi. (125 km) and is almost exclusively brackish marshes with no road access.

Fourteen shoreline types have been identified based upon ecological and geological attributes, including eleven natural types and three man-made (Table 13). Their distribution primarily reflects the impact of salinity (increasing from Lake Maurepas to Lake Borgne) and the incidence of human activities (highest in Lake Pontchartrain). The Lake Pontchartrain shoreline is more diverse than those of Lakes Borgne and Maurepas, with mostly swamp on the western side (Figure 12.2), human structures on the southern side (see Figure 8.4), a diverse mixture of both natural and man-made features (see Figure 8.3) on the northern side, and brackish marsh to the east (Figure 12.3).

Table 13 Shoreline types in the Pontchartrain basin

Shoreline Type	Lake Maurepas	Pass Manchac	Lake Pontchartrain	Lake St. Catherine	Rigolets	Lake Borgne*
Swamp (Figures 12.1, 12.2)	28.0 mi. (45.1 km)	0.1 mi. (0.2 km)	22.8 mi. (36.7 km)			
Fresh Marsh	4.0 mi. (6.4 km)	7.3 mi. (11.7 km)	1.8 mi. (2.9 km)			
Fresh Marsh and Swamp	8.4 mi. (13.5 km)	1.6 mi. (2.6 km)	4.6 mi. (7.4 km)			
Intermediate Marsh (Figure 7.1)			5.9 mi. (9.5 km)			
Intermediate Marsh and Swamp			0.3 mi. (0.5 km)			
Brackish Marsh (Figure 12.3)			30.1 mi. (48.4 km)	16.0 mi. (25.7 km)	17.7 mi. (28.5 km)	78.4 mi. (126.1 km)
Brackish Marsh and Swamp			0.1 mi. (0.2 km)			
Salt Marsh						43.4 mi. (69.8 km)
Sand Beach (Figure 12.4)			8.6 mi. (13.8 km)		0.2 mi. (0.3 km)	2.0 mi. (3.2 km)
Shell Beach (Figure 12.5)			0.3 mi. (0.5 km)			6.9 mi. (11.1 km)
Natural Bank	1.2 mi. (1.9 km)	2.5 mi. (4.0 km)	0.1 mi. (0.2 km)			
Seawall (Figure 8.4)			4.3 mi. (6.9 km)			0.8 mi. (1.3 km)
Bulkhead (Figure 8.3)	0.1 mi. (0.2 km)	0.8 mi. (1.3 km)	11.8 mi. (19.0 km)	2.9 mi. (4.7 km)	0.7 mi. (1.1 km)	0.3 mi. (0.5 km)
Riprap (Figure 12.6–12.8)	0.6 mi. (1.0 km)		34.6 mi. (55.7 km)		0.1 mi. (0.2 km)	1.1 mi. (1.8 km)
Total	42.3 mi. (68.1 km)	12.4 mi. (20.0 km)	125.3 mi. (201.6 km)	18.9 mi. (30.4 km)	19.0 mi. (30.6 km)	133.0 mi. (214.0 km)

After Beall et al. (2001)
*Includes about 55 mi. (88.5 km) of shoreline in Mississippi Sound

PHYSICAL DESCRIPTION 167

Figure 12.2 Lake Pontchartrain cypress shoreline near the mouth of the Tangipahoa River (Photograph by the author)

Figure 12.3 Brackish marsh of marshhay cordgrass (*Spartina patens*) at Northshore Beach (Photograph by the author)

168 CHARACTERISTICS OF THE ESTUARINE SYSTEM TODAY

Figure 12.4 Sand beaches near (A) Point Platte and (B) Point aux Herbes (Photographs by the author)

PHYSICAL DESCRIPTION 169

Figure 12.5 Rangia shell hash beach in Metairie (Photograph by the author)

Figure 12.6 Metairie Linear Park (Photograph by the author)

170 CHARACTERISTICS OF THE ESTUARINE SYSTEM TODAY

Figure 12.7 Riprap shoreline in Metairie (Photograph by the author)

Figure 12.8 Riprap shoreline and old bulkhead at the Washout near Frenier (Photograph by the author)

Three beach types have been recognized and make up about half of these shorelines, although typical beaches are relatively rare, because most shores are muddy (Saucier 1963). Most widespread in Lake Maurepas and western Lake Pontchartrain is a narrow (less than 25 ft. or 7.6 m wide) strip of fine to very fine sand, silt, and shell, with numerous cypress trees and stumps occurring some distance offshore. These shorelines are also the sites of abundant accumulations of "coffee grounds," the bits and pieces of organic detritus so characteristic of the lake (see Figure 6.1). More typical beach-like shores with very fine to fine sand and little shell content are present on the north shore between Mandeville and the Rigolets (Figure 12.4). Other beaches are composed almost entirely of rangia clam shells (Figure 12.5), such as near the mouth of the Tangipahoa River, east of the Tchefuncte River, and several miles south of Frenier. Some of these represent destroyed Indian middens. In addition to the permanent seawalls and bulkheads of some urban shorelines, rock or concrete rip-rap has been placed along many shorelines to reduce the rate of shoreline erosion (Figures 12.6–12.8).

Passes, Rivers, and Bayous

In addition to the deep natural passes that connect the three Lakes of Pontchartrain (Table 12), an artificial pass, the Inner Harbor Navigation Canal (completed in 1923), connects Lake Pontchartrain with the Mississippi River (but separated by a lock) and with another artificial canal, the Intracoastal Waterway, which passes through both Chef Menteur Pass and the Rigolets. Since 1963 the Mississippi River Gulf Outlet (MRGO) has connected the Inner Harbor Navigation Canal directly with Breton Sound to the southeast. The total length of the Inner Harbor Navigation Canal and MRGO system is 19 mi. (30 km), with an average depth of 25 ft. (7.5 m; Swenson 1980b). When first completed, the MRGO had a depth of 36 ft. (11 m) and a width of 500 ft. (151 m), but shoreline erosion has since increased its width to more than 2000 ft. (600 m) in places (Ledoux 1993) and it has broken through the marsh into Lake Borgne at its upper end.

Five rivers provide freshwater inflow (Amite, Blind, and Tickfaw Rivers into Lake Maurepas; Tangipahoa and Tchefuncte Rivers into Lake Pontchartrain), along with several smaller bayous (Chinchuba, Castine, Cane, Lacombe, Bonfouca, St. John, LaBranche/Trepagnier, and Piquant). In addition, the Pearl River flows into Lake Borgne. Prior to the creation of drainage ditches and levees built to protect New Orleans and Jefferson Parish from flooding, other bayous entered the lake from the south shore, but their number and locations are confused. According to various nautical charts of the lake (Table 14A), these

172 CHARACTERISTICS OF THE ESTUARINE SYSTEM TODAY

Table 14 Lake Pontchartrain place names from selected U.S. Coastal Survey nautical charts

A. Locations along the south shore of Lake Pontchartrain				
Current Name	Location*	1967 Chart (No. 1269)	1934 Chart (No. 1269)	1906 Chart (No. 193)
The Rigolets	0 mi. (0 km)	The Rigolets	Rigolets	The Rigolets
Bayou de Lesaire	3.1 mi. (5 km)	Bayou de Lesaire		
Big Cedar Bayou	5.6 mi. (9 km)	Shell Point Bayou		
Little Cedar Bayou	5.9 mi. (9.5 km)			
Chef Menteur Pass	7.5 mi. (12 km)	Chef Menteur Pass	Chef Menteur Pass	Chef Menteur Pass
Bayou Chevee	9.0 mi. (14.5 km)	Bayou Chevee		
	12.1 mi. (19.5 km)		Irish Bayou	Irish Bayou
Point aux Herbes	13.1 mi. (21 km)	Point aux Herbes	Point aux Herbes	Point aux Herbes
	13.1 mi. (21 km)			Turtle Bayou
Interstate 10	13.1 mi. (21 km)	Interstate 10		
U.S. Highway 11	13.4 mi. (21.5 km)	U.S. Highway 11	U.S. Highway 11	
Irish Bayou Lagoon	14.3 mi. (23 km)	Irish Bayou Lagoon		
South Point	14.9 mi. (24 km)	South Point	South Point	
Southern Railroad	14.9 mi. (24 km)	Southern Railroad	Southern Railroad	New Orleans and Northeastern Railroad
	15.5 mi. (25 km)			Bayou Castiglione
	17.4 mi. (28 km)		Black Bayou	Black Bayou
	18.6 mi. (30 km)		Little River	Little River
Little Woods	20.5 mi. (33 km)	Little Woods		
Lincoln Beach	21.1 mi. (34 km)	Lincoln Beach		
Edge Lake	23.6 mi. (38 km)	Edge Lake		Bayou Couchon and Little Bayou Couchon
Seabrook	24.9 mi. (40 km)	Seabrook		
Lakefront Airport	25.5 mi. (41 km)	Lakefront Airport	Airport under construction	
Inner Harbor Navigation Canal	26.7 mi. (43 km)	Inner Harbor Navigation Canal	Inner Harbor Navigation Canal	

PHYSICAL DESCRIPTION 173

Current Name	Location*	1967 Chart (No. 1269)	1934 Chart (No. 1269)	1906 Chart (No. 193)
	27.3 mi. (44 km)			Peoples Avenue Canal
Milneburg	28.0 mi. (45 km)	Milneburg	Milneburg	Milneburg
London Avenue Canal	28.9 mi. (46.5 km)	Canal	Canal	
Bayou St. John	29.2 mi. (47 km)	Bayou St. John	Bayou St. John	Bayou St. John
Orleans Canal	30.1 mi. (48.5 km)	Canal		
West End	31.1 mi. (50 km)		West End and New Canal	West End and New Canal
17th Street (Outfall) Canal	31.7 mi. (51 km)	Outfall Canal	Upper Drainage Canal	Upper Drainage Canal
Bucktown	32.0 mi. (51.5 km)	Bucktown		
Indian Beach	32.3 mi. (52 km)	Indian Beach	Indian Bayou	Indian Bayou
Bonnabel Canal and Boat Launch	32.9 mi. (53 km)		Bayou Tchoupitoulas	Bayou Tchoupitoulas
Causeway	33.6 mi. (54 km)		Bayou Le Bar	Bayou Le Bar
Suburban Canal	35.1 mi. (56.5 km)	Canal	Bayou Laurier	Bayou Laurier
Elmwood Canal	37.3 mi. (60 km)	Canal		
Pontchartrain Center	38.5 mi. (62 km)			
Duncan Canal	39.2 mi. (63 km)	Canal	Alligator Bayou	Alligator Bayou
Parish Line (Duncan) Canal	41.0 mi. (66 km)	Canal		
Bayou Piquant	42.6 mi. (68.5 km)	Bayou Piquant	Double Bayou	Double Bayou
Walker Canal	43.8 mi. (70.5 km)	Walker Canal	Walkers Canal	Walkers Canal
Bayou LaBranche	46.3 mi. (74.5 km)	Bayou LaBranche	Bayou le Branch	Bayou le Branch
Bonnet Carré Floodway	46.6 mi. (75 km)	Bonnet Carré Floodway	Bonnet Carré Spillway	
Frenier	50.3 mi. (81 km)	Frenier	Frenier	Frenier
Shell Bank Bayou	54.7 mi. (88 km)	Bayou Jasmin	Shell Bank Bayou	Shell Bank Bayou
Desert Bayou	56.6 mi. (91 km)	Desert Bayou	Bayou Desir	Bayou Desair?
Ruddock Canal	57.8 mi. (93 km)	Ruddock Canal	Ruddock Canal	Ruddock
Bayou Black	59.7 mi. (96 km)	Black Bayou		
Pass Manchac	67.1 mi. (108 km)	Pass Manchac	Pass Manchac	Pass Manchac

174 CHARACTERISTICS OF THE ESTUARINE SYSTEM TODAY

B. Locations along the north shore of Lake Pontchartrain

Current Name	Location†	1967 Chart (No. 1269)	1934 Chart (No. 1269)	1906 Chart (No. 193)
Pass Manchac	42.3 mi. (68 km)	Pass Manchac	Pass Manchac	Pass Manchac
Tangipahoa River	39.2 mi. (63 km)	Tangipahoa River	Tangipahoa River	Tangipahoa River
Port Louis	34.2 mi. (55 km)	Port Louis		
	32.3 mi. (52 km)		Black River	Black River
Tchefuncta River	31.1 mi. (50 km)	Tchefuncta River	Chefuncte River	Chefuncte River
Bayou Chinchuba	28.6 mi. (46 km)	Bayou Chinchuba		
Lewisburg	27.3 mi. (44 km)	Lewisburg	Lewisburg	Lewisburg
Causeway	27.3 mi. (44 km)	Causeway		
Mandeville	26.7 mi. (43 km)	Mandeville	Mandeville	Mandeville
Bayou Castine	24.9 mi. (40 km)	Bayou Castine	Bayou Castine	Bayou Castine
Green Point	23.0 mi. (37 km)	Green Point	Green Point	Green Point
Cane Bayou	21.8 mi. (35 km)	Cane Bayou	Big Branch	Big Branch
Goose Point	16.8 mi. (27 km)	Goose Point	Ragged Point	Ragged Point
Lacombe Bayou	14.9 mi. (24 km)	Lacombe Bayou	Bayou Lacombe	Bayou Lacombe
Point Platte	13.7 mi. (22 km)	Point Platte	Point Platte	Point Platte
	12.4 mi. (20 km)		Bayou Ruis	Bayou Ruis
Canal	11.8 mi. (19 km)	Canal		
	10.6 mi. (17 km)		Bayou du Chien	Bayou du Chien
Point du Chien	10.3 mi. (16.5 km)	Point du Chien	Point au Chien	Point au Chien
Bayou Bonfouca	9.3 mi. (15 km)	Bayou Bonfouca	Bonfouca Bayou	Bonfouca Bayou
Big Point	7.5 mi. (12 km)	Big Point	Big Point	Big Point
Northshore Beach	7.1 mi. (11.5 km)			
Southern Railroad	5.9 mi. (9.5 km)	Southern Railroad	Southern Railroad	New Orleans and Northeastern Railroad
U.S. Highway 11	5.9 mi. (9.5 km)	U.S. Highway 11		
North Shore	5.6 mi. (9 km)	North Shore		
Eden Isles	4.4 mi. (7 km)	Grand Lagoon	Grand Lagoon	Grand Lagoon
Interstate 10	4.0 mi. (6.5 km)	Interstate 10		
Howze Beach	3.7 mi. (6 km)	Howze Beach		

PHYSICAL DESCRIPTION 175

Current Name	Location†	1967 Chart (No. 1269)	1934 Chart (No. 1269)	1906 Chart (No. 193)
Little Lagoon	1.9 mi. (3 km)	Little Lagoon		
Salt Bayou	1.6 mi. (2.5 km)	Salt Bayou	Salt Bayou	Salt Bayou
Treasure Island	1.2 mi. (2 km)			
The Rigolets	0 mi. (0 km)	The Rigolets	Rigolets	The Rigolets

*Estimated shoreline distance measured on nautical chart from the Rigolets clockwise
†Estimated shoreline distance measured on nautical chart from the Rigolets counterclockwise

included in the Orleans Parish area Irish Bayou, Turtle Bayou, Bayou Castiglione, Black Bayou, Little River, Bayou Couchon, and Little Bayou Couchon. West of Bayou St. John were Indian Bayou, Bayou Tchoupitoulas, Bayou Le Bar (or Labarre), Bayou Laurier, and Alligator Bayou, as well as LaBranche/Trepagnier (also known as Bayou Tigouyou), and Piquant (once known as Double Bayou). The eastern portion of the city once drained to the east via Bayou Sauvage along Gentilly Ridge into Chef Menteur Pass and via Bayou Bienvenue into Lake Borgne.

Most of these bayous have now been replaced by the canals and pumping stations of the New Orleans, Metairie, and Kenner urban areas. Indian Bayou and Bayou Tchoupitoulas have been replaced by the Bonnabel Canal (Figure 12.9), Bayou La Bar by the Lake Pontchartrain Causeway approaches, Bayou Laurier by Suburban Canal, and Alligator Bayou by Duncan Canal. Some of the canals, including the Inner Harbor Navigation Canal, London Avenue Canal, Bayou St. John, Orleans Canal, 17th Street Canal, and St. Charles Parish Line Canal are at lake level. Others drain regions of the city that are now below sea level and have pumping stations to move their drainage into the lake (or into another canal).

Three small bayous (now blocked by the tracks of the Illinois Central Railroad) drained the swamps on the western side of the lake: Bayou Jasmine (now known as Shell Bank Bayou), Desert Bayou (once known as Bayou deSert or deSair), and Joe's Bayou (now known as Bayou Black; Laurent 1982). Coastal features and waterways along the north shore (Table 14B) and in Lakes Maurepas and Borgne have been less modified by human impacts.

The total Lake Pontchartrain drainage basin covers some 4872 sq. mi. (12,618 km^2), with a total input of fresh water averaging about 4800 cfs (136 m^3/sec; excluding flow from the Pearl River basin, with a drainage area of 8669 sq. mi. [22,453 km^2], and from periodic openings of the Bonnet Carré Spillway; Table 15). The highest levels of inflow occur in the winter and spring, especially

Figure 12.9 Bonnabel Canal pumping station in Metairie (Photograph by the author)

December and May, with the lowest flow from August to November (Xu and Wu 2006). Cry (1978) estimated the total input of water from Pass Manchac into Lake Pontchartrain to be about 4484 cfs (127 m^3/sec), with another 1942 cfs (55 m^3/sec) flowing directly into Lake Pontchartrain (for a total of 6426 cfs or 182 m^3/sec). The flushing time for Lake Pontchartrain (or the time required to replace the existing fresh water in the estuary) has been estimated to be about sixty days (Swenson 1980b).

Waldon and Bryan (1999) estimated the tributary inflow into the lake to be about 36% of the total inflow (about 1.7 cu. mi./year or 7.2 km^3/year), plus another 11% (0.5 cu. mi./year or 2.1 km^3/year) from urban stormwater, direct rainfall, and leakage from the Mississippi River (0.02, 0.24, and 0.24 cu. mi./year or 0.1, 1.0, and 1.0 km^3/year, respectively). Lake Pontchartrain is also affected significantly by outflow from the Pearl River, which flows into Lake Borgne and forms the eastern boundary of the basin. Much of its flow into Lake Borgne can be carried into the Rigolets and thence into Lake Pontchartrain (Haralampides and McCorquodale 2001). Waldon and Bryan estimated that about 20% (0.9 cu. mi./year or 3.9 km^3/year) of the total inflow of water into Lake Pontchartrain was provided by the Pearl River. The remaining 33% (average about 1.5 cu. mi./year or 6.4 km^3/year) is saline water input from its passes. Xu and Wu (2006) estimated the average annual inflow from the three major rivers (Amite, Tangipahoa, and Tickfaw) to be 0.8 cu. mi. or 3.29 km^3.

Table 15 River inputs to Lake Pontchartrain

Drainage	Basin Area	Long-Term Average Annual Flow
Amite/Comite	1819 sq. mi. (4711 km²)	2146 cfs (60.8 m³/sec)
Tangipahoa	771 sq. mi. (1997 km²)	1194 cfs (33.8 m³/sec)
Tickfaw	727 sq. mi. (1883 km²)	345 cfs (9.8 m³/sec)
Tchefuncte	450 sq. mi. (1165 km²)	166 cfs (4.7 m³/sec)
Blind/other Lake Maurepas	412 sq. mi. (1067 km²)	375 cfs (10.6 m³/sec)
Bayou Lacombe	96 sq. mi. (249 km²)	53 cfs (1.5 m³/sec)
Bayou Bonfouca/Liberty	73 sq. mi. (189 km²)	148 cfs (4.2 m³/sec)
Urban	63 sq. mi. (163 km²)	185 cfs (5.2 m³/sec)
Bonnet Carré Spillway	11 sq. mi. (28 km²)	12 cfs (0.3 m³/sec)
Bayou Chinchuba	10 sq. mi. (26 km²)	11 cfs (0.3 m³/sec)
Bayou Castine	8 sq. mi. (21 km²)	10 cfs (0.3 m³/sec)
Others (marshes and swamps)	432 sq. mi. (1119 km²)	159 cfs (4.5 m³/sec)
Total	4872 sq. mi. (12,618 km²)	4804 cfs (136 m³/sec)

Data from McCorquodale et al. (2001a)

Climate

The climate of the Pontchartrain basin is subtropical and humid, with annual average temperature at New Orleans of 68.8°F (20.4°C; U.S. Census Bureau 2006 Statistical Abstract, www.census.gov/compendia/statab/2006). Daily mean temperatures are 52.6°F (11.4°C) in January (daily minimum and maximum are 43.4 and 61.8°F or 6.3 and 16.5°C) and 82.7°F (28.2°C) in July (daily minimum and maximum are 74.2 and 91.1°F or 23.4 and 32.8°C). The lake has a tempering effect upon the surrounding land areas, with winter temperature south of the lake usually a few degrees warmer than the north shore.

Average temperatures in the open waters of Lake Pontchartrain generally range from about 41 to 50°F (5 to 10°C) in winter (December to February) to about 86°F (30°C) in summer (June to September). Winter temperatures can fall lower when cold fronts pass through, especially in shallow waters, where surfaces may freeze on rare occasions. Shallow marsh waters will also reach higher temperatures in midsummer. Mississippi River water from the Bonnet Carré Spillway and Pearl River water entering via the Rigolets can lower lake temperatures, especially in early spring (Tarver and Savoie 1976).

Table 16 Monthly average precipitation and rain days for New Orleans, Slidell, and Covington

Month	New Orleans		Slidell		Covington		Average	
	Inches	Days	Inches	Days	Inches	Days	Inches (cm)	Days
January	5.5	10	6.1	11	5.2	10	5.6 (14.2)	10.3
February	5.4	9	5.0	9	5.3	8	5.2 (13.2)	8.7
March	4.8	9	5.6	10	6.1	7	5.5 (14.0)	8.7
April	4.5	7	4.6	7	5.2	7	4.8 (12.2)	7.0
May	4.9	8	5.6	8	5.1	8	5.2 (13.2)	8.0
June	6.0	11	4.7	10	5.0	10	5.2 (13.2)	10.3
July	6.5	14	6.7	13	6.7	14	6.6 (16.8)	3.7
August	6.0	13	5.9	13	5.7	12	5.9 (15.0)	12.7
September	5.5	10	5.3	10	5.1	9	5.3 (13.5)	9.7
October	2.9	6	3.2	7	3.3	5	3.1 (7.9)	6.0
November	4.3	8	4.2	8	4.2	7	4.2 (10.7)	7.7
December	5.1	9	4.9	10	5.6	9	5.2 (13.2)	9.3

After Peters and Beall (2001)

Rainfall levels in southeastern Louisiana are high, with normal annual rainfall amounts of 60 in. (152 cm) at New Orleans. However, rainfall over the central part of the lake may be appreciably less, especially during the summer (Saucier 1963). Substantial rainfall occurs during all months, but with slight peaks from January to March and July to September (Table 16). However, because of the more extreme storm events and reduced temperatures and evapotranspiration, freshwater runoff and input to the lakes is substantially higher in the winter and spring. Late summer or autumn tropical storms can result in excessive rainfall and concomitant increased freshwater input, but they can also be associated with massive tidal surges that result in an influx of high salinity water.

At one time the basin received an annual influx of Mississippi River flood water through Bayou Manchac (by way of the Amite River), the Bonnet Carré crevasse, and possibly also via New River (by way of Blind River; Saucier 1963). These sources of fresh water are now blocked by levees on the river, although the Bonnet Carré Spillway is controlled to divert river water into the lake when the river reaches flood stage, and there is some leakage of river water through the spillway at high river levels even when it is not officially open. When the spillway is open, or in the past when crevasses have broken through the levees, tremendous quantities of Mississippi River water enter the lake, swamping the usual discharge from other sources (Table 11).

Sediments and Turbidity

The freshwater rivers and streams that enter the estuary carry suspended silts and clays from upland soil erosion and create muddy substrates of alluvial sediments within the estuary. When the sediment-laden riverine waters mix with the saline waters of the estuary, ionic reactions by the dissolved salts cause the silts and clays to flocculate, increasing their particle size and stimulating their rapid settling out of the water column (Brooks 1969). Substrates within the Lake Pontchartrain estuary are relatively uniform soft silty clay or clayey silt (Flowers and Isphording 1990), with averages of 19% sand, 38% silt, and 43% clay. The predominant bottom type has been described as silty clay (Barrett 1976), with a mean grain size increasing from Lake Maurepas to Lake Borgne (mean ϕ values of 8.5 in Lake Maurepas, 7.1 for Lake Pontchartrain, and 6.2 in Lake Borgne, approximate mean particle diameters less than 0.0039 mm, 0.0078 mm, and 0.0156 mm, respectively). Wave action or other turbulence can resuspend smaller particles, resulting in a segregation of sediments by size fraction based upon the amount of wave action or water movement in an area. Thus deeper waters, as well as shallow areas protected from wave action, tend to be characterized by finer sediments of silt and clay. The finer sediments also tend to accumulate large amounts of organic material. Shorelines with frequent wave-generated sorting of sediments tend to have more sand and less silt and clay. Thus, shorelines such as Goose Point and Point aux Herbes, can be mostly sand, whereas shorelines with less wave action are muddier, such as along the southwestern side of the lake. According to Flowers and Isphording (1990), sandy sediments are found in tidal and river deltas; near the Bonnet Carré Spillway; in near-shore areas along the northern and southern shores; in the eastern lobe of the lake; and as small, isolated patches in the open lake. Strong waves associated with stormy weather can resuspend finer sediments even from the deepest parts of the lake, so the lake is prone to periods of high turbidity associated with stormy weather.

Because of the suspended sediments and planktonic organisms in estuarine waters, they are rarely clear. However, there can be great variation in the relative clarity (or turbidity) of the water. Generally wind is a direct factor in the resuspension of bottom sediments, and thus water turbidity (Darnell 1961). Darnell considered Lake Pontchartrain highly turbid, but still recorded an average Secchi disk depth of about 4 ft. (120 cm). During the late 1980s, however, turbidity was even greater because of the extensive shell dredging being conducted in the lake, with average Secchi disk readings of 24–31 in. (60–80 cm; Francis et al. 1994; Francis and Poirrier 1999). With the banning of shell dredging in the lake in 1990, the average clarity dramatically increased for much of the lake (with average Secchi disk readings of about 50–60 in. or about 120–160 cm in 1993–1995; Francis and Poirrier 1999).

Tides and Water Movements

In most estuaries, consistent and predictable tidal changes (controlled by the lunar phases and to a lesser degree by the sun, because of their gravitational pull on the earth's surface) result in intertidal mudflats alternately flooded and exposed with each tidal cycle of 12.42 hours (semidiurnal or semidaily tides, with two successive tides each day that are about equal) or 24.84 hours (diurnal or daily tides with only one high and low each day). Diurnal tides occur along the Louisiana coast, but tidal ranges are so narrow that those in Lake Pontchartrain are almost insignificant, with a mean range of only 4.3 in. (10.9 cm; Swenson and Chuang 1983). Consequently, there are no typical intertidal mudflats in Lake Pontchartrain. Tidal ranges are highest near the Rigolets and lowest in the areas most distant from the passes (9.7 in. or 24.6 cm at the Rigolets and 3.6 in. or 9.1 cm at Pass Manchac). Even so, tidal currents normally occur in these major passes that average 13–20 in./sec (33–50 cm/sec) on the flood tide and 14–18 in./sec (35–45 cm/sec) on the ebb (Swenson 1980b). About 60% of the tidal flow entering Lake Pontchartrain passes through the Rigolets, 30% through Chef Menteur Pass, and 10% through the Inner Harbor Navigation Canal (Swenson and Chuang 1983). However, half of the volume change is due to subtidal variation, such as wind-induced flow associated with frontal passage.

Because of the narrow tidal range in Lake Pontchartrain, wind-dominated water level changes tend to be much more dramatic than lunar tides. Lunar tides predominate in moving water at wind speeds less than about 6 ft./sec (2 m/sec), and winds predominate when they are greater than about 10 ft./sec (3 m/sec; Swenson 1980b). Winds from the south or east tend to force water into the lake resulting in high water, and winds from the north or west force water out, which can result in low water. These wind-dominated water level changes usually override the relatively minor tidal changes in water depth in the lakes. They become especially dramatic during major storms such as hurricanes, when massive storm surges can cause extensive flooding. The combination of hurricane-force winds, low barometric pressure, and exceptionally large rainfall amounts can result in high water and massive flooding of low-lying areas surrounding the lakes. Because of the broad but shallow nature of the lakes, winds can push substantial amounts of water across the lakes, creating high water on one side and low water on the other. Wind-generated standing waves, or seiches, can result when waves of high water bounce off one shore and move back across the lake.

Tides for Lake Pontchartrain are not included in U.S. government tide tables, although two locations in Lake Borgne are listed (Long Point near the mouth of the Rigolets and Shell Beach at the extreme southern end of the lake). Tides at Shell Beach lag approximately two hours behind tides at Long Point. Tides within most of Lake Pontchartrain, if not affected by wind, would lag approximately seven hours behind the tides at the Rigolets (Swenson 1980a).

Public Lands and Access

Public lands and access points around Lake Pontchartrain are relatively numerous. These include city parks, such as the outstanding Lakeshore Park along the New Orleans lake front, West End Lake Shore Park and "The Point" at the end of Breakwater Drive in New Orleans, Pontchartrain Center Park at the end of Williams Boulevard in Kenner, and the Bonnabel Boat Launch Park at the end of Bonnabel Boulevard in Metairie. The remaining narrow but extensive stretch of land between the lake and the lakeshore levees of Jefferson Parish (Kenner and Metairie) is designated a linear lakefront park and is open to the public and commonly used for walking, jogging, biking, and other activities (Figure 12.6). The once-popular Pontchartrain Beach and Lincoln Beach on the Orleans Parish lakeshore were closed to swimming in the early 1960s, but they may someday be open to the public if water quality in the lake continues to improve. On the north shore is the Lakeshore Park in Mandeville, which is protected for public use by legal mandate (see Figure 8.3; Nichols 1990).

More natural areas with convenient access to the lake, its adjacent wetlands, or tributaries are Fontainebleau and Fairview Riverside State Parks in Mandeville, Big Branch Marsh National Wildlife Refuge just east of Fontainebleau, and Bayou Sauvage National Wildlife Refuge in New Orleans. Natural areas with limited access and few facilities are the Pearl River, Joyce, Manchac, Maurepas Swamp, and Biloxi Wildlife Management Areas managed by the Louisiana State Department of Wildlife and Fisheries. Another site with limited access is the Bonnet Carré Spillway, which is open to the public when not being used for flood control. Many of these and other natural sites around the lake were described in Maygarden et al. (2000). Additional public boat launch sites around the lake are located at Fort Pike on the Rigolets, in Mandeville at Castine Bayou, in Madisonville at the mouth of the Tchefuncte River, on North Pass near Manchac, at Ruddock on Highway 51, and at Frenier.

13.

Water Chemistry

The Lake Pontchartrain estuary is characterized by the mixing of fresh water from its tributary rivers and streams with saline water entering from its connections with the Gulf of Mexico. Fresh water from rivers and streams is a complex mixture of dissolved and particulate matter that can vary widely. Seawater is a complex mixture of many ionic salts and other substances dissolved in water. The combination of these mixtures results in an extremely complex chemistry in any estuary. Additional substances enter via urban runoff, diffusion from sediments, and atmospheric deposition. This chapter describes some of the more significant chemical components of waters within Lake Pontchartrain.

Salinity

Midocean surface water is composed of about 96.5% water and 3.5% dissolved salts, gases, organic compounds, and other substances, or about 35 g/kg (or parts per thousand, ppt, or ‰) of salt. Coastal waters with freshwater influx, such as the Pontchartrain estuary, usually contain the same major salts as seawater (chloride, sodium, sulfate, magnesium, calcium, potassium, bicarbonate, bromide, boric acid, and strontium), but they have much lower salinity levels and vary dramatically with a variety of changing conditions. Usually a salinity gradient exists in estuaries, with levels ranging from full seawater (35 ppt) at the mouth to fresh water (0 ppt) at the upper reaches. These salinity levels and the gradient vary with factors such as tides, amount of freshwater runoff, temperature, and evaporation rates.

The Lake Pontchartrain system is considered an "oligohaline" estuary, with relatively low salinities, usually about 0–8 ppt. Reported salinity means are 1.2 ppt on the western side of Lake Pontchartrain and 5.4 ppt in the east, but with ranges considerably greater (0 to 15.2 ppt at Little Woods; Sikora and Kjerfve 1985). Lake Maurepas has lower salinities, usually about 0–5 ppt (Hastings et al. 1987). Salinities generally range from 2 to 15 ppt in Lake Borgne and from 2 to 30 ppt in Mississippi Sound (U.S. Army Corps of Engineers 1984). Full-strength seawater of 35 ppt does not occur until some distance offshore in the Gulf of Mexico. During excessively wet years salinities are lower, and during periods of drought, such as occurred in 1999–2000, salinities can reach significantly higher levels (up to 10 ppt in Pass Manchac and Lake Maurepas). Because of the seasonal change in freshwater input to the system, with highest levels in the winter and spring, salinity levels are usually lowest in the winter and spring and gradually increase through the summer to reach a high in autumn (Hastings 2002).

In addition to its chemical effects, salinity also has important physical effects, such as increased water density. Changes in salinity can result in vertical water mass movements because of density differences. Saline waters may sink and move below fresher waters, causing stratification or a salt wedge. Stratification is generally slight in the Lake Pontchartrain system because of the relatively shallow depths and high degree of mixing (Swenson 1980a), but it does occur in the deeper dredge holes (Poirrier 1978b; Georgiou and McCorquodale 2001). Salt wedges can also move into the lake from the Mississippi River Gulf Outlet and Inner Harbor Navigational Canal, so that there are usually plumes of higher salinity water in the lake adjacent to this canal (Poirrier 1978b).

Salinity has important osmotic pressure effects on living organisms, which affect the ionic equilibrium of their body fluids. Organisms that occur in estuaries must be able to survive frequent changes in salinity, as well as tolerate a wide range of salinities, a characteristic referred to as "euryhaline." Osmoregulation, or physiological control of body salt and water balance, is very important for such organisms.

Dissolved Oxygen

Dissolved oxygen (O_2) is important to sustain aquatic life, but its concentration may vary in estuarine waters such that it may become limiting to living organisms (that is, low enough to prohibit their survival). Although abundant in the atmosphere (210 mg/L), oxygen's solubility in water is low, with a maximum of about 14.6 mg/L (or parts per million, ppm) in saturated distilled water at 32°F

(0°C; the saturation point decreases as temperature and salinity increase; Kalff 2002). Fresh water at a temperature of 77°F (25°C) has a saturation point of 8.2 mg/L, while estuarine water at a salinity of 10 ppt would reach saturation at 7.8 mg/L. Increased temperature further decreases the solubility of oxygen in water.

There are two sources of oxygen in water: surface exchange with the atmosphere and photosynthetic production. Atmospheric input is enhanced by surface turbulence or wave action, and photosynthesis must occur in the presence of light. Thus, oxygen levels may decline during periods of calm water (especially with warm temperatures) and at night or on overcast days, especially in deeper waters. The amount of organic material in the water generates a need for oxygen as bacteria and other living organisms decompose that organic material, a measure defined as biological or biochemical oxygen demand. In waters where there is excessive biological oxygen demand, oxygen levels can be reduced to hypoxic or anoxic levels. Such reductions are usually caused by high organic content, rapid bacterial decomposition, and poor water circulation such as during summer stratification of the water column (Darnell 1992).

Surface dissolved oxygen levels recorded in Lake Pontchartrain are about 5.6–10.3 mg/L, with the lowest levels generally occurring during warm water months (Schurtz and St. Pé 1984). Oxygen levels near the bottom can reach a minimum of 1.4 mg/L (or lower), with the lowest levels in June, July, and August. Such hypoxic areas, defined as areas with dissolved oxygen levels of 1–4 ppm, have been reported in Lake Pontchartrain near the Inner Harbor Navigation Canal, resulting from salinity stratification caused when high-salinity water enters the lake from the canal (Poirrier 1978b; Sikora and Sikora 1982; McCorquodale et al. 2001b). Shallow marsh canals and pools usually become hypoxic during the summer because of high detrital decomposition and high water temperatures.

Carbon

Among the other important chemicals contained within estuarine waters, carbon is especially significant. It is abundant in two forms, as inorganic carbon (or carbon dioxide, CO_2) and as organic carbon (associated with living organisms). The concentration of carbon dioxide in water can be much higher than in air because of its tendency to combine with water or other substances to form carbonates (such as calcium carbonate). The greenhouse effect, or buildup of carbon dioxide in the atmosphere, would be much greater if not for this capacity of the world's oceans to take up large quantities of carbon dioxide.

When carbon dioxide enters water, primarily by diffusion from the air or as a by-product of respiration, it combines with water molecules to form carbonic acid (H_2CO_3). The carbonic acid then ionizes to form bicarbonate (HCO_3^-) and carbonate ions ($CO_3^=$). The presence of these ions buffers the water against rapid changes in pH, or hydrogen ion concentration (the acidity or alkalinity). The pH levels recorded in Lake Pontchartrain are almost always 7.0 to 8.5, and inorganic carbon concentrations range from 0.17 to 2.36 mg-at C/L (milligram-atoms carbon per liter), with a mean of 0.85 mg-at C/L (Stoessel 1980).

Carbon dioxide is also of critical importance as a raw material for photosynthesis. Green plants, in the presence of light, combine carbon dioxide and water to form carbohydrates or sugars ($C_6H_{12}O_6$). These simple sugars then become the building blocks for more complex organic carbon compounds in living cells. This organic carbon can be released into the water with the death and decomposition of the living organisms to form dissolved organic carbon (DOC) and particulate organic carbon (POC, or detritus). Reported levels are 0.03–8.5 mg-at C/L DOC (mean, 1.16) in Lake Pontchartrain, 0–20 mg C/L DOC (mean, 7.0) in Lake Maurepas, and up to 28 mg-at C/L DOC in some tributary waters (Stoessel 1980; Childers et al. 1985; Argyrou et al. 1997; Bianchi and Argyrou 1997). The dominant sources of DOC into Lake Pontchartrain were shown to be riverine discharge (2.8×10^{10} g C/year) and benthic fluxes (8.8×10^{10} g C/year), with the highest levels during winter and early summer correlated with maximum freshwater input. Much of this was derived from terrestrial sources. Levels of POC in Lake Pontchartrain are 0.00–1.94 mg-at C/L (mean, 0.25).

The productivity level of aquatic systems is usually expressed in terms of grams (or micrograms) of carbon per square meter (or liter) per day (or hour) fixed by photosynthetic organisms such as aquatic diatoms. Average lakewide plankton productivity levels measured in the Lake Pontchartrain basin ranged from 18.6 µg C/L/hour in October to 46.3 µg C/L/hour in April (Dow and Turner 1980). Marsh plants growing in wetlands surrounding the estuary are also an important source of organic carbon, with productivity levels as high as 3000 g C/m²/year (Turner 1976).

Calcium

Calcium compounds, and especially calcium carbonate, are important to marine and estuarine organisms as a major component of their shells. Many abundant groups of organisms, including Foraminifera, Mollusca, Porifera, and Crustacea, remove enormous quantities of calcium carbonate from the water. Large quantities of rangia clam shells, composed primarily of calcium carbonate, have accumulated on the bottom of Lake Pontchartrain in deposits sufficiently vast to support commercial industries dating back to the earliest European settlements. Calcium is continually resupplied to the estuary by erosion of limestone and other terrestrial sources, as well as erosion of the accumulated shells in the lake. Garrison (1999) reported values of dissolved calcium in Lake Pontchartrain of 0.5–150 mg/L (means, 14–48 mg/L) at eleven stations sampled between 1943 and 1995.

Silicon

Silicon compounds (or silicates) are another important substance as a component of the shells of some aquatic organisms, such as diatoms and radiolarians. Silicon levels, with recorded ranges in Lake Pontchartrain of 5–145 µg-at Si/L (mean, 48.5 µg-at Si/L), are usually high in the spring, low in summer, and increase in autumn (Stoessel 1980).

Sulfur

Sulfur compounds (or sulfates) are common in coastal waters and are important to the metabolism of plants in the formation of amino acids and proteins. These compounds can be abundant in sediments rich in organic material. In the presence of oxygen, heterotrophic bacteria may decompose organic compounds to again release sulfate. Garrison (1999) reported sulfate values in Lake Pontchartrain of 1.4–1100 mg/L (means, 35–250 mg/L at eleven stations). Levels in Lake Maurepas water samples were 0–165 mg/L (mean, 22.9 mg/L) and sediments 18–162 mg/L dry weight (mean, 72 mg/L; Childers et al. 1985).

Under anoxic or anaerobic conditions, such as in stagnant marsh pools or organic-rich sediments, sulfates are reduced to sulfides such as hydrogen sulfide, a waste product of sulfate-reducing bacteria. The hydrogen sulfide then reacts with iron (or ferrous) compounds and water to produce ferrous sulfide (FeS), hydrotroilite (FeS-nH_2O), and pyrite (FeS_2). The presence of these sulfur compounds gives the estuarine muds their characteristic black color and strong odor. On the bottom of Lake Pontchartrain, the surface sediments are oxidized, making them light brown in color, while those just below the surface are reduced and black.

Nitrogen and Phosphorus

Among the most important chemicals dissolved in estuarine waters are nitrogen compounds, such as ammonia (NH_3), nitrites (NO_2), and nitrates (NO_3), and phosphorus compounds or phosphates (PO_4). The nitrates and phosphates are important nutrients for plants and may limit their growth if not present in sufficient quantities. They can also stimulate plant growth or "blooms" if abundant. Recorded nitrogen levels in Lake Pontchartrain were 0–26.5 µg-at N/L for nitrates plus nitrites (mean, 3.57 µg-at N/L) and 0–40.2 µg-at N/L for ammonia (mean, 3.09 µg-at N/L; Stoessel 1980). Nitrogen levels are usually high in the spring, apparently related to maximum river input, and low in the summer and autumn as a result of assimilation by phytoplankton. The phytoplankton in Lake Pontchartrain are nitrogen limited in the summer and autumn (Dow and Turner 1980). Nitrogen gas (N_2) is also abundant in most waters but is inert, although some bacteria and blue-green algae (or cyanobacteria) such as *Anabaena* can convert molecular nitrogen to ammonia, a process referred to as nitrogen fixation.

Phosphorus levels in Lake Pontchartrain are usually high in the spring, low in summer, and then increase in autumn (Stoessel 1980). Recorded ranges were 0.03–5.88 µg-at P/L for phosphates (mean, 0.94 µg-at P/L) and 0–6.55 µg-at P/L for dissolved phosphorus (mean, 1.17 µg-at P/L). The autumn increase possibly results from increased suspension of bottom sediments as a result of increased lake turbulence. Dow and Turner (1980) suggested that phytoplankton may be phosphorus limited in late spring.

Bianchi and Argyrou (1997) concluded that phytoplankton should be nitrogen-limited in Lake Pontchartrain based upon the low recorded nitrogen-to-phosphorus ratios of 2.3 to 8.3, which were positively correlated with freshwater discharge into the estuary. (A nitrogen-to-phosphorus ratio of 16/1, the Redfield ratio, is considered ideal for balanced phytoplankton growth [Redfield et al. 1963].) However, light limitation was considered more important in the upper estuary (because of increased turbidity associated with high levels of suspended particulate matter), while nitrogen limitation was more significant in the lower estuary.

Nutrients such as nitrogen and phosphorus compounds enter the estuary from freshwater input and urban runoff, as well as other sources, such as aerial deposition. There has been an estimated 10-fold increase in nitrogen loading in the Lake Pontchartrain basin during the past 180 years as a result of anthropogenic influences (agriculture and urbanization; Turner et al. 2002). The estimated annual amounts of nitrogen loading to the lake from various sources total 24 million lb. (10.9 million kg) for an average year (with no spillway opening and normal rainfall), including 17 million lb. (7.77 million kg, 71%) from river discharges from the watershed, 2.8 million lb. (1.25 million kg, 11%) from the atmosphere (+ 0.4 million lb. or 0.18 million kg entering Lake Maurepas, 2%), 2.2 million lb. (1.01 million kg, 9%) from urban runoff, and 1.1–2.0 million lb.

(0.5–0.9 million kg, 1%) from leakage of the Bonnet Carré Spillway, plus a relatively minor amount of 0.2–0.4 million lb. (0.1–0.16 million kg during a normal year, 1%) from nitrogen fixation by living organisms (Turner 2001; Turner et al. 2002). In estuaries of the eastern U.S. coast, including the eastern Gulf of Mexico, from 10% to 40% of the nitrogen entering the estuaries comes from atmospheric deposition of nitrogen, which is dominated by nitric acid and nitrates from fossil fuel combustion (Paerl et al. 2002). However, ammonia (NH_3), ammonium (NH_4), and organic nitrogen can also be important.

An opening of the Bonnet Carré spillway can add 35–53 million lb. (16–24 million kg) of nitrogen to the lake and thus triple the annual total in the space of one or two months. The average total nitrogen and phosphorus levels in the Mississippi River are about 3.5 and 4.0 times higher than those in Lake Pontchartrain (Waldon and Bryan 1999). Such massive increases in the nitrogen input can trigger algal blooms and subsequent fish kills, as occurred following spillway openings in 1995 and 1997 (Day et al. 1999; Turner et al. 2002).

Pollutants

As with most water bodies adjacent to urban areas, Lake Pontchartrain has suffered environmental abuse with substantial input of a variety of pollutants, such as untreated or partially treated sewage and urban runoff containing oil and grease, heavy metals, pesticides, and other chemicals, in addition to sewage (see Chapter 10). Because most of the pollution in Lake Pontchartrain comes from terrestrial and tributary sources, water quality in the middle of the lake some distance from shore has generally been relatively good (Coastal Environments, Inc. 1984a), with the greatest concerns for swimmer safety being near the southern shore and the mouths of rivers. In recent years levels of microbial indicator organisms (fecal coliform, *Escherichia coli*, and enterococci) were within satisfactory water quality limits during dry weather, but they increased significantly following stormwater events and remained high for about three days (Jin et al. 2004; Jeng et al. 2005). The water quality monitoring program conducted by the Lake Pontchartrain Basin Foundation showed that conditions were so improved by the close of the century that public swimming could be once again considered feasible. In February 2002, the foundation declared the lake "recovered" and safe for swimming based upon water quality testing during the previous year (*Baton Rouge Advocate*, February 21, 2002). However, water quality degradation has been, and continues to be, one of the major environmental problems in the Pontchartrain basin, and Lopez (2003) suggested that serious water quality impairment had not yet peaked and overall water quality may still be declining.

14.

Biota of the Pontchartrain Basin

The generally variable conditions of changing salinity levels, temperature, water level, currents, oxygen, and other factors create conditions in Lake Pontchartrain and other estuaries that make survival for most aquatic organisms difficult. Consequently this rigorous environment is occupied by relatively few species. However, the freshwater runoff entering the system carries with it dissolved chemicals such as nitrates and phosphates that are important nutrients for aquatic plants. Therefore estuaries are usually characterized by very high biological productivity, much higher than in the open ocean or in fresh water. The relatively few species that can tolerate the variable conditions can take advantage of the high productivity and become abundant. Estuaries such as Lake Pontchartrain support tremendous populations of some species, including commercially valuable fish and shellfish such as spotted seatrout (*Cynoscion nebulosus*), blue crabs (*Callinectes sapidus*), and white and brown shrimp (*Litopenaeus setiferus* and *Farfantepenaeus aztecus*).

Darnell (1962) suggested that biodiversity in Lake Pontchartrain may be somewhat high compared to many estuaries because of its subtropical location and number of rare transient species that may occasionally enter the system. However, he recognized only four species that maintain large endemic populations as year-round residents of Lake Pontchartrain. These are the clam *Rangia cuneata* (Figure 14.1), the mud crab *Rhithropanopeus harrisii* (Figure 14.2), the copepod *Acartia tonsa* (Figure 14.3), and the bay anchovy *Anchoa mitchilli* (Figure 14.4). Darnell emphasized the marine origin of most estuarine animals and noted that other dominant marine species in Lake Pontchartrain were seasonal in their occurrence, entering the lake in larval or juvenile stages, with great

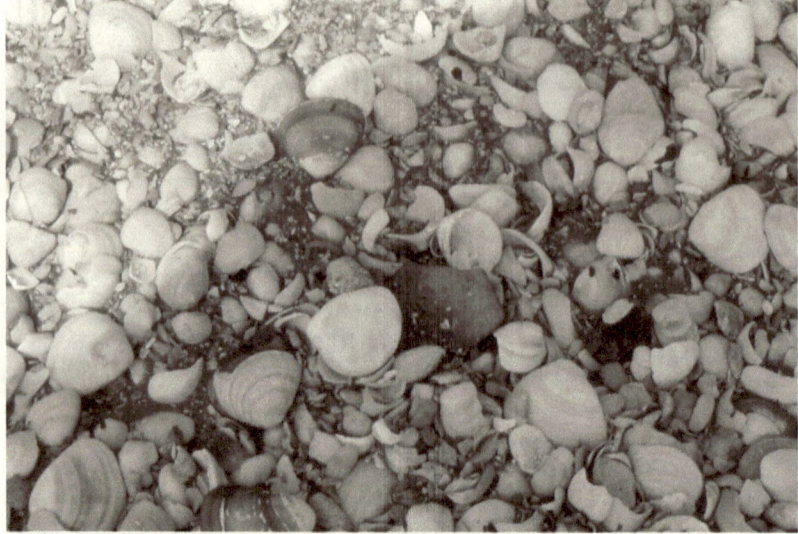

Figure 14.1 *Rangia cuneata* shells near the mouth of the Tangipahoa River (Photograph by the author)

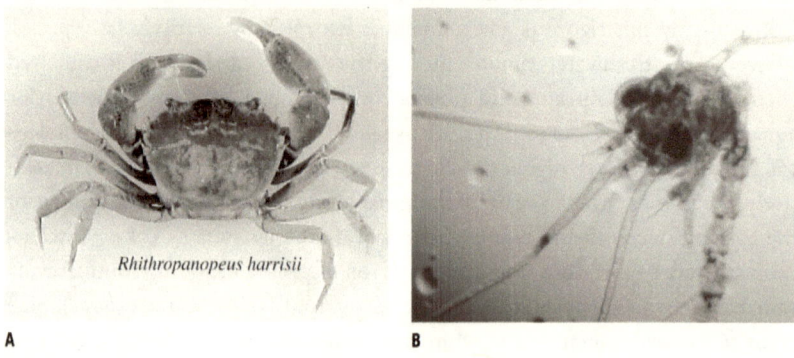

Figure 14.2 Harris's mud crab (*Rhithropanopeus harrisii*): (A) adult and (B) zoea larva (Photo A used with permission of the photographer, Dr. Donald E. Keith; photograph B by the author)

variation in species composition and population levels from season to season and year to year. Freshwater species were common only when water conditions were almost fresh. Even in Lake Maurepas, where salinity is very low, the fish fauna is about half freshwater- and half marine-associated species (Hastings et al. 1987). During years when salinities are higher than normal, a larger proportion of marine species is present.

BIOTA OF THE PONTCHARTRAIN BASIN   191

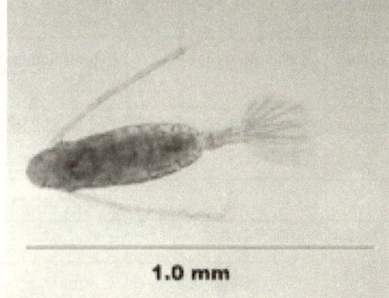

Figure 14.3   The copepod *Acartia tonsa* (Used with permission of the photographer, Dr. William Johnson; http://www.zooplankton-online.net/gallery.html)

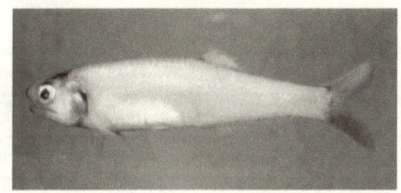

Figure 14.4   Bay anchovy (*Anchoa mitchilli*) (Photograph by the author)

Major Geomorphic Regions

Three major geomorphic regions are recognized in the Pontchartrain basin: the Marginal Deltaic Basin, which includes Lakes Pontchartrain and Maurepas; the Mississippi River Deltaic Plain, which includes the Lake Borgne area and its surrounding wetlands; and the Pleistocene Terraces, which include the forested habitats that abut the northern side of the lakes and contribute to the Pontchartrain drainage basin (Penland et al. 2001c). The Marginal Deltaic Basin is further subdivided into eight distinct areas based upon habitat characteristics, plant communities, and faunal assemblages: the Maurepas swamp, the Manchac land bridge, the southwest Pontchartrain area, the Lake Pontchartrain area proper, the north-shore marshes, Bayou Sauvage area, East Orleans land bridge, and Pearl River mouth area. Lake Maurepas proper could be added as another distinct area.

Ecological Communities

Within these geomorphic regions and their subdivisions, several major ecological communities may be recognized, based upon the general living conditions, habitat characteristics, and living organisms present, although there is much overlap and many species occupy more than one community. In most cases,

Table 17 Natural and ecological communities of the Pontchartrain basin

Community System	Community Type	Natural Community	Comparable Ecological Communities Discussed Here
Estuarine	A. Intertidal emergent vegetation	1. Salt marsh	Marsh community
		2. Brackish marsh	
		3. Intermediate marsh	
	B. Subtidal aquatic bed	4. Submergent algal vegetation	—
		5. Submergent vascular vegetation	Grassbeds community
	C. Intertidal flat	6. Intertidal sand/shell flat	Shoreline areas
		7. Intertidal mud/organic flat	
		8. Intertidal mollusk reef	—
	D. Subtidal open water	9. Bay	Open-water estuarine community + soft-bottom benthic community + hard substrate community
		10. Tidal channel/creek	
		11. Tidal pass	
Lacustrine	A. Limnetic open water	12. Upland lake	Freshwater lakes and ponds
	B. Littoral open water	13. Marsh lake	
		14. Swamp lake	
Palustrine	A. Aquatic bed	15. Submergent algal bed	—
		16. Submerged/floating vascular vegetation	—
	B. Emergent vegetation	17. Freshwater marsh	Marsh community
		18. Hillside bog	—
	C. Scrub/shrub wetland vegetation	19. Scrub/shrub swamp	—
		20. Shrub swamp	—
	D. Forested wetland	21. Bald cypress-tupelo swamp	Cypress-tupelo swamps
		22. Bald cypress swamp	
		23. Tupelo–black gum swamp	
		24. Batture	—
		25–29. Bottomland forest	Bottomland hardwood forests
		25. Overcup oak–water hickory	
		26. Sugarberry–American elm–green ash	

Community System	Community Type	Natural Community	Comparable Ecological Communities Discussed Here
		27. Sycamore-sweetgum–American elm	
		28. Sweetgum–water oak	
		29. Live oak forest	
		30. Wooded seep	—
		31. Bayhead swamp	—
		32. Slash pine–cypress/hardwood forest	—
		33. Pine flatwoods	—
		34. Wet hardwood flatwoods	—
		35. Wet/mesic spruce pine/hardwood flatwoods	—
		36. Pine savannah	—
		37. Riparian forest	—
Riverine	A. Riverine subtidal channel	38. Tidal mud flat	Freshwater tributaries
		39. Subtidal open water	
	B. Riverine lower perennial channel	40. Sand/gravel beach/bar	
		41. Mud bar	
		42. Lower perennial open water	
	C. Aquatic bed	43. Submerged/floating vascular vegetation	
Terrestrial	A. Deciduous forests	44. Hardwood slope forest	Upland forest communities
	B. Mixed evergreen/deciduous forests	45. Shortleaf pine/oak-hickory forest	
		46. Mixed hardwood-loblolly forest	
		47. Slash pine/post oak forest	
		48. Live oak–pine–magnolia forest	
	C. Evergreen forests	49. Upland longleaf pine forest	
	D. Woodland	50. Sandy woodland	

Modified from Louisiana Natural Heritage Program (1988)

one community gradually merges with others. The Manchac land bridge area between Lake Pontchartrain and Lake Maurepas and extending east along the north shore to the Tchefuncte River, as well as most of the south shore, was once primarily cypress swamp, with some bottomland hardwood forest and some fresh to intermediate marsh. Logging of the old-growth cypress-tupelo swamps began in the 1700s, but they were devastated in the late 1800s and early 1900s. Some areas have never recovered and have converted to marsh. In recent decades, much of the fresh marsh habitat has converted to intermediate marsh with increased saltwater intrusion (Penland et al. 2001c). The Maurepas swamp was also logged in the past but has mostly recovered with second-growth cypress and tupelo and some areas of bottomland hardwood forest and fresh marsh, although some areas once forested have converted to marsh. The southwestern Pontchartrain area, including the LaBranche Wetlands and the Bonnet Carré Spillway, is similar to the Manchac area, with a mixture of swamps, forests, and fresh and intermediate marshes, but the area has also suffered severely from subsidence and ditching.

The Bayou Sauvage area to the east of New Orleans was once largely brackish marsh, with bottomland hardwood forests on the slightly higher ridges. Today much of the area has been impounded by levees, converting the brackish marshes to fresh marshes, and the ridges have been largely developed for human occupation. The remainder of the East Orleans land bridge between Lake Pontchartrain and Lake Borgne is still almost exclusively brackish marsh, but with some residential development and camps, especially along Highway 90 and along Chef Menteur Pass, the Rigolets, and Lake St. Catherine. The wetlands surrounding the remainder of Lake Borgne are almost exclusively brackish marshes, but many have suffered from subsidence or have been dissected by numerous canals and ditches, increasing the amount of aquatic habitat.

The north-shore marshes that rim the lakeshore from Mandeville to Slidell, composed of both intermediate and brackish marshes, have been reduced in extent by subsidence, ditching, and filling, especially in the Slidell area. The bottomlands of most rivers and bayous entering the lake are now occupied by numerous camps and residential developments. Most of the Pearl River basin remains in a relatively natural condition, with the area near its mouth of intermediate marshes adjacent to Lake Borgne, fresh marshes upstream, and then cypress swamps and bottomland hardwood forests further upriver.

Five natural community systems, as defined by the Louisiana Natural Heritage Program (1988) primarily on the basis of dominant vegetation present, can be identified in the Pontchartrain basin, which are further subdivided into seventeen natural community types and then fifty natural communities (Table 17).

These categories, however, tend to emphasize terrestrial, vegetated communities, rather than aquatic communities, and they are not especially appropriate for estuarine environments. For simplicity, only ten categories will be recognized:

Estuarine system (saline environments)
1. Open-water estuarine community
2. Soft-bottom benthic community
3. Shoreline areas
4. Hard substrate community
5. Grassbeds community
6. Marsh community

Palustrine system (freshwater wetlands)
7. Cypress-tupelo swamps and bottomland hardwood forests

Riverine and lacustrine systems (freshwater rivers, streams, and lakes)
8. Freshwater tributaries
9. Freshwater lakes and ponds

Terrestrial system (upland areas)
10. Upland forest communities

In subsequent chapters, these community types will be discussed with emphasis on their current condition and characteristics.

15.

The Estuarine Communities

The large volume of open water in the three lakes of the Pontchartrain estuary, as well as the water and substrate surfaces, shoreline, and adjacent marshes, provides a large amount of estuarine living space available to aquatic organisms. Most of these organisms are euryhaline and able to tolerate a wide range of salinity variation and are therefore widely distributed in the lakes. However, there is also some variation in species distribution with salinity, so that more freshwater species tend to occur in Lake Maurepas, while more marine species occupy Lake Borgne and eastern Lake Pontchartrain. During periods of higher salinity, more marine species move further into the upper estuary. Within this estuarine system, we can recognize several different habitat or community types with distinct species assemblages but with much overlap.

Open-Water Estuarine Community

Because of the three-dimensional aquatic living space in this open-water environment, both free-swimming and planktonic drifting organisms are important components of estuaries, as well as the entire marine environment. These include microscopic one-celled diatoms, protozoans, and bacteria; larger invertebrates such as copepods, rotifers, and cladocerans; and open-water fishes. Small planktonic organisms, with little or no swimming ability, drift in the water with virtually no control over their movements. Many benthic organisms, such as crabs, shrimp, and sponges, as well as larger swimming organisms have planktonic eggs or larvae as a means of enhancing their dispersal to new habitats. Thus, these organisms are temporary residents of this open-water community.

PHYTOPLANKTON

The dominant phytoplankton of Lake Pontchartrain include both marine and brackish and freshwater forms, dominated by green algae (Chlorophyceae) and diatoms (Chrysophyceae) during most of the year, and blue-green algae (Cyanophyceae or Cyanobacteria) during summer plankton blooms (Bianchi and Argyrou 1997). Stone et al. (1980) also recognized the freshwater cryptomonad *Cryptomonas* (Cryptophyceae) as being important in the lake.

Stone et al. (1980) identified sixty-four taxa (mostly genera) of phytoplankton in Lake Pontchartrain, thirty-two of which were freshwater forms of green algae, with *Ankistrodesmus* being most important. However, the most abundant forms were euryhaline and brackish water taxa, including *Chlamydomonas* and *Phacotus*. *Sphaerocystis* has been reported as dominant on the southern side of the lake (Stern and Stern 1969).

Diatoms were considered abundant by Stone et al. (1980) but were not identified to genus or species. The genera *Chaetoceros* and *Coscinodiscus* have been reported as abundant in other Lake Pontchartrain surveys (Suttkus et al. 1954; Darnell 1961; Stern and Stern 1969). Suttkus et al. (1954) considered the diatoms marine forms and less numerous in the fresher areas of the lake. They suggested that heavy blooms of diatoms occurred in Lake Borgne but only occasionally in Lake Pontchartrain.

In terms of abundance, blue-green algae have been dominated by euryhaline and brackish water forms, including *Oscillatoria*, *Microcystis*, and *Lyngbya*, and freshwater *Anabaena* (Stone et al. 1980). Suttkus et al. (1954) reported *Anabaena* in the lake as including at least seven species, with the heaviest blooms (including thick scums in late summer and early autumn) in the western half of the lake. Major blooms have become a regular occurrence in Lake Pontchartrain, with the predominant species being *Anabaena circinalis* and *Microcystis aeruginosa* (Day et al. 1999; Dortch et al. 1999; Turner et al. 2002). The largest blooms occur in response to openings of the Bonnet Carré Spillway, although Dow and Turner (1980) reported a maximum standing crop in May 1978, associated with a bloom of *Anabaena* in fresh water emanating from the Tchefuncte River and Pass Manchac. Conversely, blooms should not occur during years when salinity is above those tolerated by *Anabaena* (Turner et al. 2002).

Several dinoflagellates (*Ceratium furca*, *Ceratium fusus*, and *Peridinium divergens*) have been reported from Lake Pontchartrain (Suttkus et al. 1954), but these are generally more characteristic of higher salinity waters. Some species can cause red tides when they become extremely abundant (2–8 million cells/L) during blooms and can produce toxins that cause fish kills. However, such blooms of dinoflagellates rarely if ever occur in Lake Pontchartrain, although a bloom of *Karenia* (*Gymnodinium*) *breve* did extend into the coastal waters of Mississippi Sound in 1996, the first ever occurrence for Louisiana and Mississippi (Dortch et al. 1999).

Although technically not part of the plankton community, several small floating plants are characteristic of Lake Pontchartrain and drift on the surface under the influence of wind and currents. These include several species commonly referred to as duckweed (*Lemna minor, Spirodela polyrrhiza*, and *S. oligorrhiza*), bogmat (*Wolffiella floridana*), and watermeal (*Wolffia columbiana*), which often form dense masses of green scum on the water's surface. These and other aquatic plants, including the nonnative water lettuce (*Pistia stratiotes*), alligatorweed (*Alternanthera philoxeroides*), common salvinia (*Salvinia minima*), and water hyacinth (*Eichhornia crassipes*), are usually more abundant in sheltered waters but can be carried into the open lake by wind and currents. Such floating plants can also be carried into Lake Borgne by freshwater washouts from Lake Pontchartrain (Hawes and Perry 1978).

ZOOPLANKTON

The zooplankton of Lake Pontchartrain are a diverse assortment of many different groups, including protozoa, rotifers, copepods, cladocerans, and the larval forms of many crustaceans, mollusks, annelid worms, and fish. Several species are usually dominant, but their abundance can vary with changes in water conditions such as salinity. Suttkus et al. (1954) recognized four elements comprising the zooplankton of the lake: (1) brackish water plankton, including tintinnids, rotifers (*Brachionus plicatilis, Filinia longiseta, Pedalia fennica, Synchaeta bicornis*, and *Synchaeta littoralis*), and copepods (*Acartia tonsa, Eurytemora affinis*, and *Halicyclops* sp.); (2) larval forms of brackish water adults, including barnacles, crabs, mollusks, annelids, and copepods; (3) adventitious marine forms, such as tintinnids, dinoflagellates, a rotifer (*Synchaeta cecilia*), and copepods (*Canuella* sp., *Oithona brevicornis*, and *Paracalanus crassirostris*); and (4) adventitious freshwater or sporadic brackish forms, such as colonial flagellated Protista (Protozoa of Suttkus et al.; *Gonium pectorale, Eudorina elegans, Pandorina morum, Platydorina caudata*, and *Volvox tertius*), rotifers (*Brachionus angularis, Brachionus calyciflorus, Brachionus havanaensis, Keratella gracilenta, Keratella valga, Polyarthra trigla*, and *Sinantherina semibullata*), and a cladoceran (*Bosmina longirostris*). They reported large populations of a few brackish water species and low densities or localized populations of many freshwater and littoral marine species.

According to Stone et al. (1980), the zooplankton in Lake Pontchartrain were dominated by rotifers, copepods, cladocerans, and decapod crustacean larvae. Most of the taxa were freshwater forms, but several of the more abundant were characteristic of brackish waters. The most abundant forms were the rotifers *Synchaeta* spp., *Brachionus plicatilis, Brachionus angularis, Brachionus deitersi, Filinia pejleri, Keratella cochlearis,* and *Conochilus* sp.; copepods *Acartia tonsa, Eurytemora affinis,* and *Diaptomus* sp.; larvae of the phantom midge *Chaoborus* sp.; zoea larvae of the benthic mud crab *Rhithropanopeus harrisii* (Figure 14.2); and the mollusk *Texadina sphinctosoma.* The last species is normally benthic, but apparently at times it can be suspended in the water column in large numbers (that is, tychoplanktonic).

Hawes and Perry (1978) described zooplankton populations at two stations in extreme southeastern Lake Pontchartrain and at twelve stations in Lake Borgne and adjacent Mississippi Sound during a period when the Bonnet Carré Spillway was opened to divert Mississippi River water into Lake Pontchartrain (April to June 1973). Salinity in the Lake Pontchartrain area was near fresh (0–1.3 ppt) throughout their sampling period. In April and May, their samples from Lake Pontchartrain were dominated by zoea larvae of the mud crab. Copepods were rare until June, when forms characteristic of fresh water (*Diaptomus, Cyclops,* and *Mesocyclops*) became common to abundant. The usually abundant and dominant *Acartia tonsa* was rare. Freshwater cladocerans (*Diaphanosoma brachyurum, Moina micrura,* and *Bosmina coregoni*) became dominant. In Lake Borgne, salinities were slightly higher, ranging from 0.0 to 4.5 ppt from April through June, then increased significantly in July (0.3–10.0 ppt). Mud crab zoea were abundant throughout the sampling period (April to July). *Acartia tonsa* was abundant, especially in June. Copepods of the genus *Ergasilus* were also common in June, as were the cladocerans *D. brachyurum* and *M. micrura.* In summary, Hawes and Perry noted that the Bonnet Carré Spillway waters had a dramatic but short-term impact on the plankton populations, especially with the addition of numerous freshwater and oligohaline species, which were eliminated as salinities returned to normal levels.

Several studies have documented the significance of the copepod *Acartia tonsa* in Lake Pontchartrain. Most studies have determined this to be the most abundant copepod in the lake (Suttkus et al. 1954; Darnell 1962; Tarver and Dugas 1973; Tarver and Savoie 1976; Stone et al. 1980). In macrozooplankton samples, Stone et al. (1980) found copepod nauplii ("probably *Acartia tonsa,*" 41,856 individuals per 100 m^3) and *Acartia tonsa* (27,986 per 100 m^3) far exceeded the next most abundant taxon (*Eurytemora affinis*; 990 per 100 m^3). The zooplankton in marsh waterways of upper Lake Borgne were also dominated by *A.*

tonsa and *E. affinis* (as *E. hirundoides*), but with the former nearly twenty-five times more abundant than the latter (Cuzon du Rest 1963).

At times the comb jellyfish or ctenophore *Mnemiopsis mccradyi* may be abundant in the lake (Tarver and Dugas 1973; Tarver and Savoie 1976; Hawes and Perry 1978; Fannaly 1980), especially during periods of higher salinity, such as during the autumn of 2000 when large numbers were observed in Lake Maurepas (Hastings, personal observation). The comb jellyfish has generally not been enumerated in plankton studies, but instead is considered a nuisance because it clogs nets and interferes with sampling.

Many species of benthic organisms such as copepods, isopods, mysids, and shrimp make regular vertical migrations from the bottom to near surface waters, especially at night. Other species most characteristic of protected waters or benthic habitats may be carried into open waters by floods or turbulent weather or when clinging to drifting plants or other debris.

The early larval or juvenile stages of many fishes and crustaceans are also planktonic for a part of their life cycle (that is, meroplanktonic). Fannaly (1980) reported thirty-seven species of fish and twelve species of crustaceans collected in plankton nets set in the Rigolets, Chef Menteur Pass, and the Inner Harbor Navigation Canal. Many of these have also been collected as they move through Pass Manchac at the upper end of Lake Pontchartrain (Hastings, personal observation).

NEKTON

The free-swimming or nektonic component of the open lake waters includes mostly fishes and crustaceans. Approximately 126 species of fish have been reported from Lakes Pontchartrain and Maurepas and surrounding marshes, and many of these occupy the open waters of the lakes (Thompson and Verret 1980; Hastings et al. 1987; Hastings 2002). Of sixty-seven fish species reported for Lake Maurepas, about half are freshwater (49%) and half marine (9%) or estuarine (42%) species (Hastings et al. 1987). The major freshwater species were considered year-round residents, whereas most of the marine and estuarine species were seasonally present. The number of marine species also tended to increase during autumn or during years when salinities were higher (such as 1999–2000). The jellyfish *Chrysaora (Dactylometra) quinquecirrha* and squids *Loligo pealii* and *Lolliguncula brevis* may also be common in the lake during periods of increased salinity (Darnell 1962). *Lolliguncula brevis* has been described as abundant in Lake Borgne and common in Lake Pontchartrain (Pattillo et al. 1997).

Few fish species in the Lake Pontchartrain system are completely independent of substrate contact for feeding or resting, but some of these are quite abundant in the open waters of the lakes. Most notable are the bay anchovy (*Anchoa mitchilli*), Gulf menhaden (*Brevoortia patronus*), and skipjack herring (*Alosa chrysochloris*). Other common species are the paddlefish (*Polyodon spathula*), ladyfish (*Elops saurus*), gizzard shad (*Dorosoma cepedianum*), threadfin shad (*Dorosoma petenense*), and Atlantic needlefish (*Strongylura marina*). Many other fishes, as well as some larger invertebrates, may feed primarily near the substrate but can swim freely in the open waters of the lake and be considered part of this community. This would include the benthic blue crab (*Callinectes sapidus*) and shrimp (*Farfantepenaeus aztecus* and *Litopenaeus setiferus*) that often swim to the surface, especially at night. Many of the open lake fishes are most common near the bottom (demersal) or in nearshore areas or other sheltered locations. Among these are the spotted and alligator gar (*Lepisosteus oculatus* and *Atractosteus spatula*), yellow bass (*Morone mississippiensis*), sheepshead (*Archosargus probatocephalus*), pinfish (*Lagodon rhomboides*), freshwater drum (*Aplodinotus grunniens*), sand seatrout (*Cynoscion arenarius*), spotted seatrout (*Cynoscion nebulosus*), red drum (*Sciaenops ocellatus*), spot (*Leiostomus xanthurus*), Atlantic croaker (*Micropogonias undulatus*), silver perch (*Bairdiella chrysoura*), black drum (*Pogonias cromis*), and striped mullet (*Mugil cephalus*). Most of these more common species are estuarine or marine, rather than freshwater species.

Suttkus et al. (1954) listed Atlantic croaker (43.8%) and bay anchovy (36.5%) as the most abundant species in their trawl catches in Lake Pontchartrain. Other numerically dominant species were spot (4.2%), hardhead catfish (*Ariopsis* [*Arius*] *felis*, 2.8%), hogchoker (*Trinectes maculatus*, 2.5%), channel catfish (*Ictalurus punctatus*, 2.0%), sand seatrout (1.7%), and blue catfish (*Ictalurus furcatus*, 1.1%). The major species recorded by Thompson and Verret (1980), using a variety of gear, were bay anchovy (35.2%), Atlantic croaker (18.2%), Gulf menhaden (14.5%), inland silverside (*Menidia beryllina*, 9.8%), Gulf pipefish (*Syngnathus scovelli*, 3.5%), sheepshead minnow (*Cyprinodon variegatus*, 2.6%), spot (2.2%), and hardhead catfish (1.8%).

In Lake Maurepas, Hastings et al. (1987) listed bay anchovy (85%), blue catfish (3.4%), channel catfish (3.0%), Atlantic croaker (2.8%), Gulf menhaden (2.8%), freshwater drum (1.2%), and hogchoker (0.8%) as the most numerous species in trawls.

Other less common but large and quite interesting species also occur in the open lake, including bull sharks (*Carcharhinus leucas*) and Gulf sturgeon (*Acipenser oxyrinchus desotoi*). Bottlenose dolphins (*Tursiops truncatus*) occasionally stray into Lake Pontchartrain, especially during periods of high salinity. Other rare strays include sea turtles (*Lepidochelys kempi*) and manatees (*Trichechus manatus*). The sighting or capture of any of these large and relatively rare animals in Lake Pontchartrain is usually cause for newspaper headlines or other publicity. Several alleged shark attacks occurred at Pontchartrain Beach during the summer of 1953 (Darnell 1958).

The manatee is generally regarded as a stray from more southern waters and is one of the most unique animals found in Lake Pontchartrain. Single individuals (or occasionally pairs) have been sighted in the lake or its tributaries every few years since 1975, with the most frequent sightings in 1995 (Louisiana Natural Heritage Program, undated report), 1999 (LPBF 2000a), and 2005 (LPBF, website report). There is some indication that manatees have become more frequent in the northern Gulf in recent years. With continued improvement in water quality in Lake Pontchartrain and restoration of extensive grassbeds, these large herbivores could become more common.

The most popular species of marine food or game fish caught in Lake Pontchartrain are spotted seatrout (or speckled trout), sand seatrout (or white trout), southern flounder (*Paralichthys lethostigma*), black drum, sheepshead, red drum (or redfish), Atlantic croaker, jack crevalle (or jack fish, *Caranx hippos*), and gafftopsail catfish (*Bagre marinus*; Davis 1978, 1983, 1988). In fresher waters of the upper estuary, freshwater species such as largemouth bass (*Micropterus salmoides*, known locally as green trout), crappie (or sac-a-lait, *Pomoxis annularis* and *P. nigromaculatus*), catfish (especially blue catfish, channel catfish, and flathead catfish, *Pylodictus olivaris*), freshwater drum (or gaspergou), and sunfish (known locally as bream or perch, *Lepomis* spp.) are caught. Commercial fishing for finfish in the lakes is dominated by spotted seatrout and freshwater catfish, especially blue and channel catfish (Thompson and Stone 1980).

Lake Pontchartrain has been known in the past for its tarpon (*Megalops atlanticus*) fishing, and many of the state's largest tarpon have been taken from Lake Pontchartrain and Lake Borgne. Duffy (1975) suggested that there is a definite migration of tarpon into Lake Pontchartrain in late August and September each year. According to Davis (1988), the southern shore from Lincoln Beach to the Rigolets is noted for excellent tarpon fishing, and the dredge holes in this area have become important haunts for tarpon up to 200 lb. (91 kg). Some species such as the anadromous Alabama shad (*Alosa alabamae*) and striped bass (*Morone saxatilis*), which had been important commercial and sport fish in the lake and adjacent rivers in the past, have virtually disappeared from the Pontchartrain system (Davis et al. 1970; Gunning and Suttkus 1990).

O'Connell et al. (2004) assessed the stability of fish assemblages in Lake Pontchartrain over the previous fifty years and concluded that there were significant changes. The most pronounced changes have occurred in demersal species (Atlantic croaker, spot, and hardhead catfish), which have become less dominant since 1954. In contrast, open-water planktivorous species have become more dominant (bay anchovy) or remained equally represented over time (Gulf menhaden), and nearshore assemblages have remained stable. They suggested that anthropogenic environmental degradation in the lake, such as shell dredging, had a greater effect on demersal habitats than on pelagic (open-water) and nearshore habitats.

BIRDS OF THE OPEN LAKE

Several species of birds are characteristic of the open lake or its shoreline areas. Those most often seen in the open lake are the common fish-eating predators such as brown pelican (*Pelecanus occidentalis*); double-crested cormorant (*Phalacrocorax auritus*); terns, including Forster's tern (*Sterna forsteri*), least tern (*Sterna antillarum*), royal tern (*Sterna maxima*), and Caspian tern (*Sterna caspia*); gulls, including laughing gull (*Larus atricilla*) and ring-billed gull (*Larus delawarensis*); and black skimmer (*Rynchops niger*). Laughing gulls, Forster's terns, gull-billed terns (*Sterna nilotica*), royal terns, and black skimmers have been reported as nesting on islands in Lake Borgne, but not in Lakes Pontchartrain or Maurepas, where suitable sand or shell nesting habitat is not present (Portnoy 1977; Martin and Lester 1990).

Several species of ducks are common on the lakes or adjacent marshes, but by far the most abundant species in the open lake is lesser scaup (*Aythya affinis*), which occurs in tremendous flocks on Lake Pontchartrain in autumn and winter. They feed upon the abundant benthic mollusks, especially *Rangia cuneata* (Bowman 1973; Mulholland 1985; Melancon 1995). Other common species are red-breasted merganser (*Mergus serrator*) and bufflehead (*Bucephala albeola*). Although other species of ducks may occur frequently on the lakes, they usually prefer more sheltered marsh habitats. Among the more common are green-winged teal (*Anas crecca*), mottled duck (*Anas fulvigula*), mallard (*Anas platyrhynchos*), blue-winged teal (*Anas discors*), northern shoveler (*Anas clypeata*), gadwall (*Anas strepera*), American wigeon (*Anas americana*), and ring-necked duck (*Aythya collaris*). These tend to be most numerous in autumn and winter.

Occasional ospreys (*Pandion haliaetus*) and bald eagles (*Haliaeetus leucocephalus*) are seen flying over or capturing fish in the lakes, and several nests are known in the area. Both species have increased in numbers in recent decades, having recovered significantly from the detrimental effects of widespread DDT use during the 1940s and 1950s.

Lake Pontchartrain is noted for its purple martin (*Porgne subis*) refuge at the southern end of the causeway, where thousands of purple martins gather and roost in preparation for their late summer migration south (Graham 1991). Large numbers of tree swallows (*Tachycineta bicolor*) arrive for winter, when they fly over the lakes and adjacent waterways. Barn swallows (*Hirundo rustica*) nest under most bridges and trestles crossing the lake and fly over the lakes capturing insects.

Soft-Bottom Benthic Community

The soft bottom sediments of the three lakes, as well as any estuary, provide habitat for numerous organisms, as well as food sources for benthic, burrowing, and demersal species. Sediments can vary in many ways, including grain size, origin, and chemical composition, and this variation may determine the dominant species in an area. In addition, water depth and related factors such as wave action, light penetration, and oxygen levels may affect community composition. These factors can affect the distribution of various organisms and yield distinct differences in community types, such as inshore or littoral areas versus offshore deep-water areas. In virtually every estuary, burrowing organisms such as annelid worms and clams will live within the sediments (the infauna). Benthic crabs, shrimp, snails, and some fishes live on the surface of the sediments. Demersal fishes swim near the bottom, where they find abundant food sources. Photosynthetic algae, diatoms, and bacteria may grow on the surface of the substrate in water shallow and clear enough to allow sufficient sunlight penetration. Submersed aquatic vegetation beds may be present in areas with sufficient light penetration to allow photosynthesis (to be discussed later as the grassbeds community).

Lake Pontchartrain estuary bottoms have been described as relatively depauperate in terms of species richness and density of macrofauna (Bahr et al. 1980). By far the dominant and most obvious benthic organism is the clam *Rangia cuneata*. Its biology and distribution in Lake Pontchartrain has been extensively studied (Fairbanks 1963; Tarver 1972; Tarver and Dugas 1973; Dugas et al. 1974; Tarver and Savoie 1976; Sikora and Sikora 1982; Abadie and Poirrier 2000, 2001). *Rangia cuneata* is a keystone species in the lake, contributing to substrate formation, water quality, and food sources for many other species. It is the dominant food for many of the more common species in the lake, including blue crab, freshwater drum, black drum, and lesser scaup (Darnell 1958; Bowman 1973; Mulholland 1985; Melancon 1995). Abadie and Poirrier (2001) estimated that the rangia clams in Lake Pontchartrain could filter the entire volume of water in the lake every four days and could produce more than 1 million tons of shell per year.

The rangia clams have been so abundant in Lake Pontchartrain and other coastal waters that massive deposits of "fossil" shell have accumulated. The shells along the shoreline and in Indian middens were recognized as commercially valuable for the production of lime cement as early as the mid-1700s. Beginning in the 1930s, commercial dredging of the clam shells below the lake began in earnest, and this practice had a profound effect on substrate and water quality, as well as the populations of live *Rangia* and other biota. The dredging had a much greater effect on benthic and demersal habitats than on pelagic (open-water) and nearshore habitats. However, the turbidity caused by the dredging affected virtually all aspects of the lake environment.

Studies have indicated that the adult *Rangia* population was severely reduced by dredging in most parts of the lake, with the exception of areas closed to dredging, such as those within 1 mi. (1.6 km) of shore (Bahr et al. 1980). With the cessation of shell dredging in 1990, there was a dramatic increase in the abundance of large clams (more than 20 mm), except in the southeastern portion of the lake off the Inner Harbor Navigation Canal, which is often impacted by hypoxic conditions (Abbadie and Poirrier 2000, 2001). However, there was a decrease in the abundance of *Rangia* during the drought and associated salinity increase in 1997–2001, and then widespread mortality of *Rangia* occurred following Hurricane Katrina in 2005 (Poirrier et al. 2006). The latter mortality was attributed to salinity stratification and hypoxic conditions similar to that occurring off the Inner Harbor Navigation Canal.

Two small gastropods, *Texadina sphinctostoma* and *Probythinella protera* (*Probythinella* or *Vioscalba louisianae*), are abundant in the lake but rarely observed because of their almost microscopic size (less than 3 mm). Bahr et al. (1980) and Sikora and Sikora (1982) found them to be the dominant benthic organisms in both numerical abundance (4000–11,000 per m^2) and biomass (2–3 g/m^2) during a period when the populations of adult *Rangia* were apparently reduced by shell dredging. In spite of their diminutive size, the two species could be important in the reworking and enrichment of estuarine sediments (Heard 1979). *Texadina barretti*, another similar gastropod, has been reported in Lake Pontchartrain, but it occurs in lesser numbers (Morrison 1965).

The dwarf surf clam (*Mulinia pontchartrainensis*) was fourth in abundance in the samples of Sikora and Sikora (1982) taken during 1978–1980, but second to *Probythinella protera* in 1978 (March to May) samples (Bahr et al. 1980). Dugas et al. (1974) reported *M. pontchartrainensis* in 95% of their collections from Lake Pontchartrain and second to *Rangia* in overall abundance. The species (as *Mulinia* sp.) was first in abundance in the collections of Poirrier et al. (1984). This small species (less than 10 mm long) was referred to by Fairbanks (1963) as *Rangianella* and subsequently described as a new species based upon collections from Lake Pontchartrain (Morrison 1965).

Other dominant benthic organisms reported by Sikora and Sikora (1982) as abundant in the Lake Pontchartrain sediments are the polychaetes *Hobsonia* (*Hypaniola*) *florida* and *Mediomastus californiensis*, chironomid insect larvae of the genus *Ablabesmyia*, the dark false mussel (*Mytilopsis* [*Congeria*] *leucophaeta*), the amphipod *Cerapus benthophilus*, and nematodes. The dark false mussel does not normally occur in soft sediments but attaches by byssal threads to a hard substrate, such as rangia clam shells or submerged logs. The American oyster (*Crassostrea virginica*), also characteristic of hard substrates but capable of forming colonial reefs on soft sediments, is common in Lake Borgne and the higher salinity eastern portions of Lake Pontchartrain.

Fleeger et al. (1983) recorded fifteen species of bottom-dwelling meiobenthic copepods in lake sediments, but noted that this group was dominated by species often associated with the water column. True infaunal species (living within the sediment interstitial spaces) were rare, possibly because of the unstable nature of the lake sediments, which were readily resuspended by wind-generated scour. Four species were considered common and comprised 90% of all individuals collected. The most common was *Scottolana canadensis*, considered epibenthic (living at the water-sediment interface) as adults, but planktonic as nauplii. Two other common species, *Acartia tonsa* and *Halicyclops fosteri*, were abundant planktonic species in the water column. The fourth common copepod was an unidentified species of *Pseudobradya*.

Four distinct benthic zones were identified along a transect on the northern side of the lake based upon the dominant species (Roberts 1981): (1) lake edge within 0.25 mi. (0.4 km) from shore: meiofauna dominated by nematodes, macrofauna rare; (2) nearshore, 0.25–1.00 mi. (0.4–1.6 km) from shore: meiofauna dominated by nematodes, macrofauna dominated by *Rangia cuneata* and *Probythinella protera*; (3) open lake, 1.25–7 mi. (2.0–11.3 km) from shore: meiofauna dominated by copepods, macrofauna dominated by *Mulinia pontchartrainensis* and *Texadina sphinctostoma*; and (4) causeway zones, 7–9 mi. (11.3–14.5 km) from shore: meiofauna dominated by nematodes, macrofauna dominated by *R. cuneata, M. pontchartrainensis, P. protera, T. sphinctostoma, Mytilopsis leucophaeta*, and chironomid midge larvae. Other species listed by Roberts included the clam *Macoma mitchilli*, the isopods *Edotea montosa* and *Cyathura polita*, the amphipods *Monoculoides edwardsii, Corophium lacustre*, and *Grandidierella bonnieroides*, the opossum shrimp *Mysidopsis almyra*, and the mud crab *Rhithropanopeus harrisii*.

Otvos (1978a, 1978b) studied the benthic foraminiferal fauna of Lake Pontchartrain and found it dominated by *Ammotium salsum* and *Ammonia beccarii*, both characteristic of oligohaline environments. The surveys suggested, however, that the influx of higher salinity waters through the Mississippi River Gulf Outlet had introduced several open marine species into the lake.

Among the dominant macroinvertebrates that commonly rest on the lake substrate are various crustaceans, including the commercially important blue crab (*Callinectes sapidus*) and brown and white shrimp (*Farfantepenaeus aztecus* and *Litopenaeus setiferus*). The freshwater river shrimp (*Macrobrachium ohione*) is a common resident of fresher areas of the lakes (Darnell 1958; Tarver and Savoie 1976), and the mud shrimp (*Callianassa jamaicense*) may be common in more saline parts of Lake Pontchartrain and Lake Borgne (Darnell 1961; Bahr et al. 1980; Fannaly 1980; Sikora and Sikora 1982). Five species of grass shrimp (*Palaemonetes* spp.) have been recorded from the lakes (Suttkus et al. 1954; Fannaly 1980; Sikora and Sikora 1982), but are more characteristic of vegetated areas such as marshes and grass beds.

The blue crab is one of the most characteristic organisms in Lake Pontchartrain. The adults are benthic, but can swim (the genus name *Callinectes* means "beautiful swimmer"). They are euryhaline, being able to survive in salinities of 0–35 ppt. Blue crabs consume a wide range of foods in Lake Pontchartrain and have been described as "a detritivore, bottom predator, and general scavenger" (Darnell 1958). The adults mate while the female is in a soft, post-molt condition, and then the females migrate to higher salinity water (20+ ppt) outside of Lake Pontchartrain. The species generally requires a salinity range of 21–28 ppt for successful spawning. Blue crabs in Lake Pontchartrain are apparently mostly spawned in Lake Borgne and Chandeleur Sound, where egg-bearing females are common, and not in Lake Pontchartrain (Darnell 1959). The sex ratio in the lake is about equal only in June and July, with females least numerous during February to March and August to September, suggesting two spawning peaks each year. The eggs, which number about 2 million per female, are carried on swimmerets on the underside of the female's apron, at which time she is referred to as a "sponge" or "berry" crab. The eggs hatch after about two weeks, as zoea larvae that are planktonic and stenohaline (requiring a salinity of 20+ ppt). The zoea go through a series of seven molts during a period of about four to six weeks, and then enter the megalops stage, when they are still planktonic but euryhaline and are carried into the estuary by tidal currents. After two additional molts, over a period of six to nine days, the megalops become juvenile crabs, which are able to swim and continue their migration into the estuary; they eventually become more benthic.

The blue crab dominates the commercial fishery of Lake Pontchartrain, with large numbers caught each year, primarily in wire-mesh crab traps marked by round, styrofoam floats that are scattered all over the lake. Frequently the styrofoam floats break loose, ending up among the windrows of litter and other flotsam along the lakeshore, and the "ghost" traps continue capturing and killing crabs and fish. They also become artificial hard substrate for colonies of hydroids, sponges, and other encrusting organisms.

Based upon National Marine Fisheries Service catch statistics, there was a general decline in crab production in the lakes between 1960 and 1980, from an average of 2.6 million lb. (1.2 million kg) annually in 1959–1963, with a high in 1961 of 2.96 million lb. (1.3 million kg), to an average during 1974–1978 of about 1.4 million lb. (0.6 million kg). Roberts and Thompson (1982) suggested that negative impacts from openings of the Bonnet Carré Spillway (in 1974 and 1978) and reduced water quality in the lakes may have been associated with this decline. They also suggested, however, that the National Marine Fisheries Service data grossly underestimate the total catch (including part-time commercial and recreational crabbers). Roberts and Thompson estimated the 1980 total catch of blue crabs in Lake Pontchartrain and Lake Borgne to be 9.8 million lb. (4.4 million kg), with a total economic impact of $13.4 million, several times larger than the published federal catch statistics for the lakes. Blue crabs accounted for 67% of the value and 79% of the volume of commercial fisheries in Lake Pontchartrain between 1965 and 1975 (Thompson and Stone 1980). The soft-shell crab industry has also been important and lucrative in the Lake Pontchartrain system (Gilbert 1989).

Trawling for shrimp (including white shrimp, *Litopenaeus setiferus*, and brown shrimp, *Farfantepenaeus aztecus*) in Lake Pontchartrain and Lake Borgne is an important commercial fishery, as well as a popular recreational activity. The pink shrimp (*Farfantepenaeus duorarum*) has also been reported in Lake Pontchartrain and Lake Borgne but in small numbers (Darnell and Williams 1956). Bottom trawls are used for shrimp fishing in the open lake, and wing nets or butterfly nets towed at the surface are used in the passes at night when the shrimp are migrating. Shrimp represented about 19% of the commercial fisheries value for Lake Pontchartrain between 1963 and 1975 (Thompson and Stone 1980). Both brown (beginning late May to early June) and white shrimp (August) seasons are recognized, but the commercial catch of brown shrimp (average annual catch 1965–1973 was 195,000 lb. or 88,000 kg) has far exceeded that of white shrimp (26,000 lb., 12,000 kg) in Lake Pontchartrain (Tarver and Savoie 1976). In contrast, white shrimp dominated the shrimp harvest in coastal Louisiana, including Lake Pontchartrain, prior to about 1950 (Condrey and

Fuller 1992). Suggested causes for the "cataclysmic drop" in abundance of white shrimp include overfishing, severe drought, restricted flow of the Mississippi River into the marshes, pesticide spraying of sugar cane fields, early oil and gas exploration, and manufacturing activities.

Part of the eastern portion of Lake Pontchartrain and Lake St. Catherine is designated a marine preserve (Louisiana House Bill 1527, 1999), where trawling for shrimp, fish, and crabs is banned from the shore areas (from the shoreline to 1.25 mi. [2 km] out) from the Jefferson/Orleans Parish line east to the eastern shore of South Point, from South Point to North Shore along the railroad bridge and between the railroad bridge and Interstate 10, and then west from North Shore to Goose Point. Trawling is also prohibited in Lake Maurepas.

The two commercially important shrimp species in Lake Pontchartrain are similar in habits but have distinct reproductive cycles and occurrence patterns in the lake. Both are benthic detritivores that can burrow and swim (especially at night and during migratory movements). Some shrimp spawning may occur throughout the year, but there is a distinct peak spawn in autumn. The eggs are fertilized internally, then released into the water (0.5–1 million eggs per female), where they hatch within twenty-four hours. The eggs are buoyant, remaining near the surface, and the larvae are planktonic. During the first several weeks of life, the shrimp pass through several larval stages including nauplius (five stages), protozoea (three stages), mysis (three stages), and postlarva. The latter is about 0.2–0.5 in. (5.5–12.5 mm) long, migrates inshore and into the estuary, and becomes benthic. The brown shrimp tend to spawn further offshore than white shrimp (in Gulf waters deeper than 60 ft. or 18 m) and enter the estuary in March to May. By this time the juveniles are about 1 in. (25 mm) long, and they continue to grow about 2 in. (50 mm) per month. The adults are about 3 in. (75 mm) and larger. The spring shrimping season (mostly for brown shrimp) is opened when 75% of the shrimp are 4 in. (100 mm) long (68 per lb.), which usually occurs in late May or early June. The adults emigrate to offshore waters in June to October, and few are left inshore by November. Most do not survive more than one year, but provide prey for many other species.

The white shrimp are similar in most respects, but spawn closer to shore (from inshore waters to depths of about 100 ft. or 30 m) and are more characteristic of low salinity waters (almost fresh). They are also less likely to burrow and are more active during daylight. Their postlarval migration inshore occurs in summer (late June to September) following the brown shrimp, and supports a fall shrimp season (mostly for white shrimp) that begins in August. The adults then move offshore to overwinter (following cold fronts in early winter) and return in the spring.

Many species of demersal or benthic fishes are associated with the substrate in Lake Pontchartrain. Common species include Atlantic stingray (*Dasyatis sabina*), American eel (*Anguilla rostrata*), speckled worm eel (*Myrophis punctatus*), blue catfish (*Ictalurus furcatus*), channel catfish (*Ictalurus punctatus*), flathead catfish (*Pylodictus olivaris*), hardhead catfish (*Ariopsis felis*), gafftopsail catfish (*Bagre marinus*), skilletfish (*Gobiesox strumosus*), chain pipefish (*Syngnathus louisianae*), Gulf pipefish (*Syngnathus scovelli*), naked goby (*Gobiosoma bosc*), southern flounder (*Paralichthys lethostigma*), and hogchoker (*Trinectes maculatus*). In addition, many of the free-swimming fishes that occupy Lake Pontchartrain tend to orient near the bottom, especially to feed. Blue catfish and channel catfish are the dominant demersal species in Lake Maurepas and support a significant commercial fishery (McElroy et al. 1990; Hastings 2002).

Shoreline Areas

Shoreline areas tend to have their own unique biota, consisting of species not often found in deeper offshore waters. The shallower areas of the lake may support scattered mats of filamentous algae (such as *Cladophora*, *Oedogonium*, *Rhizoclonium*, and *Spirogyra*) and various benthic diatoms (including *Biddulphia*, *Terpsinoe*, *Cymbella*, *Navicula*, and *Pinnularia*; Darnell 1958), which cannot survive in deeper waters because of the lack of light penetration to the bottom. The intertidal mudflat community so characteristic of most estuaries with predictable periods of flooding and drying is almost nonexistent in Lake Pontchartrain because of the very narrow and unpredictable tidal ranges. However, during irregular periods of low water, extensive shallow areas of mud or sandy mud mixed with shell fragments may be temporarily exposed, especially along shorelines.

Beaches are considered the primary habitat of Gulf killifish (*Fundulus grandis*) and inland silverside (*Menidia beryllina*) and secondary habitat of bay anchovy (*Anchoa mitchilli*), juvenile Gulf menhaden (*Brevoortia patronus*), juvenile striped mullet (*Mugil cephalus*), juvenile hardhead catfish (*Ariopsis felis*), and sheepshead minnow (*Cyprinodon variegatus*) in Lake Pontchartrain (Thompson and Verret 1980). In seine collections along shoreline sites in Lake Pontchartrain, Suttkus et al. (1954) listed the dominant species as Atlantic croaker (20.9%), Gulf menhaden (26.0%), spot (8.6%), silver perch (8.5%), hardhead catfish (6.2%), and inland silverside (5.5%). Most of these species are also common in the open lake waters.

In the upper parts of Lake Pontchartrain, and especially in Lake Maurepas, the shoreline areas are characterized by cypress swamps with numerous cypress trees and knees standing in the water and numerous stumps of ancient cypress trees either submerged or slightly emergent above the water surface (see Figure 9.1). Catfishes (*Ictalurus* sp. and *Pylodictus olivaris*) may hide in the protective shelter of holes under the stumps. Fishermen often string trotlines from stump to stump (known locally as "birdlines") to catch catfish, which may often reach impressive sizes of 40–50 lb. (18–23 kg).

Hastings et al. (1987) used rotenone to collect fishes in shoreline areas of Lake Maurepas, where seining was not productive because of the numerous cypress stumps and other snags. The most numerous species of fish were Gulf menhaden (56.8%), inland silverside (4.4%), hogchoker (2.7%), naked goby (2.5%), longear sunfish (*Lepomis megalotis*, 2.3%), bay anchovy (1.3%), bluegill (*Lepomis macrochirus*, 1.1%), least killifish (*Heterandria formosa*, 1.1%), mosquitofish (*Gambusia affinis*, 1.0%), Gulf killifish (0.8%), and Gulf pipefish (0.7%). Other species that may be common along shorelines in the lakes include largemouth bass (*Micropterus salmoides*), Atlantic needlefish (*Strongylura marina*), spotted gar (*Lepisosteus oculatus*), rainwater killifish (*Lucania parva*), sailfin molly (*Poecilia latipinna*), and pinfish (*Lagodon rhomboides*).

Several common shorebirds are associated with Lake Pontchartrain shorelines and adjacent wetlands, including black-bellied plover (*Pluvialis squatarola*), killdeer (*Charadrius vociferus*), black-necked stilt (*Himantopus mexicanus*), greater yellowlegs (*Tringa melanoleuca*), lesser yellowlegs (*Tringa flavipes*), spotted sandpiper (*Actitis macularia*), semipalmated sandpiper (*Calidris pusilla*), western sandpiper (*Calidris mauri*), least sandpiper (*Calidris minutilla*), pectoral sandpiper (*Calidris melanotos*), short-billed dowitcher (*Limnodromus griseus*), and long-billed dowitcher (*Limnodromus scolopaceus*).

Hard Substrate Community

Hard substrates are important habitat for many benthic marine organisms, especially as attachment sites for sessile forms that never move once they become attached. However, natural hard substrates are not common in the Lake Pontchartrain system or in most of the north-central Gulf of Mexico. But their potential importance as habitat even in such areas is demonstrated by the rapidity with which artificial substrates such as boat bottoms and pilings become "fouled" with benthic organisms. This fouling results from the large number of planktonic larvae of benthic organisms carried to all parts of the marine environment as a means of dispersal to new habitats. Filamentous algae such as *Cladophora*, *Oedogonium*, and *Rhizoclonium* and many of the benthic animals that produce moss-like colonies (such as hydroids and bryozoans), then provide hiding places and food sources for other small benthic invertebrates such as protozoans, polychaetes, and crustaceans (amphipods, isopods, and tanaids).

The most significant natural hard substrate habitats in the Pontchartrain basin are the oyster reefs of the higher salinity portion of Lake Pontchartrain and Lake Borgne, accumulations of rangia clam shells in other parts of the system, and the many cypress stumps, logs, and other wood pieces washed into the lake. However, there are also many sources of artificial substrate associated with human activities now present in the lake. In fact, virtually any hard object placed in the lake, such as crab traps, glass bottles, metal cans, or other junk, if not buried in the sediments, can become the site of a small hard substrate community. Posts and pilings used for bridges, piers, and camps usually become encrusted with algae, barnacles, and other benthic organisms. Bulkheads, seawalls, and groins, as well as the numerous rock piles and other shoreline protection materials around the lake provide substrate to which such organisms can attach. An estimated 36–40% of the shoreline is armored with potential hard substrate (Lopez 2003). The concrete pilings supporting the Pontchartrain Causeway and Interstate 10 bridges, as well as other bridges and powerline supports, provide extensive artificial hard substrate. Since 2001 several artificial reefs have been constructed in the lake specifically to increase available hard substrate and hiding places for benthic invertebrates and fish (LPBF 2001a, 2001d).

The American oyster (*Crassostrea virginica*) can form extensive oyster reefs providing hard substrate for a variety of other benthic species, but this species is found only in the extreme eastern end of Lake Pontchartrain and in Lake Borgne, although planktonic oyster larvae can be collected throughout Lake Pontchartrain and in Lake Maurepas (Tarver and Savoie 1976). Because the American oyster requires a salinity range of 10–28 ppt, there are no reefs developed within Lake Pontchartrain. However, they are well-developed in Lake Borgne and the adjacent Mississippi Sound, where oysters are commercially harvested. Only small patches of scattered oysters occur in the lower portions of Lake Pontchartrain near the tidal passes. Where they do occur, oyster reefs provide significant hard-bottom habitat for a variety of benthic organisms such as sponges, hydroids, bryozoans, worms, mollusks, and barnacles. Many demersal predators also feed around oyster reefs because of this abundance of benthic prey. Important species are black drum (*Pogonias cromis*), which can reach sizes up to 150 lb. (68 kg), sheepshead (*Archosargus probatocephalus*), and blue crab (*Callinectes sapidus*). The black drum has large molariform pharyngeal teeth with which it can crush the shells of its prey. The sheepshead has strong incisors and molariform teeth for scraping its prey off hard substrates and crushing it. The Gulf stone crab (*Menippe adina*, as *M. mercenaria*) and pistol shrimp

THE ESTUARINE COMMUNITIES 213

Figure 15.1 Cypress stump with *Sphaeroma* damage near the mouth of the Tangipahoa River (Photograph by the author)

(*Alpheus estuariensis*, as *A. heterochaelis*), species often associated with oyster reefs, have been recorded in Lake Borgne (Davis et al. 1970), although Pattillo et al. (1997) listed the Gulf stone crab as rare in both Lake Pontchartrain and Lake Borgne.

The most common species identified in a series of studies on epifaunal invertebrates in Lake Pontchartrain (Poirrier and Mulino 1975, 1977; Poirrier 1976, 1978a; Poirrier and Partridge 1979) include hydroids (*Garveia* [*Bimeria*] *franciscana* and *Cordylophora caspia*), sponges (*Spongilla alba* and *Trochospongilla leidii*), barnacles (*Balanus subalbidus*), nematodes, bryozoans or ectoprocts (*Victorella pavida* and *Membranipora* sp.), polychaete worms (*Polydora websteri*), and tube-building amphipods (*Corophium lacustre*). The tanaid crustacean *Hargeria rapax* may also be common on hard substrates, as well as soft sediments. Two mussels (*Mytilopsis leucophaeta* and *Ischadium recurvum*) are most characteristic of hard substrates, to which they attach by byssal threads, and they may become abundant in places. The hydroid *G. franciscana* has been described as widely distributed in Lake Pontchartrain, but especially in areas of high bottom organic content and moderate current; it attaches to various substrates including clam shells, logs, sticks, and posts, as well as silt and sandy silt bottoms (Crowell and Darnell 1955).

Among the natural woody substrates entering the lake, cypress logs and stumps are especially important. Because of the dense resins accumulated in old-growth cypress trees, their wood is especially resistant to decay and can survive for hundreds of years when submerged. However, a small isopod crustacean (*Sphaeroma terebrans*) bores holes into the wood. Stumps standing in the water can have an eroded appearance below the normal water line because of the effects of these small organisms (Figure 15.1). In higher salinity areas (greater than 5 ppt) the wood-boring mollusk or "ship worm" *Teredo navalis* is common. Wood submerged for extended periods can become extensively eroded and tunneled by these boring invertebrates, and the openings and crevices then become important hiding places for other benthic animals, such as the naked goby (*Gobiosoma bosc*), skilletfish (*Gobiesox strumosus*), and mud crab (*Rhithropanopeus harrisii*), which may be especially common on the stumps and logs.

Grassbeds Community

In locations of Lake Pontchartrain sufficiently shallow to allow light penetration to the bottom, submersed vegetation such as seagrasses and algae can occur. The major grassbeds are located along the northeastern shoreline near Goose Point from the Tchefuncte River east to Point du Chien and in a small area near Lincoln Beach (Cho and Poirrier 2001), and they are dominated by water celery or eelgrass (*Vallisneria americana*) and widgeon grass (*Ruppia maritima*). Other aquatic plants reported from the lake (Montz 1978) include clasping pondweed (*Potamogeton perfoliatus*), southern naiad (*Najas guadalupensis*), horned pondweed (*Zannichellia palustris*), dwarf spikerush (*Eleocharis parvula*), as well as the nonnative Eurasian watermilfoil (*Myriophyllum spicatum*; Cho and Poirrier 2001). Burns et al. (1995) reported a relatively large bed (4.4 acres or 1.8 ha) of clasping pondweed in northeastern Lake Pontchartrain near Point Platte, but *P. perfoliatus* has not been found in Lake Pontchartrain since 1998 (Cho and Poirrier 2005). Other aquatic species, which tend to be more characteristic of adjacent canals or passes and lower salinities, include coontail (*Ceratophyllum demersum* and *C. echinatum*), fanwort (*Cabomba caroliniana*), frogbit (*Limnobium spongia*), muskgrass (*Chara vulgaris*), white waterlily (*Nymphaea odorata*), and yellow waterlily or spatterdock (*Nuphar lutea advena*). *Myriophyllum spicatum* is also very common in some sheltered waters. Pieces of these plants may be occasionally flushed into the lake by high water, as are many floating aquatic plants common in protected waters of the basin (Montz 1978). Other species that may occasionally occur are floating waterprimrose (*Ludwigia peploides*) and water paspalum (*Paspalum fluitans*).

Grassbeds were once more widely distributed in Lake Pontchartrain but have declined because of environmental degradation, especially the increased turbidity associated with shell dredging (Table 10). After shell dredging was banned from Lake Pontchartrain in 1990, the water clarity significantly improved (Francis and Poirrier 1999) and the grassbeds began to recover. However, water quality changes continue to affect the occurrence of these submersed aquatic plants. Decreased salinity and water clarity associated with the opening of the Bonnet Carré Spillway in March 1997 resulted in a significant decrease in the distribution of *Ruppia maritima* (Poirrier et al. 1999; Cho and Poirrier 2001, 2005) and a reduction in the maximum water depth (to less than 1 m) for all submersed aquatic vegetation. In contrast, there was a significant increase in the occurrence of *Ruppia* during the drought years of 1999 and 2000, when salinity and water clarity were higher, so that *Ruppia* extended to depths of 2.0 m and eventually surpassed *Vallisneria* as the most abundant species. However, the abundance of *Ruppia* tended to decrease significantly in 2003 with decreasing salinity, and freshwater species (*Vallisneria* and *Najas*) increased.

The grassbeds are important habitat and sources of food for a variety of benthic invertebrates and fishes, especially as juveniles, including the most valuable commercial species in the lake (blue crab, *Callinectes sapidus*; brown shrimp, *Farfantepenaeus aztecus*; and spotted seatrout, *Cynoscion nebulosus*; Thompson and Stone 1980). Young-of-the-year spotted seatrout (or speckled trout), which move into the lake between June and September, are found exclusively in the grassbeds (Thompson and Verret 1980). The grassbed plants also provide substrate for various epiphytic organisms, such as the alga *Cladophora*, which can become so abundant during excess nutrient events that it may inhibit the growth of or kill the macrophytic plants (Poirrier et al. 1999). Four species of fish, rainwater killifish (*Lucania parva*), naked goby (*Gobiosoma bosc*), Gulf pipefish (*Syngnathus scovelli*), and clown goby (*Microgobius gulosus*), are dominant in Lake Pontchartrain vegetation beds (Duffy and Baltz 1998). Gulf pipefish are especially characteristic of these grass beds and can be quite common in the lake (Joseph 1957). Darnell (1961) noted that the *Vallisneria* beds adjacent to streams of the north shore were denuded by turtles (*Pseudemys* sp., probably *Pseudemys floridana*; Dundee and Rossman 1989).

Grass shrimp (*Palaemonetes* spp.) are especially characteristic of the vegetation beds, although Tarver and Savoie (1976) reported the dominant species *P. pugio* at all stations sampled, including open lake stations, and it is especially common in marsh pools and ditches. *Palaemonetes intermedius*, *P. kadiakensis*,

P. paludosus, and *P. vulgaris* have also been reported from the lake (Suttkus et al. 1954; Fannaly 1980; Sikora and Sikora 1982). According to Heard (1982) and Anderson (1985), *P. paludosus* and *P. kadiakensis* are more characteristic of freshwater and oligohaline areas, whereas *P. pugio*, *P. intermedius*, and *P. vulgaris* are brackish water forms. A variety of other benthic invertebrates and epiphytic organisms are also common in grassbeds but have not been studied in Lake Pontchartrain.

16.

The Marsh Communities

Surrounding almost all estuaries is a vast expanse of emergent marsh vegetation that benefits from the rich nutrients provided in the estuarine water and sediments, plus the high level of direct solar radiation needed for photosynthesis, to produce one of the most biologically productive ecological communities on earth. The marshes are dominated by various species of grasses, sedges, and rushes, depending upon salinity levels. The salinity gradient across the estuary determines the species of dominant plants characteristic of the marshes, although there are no clear dividing lines and one type tends to gradually merge with another. In addition, the salinity gradient can be affected by freshwater inflow, which can determine the local distribution of marsh species. There is also a vegetation gradient with slight changes in elevation.

Penfound and Hathaway (1938) defined four types of marshes of southeastern Louisiana: (1) strictly freshwater marsh, with no trace of salt; (2) nearly fresh or faintly brackish marsh, with salinities less than 5 ppt; (3) brackish marsh, with salinities of 5–20 ppt; and (4) saline marsh, with salinities greater than 20 ppt. These definitions approximate the divisions recognized by the Louisiana Natural Heritage Program (1988), as well as Handley et al. (2001), as fresh marsh, intermediate marsh, brackish marsh, and saline marsh. There are about 483,400 acres (195,629 ha) of wetlands in the Pontchartrain basin, including 38,500 acres (15,581 ha) of fresh marsh, 28,600 acres (11,574 ha) of intermediate marsh, 116,800 acres (47,268 ha) of brackish marsh, 83,900 acres (33,954 ha) of saline marsh, and 215,600 acres (87,252 ha) of cypress swamp (Louisiana Coastal Wetlands Conservation and Restoration Task Force 1993).

Figure 16.1 Wildflowers of the Manchac marshes: (A) bulltongue (*Sagittaria lancifolia*), (B) deerpea (*Vigna luteola*), (C) Louisiana or Virginia iris (*Iris virginica*), (D) spider lily (*Hymenocallis occidentalis*), (E) marsh morning glory (*Ipomoea sagittata*), (F) marsh mallow (*Hibiscus lasiocarpus*), (G) saltmarsh mallow (*Kosteletzkya virginica*) (Photographs by the author)

Saline marshes occur only in the extreme outer limits of the basin and are beyond the scope of this book.

Fresh marshes occur at the upper freshwater end of the salinity gradient within the Pontchartrain basin, mostly around Lake Maurepas at the western end of the basin and within river tributaries (Louisiana Natural Heritage Program 1988). These marshes are dominated by plants such as maidencane or paille fine (*Panicum hemitomon*), spikesedge or spikerush (*Eleocharis* spp.), bulltongue, also known as lance-leaf arrowhead or paddleweed (*Sagittaria lancifolia* = *S. falcata*; Figure 16.1A), marshhay cordgrass (*Spartina patens*; see Figure 12.3), common reed or roseau cane (*Phragmites australis*), fragrant flatsedge (*Cyperus odoratus*), pickerelweed (*Pontederia cordata*), arrow arum (*Peltandra virginica*), cattails (*Typha angustifolia* and *T. latifolia*), deerpea or hairypod cowpea (*Vigna luteola*; Figure 16.1B), southern wild rice or giant cutgrass (*Zizaniopsis miliacea*), and smartweed (*Polygonum* spp.). Annual wild rice (*Zizania aquatica*) may grow along some waterways. Louisiana or Virginia iris (*Iris virginica*; Figure 16.1C), swamp lilies (*Crinum americanum*), and spiderlilies (*Hymenocallis caroliniana*; Figure 16.1D) are common in places. A nonnative marsh species that has become common in some areas of the Pontchartrain basin is the tropical wild taro (*Colocasia esculenta*), which is also commonly referred to as elephant ear (but not *Xanthosoma sagittifolium*, which does not appear to be established outside of cultivation in the Pontchartrain basin).

Most of the marshes bordering the central part of the basin are considered intermediate marshes (brackish-freshwater) dominated by either marshhay cordgrass (Louisiana Natural Heritage Program 1988) or sawgrass (*Cladium jamaicense*; Penfound and Hathaway 1938). Other significant associated species include roseau cane, bulltongue, spikesedge, common three-cornered grass (*Scirpus americanus* = *S. olneyi*), giant bulrush (*Scirpus californicus*), deerpea, seashore paspalum (*Paspalum vaginatum*), switch grass (*Panicum virgatum*), bearded sprangletop (*Leptochloa fusca* = *L. fascicularis*), camphor-weed (*Pluchea camphorata*), walter millet (*Echinochloa walteri*), fragrant flatsedge, and big cordgrass (*Spartina cynosuroides*). Nonnative alligatorweed (*Alternanthera philoxeroides*) may be common. The fresh and intermediate marshes are noted for the striking beauty of their abundant wildflowers, which at times cover the marshes with contrasting whites, yellows, blues, and pinks against a background of bright green foliage (Figure 16.1).

At the extreme eastern end of the lake and bordering Lake Borgne are brackish water marshes (Louisiana Natural Heritage Program 1988), with dominant vegetation including marshhay cordgrass (see Figure 12.3), black rush (*Juncus roemerianus*), and saltmarsh cordgrass (*Spartina alterniflora*). Other significant associated species include salt grass (*Distichlis spicata*), common three-cornered grass, salt marsh bulrush (*Scirpus robustus*), dwarf spikesedge (*Eleocharis parvula*), widgeon grass (*Ruppia maritima*), seashore paspalum, coastal water hyssop (*Bacopa monnieri*), and big cordgrass.

At a site considered to be a brackish marsh (their "oak island" transect near the lower Pearl River), Penfound and Hathaway (1938) recognized two community types dominated by marsh vegetation, the cane zone and the brackish marsh. The brackish marshes (said to stretch "away for miles" and "perhaps the most widespread of all" marsh types) were dominated by marshhay cordgrass and salt grass, with saltmarsh cordgrass ("salt cane") and saltmarsh bulrush ("three-cornered rush") around the borders of lagoons. The adjacent cane zone, only 2 in. (5 cm) higher than the brackish marsh, was dominated by big cordgrass ("quill cane") and switch grass, but also with much marshhay cordgrass and salt grass.

At a nearby slightly brackish or almost freshwater marsh transect near Slidell, Penfound and Hathaway (1938) described the community as sawgrass marsh, with an almost pure stand of sawgrass, but with some broadleaf cattail (*Typha latifolia*), narrowleaf cattail (*Typha augustifolia*), and giant bulrush.

Over a distance of about 3 mi. (5 km), Taylor and Grace (1995) identified sites near the mouth of the Pearl River as fresh marsh (salinity always near zero) dominated by switch grass and big cordgrass, oligohaline marsh (salinity 0–4 ppt) dominated by marshhay cordgrass and bulltongue, and mesohaline marsh (salinity 0–6 ppt) dominated by saltmarsh cordgrass.

Also in the lower Pearl River basin, White (1983) studied plant communities in the transition from floodplain forest to open marsh adjacent to Lake Borgne, over a distance of approximately 19 mi. (30 km). He recognized five communities as hardwood bottom forest, cypress-tupelo forest, scrub, fresh marsh, and saline marsh. The fresh marsh was dominated by bulltongue, dotted smartweed (*Polygonum punctatum*), spikesedges, and panic grasses (*Panicum* spp.). Most of the herbaceous species of the adjacent scrub community (smartweed, *Polygonum* spp., mostly *P. punctatum*; bulltongue; sawgrass; spikesedge; switch grass; lizard's tail, *Saururus cernuus*; pickerelweed; royal fern, *Osmunda regalis*; and marsh fern, *Thelypteris palustris*) also occurred in the fresh marshes, but the woody species did not. The saline marsh (with mean salinity of 1.5 ppt, and thus equivalent to the "intermediate" marshes of Louisiana Natural Heritage Program [1988] and Handley et al. [2001]) was dominated by marshhay cordgrass, which in some places was present in nearly pure stands, salt grass, and Roseau cane. Other important species were black rush and saltmarsh cordgrass. Deerpea was described as "smothering" these marshes in late summer.

Conner et al. (1980) sampled marsh vegetation at several sites on the north shore of Lake Pontchartrain, from near the mouth of the Tchefuncte River to Little Lagoon near the Rigolets. They noted the salinity gradient reflected in the vegetation composition of the marshes. At their lakeshore sites, marshhay cordgrass was by far the dominant vegetation. This was also the dominant species at two inland sites (Cane Bayou and Bayou Bonfouca). Common three-cornered grass was also important at most lakeshore sites. In contrast, bulltongue was the dominant species at two inland fresh marsh locations (Tchefuncte Canal and Bayou Powell) and was present at the westernmost lakeshore site (Tchefuncte Marsh) but not to the east, where salinities were higher. The two fresh marsh sites had the highest species diversity.

Brewer and Grace (1990) noted a gradient of vegetation types upstream from Lake Pontchartrain along the Tchefuncte River, but they suggested that the gradient was best correlated with distance from the lake, as well as elevation (decreased up to 6 in. or 15 cm with distance away from the lake) and substrate organic matter (increased with distance away from the lake), rather than soil salinity. However, their dominant vegetation types, marshhay cordgrass nearest the lake, bulltongue farther inland, and sawgrass farthest inland, were also distributed in order of decreasing salinity tolerance. The sawgrass marsh was bordered to the north by bald cypress swamp. Storm-generated salinity pulses, with short-lived but strong salinity gradients, were considered more significant in determining species distribution than were background soil salinities (which were generally less than 5 ppt). Other common species recorded (from a total list of thirty-seven) were alligatorweed, softstem bulrush (*Scirpus tabernaemontani* = *S. validus*), salt marsh bulrush, annual saltmarsh aster (*Symphyotrichum* [*Aster*] *subulatus*), barnyard grass (*Echinochloa crus-galli*), bearded sprangletop, and deerpea.

Baldwin and Mendelssohn (1998) included a list of thirty-one species recorded in their study of *Sagittaria* and *Spartina* communities of the Tchefuncte area. In the *Sagittaria* community, they recognized bulltongue and dotted smartweed as codominant and alligatorweed, saltmarsh aster, Virginia buttonweed (*Diodia virginiana*), creeping spikerush (*Eleocharis fallax*), marsh morning glory (*Ipomoea sagittata*; Figure 16.1E), wand loosestrife (*Lythrum lineare*), turkey tangle fogfruit (*Phyla nodiflora*), mock bishopsweed (*Ptilimnium capillaceum*), and deerpea as subdominant. In contrast they considered the *Spartina* community a monoculture of marshhay cordgrass, with softstem bulrush, deerpea, and groundsel bush (*Baccharis halimifolia*) as subdominant but occurring at low densities.

Farther to the west, the land bridge separating Lakes Pontchartrain and Maurepas was once covered with a dense forest of cypress-tupelo swamp, which was logged around the turn of the twentieth century and much of the area has converted to open marsh. It is now the location of the Manchac Wildlife Management Area and the Turtle Cove Environmental Research Station, where research has addressed various ecological aspects of this marsh community. The area is classified as intermediate marsh, with salinities usually less than 5 ppt. Platt (1988) listed eighty-seven plant species recorded on the Manchac Wildlife Management Area, and noted that bulltongue, dotted smartweed, deerpea, and marsh morning glory were the dominant species. The vines of deerpea and marsh morning glory tended to overgrow and form a dense mat covering other marsh species in July and August. Other major species mentioned were sicklepod or coffeeweed (*Sesbania herbacea*), annual marsh aster, perennial saltmarsh aster (*Symphyotrichum tenuifolium*), seashore paspalum, walter millet, and fall panicum (*Panicum dichotimiflorum*). Marshhay cordgrass was dominant in a limited area. Surrounding the open-water area known as the "Prairie" was floating marsh comprised of bearded sprangletop. The Prairie was once a continuous terrestrial marsh but is now almost completely flooded because of subsidence. Myers et al. (1995) added alligatorweed and leafy threesquare (*Scirpus maritimus*) as dominant species in the marshes of the Manchac Wildlife Management Area.

Within each of these marsh types, slight increases in elevation may allow other species to grow, especially shrubs but also trees if elevations are substantial enough. Shrubs such as marsh elder (*Iva frutescens*), groundsel bush, wax myrtle (*Morella cerifera*), rattlebox (*Daubentonia drummondii*), sicklepod, marsh mallow (*Hibiscus lasiocarpus*; Figure 16.1F), saltmarsh mallow (*Kosteletzkya virginica*; Figure 16.1G), and buttonbush (*Cephalanthus occidentalis*) are usually scattered through these marsh areas on slightly higher ground. Areas in the marshes with increased elevation of only a few centimeters may be unique microhabitats with highly diverse plant communities, as Kidder (1998) noted for shell midden sites. However, much of that diversity has been reduced in recent years by the invasive Chinese tallowtree (*Triadica* or *Sapium sebiferum*), which has taken over much of the higher ground in the marshes. As elevation continues to increase, typical upland vegetation begins to appear, such as the typical forest types indigenous to the area.

At their "oak island" marsh transect near the lower Pearl River, Penfound and Hathaway (1938) noted that a shrub belt occurred 8 in. (20 cm) and 6 in. (15 cm) higher than the adjacent marsh and cane zone, respectively. The shrub belt was characterized by marsh elder, groundsel bush, and dwarf palmetto (*Sabal minor*). Other significant plants were marshhay cordgrass, marsh bindweed (*Convolvulus repens*), marsh morning glory, switch grass, and seaside goldenrod

(*Solidago mexicana*). The oak forest (22 in. or 55 cm higher than the marshes) was dominated by live oak (*Quercus virginiana*) and sweetgum (*Liquidamber styraciflua*) but included a diversity of tree, shrub, and herbaceous species.

On slightly elevated sites in the Manchac marshes, such as spoil banks along canals and on the natural levee along the Lake Pontchartrain shoreline and Pass Manchac, scattered trees and shrubs occurred (Platt 1988). The few remnant cypress trees (*Taxodium distichum*) were most numerous on these higher places, along with ashes (*Fraxinus caroliniana, F. pennsylvanica,* and *F. profunda* [as *F. tomentosa*]), water tupelo (*Nyssa aquatica*), black tupelo (*Nyssa sylvatica*), swamp red maple (*Acer rubrum* var. *drummondii*), groundsel bush, wax myrtle, and Chinese tallow tree. Common understory plants were poison ivy (*Rhus radicans*), dwarf palmetto, and dewberry (*Rubus trivialis*).

Efforts to stimulate cypress regeneration in the Manchac marshes have involved extensive planting of cypress seedlings in the vicinity of the Turtle Cove Environmental Research Station and numerous studies to document their success and failure (Brantley and Platt 1992; Llewellyn and Shaffer 1993; Myers et al. 1995; Souther and Shaffer 2000). Although partially successful initially, only time will tell if these cypress trees can survive the combined stresses of subsidence (and associated increased flooding), saltwater intrusion, and herbivory by nutria and eventually mature as 150-year-old trees.

The marshes surrounding the Lake Pontchartrain system provide important food sources for many species of both aquatic and terrestrial herbivores. In addition, their seasonal decomposition adds detritus, to the estuary, providing an important source of productivity. Much of the sediment in an estuary is composed of detritus from these wetland plants. Masses of detritus, consisting of small bits and pieces of marsh plants, wood, and other plant pieces, accumulate along most shorelines in deposits up to several feet thick (see Figure 6.1). Darnell (1961) considered marsh erosion to be a major source of this material.

The marsh areas contain extensive aquatic habitats in the form of small pools or ponds, bayous, and ditches, many of which also extend into adjacent swamp habitats. Additional waterways have been created as logging canals and ditches, boat navigational canals, and oil and gas exploration and drilling canals (see Figure 7.1). Most of these enclosed waterways, whether natural or man-made, are habitat for a number of organisms usually not common in the open waters of the lake. Most, and especially those with lower salinities, are densely vegetated with submersed plants such as yellow pondlily (*Nuphar lutea advena*), white waterlily (*Nymphaea odorata*), southern naiad (*Najas guadalupensis*), horned pondweed (*Zannichellia palustris*), clasping pondweed (*Potamogeton perfoliatus*), coontail (*Ceratophyllum demersum*), fanwort (*Cabomba caroliniana*), floating waterprimrose (*Ludwigia peploides*), water paspalum (*Paspalum fluitans*), pennywort (*Hydrocotyle* spp.), and bladderworts (*Utricularia* spp.). The nonnative alligatorweed (*Alternanthera philoxeroides*) and Eurasian watermilfoil (*Myriophyllum spicatum*) are also abundant. Several floating plants may completely cover the water surface in some areas, including duckweed (*Lemna minor* and *Spirodela polyrhiza*), bogmat (*Wolffiella floridana*), floating liverwort (*Riccia fluitans*), frogbit (*Limnobium spongia*), and water fern (*Azolla caroliniana*). The nonnative water hyacinth (*Eichhornia crassipes*) and common salvinia (*Salvinia minima*) almost completely block some waterways. Gaston (1999) noted that floating plants in bayous were especially rich in invertebrate species and supported abundant populations (more than 30,000 per m^2 in Bayou LaBranche). Broken pieces or mats of these plants may drift into the open lakes, but they are usually less common in these often-turbulent waters than they are in more sheltered waters. In a few places, dense stands of wild rice (*Zizania aquatica*) grow in shallow water along the margins of the waterways. Their abundant seeds attract large flocks of redwinged blackbirds (*Agelaius phoeniceus*) and other seed-eating birds in autumn.

The submersed vegetation beds in these protected waterways provide habitat and shelter for numerous invertebrates, including many aquatic insects; aquatic larvae and nymphs of flying insects such as midges, damselflies, and dragonflies; snails (*Physella gyrina* and *Planorbella* or *Helisoma*); amphipods; grass shrimp (*Palaemonetes pugio* and *P. kadiakensis*); crayfish; and other crustaceans. By far the dominant crayfish species is the red swamp crayfish or mudbug (*Procambarus clarkii*), which is also the economically important crawfish of Louisiana fame. This abundant species is most characteristic of marshes and marsh pools and swamps and swamp pools (Penn 1956). Dominant invertebrates recorded in Bayou LaBranche (listed in order of numerical density; Gaston 1999) were ostracods, nematodes, oligochaete worms, chironomid midges, the polychaete *Hobsonia florida*, clam shrimp (Conchostraca), amphipods (*Grandidierella bonnieroides*, *Corophium louisianum*, and *Gammarus mucronatus*), biting midges (Ceratopogonidae), the mysid *Taphromysis louisianae*, the isopod *Cyathura polita*, physid snails, hydrobiid snails, the clam *Rangia cuneata*, and leeches (Hirudinea).

Many species of small fish are abundant in the canals, ditches, and bayous. Most significant of these are the killifishes (from *kill*, the Dutch word for canal; families Fundulidae, Cyprinodontidae, and Poeciliidae). Of thirty-seven fish species collected in canals and ditches of the Manchac Wildlife Management Area, by far the dominant species were western mosquitofish (*Gambusia affinis*), sailfin molly (*Poecilia latipinna*), sheepshead minnow (*Cyprinodon variegatus*), and least killifish (*Heterandria formosa*; Hastings 1987). Other common species were inland silversides (*Menidia beryllina*), rainwater killifish (*Lucania parva*), bayou killifish (*Fundulus pulvereus*), bay anchovy (*Anchoa mitchilli*), Gulf menhaden (*Brevoortia patronus*), and spotted gar (*Lepisosteus oculatus*). The dominant fish species in Bayou Trepagnier and Bayou LaBranche, in order of abundance were mosquitofish, Gulf menhaden, sailfin molly, sheepshead minnow, bayou killifish, striped mullet (*Mugil cephalus*), spotted gar, rainwater killifish, inland silversides, and red-spotted sunfish (*Lepomis miniatus*; Cashner et al. 1994).

Also common in the marshes are several species of frogs, turtles, and water snakes, as well as alligators. Seven species of frogs and toads and twenty species of reptiles have been recorded on the Manchac Wildlife Management Area (Platt et al. 1989). The most numerous frogs are the green treefrog (*Hyla cinerea*) and the northern cricket frog (*Acris crepitans*). Other species of amphibian recorded were Gulf coast toad (*Bufo valliceps*), eastern narrow-mouthed toad (*Gastrophryne carolinensis*), bullfrog (*Rana catesbeiana*), pig frog (*Rana gryllio*), and southern leopard frog (*Rana sphenocephala*). Only four species of turtles have been reported, with red-eared slider (*Trachemys scripta*) by far the most common species. In the spring, large females are frequently seen searching the Manchac area for high ground to dig holes and lay eggs where they will be safe from flooding. However, many of the turtle nests are dug up and destroyed by raccoons and other predators. Other species were common snapping turtle (*Chelydra serpentina*), alligator snapping turtle (*Macrochelys temmincki*), and stinkpot (*Sternotherus odoratus*). The eastern mud turtle (*Kinosternon subrubrum*) was noted as common in nearby areas. Alligator snapping turtles were once common in the Manchac area and other parts of the Pontchartrain basin, but they are less common now, possibly because of excessive trapping for human consumption (Dobie 1971). The species has been protected from commercial harvesting since 2004 and seems to have experienced some population recovery (Boundy and Kennedy 2006).

Of twelve snake species reported on the Manchac Wildlife Management Area (Platt et al. 1989), seven are most characteristic of aquatic or semi-aquatic habitats. Of these, broad-banded water snake (*Nerodia fasciata*), diamond-backed water snake (*Nerodia rhombifera*), western green water snake (*Nerodia cyclopion*), and Gulf coast ribbon snake (*Thamnophis proximus*) were most common. Less frequently seen were cottonmouth (*Agkistrodon piscivorus*), yellow-bellied water snake (*Nerodia erythrogaster*), and delta crayfish snake (*Regina rigida*). The mud snake (*Farancia abacura*) was reported as frequently seen in nearby areas. Other snakes that are quite common in adjacent higher ground with shrubs and trees are rough green snake (*Opheodrys aestivus*), black-masked racer (*Coluber constrictor*), Texas rat snake (*Elaphe obsoleta*), and speckled kingsnake (*Lampropeltis getulus*). The green anole (*Anolis carolinensis*) is abundant in shrub and forested habitats throughout most of the Pontchartrain basin, including the marshes. The five-lined skink (*Eumeces fasciatus*), broad-headed skink (*Eumeces laticeps*), and ground skink (*Scincella lateralis*) also occur in the area.

Alligators (*Alligator mississippiensis*) are common and characteristic of the Lake Pontchartrain system, at times venturing into the open lake but usually remaining in sheltered shoreline or inland waters of the marshes and swamps. Their numbers were so severely reduced by overhunting and poaching in the early 1900s that there was concern that the species might become extinct (Dundee and Rossman 1989). Consequently, all hunting and trapping of alligators in Louisiana was banned in 1963. Subsequent protection and management programs were so successful and alligators became so numerous, that in 1972 Louisiana established an experimental alligator harvest program (initially in southwestern Louisiana; Palmisano et al. 1973). A strictly regulated harvest of alligators continues annually during the month of September in Louisiana, including the Pontchartrain basin. Raccoons are major predators on alligator eggs, but adverse weather events can also severely affect reproductive success, such as in August 1988, when all monitored nests were destroyed by floodwaters generated by tropical storm Beryl (Platt et al. 1997).

As the major large predator in the Lake Pontchartrain basin, alligators are significant in affecting the populations of other species. Adults (larger than 5 ft. or 1.5 m in length) from the southeastern side of the lake were found to feed primarily upon nutria (*Myocastor coypus*) and muskrat (*Ondatra zibethicus*), with nutria by far the dominant food by weight (59.6%; Wolfe et al. 1987). Muskrats accounted for 24.0% of the food by weight and fishes (especially garfish and drum) 10.9%. Nutria are the most abundant semi-aquatic mammals occurring in the marsh waterways of the Manchac area and by far the dominant food of adult alligators taken during the September hunting season (Hastings, personal observation). In contrast, juvenile alligators (19–48 in., 49–121 cm) in the Manchac area fed primarily upon crustaceans (35.6% by weight, especially crayfish [Cambaridae]; grass shrimp [*Palaemonetes*]; and blue crabs [*Callinectes sapidus*]), insects (19.1%, especially water beetles [Coleoptera] and water bugs [Hemiptera]), and small fishes (16.7%, Fundulidae and Poeciliidae; Platt et al. 1990).

Trapping of fur-bearing mammals in the wetlands surrounding the lakes has in the past been an important industry, especially in the marsh areas adjacent to Lake Borgne. Fur trapping boomed in the 1920s, with muskrat comprising over 90% of the harvest (Gomez 2001). Other important species have been mink (*Mustela vison*), raccoon (*Procyon lotor*), opossum (*Didelphis virginiana*), and otter (*Lutra canadensis*). In 1926–1927, 80% of the state's muskrat harvest came from St. Bernard Parish, or 2.4 million pelts worth an average of $1.20 per pelt (for a total value of about $2.9 million). Muskrat continued to be the major fur producer in Louisiana through the early 1950s (Davis, Donald W. 1978). Surprisingly, O'Neil (1949) suggested that muskrat may have been uncommon (or absent) from Louisiana coastal marshes prior to about 1850 and did not become important in the trapping industry until the early 1900s. However, their bones have been reported as remains in prehistoric middens of the Lake Pontchartrain area (Duhe 1976; Shenkel 1984). Today, muskrats are common in some areas, such as in the Lake Borgne marshes (Davis 1978), and Chabreck et al. (1989) studied their movement patterns in marshes on the north shore of Lake Pontchartrain. They are now absent from the western side of Lake Pontchartrain and appear to have been displaced from some areas by the introduced nutria. Although Lowery (1974a) suggested that the two mainly live in different kinds of marshes (muskrat in salt or brackish marshes and nutria in freshwater marshes), he did acknowledge an apparent correlation of the dramatic decline in numbers of muskrat trapped in the state (from more than 8 million in 1945–1946 to 200,000 in 1964–1965) with the increase in numbers of nutria trapped. Nutria, one of the most conspicuous mammals in much of coastal Louisiana, are now abundant in salt and brackish marshes along the coast, as well as freshwater marshes.

Other mammal species common in the Lake Pontchartrain marshes, especially where high ground is available for resting, include armadillo (*Dasypus novemcinctus*), swamp rabbit (*Sylvilagus aquaticus*), marsh rice rat (*Oryzomys palustris*), long-tailed weasel (*Mustela frenata*), white-tailed deer (*Odocoileus virginianus*), and feral pigs (*Sus scrofa*). Others present in areas adjacent to forested swamp or upland habitats where trees are available for shelter include raccoon and opossum. Raccoons are often seen foraging along the edges of the marsh waterways, and otters are also frequently seen swimming in the marsh canals and bayous. At one time, American bison (*Bison bison*) were common in the marshes, but have been rare or absent from southern Louisiana since the last half of the eighteenth century (Lowery 1974a). The last bison in Louisiana died in 1803.

Among the most abundant birds in the marshes surrounding Lake Pontchartrain are red-winged blackbirds (*Agelaius phoeniceus*), boat-tailed grackle (*Quiscalus major*), and common grackle (*Quiscalus quiscla*). Numerous wading birds are common and characteristic of the marshes. Among the most common are the great blue heron (*Ardea herodias*), little blue heron (*Florida caerulea*), tricolored heron (*Egretta tricolor*), green heron (*Butorides virescens*), black-crowned night-heron (*Nycticorax nycticorax*), yellow-crowned night-heron (*Nyctanassa violacea*), great egret (*Casmerodius alba*), snowy egret (*Egretta thula*), cattle egret (*Bubulcus ibis*), white ibis (*Eudocimus albus*), glossy ibis (*Plegadis falcinellus*), white-faced ibis (*Plegadis chihi*), common moorhen (*Gallinula chloropus*), and purple gallinule (*Porphyrio martinica*). Several species of rails are also common, including clapper rail (*Rallus longirostris*), king rail (*Rallus elegans*), Virginia rail (*Rallus limicola*), and sora (*Porzana carolina*). Northern harriers or marsh hawks (*Circus cyaneus*) are frequently seen flying low over the marshes in search of prey. Other common predatory birds frequently seen perched in trees adjacent to the lakes or in the marshes are red-shouldered hawk (*Buteo lineatus*), red-tailed hawk (*Buteo jamaicensis*), barred owl (*Strix varia*), and great horned owl (*Bubo virginianus*).

Several species of birds are closely associated with the marsh ponds and waterways. Among the most common are wood duck (*Aix sponsa*), green-winged teal (*Anas crecca*), mottled duck (*Anas fulvigula*), mallard (*Anas platyrhynchos*), blue-winged teal (*Anas discors*), northern shoveler (*Anas clypeata*), gadwall (*Anas strepera*), American wigeon (*Anas americana*), ring-necked duck (*Aythya collaris*), American coot (*Fulica americana*), and belted kingfisher (*Ceryle alcyon*). Hunting for waterfowl in the Lake Pontchartrain marshes, as well as for other species such as rail and white-tailed deer, have been important human activities from prehistoric times until the present.

Many smaller birds are common in the marshes, especially where there are trees or shrubs for perching. Among the most common are red-bellied woodpecker (*Melanerpes carolinus*), pileated woodpecker (*Dryocopus pileatus*), blue jay (*Cyanocitta cristata*), fish crow (*Corvus ossifragus*), Carolina chickadee (*Parus carolinensis*), tufted titmouse (*Parus bicolor*), Carolina wren (*Thryothorus ludovicianus*), ruby-crowned kinglet (*Regulus calendula*), blue-gray gnatcatcher (*Polioptila caerulea*), American robin (*Turdus migratorius*), northern mockingbird (*Mimus polyglottos*), white-eyed vireo (*Vireo griseus*), red-eyed vireo (*Vireo olivaceus*), northern parula (*Parula americana*), yellow-rumped warbler (*Dendroica coronata*), prothonotary warbler (*Protonotaria citrea*), northern cardinal (*Cardinalis cardinalis*), swamp sparrow (*Melospiza georgiana*), and white-throated sparrow (*Zonotrichia albicollis*).

The marshes are also important habitat for a diverse assortment of invertebrates, but these have for the most part not been inventoried nor studied in any detail. One of the most obvious and distinctive species is the eastern lubber grasshopper (*Romalea guttata*). It occurs in various habitats throughout the southeastern United States but seems to be especially abundant in the wetlands of southeastern Louisiana. In about mid-March, groups of small black grasshoppers with bold yellow stripes begin to appear after hatching from egg clutches in the soil. They feed on a variety of marsh plants, often denuding areas by the end of the summer, when they are about 2–3 in. (6–8 cm) long. The adults are mostly yellowish with black markings and have two pairs of wings, the first the same color as the body, but the second bright red or rose. The grasshoppers cannot fly but use their wings as a threat display against potential predators, a warning that the lubber is toxic. The adults mate in late summer, then the females lay masses of up to seventy eggs about 2 in. (6 cm) deep within the soil. The adults die soon after, and the eggs remain to hatch as a new generation the following spring.

17.

Estuarine Food Webs

Among the most significant features of any ecosystem are the various feeding or trophic relationships among the numerous species and the pathways by which resources are transferred from one trophic level to another as foods. Such patterns of energy transfer are commonly referred to as food chains or webs. Food webs are usually quite complex and difficult to generalize, but several major features can be recognized. Trophic relationships in Lake Pontchartrain are based primarily upon two studies of feeding habits of fishes or larger invertebrates. Darnell (1958, 1961) analyzed the stomach contents of thirty-five of the most important consumer species, including thirty-one fishes and four invertebrates, and Levine (1980) studied the gut contents of forty-four fish species.

Producers

The communities of living organisms in any ecosystem are ultimately dependent upon primary producers (or autotrophs) as a source of energy. These are the organisms able to produce their own food through chemical means and thus convert energy, usually from sunlight, into chemical compounds. The most important of these chemical processes is photosynthesis.

In estuaries, primary production through photosynthesis is usually associated with four major categories of autotrophs: phytoplankton (especially diatoms, green algae, and blue-green algae), benthic algae, submersed macrophytes (especially grass beds), and emergent macrophytes (marsh and terrestrial plants). Darnell (1961) classified the primary producers contributing to the Lake Pontchartrain food webs into eight categories:

Autochthonous (originating within the lake)
1. Phytoplankton
2. Marginal submersed vegetation, including vascular plants, filamentous algae, and benthic diatoms
3. Bacteria

Allochthonous (originating outside the lake)
4. Marginal marsh vegetation
5. Phytoplankton (from adjacent passes)
6. Mississippi River overflow material
7. Woody swamp vegetation
8. Wind-blown material

In the waters of Lake Pontchartrain, there are abundant photosynthetic phytoplankton, including diatoms, blue-green algae (or cyanobacteria), green algae, and dinoflagellates. The abundance of phytoplankton can vary, being increased by high nutrient levels, such as nitrates and phosphates, but decreased by turbidity, which reduces light penetration and limits photosynthesis. There is a direct relationship between the clarity of the water and how deep light-dependent photosynthesizers can occur. The phytoplankton community is frequently light-limited due to high levels of suspended particulate matter (Bianchi and Argyrou 1997).

As described previously, primary production levels in estuaries such as Lake Pontchartrain are normally quite high because of the continuous source of nutrients coming in from freshwater tributaries. However, phytoplankton blooms can occur when masses of nutrient-rich water, such as from the Bonnet Carré Spillway, enter the lake. The lake can then turn green or turquoise, depending upon the algal species involved (see Figure 10.3). Some can produce toxins that cause potential health threats. One of the most significant blooms occurred in 1997 following a prolonged opening of the spillway, when large masses of *Anabaena* (primarily *A.* cf. *circinalis*; Turner et al. 2002) covered much of the lake. Subsequent death and decomposition of these algae resulted in low-oxygen conditions that killed many fish. Blooms can occur almost every year but in more limited extent and duration. Some species of fish, such as striped mullet (*Mugil cephalus*), Gulf menhaden (*Brevoortia patronus*), and possibly threadfin shad (*Dorosoma petenense*), may feed upon the abundant blue-green algae (Darnell 1958, 1961). According to Darnell, these cyanobacteria can also contribute to the organic detritus in the lake and become an important food source for animals such as rangia clams and river shrimp (*Macrobrachium ohione*).

Benthic diatoms and other algae can be abundant, but they are restricted to relatively shallow water by turbidity. The clearer the water, the deeper they can occur. Benthic diatoms can be especially important on shallow mud flats. These benthic species provide food for some bottom-feeding fishes and invertebrates, such as pinfish (*Lagodon rhomboides*), striped mullet, spot (*Leiostomus xanthurus*), and river shrimp (Darnell 1958). However, the absence of extensive mud flats in Lake Pontchartrain makes benthic diatoms (and other benthic algae) relatively unimportant as primary producers (Darnell 1961).

Aquatic bacteria (other than cyanobacteria) tend to be associated with surfaces, including both benthic substrates and particulate matter in the water. The latter could be considered a part of the plankton. Some species are autotrophic (such as green and purple sulfur bacteria), forming their own foods through photosynthetic processes, but have not been reported as common in Lake Pontchartrain. Other bacteria, which are abundant in both water and mud, can use chemosynthetic methods to produce their foods, even when light is not present. They are especially abundant in muds, where they can survive in anaerobic or anoxic conditions. Chemoautotrophic bacteria obtain energy from chemical compounds such as hydrogen sulfide. They in turn provide food for nematodes and other small but abundant consumers. The most important bacteria in the lake, however, may be the decomposers, which attach to detritus particles and become food for fish and other organisms feeding upon the detritus (Darnell 1961).

Submersed aquatic vegetation, or seagrasses, is another group of primary producers important in many estuarine areas. These plants are limited to shallow water (less than 6 ft. or 2 m in Lake Pontchartrain; Darnell 1961) by turbidity and the depth of light penetration. Other submersed aquatic plants are abundant in the more protected waters of rivers, bayous, and canals. Patches of filamentous green algae can also occur in shallow waters but are usually not extensive. Darnell (1961) considered submersed vegetation "a very minor source of organic matter in Lake Pontchartrain." A more significant function of submersed aquatic plants is to serve as habitat and shelter (as well as food) for many juvenile and cryptic aquatic organisms.

By far the most important primary producers in many estuarine systems, including Lake Pontchartrain, are the emergent macrophytes, or marsh plants, that surround the perimeter of the estuary. Because these plants grow with their roots within the nutrient-rich organic muds of the estuary, but have their leaves in the air and exposed to the full radiant energy of sunlight, they can generate extremely high levels of productivity. These primary productivity levels, generally measured as grams of carbon per square meter per year (g C/m^2/year), can reach levels equivalent to cultivated farm crops. Measured levels of production in the Lake Pontchartrain marshes of marshhay cordgrass (*Spartina patens*) are generally estimated to be about 3000 g C/m^2/year and may exceed 5500 g C/m^2/year (Turner 1976; Cramer et al. 1981). These plants grow and photosynthesize, incorporating chemical energy into their cellular material or biomass. As they subsequently die and decompose, pieces fall into the water to become detritus and accumulate as part of the mud sediments, or if they remain on the marsh surface, the dead plants form peat deposits. They are further broken down by bacteria and some animal consumers.

Because of the limited light penetration in turbid waters of Lake Pontchartrain, deeper areas may be devoid of plant life, and detritus generated by these extensive marshes may be the major source of primary production (Darnell 1961, 1962). The bare mud bottoms are rich in organic material derived from the bits and pieces of macrophytes from the marshes. A prominent form of detritus in Lake Pontchartrain is the "coffee grounds" that accumulate in places around the perimeter of the lake (see Figure 6.1). No detailed studies of the biological significance of the "coffee grounds" to the economy of the lake have been conducted, but it could be important as suggested by Darnell (1958, 1961, 1962). This material was considered a possible major food source for Gulf menhaden in the lake, as well as other species including Atlantic croaker (*Micropogonias undulatus*), hardhead catfish (*Ariopsis felis*), striped mullet (*Mugil cephalus*), penaeid shrimp (*Litopenaeus setiferus* and *Farfantepenaeus aztecus*), and blue crabs (*Callinectes sapidus*).

Darnell (1961) considered Lake Pontchartrain food webs to be based mostly upon primary productivity from allochthonous sources, or sources outside the lake. These include plankton entering from the adjacent passes, as well as the organic marsh humus entering the lake from eroded shores. Bianchi and Argyrou (1997) provided further evidence regarding the importance of allochthonous detritus to the lake. Bacterial decomposition of the detrital material can make its organic content available to other organisms.

Other sources of primary production to the lake, including phytoplankton from adjacent passes and rivers, Mississippi River overflow material, woody swamp vegetation, and wind-blown material, are apparently relatively minor, according to Darnell (1961). However, the addition of nutrients from the Mississippi River and adjacent passes and rivers enhances production levels in the lake and at times stimulates major algal blooms.

Consumers

Consumers are the animals that feed upon the primary producers or one another. They are also referred to as heterotrophs (meaning "different feeders") because they do not produce their own foods, as the autotrophs do. In any estuary, consumers are a mixed fauna of marine, freshwater, and brackish water organisms, as well as some terrestrial animals, including birds that may feed on the surface or along the lake shoreline. Darnell (1961) recognized seven major food groups for consumers in Lake Pontchartrain: organic detritus (and bacteria), zooplankton, micro-bottom animals, macro-bottom animals, free-swimming fishes, submersed vascular plants, and phytoplankton. He emphasized that only a few key species were targets for intense predation.

The major aquatic primary consumer animals (that is, herbivores, or those that feed upon primary producers) in estuaries such as Lake Pontchartrain include copepods, which live in the plankton and consume diatoms, other microscopic plants, and detrital particles using specialized appendages with setae to filter the water and capture their prey (see Figure 14.3). Copepods are small (less than a few millimeters long) but comprise some 70–90% of herbivore biomass in the open oceans. They are also quite important in estuarine waters and provide an important link between phytoplankton and larger carnivores. They may even control phytoplankton population size. Darnell (1961) considered Lake Pontchartrain to be dominated by the calanoid copepod *Acartia tonsa*.

Other important aquatic primary consumers in Lake Pontchartrain are protozoans, rotifers, mysids or opossum shrimp (*Mysidopsis almyra*), and larval forms of mollusks, annelids, crustaceans, and fishes, which are also planktonic. These in turn provide food for a variety of secondary consumers. According to Levine (1980), the mysid is considered by some to be the single most important fish food organism in the mid-Gulf estuarine zone. Rotifers were important foods for young bay anchovies (*Anchoa mitchilli*) and threadfin shad (*Dorosoma petenense*). Darnell (1961) noted the great importance of zooplankton as food for juvenile fish. Among the major fish species that fed primarily upon zooplankton were bay anchovy (juveniles and adults), Atlantic croaker (young and juveniles), sand seatrout (*Cynoscion arenarius*, juveniles), threadfin shad (juveniles), blue catfish (*Ictalurus furcatus*, juveniles), silver perch (*Bairdiella chrysoura*, adults), spotted seatrout (*Cynoscion nebulosus*, juveniles), and yellow bass (*Morone mississippiensis*, adults).

Darnell (1961, 1962) concluded that nearly all of the larger consumers had ingested some detritus and that this material made up at least 5% of the food of twenty-five species of fish and invertebrates studied (of a total of thirty-five). He stated that detritivorous fishes and invertebrates were among the most successful species in the lake and concluded that many of the consumers were omnivores or detritivores, including some that are generally regarded as strict carnivores. Because he considered detritus "the most important single food material ingested by fish and invertebrate consumers" in Lake Pontchartrain, Darnell (1961) considered the heterotrophic (or decomposer) bacteria that adhere to and break down detrital particles to be the chief primary consumers, which were then ingested by fish and invertebrate consumers, along with the detritus. The major nutritive value of such material was considered to be derived from the abundant bacteria associated with the detrital particles. Based upon his results, Darnell (1961) recognized two consumer groups among the most abundant fish and invertebrate species of the lake: those forms that feed largely upon organic detritus, including rangia clams (*Rangia cuneata*), striped mullet, Gulf menhaden, white shrimp (*Litopenaeus setiferus*), and hogchoker (*Trinectes maculatus*); and those that consume a wide range of foods, including detritus (omnivores), such as hardhead catfish, bay anchovy, spot, Atlantic croaker, and blue crab.

Levine (1980) and others (such as Odum et al. 1973) have challenged Darnell's conclusions because he included some "undetermined organic material" as detritus and because 5% detritus could have been ingested incidental to other feeding activity. Indeed, Darnell (1967) defined detritus as "all types of biogenic material in various stages of microbial decomposition which represent potential energy sources for consumer species," which could include the carcasses of dead animals. Other researchers have defined detritivores as those species consuming more than 20% identifiable plant detritus. Among the species studied by Darnell (1961) for which he considered detritus to constitute over 20% of their stomach contents were Gulf menhaden (juveniles), striped mullet (juveniles and adults), rangia clams (adults), Atlantic croaker (juveniles and adults), white shrimp (adults), hardhead catfish (juveniles and adults), river shrimp (adults), gizzard shad (adults), hogchoker (adults), blue catfish (juveniles and adults), bay anchovy (juveniles and adults), spot (juveniles and adults), Atlantic needlefish (*Strongylura marina*, adults), channel catfish (*Ictalurus punctatus*, juveniles), blue crab (juveniles and adults), and pinfish (adults). The first nine of these species had more than 50% detritus in their stomachs. Several of these fish are commonly regarded as carnivores.

Odum and Heald (1975) contrasted their results for the North River in the Florida Everglades with the findings of Darnell. They suggested that of the fish species studied, only Gulf menhaden and striped mullet could derive much nourishment from detritus particles (defined as vascular plant particles). They recognized detritus as being important to consumers in the estuary, but only for a few abundant species of herbivorous and omnivorous crustaceans, mollusks, insect larvae, nematodes, polychaetes, and a few fishes. Odum et al. (1973) suggested that fishes were less important as detritivores when compared to crustaceans (amphipods, mysids, cumaceans, ostracods, copepods, shrimp, and crabs), mollusks (filter-feeding bivalves), and insect larvae (chironomids). Levine (1980) also recognized the importance of detritus to Lake Pontchartrain, but because of detritivores such as amphipods, mysids, polychaetes, and chironomid larvae, rather than fishes. He also concluded that striped mullet and Gulf menhaden were the only fish species in the lake that definitely derive nourishment from directly ingested detritus.

The actual importance of various sources of detritus, as well as its value as a food source, has been the subject of much research and controversy (Boesch and Turner 1984; Day et al. 1989), and many of Darnell's conclusions have been rejected. The role of detritus in estuaries is certainly complex and will vary with many factors, including both producer species and consumers. However, Day et al. (1989) concluded that "the bulk of the evidence continues to support the fundamental role of the detrital food web in estuarine trophic dynamics."

Micro-bottom (or small benthic) animals such as mollusks and crustaceans are important foods for many fishes in the lake. Primary components according to Darnell (1961) were small mollusks (*Rangia cuneata* and *Mytilopsis leucophaeta*), isopods and amphipods, small crabs, and chironomid larvae. Foraminifera were found to be a major food of gizzard shad. Other species that fed largely upon microbenthic invertebrates were spot (juveniles and adults), inland silversides (*Menidia beryllina*, adults), channel catfish (juveniles), pinfish (juveniles and adults), blue crab (juveniles and adults), hogchoker (adults), freshwater drum (*Aplodinotus grunniens*, juveniles), blue catfish (juveniles and adults), Atlantic croaker (juveniles and adults), hardhead catfish (juveniles and adults), sheepshead (*Archosargus probatocephalus*, adults), river shrimp (adults), spotted seatrout (juveniles), and white shrimp (adults). Darnell considered annelid worms negligible as food for species in Lake Pontchartrain, but Levine (1980) considered them one of six major benthic and infaunal food taxa, being fed upon by at least sixteen fish species.

Macro-bottom (or larger benthic) animals of greatest importance were subadult blue crabs and adult mud crabs (*Rhithropanopeus harrisii*), with adult rangia clams and other crustaceans being of secondary importance. The abundant rangia clams were important in the diets of black drum (*Pogonias cromis*) and freshwater drum, which were capable of crushing their thick shells (Darnell 1958). Levine (1980) also found numerous bivalves, including *Rangia*, in blue catfish, spot, and Atlantic croaker. Darnell considered the various shrimp species in the lake to be poorly utilized by lake predators, possibly being inaccessible because of turbid water on the bottom of the lake. Crabs, in contrast, suffered very heavy predation and were considered of great importance as food for larger predators. Species that fed heavily upon larger benthic invertebrates were black drum, largemouth bass (*Micropterus salmoides*), spotted gar (*Lepisosteus oculatus*), alligator gar (*Atractosteus spatula*), red drum (*Sciaenops ocellatus*), freshwater drum, yellow bass, hardhead catfish, silver perch, sheepshead, Atlantic croaker, blue crab, spotted seatrout, and blue catfish.

Although many species of fish provide food for the various secondary consumers in Lake Pontchartrain, Darnell (1961) recognized only four as primary components: Gulf menhaden, bay anchovy, Atlantic croaker, and striped mullet. These are also among the most abundant species in the lake. The bay anchovy provides food for at least ten major predatory fish in the lake and is the subject of heavy predation, along with menhaden and young Atlantic croaker.

Submersed vascular plants were major foods for only a few species of fish, such as sheepshead and pinfish, but also species that Darnell (1961) considered omnivores, such as blue catfish. However, the grassbeds provide important habitat, as well as food, for many small invertebrates, such as shrimp and amphipods, as well as small fish, especially juveniles. Turtles (*Pseudemys* sp.) may also be important consumers of water celery, the common submersed aquatic plant in the lake.

According to Darnell (1961), few fishes and larger invertebrates consume phytoplankton in Lake Pontchartrain, although it could be more important to larvae and juveniles of clupeids, engraulids, and atherinids (which were not studied by Darnell). However, during seasonal blooms of blue-green algae, *Anabaena* and *Microcystis* were important foods for striped mullet, Gulf menhaden, and possibly also threadfin shad.

Darnell (1958) concluded that there were two primary food chains for the consumers in Lake Pontchartrain. One originates with copepods (*Acartia*), which are consumed by small fishes such as anchovies, menhaden, and young drums (Sciaenidae), which in turn provide food for larger predators. The second involves small benthic invertebrates that provide food for larger benthic invertebrates, then small bottom-dwelling fishes (catfishes and young sciaenids), and finally larger predators. For both chains he considered detritus to be an important base nutrient source.

Levine (1980) emphasized a lesser role for detritus in the foods of Lake Pontchartrain fishes and broader, overlapping and less exclusive "predator-prey pathways" than Darnell (that is, food webs versus food chains). In spite of several significant differences from Darnell's results, Levine's two predator-prey pathways are quite similar to those of Darnell: one based upon planktonic and nektonic forms, with four major food taxa, and the other based upon benthic or infaunal organisms, with six major food taxa. The major foods of the plankton/nekton group were mysids (primarily *Mysidopsis almyra*), copepods, decapods (primarily *Palaemonetes* spp. and *Callinectes sapidus*), and fishes (especially *Anchoa mitchilli* and *Gobiosoma bosc*). These groups in turn were considered to feed primarily upon detritus, algae, diatoms, crustaceans, fishes, and insects. The major foods of the benthic/infaunal group were polychaetes, mollusks, mud crabs, chironomid larvae, amphipods (notably *Corophium lacustre* and *Gammarus* spp.), and the isopod *Cyathura polita*. The major foods of these groups were considered to be detritus, algae, diatoms, crustaceans, and vascular plants.

18.

The Palustrine Communities

Cypress-Tupelo Swamps and Adjacent Bottomland Hardwood Forests

The major vegetation type of the Pontchartrain basin forested wetlands is bald cypress (*Taxodium distichum*) and tupelo (*Nyssa aquatica* and *N. sylvatica*) swamps. These cypress-tupelo swamps are characteristic of coastal Louisiana and the Southeast where wetlands occur with salinities averaging below about 4 ppt. However, several different community types may be recognized based upon the dominant trees. For example, the Louisiana Natural Heritage Program (1988) defined three types: bald cypress–tupelo swamps, where the two species are codominants; bald cypress swamps, where cypress is dominant; and tupelo–black gum swamps, where *Nyssa aquatica* and *N. sylvatica* var. *biflora* are codominants. Other significant associated species in most of these swamps are swamp red maple (*Acer rubrum* var. *drummondii*), black willow (*Salix nigra*), pumpkin ash (*Fraxinus profunda*), green ash (*Fraxinus pennsylvanica*), waterelm (*Planera aquatica*), water locust (*Gleditsia aquatica*), Virginia willow (*Itea virginica*), and buttonbush (*Cephalanthus occidentalis*). Also present in the tupelo–black gum swamps are swamp privet (*Forestiera acuminata*), laurel oak (*Quercus laurifolia*), sweetbells or leucothoe (*Leucothoe racemosa*), swamp cyrilla or titi (*Cyrilla racemiflora*), and swamp dogwood (*Cornus foemina*). In this and other forested areas of the Pontchartrain basin, Spanish moss (*Tillandsia usenoides*) usually adds a picturesque mantle to the large trees.

These wetland forests cover an estimated 844,212 acres (341,648 ha) in the Pontchartrain basin, plus another 46,874 acres (18,970 ha) defined as wetland shrub/scrub vegetation (Handley et al. 2001). The latter appears to largely

Figure 18.1 Ancient cypress tree along the lower Tangipahoa River (Photograph by the author)

represent areas once forested but now logged out and never reforested. Wetland shrub/scrub vegetation is characterized by swamp red maple, buttonbush, groundsel bush (*Baccharis halimifolia*), dwarf palmetto (*Sabal minor*), wax myrtle (*Morella cerifera*), marsh elder (*Iva frutescens*), and dull-leaf indigo or lead plant (*Amorpha fruticosa*).

The Pontchartrain swamps have changed dramatically with the increased human population. Virtually all of the virgin cypress swamps have been destroyed, and where regeneration has occurred, only small, relatively young trees of only a hundred or so years of age are now present. Only a few scattered large, ancient trees survive, mainly because they are hollow and considered not worth cutting for lumber. Some trees up to 1300 years old have been reported from the area (Figure 18.1), and some more than 2000 years old may still exist (Van Deusen et al. 1993) as the oldest trees in eastern North America (Stahle et al. 1988).

The remaining swamps are extremely valuable to coastal Louisiana as wildlife habitat, for water quality improvement, and as hurricane protection buffers. However, they continue to be destroyed by logging, saltwater intrusion, and increased flooding. In addition, lightning strikes kill a number of cypress trees each year. In many of the former cypress swamps, small trees left standing by loggers have subsequently died and can still be seen in places as standing dead snags. In most cases, such mortality has been attributed to saltwater intrusion.

The cypress-tupelo swamps that remain are restricted to areas with the lowest salinity (that is, almost fresh water). Montz and Cherubini (1973) reported that 56% of the cypress trees in the LaBranche Wetlands area were dead, and they noted an absence of young saplings, indicating a lack of successful germination. However, Cramer and Day (1980) studied production levels at a swamp site in the LaBranche area dominated by relatively small cypress and considered it healthy with production values comparable to those of other similar Louisiana swamps. The only other tree species recorded along their transects was small swamp red maple. At a second study site approximately 7.5 mi. (12 km) southwest of Lake Maurepas near Blind River, water tupelo, red maple, and ash (*Fraxinus* spp.) were dominant, with only a few bald cypress, although the latter were substantially larger than those at the LaBranche site. The low productivity level recorded here was attributed to the effects of intensive logging, continual flooding, and possibly heavy insect grazing.

The vast cypress-tupelo swamps that once characterized the Manchac area have been replaced by open bulltongue (*Sagittaria lancifolia*) marshes, still scarred by the numerous logging canals and pull-boat runs where the large logs were dragged out of the swamps (see Figure 7.1). Scattered stumps and logs remain to remind us of the large and impressive cypress trees that once dominated this area. Large sinker cypress logs can be found buried in the mud bottoms of swamp canals and bayous, and these are now quite valuable as the only remaining source of the ancient tidewater cypress that once provided top-quality rot-resistant lumber to southeastern Louisiana (Kemp 1996).

As in marsh areas, slight changes in elevation in forested wetlands of the Pontchartrain basin can result in significant changes in vegetation and additional community types. Originally the natural levee vegetation was comprised of hardwoods such as cottonwood (*Populus deltoides*), sycamore (*Platanus occidentalis*), sweetgum (*Liquidambar styraciflua*), sugarberry (*Celtis laevigata*), magnolia (*Magnolia grandiflora*), pecan (*Carya illinoensis*), and various oaks, especially live oak (*Quercus virginiana*), with switch cane (*Arundinaria gigantea*) and dwarf palmetto understory (Saucier 1963). This levee vegetation graded into the cypress-tupelo swamps in the lower ground at the levee margins. The lower areas between the natural levees were generally less than about 1 ft. (30 cm) above sea level and had gradually accumulated through continued deposition sediments and organic materials that are usually about 5–10 ft. (1.5–3.0 m) thick, but up to 22 ft. (6.7 m) in places.

Hall and Penfound (1939) described the vegetation of a relatively young cypress-gum swamp known as Indian Village Swamp on the lower Pearl River (approximately 10 mi. or 16 km from its mouth). Cypress trees averaged eighty-five years of age, with an average diameter (at head height) of only 5.4 in. (13.7 cm). On natural levee ridges along the river, they described a deciduous forest of wax myrtle, water oak (*Quercus nigra*), dwarf palmetto, bald cypress, "swamp tupelo" or black gum, water tupelo, and swamp red maple. Also abundant on the ridges were vines such as yellow jessamine (*Gelsemium sempervirens*), eastern poison ivy (*Toxicodendron radicans*), and coral greenbrier (*Smilax walteri*). Beyond the ridges were the swamps of swamp tupelo, water tupelo, bald cypress, and swamp red maple. Other common tree species were green ash, common buttonbush, and Virginia willow. The most significant herbaceous understory species were marsh mermaid weed (*Proserpinaca palustris*), spider lily (*Hymenocallis caroliniana*, as *H. occidentalis*), shade mudflower (*Micranthemum umbrosum*), and common bladderwort (*Utricularia macrorhiza*). Around the periphery of the swamp, lizard's tail (*Saururus cernuus*) and pickerelweed (*Pontederia cordata*) were conspicuous. Beyond the swamps were the freshwater marshes dominated by sawgrass (*Cladium jamaicense*) and further downriver brackish water marshes dominated by marshhay cordgrass (*Spartina patens*). Beyond the swamps and marshes were the coastal plain pinelands.

Penfound and Howard (1940) studied an "evergreen oak forest" community occurring on slightly elevated sites along natural levees or ridges of Bayou Sauvage, at a site called Lyon Villa in the area now known as New Orleans East. This community was described as a well-developed second-growth stand on a former sugar cane field abandoned in 1886. The most numerous tree species were water oak, live oak, sugarberry, and American elm (*Ulmus americana*). Spanish moss was common on the large trees. The only common shrub was dwarf palmetto, although yaupon (*Ilex vomitoria*), beautyberry (*Callicarpa americana*), elderberry (*Sambucus canadensis*), and pawpaw (*Asimina triloba*) were also noted as present. The herbaceous layer was dominated by oak forest grass or shortleaf basketgrass (*Oplismenus setarius*).

Approximately sixty years later, Wall and Darwin (1999) studied woody vegetation along elevational gradients adjacent to Bayou Sauvage (within Bayou Sauvage National Wildlife Refuge), at a site roughly 2.5 mi. (4 km) northeast of Penfound and Howard's study site (which had been cleared for housing development). Although the two study sites were similar, there were significant differences. The most notable was the invasion and domination of the area by Chinese tallow trees (*Triadica* or *Sapium sebiferum*), an exotic species not yet introduced at the time of Penfound and Howard's (1940) study. Wall and Darwin suggested that differences in native species could reflect elevational differences, successional changes (50 years vs. 109 years following clearcutting), or competition from the introduced tallow trees. Among native species, live oak and sugarberry were codominant. The next most numerous species were black willow, red maple, common persimmon (*Diospyros virginiana*), and rattlebox (*Daubentonia drummondii*). A few large bald cypress were also present. The understory was dominated by dwarf palmetto and possumhaw or deciduous holly (*Ilex decidua*). Three community types were recognized: the ridge forest community composed of fifteen species; the black willow community characteristic of bayou margins; and the rattlebox community bordering open freshwater marsh.

At higher elevations (greater than 24 in. or 60 cm above sea level) the characteristic woody plants were slippery elm (*Ulmus rubra*), live oak, wax myrtle, roughleaf dogwood (*Cornus drummondii*), sugarberry, sweetgum, yaupon, swamp-bay (*Persea palustris*), and water oak. Species most common at intermediate elevations (16–22 in. or 40–56 cm above sea level) were red maple, white ash (*Fraxinus americana*), groundsel bush, common persimmon, honey-locust (*Gleditisia triacanthos*), water hickory (*Carya aquatica*), and possumhaw. Lower elevations (less than 10 in. or 25 cm above sea level) were characterized by rattlebox, black willow, bald cypress, and buttonbush. Chinese tallow trees and dwarf palmetto occurred at all elevations except in standing water.

Of the five plant communities recognized by White (1983) in the lower Pearl River basin adjacent to Lake Borgne (in the transition from floodplain forest to open marsh), three may be considered palustrine communities: hardwood bottom forest, cypress-tupelo forest, and scrub. Other rivers entering the Pontchartrain system demonstrate similar patterns of vegetation change. The hardwood bottom forest, located at the upstream portion of the study area, was dominated by four overstory tree species (water oak, laurel oak, sweetgum, and black gum) and was characterized by infrequent flooding. Other common species included swamp red maple, American hornbeam (*Carpinus caroliniana*), possumhaw holly, hickory (*Carya* spp.), and ash (*Fraxinus* spp.). Less common but significant species were basket oak (*Quercus michauxii*), American holly (*Ilex opaca*), sweetbay (*Magnolia virginiana*), persimmon, American elm, overcup oak (*Quercus lyrata*), bald cypress, water tupelo, waterelm (*Planera aquatica*), American beech (*Fagus grandifolia*), river birch (*Betula nigra*), swamp cottonwood (*Populus heterophylla*), and swamp dogwood. Vines of Alabama supplejack or rattan vine (*Berchemia scandens*), peppervine (*Ampelopsis arborea*), and grape (*Vitis* spp.) were also common. There was little herbaceous cover in this and the cypress-tupelo forest community.

The cypress-tupelo forest was dominated by bald cypress, water tupelo, and pumpkin ash. Carolina ash (*Fraxinus caroliniana*), black gum, swamp red maple, buttonbush, wax myrtle, and laurel oak were also common in this community. Common vine species included climbing hempvine (*Mikania scandens*), Atlantic poison oak (*Toxicodendron pubescens*), trumpet creeper (*Campsis radicans*), and greenbriar (*Smilax* spp.).

The scrub community was described as transitional between the forest communities and the marshes. The dominant species were wax myrtle, swamp red maple, and marsh elder. Other common woody species were bald cypress, red-bay (*Persea borbonia*), dwarf palmetto, and black gum. Hempvine, Atlantic poison oak, trumpet creeper, and greenbriar were also common here. Common herbaceous species included smartweed (*Polygonum* spp., mostly dotted smartweed, *P. punctatum*), bulltongue, royal fern (*Osmunda regalis*), lizard's tail, pickerelweed, sawgrass, spikerush (*Eleocharis* spp.), switchgrass (*Panicum virgatum*), and marsh fern (*Thelypteris palustris*).

Along two small bayous on the north shore of Lake Pontchartrain (Castine and Chinchuba), Brantley et al. (2008) described swamp forest communities dominated by swamp black gum in the headwaters and water tupelo and bald cypress in the middle and downstream portions. Red maple and Carolina ash were also present but less dominant.

The swamps and other forested habitats of the Pontchartrain basin provide shelter and denning sites for a diversity of terrestrial animals, most of which are not restricted to a specific forest type. Most of the species listed above as occurring in the marsh habitats could also be expected in the adjacent swamps, and those occurring in the marsh waterways could also occur in the swamp waterways. A fish species observed to be abundant in swamp pools of the Manchac area but absent from the marshes is the banded pygmy sunfish (*Elassoma zonatum*; Hastings, personal observation). Surprisingly, there have not been any detailed studies documenting the significance of the cypress swamps as habitat for specific animals, nor on the effects of swamp removal on populations of these animals. Sharitz and Mitsch (1993) reviewed the general characteristics of animal communities in southern floodplain forests and emphasized their importance to wildlife as compared to the adjacent upland areas. They also noted the "edge effect" as a significant feature of floodplain systems, with increased diversity and abundance of species at the edge between two distinct ecosystems (the ecotone). In the case of cypress swamps, there are several edges: between river or lake and swamp, between marsh and swamp, and between upland forests and swamp.

Certainly mature trees with nesting cavities are important to a variety of species and should also provide important shelter from storms and flooding. Many species such as raccoons (*Procyon lotor*) and opossums (*Didelphis virginiana*) use the trees as shelter, but may forage in the adjacent marsh habitats. Other more arboreal species such as gray squirrels (*Sciurus carolinensis*) and flying squirrels

(*Glaucomys volans*) are common in the swamps, as well as adjacent upland forests, but not in the marshes. Other mammals common in the swamps are mink (*Mustela vison*), river otter (*Lutra canadensis*), bobcat (*Lynx rufus*), swamp rabbit (*Sylvilagus aquaticus*), white-tailed deer (*Odocoileus virginianus*), and feral hogs (*Sus scrofa*), as well as the ubiquitous nutria (*Myocastor coypus*). In contrast, beaver (*Castor canadensis*), so characteristic of upland forested wetland habitats, do not live in the cypress swamps surrounding the lakes.

Many wading and water birds characteristic of the waterways and open marshes seek shelter in rookeries of the adjacent swamps for nesting and roosting (Portnoy 1977; Keller et al. 1984; Martin and Lester 1990). These include great blue heron (*Ardea herodias*), little blue heron (*Egretta caerulea*), tricolored (or Louisiana) heron (*Egretta tricolor*), yellow-crowned night-heron (*Nyctanassa violacea*), black-crowned night-heron (*Nycticorax nycticorax*), great egret (*Ardea alba*), snowy egret (*Egretta thula*), cattle egret (*Bubulcus ibis*), anhinga (*Anhinga anhinga*), white-faced ibis (*Plegadis chihi*), glossy ibis (*Plegadis falcinellus*), and white ibis (*Eudocimus albus*). A colony of white ibis located just northeast of Lake Maurepas was estimated to include 60,000 nesting adults in 1976 and 20,000 in 1990. The large flocks of white ibis flying from their nocturnal roosting sites to diurnal feeding sites, or returning, is an impressive sight in the Manchac area. Many other tree-dwelling birds commonly occur in the swamps, as well as surrounding forests. Among the most characteristic birds of cypress swamp habitats are prothonotary warbler (*Protonotaria citrea*), northern parula (*Parula americana*), pileated woodpecker (*Dryocopus pileatus*), and wood duck (*Aix sponsa*).

The remaining cypress swamps are important habitat for many species, but they are quite different from the virgin cypress swamps with numerous large mature trees. Loss of these primeval swamp forests must have eliminated important habitat for many animals and greatly reduced their numbers.

19.

The Riverine and Lacustrine Communities

Freshwater Tributaries

The major freshwater tributaries to the Lake Pontchartrain system include the Blind River, Amite River, and Tickfaw River, which flow into Lake Maurepas, and the Tangipahoa River, Tchefuncte River, Bayou Lacombe, and Bayou Bonfouca, as well as several smaller bayous (Chinchuba, Castine, and Cane) that flow into Lake Pontchartrain. The Pearl River has a direct impact on Lake Borgne, as well as an indirect effect on Lake Pontchartrain. On the southern shore, the natural bayous have mostly been converted into drainage ditches that drain the New Orleans metropolitan area, although Bayous LaBranche/Trepagnier and St. John still retain some semblance of natural waterways. Most of these Lake Pontchartrain tributaries are listed as Louisiana natural and scenic streams. Leakage of Mississippi River water through the Bonnet Carré Spillway when the river is above the minimum level of the spillway adds additional fresh water to the system (usually only in the spring). When the spillway is opened, the Mississippi River becomes the dominant source of fresh water into the lake, at times tripling the total rate of flow into the system.

The typical freshwater stream entering Lake Pontchartrain from the north is a relatively clear, shallow, sand- and gravel-bottomed stream with moderate flow rates in its upper and middle reaches, gradually grading into a deeper, more turbid, sluggish bayou-type waterway with silt and mud bottom as it approaches the lake (and enters the cypress-tupelo swamps bordering the lake; Knight and Hastings 1994). Dominant aquatic plants include water celery or eelgrass (*Vallis-*

neria americana), watermilfoil (*Myriophyllum spicatum*), water lilies (*Nymphaea odorata* and *Nuphar lutea advena*), and bushy pondweed (*Najas guadalupensis*).

In contrast, the south shore streams that remain at least semi-natural (Blind River, Bayou LaBranche, and Bayou St. John) are sluggish water bayous, with their entire reaches more comparable to the downstream portions of the rivers of the north shore. These low-relief areas tend to have fewer species and seem to have greater estuarine characteristics. The dominant aquatic marginal vegetation in Blind River is fanwort (*Cabomba caroliniana*), coontail (*Ceratophyllum demersum*), water hyacinth (*Eichhornia crassipes*), and spatterdock (*Nuphar lutea advena*; Watson et al. 1981).

The rivers and streams of the north shore are habitat for at least 105 species of freshwater fishes, as well as another 27 or so marine species that either frequently or occasionally stray into fresh water from the estuary (Davis et al. 1970; Douglas 1974; Lee et al. 1980; Knight and Hastings 1994; Ross 2001). The dominant families are Cyprinidae (twenty-two species), Percidae (fifteen species), Centrarchidae (fifteen species), Catostomidae (ten species), Ictaluridae (ten species), and Fundulidae (six species, plus three marine).

The Lake Pontchartrain basin (and the Mississippi River) represents the boundary to a biogeographic division between east and west. Many species of freshwater fishes, as well as other aquatic groups, occur in the Pearl River but not in the Pontchartrain drainages nor in many cases further west (Douglas 1974; Ross 2001). One species is considered endemic to the Pontchartrain basin, the broadstripe topminnow (*Fundulus euryzonus*), which is found only in the Tangipahoa and Amite Rivers (Suttkus and Cashner 1981).

The rivers of the north shore are also habitat for a variety of invertebrates, most of which have been poorly studied. Forty species of native freshwater mussels (Unionidae) have been reported from the rivers of the Pontchartrain basin (Miller et al. 1986; Hartfield 1989; Vidrine 1993; Brown and Curole 1997; Brown and Banks 2001), in addition to the abundant exotic Asian clam, *Corbicula fluminea*, which is found in virtually all rivers of the area. The Pearl River was named by early French explorers because of its pearl-bearing mussels. The most common mussel species in the Amite River (according to Brown and Banks 2001) were elephant ear (*Elliptio crassidens*), purple pimpleback (*Quadrula refulgens*), yellow sandshell (*Lampsilis teres*), southern pocketbook (*Lampsilis ornate*), bleufer (*Potamilus purpureus*), and little spectaclecase (*Villosa lienosa*). Most common in the Tangipahoa were purple pimpleback, yellow sandshell, southern pocketbook, bleufer, southern fatmucket (*Lampsilis straminea* or *L. claibornensis*), and fragile papershell (*Leptodea fragilis*). In the West Pearl River, bleufer, purple pimpleback, mapleleaf (*Quadrula quadrula*), threehorn wartyback (*Obliquaria reflexa*), round pearlshell (*Glebula rotundata*), and bankclimber (*Plectomerus dombeyanus*) were common. Many of the native mussels have been extirpated from former habitats and are considered threatened or endangered. The Louisiana Natural Heritage Program (www.wlf.louisiana.gov/experience/naturalheritage) lists twelve as "species of conservation concern" in the state. The inflated heelsplitter mussel (*Potamilus inflatus*), which is federally listed as "threatened," once occurred in the Tangipahoa River and the Pearl River, but is now known in Louisiana only from the Amite River. This and other species have suffered serious declines in number because of the gravel mining and other disturbances in these rivers (Brown and Curole 1997; Brown and Banks 2001).

At least seventeen species of freshwater crayfish (Cambaridae, known in Louisiana as crawfish or mudbugs) occur in the Pontchartrain basin (Penn 1950, 1952, 1956, 1959; Penn and Marlow 1959; Hobbs 1989). Some of these live in the streams, rivers, and bayous, whereas others are burrowing forms that occur in swamps, marshes, and other wetlands, creating the characteristic mud chimneys at the entrance to the burrows. Their extensive underground burrow system into the water table provides habitat for a variety of subterranean aquatic forms. The only species that has been reported from Lake Pontchartrain itself is the red swamp crawfish (*Procambarus clarkii*), which is also abundant in adjacent marsh and bayou habitats.

Freshwater Lakes and Ponds

There are no natural upland lakes, with lacustrine habitat, in the Pontchartrain basin, but several streams and rivers have been dammed to create artificial lakes. In addition, numerous borrow pit ponds have been created along some major highways and along rivers such as the Amite and Tangipahoa where extensive gravel mining has occurred. These waters have received only limited study and are considered beyond the scope of this book.

A few swamp lakes (or ponds) that represent lacustrine environments occur in the Pontchartrain basin, but these are generally small. Their flora and fauna is similar to that described above for marsh waterways. Dominant plants include coontail (*Ceratophyllum demersum*), fanwort (*Cabomba caroliniana*), duckweeds (*Lemna* spp., *Spirodella* spp., *Wolffia* spp., *Wolffiella* spp.), water hyacinth (*Eichhornia crassipes*), water lettuce (*Pistia stratiotes*), and mosquito fern (*Azolla caroliniana*; Louisiana Natural Heritage Program 1988). *Salvinia minima* has also become abundant in some swamp lakes in recent years.

20.

The Terrestrial Communities

Upland Forest Communities

Of the various community types present in the Pontchartrain basin, the upland forested areas have changed the most during the 300 years since European settlement. The prairie terrace to the north of Lake Pontchartrain, deposited during the Pleistocene, has been described as covered originally by an almost homogeneous forest of longleaf pine (*Pinus palustris*) and slash pine (*Pinus elliotti*), with mixed hardwoods along the streams. Although certainly oversimplified, such a description does demonstrate the dominance of longleaf pine in the upland areas north of Lake Pontchartrain. Of course, much of this original forested land is quite different today. Virtually none of the virgin forests of the Pontchartrain basin remain, having been cut for timber or cleared for agriculture and construction as the human population of the area increased.

Penfound and Watkins (1937) described the forests of the north shore as longleaf pine flats dominated by pure stands of longleaf pine or mixed with loblolly (*Pinus taeda*) or slash pine (*Pinus elliotti*, as *P. caribaea*), as well as infrequent shortleaf pine (*Pinus echinata*), with extensive shallow swamps and sloughs characterized by slash pine and pond cypress (*Taxodium ascendens*, considered a variety of *T. distichum* by some authorities). The pure stands of longleaf pine have been described as "park-like," with few or no small trees or shrubs.

Today, the dominant trees in the remnant reforested areas are loblolly and slash pine with scattered magnolia (*Magnolia grandiflora*), pecan (*Carya illinoensis*), hickory (*Carya ovata*), sweetgum (*Liquidamber styraciflua*), American elm (*Ulmus americana*), and oaks (red, *Quercus falcata*; blackjack, *Q. marilandica*;

water, *Q. nigra*; post, *Q. stellata*; live, *Q. virginiana*). In the lower stream bottom areas are swamp red maple (*Acer rubrum* var. *drummondii*), water hickory (*Carya aquatica*), chinquapin (*Castanea pumila*), beech (*Fagus grandifolia*), sweetgum, yellow poplar (*Liriodendron tulipifera*), magnolia, sweetbay (*Magnolia virginiana*), swamp tupelo or swamp black gum (*Nyssa sylvatica* var. *biflora*), sycamore (*Platanus occidentalis*), red oak, water oak, cherrybark oak (*Quercus pagoda*), live oak, and black willow (*Salix nigra*), as well as slash pine and loblolly pine (Saucier 1963).

The Louisiana Natural Heritage Program (1988) recognizes at least nine different pine forest communities on the north shore, including pine flatwoods, pine savannahs, and slash pine–cypress/hardwood forest in the wetlands and upland longleaf pine forest, shortleaf pine/oak-hickory forest, mixed hardwood-loblolly forest, slash pine/post oak forest, live oak-pine-magnolia forest, and sandy woodlands in drier areas (Table 17). In addition, other communities occur within these forest types, such as bottomland forests along rivers and streams, wooded seeps and bayhead swamps, and hardwood slope forests.

Rylander (1969) identified 325 species of plants and recognized ten distinct vegetation groups (associes) in a second-growth loblolly pine forest at the Delta Regional Primate Research Center, a 500-acre (202-ha) area that had originally been longleaf and slash pine forest (for a list of species, see Table 18). These vegetation groups and their dominant species are probably typical of most second-growth sites on the north shore of Lake Pontchartrain that have not become urbanized. The vegetation groups identified were pine forest, pine and hardwood forest, mixed bottomland hardwood forest, cypress swamp, immature pine forest, shrub and immature pine, shrub and old field, roadside ditches and fences, cleared areas in the forest, and river and canal aquatic vegetation. Not surprisingly, exotic species have become a dominant part of the flora in such locations. Nonnative species recorded by Rylander include white mulberry (*Morus alba*), Japanese climbing fern (*Lygodium japonicum*), Japanese honeysuckle (*Lonicera japonica*), wisteria (*Wisteria macrostachya*), silk tree or mimosa (*Albizzia julibrissin*), elderberry (*Sambucus canadensis*), water hyacinth (*Eichhornia crassipes*), alligatorweed (*Alternanthera philoxeroides*), Chinaberry tree (*Melia azedarach*), Chinese tallow tree (*Triadica* or *Sapium sebiferum*), and Chinese privet (*Ligustrum sinense*). Many of these exotic species create significant environmental problems because of their invasive nature and tendency to displace native species.

Today, instead of a homogeneous forest dominated by longleaf pine, the north-shore area is a mixed patchwork of much reduced pine forests dominated by loblolly, cleared agricultural and pasture lands, and scattered urban and

Table 18 Plant species recorded at Delta Primate Center, St. Tammany Parish, Louisiana

Vegetation Group	Major Trees	Understory Species
Pine forest	Loblolly pine (*Pinus taeda*)	Poison ivy (*Rhus radicans*)
		Oak saplings (*Quercus* spp.; see below for major species)
		Blackberry or dewberry (*Rubus* spp.)
		Small magnolia (*Magnolia virginiana*)
		Virginia creeper (*Parthenocissus quinquifolia*)
		Wax myrtle (*Myrica cerifera*)
		Red maple (*Acer rubrum*)
		Sweetgum (*Liquidamber styraciflua*)
Pine and hardwood forest	Loblolly pine (*Pinus taeda*)	Flatwoods plum (*Prunus umbellata*)
	Black gum (*Nyssa sylvatica*)	Southern arrow-wood (*Viburnum dentatum*)
	Oaks (*Quercus* spp.; see below for major species)	Poison ivy (*Rhus radicans*)
	Mockernut hickory (*Carya tomentosa*)	Beautyberry or French mulberry (*Callicarpa americana*)
	Red maple (*Acer rubrum*)	Small magnolia (*Magnolia virginiana*)
	Sweetgum (*Liquidamber styraciflua*)	Summer grape (*Vitis aestivalis*)
	Yaupon (*Ilex vomitoria*)	Muscadine (*Vitis rotundifolia*)
	Dahoon (*Ilex cassine*)	Greenbriar (*Smilax rotundifolia*)
	American holly (*Ilex opaca*)	Catbriar (*Smilax glauca*)
	Farkle berry (*Vaccinium arboreum*)	Cross vine (*Anisostichus* [*Bignonia*] *capreolata*)
	Hawthorn (*Crataegus marshallii*)	Evening trumpet flower (*Gelsemium sempervirens*)
	Flowering dogwood (*Cornus florida*)	Peppervine (*Ampelopsis arborea*)
	Red ash (*Fraxinus pennsylvanicus*)	Deerberry (*Vaccinium stamineum*)
	Red mulberry (*Morus rubra*)	Elliott's blueberry (*Vaccinium elliottii*)
	White mulberry (*Morus alba*)*	Anise (*Illicium floridanum*)

THE TERRESTRIAL COMMUNITIES 253

Vegetation Group	Major Trees	Understory Species
		Horse sugar (*Symplocos tinctoria*)
Mixed bottomland hardwood forest	Post oak (*Quercus stellata*)	Rhododendron (*Rhododendron serrulatum*)
	Blackjack oak (*Quercus marilandica*)	Southern arrow-wood (*Viburnum dentatum*)
	Cow oak (*Quercus prinus*)	Witch hazel (*Hamamelis virginiana*)
	Water oak (*Quercus niger*)	Beech (*Fagus grandifolia*)
	Live oak (*Quercus virginiana*)	Alder (*Alnus serrulata*)
	Loblolly pine (*Pinus taeda*)	Elephant's foot (*Elephantopus nudatus*)
	Spruce pine (*Pinus glabra*)	Tick-trefoil (*Desmodium paniculatum* and *D. nudiflorum*)
	Short-leaf pine (*Pinus echinata*)	Anise (*Illicium floridanum*)
	Red maple (*Acer rubrum*)	Flatwoods plum (*Prunus umbellata*)
	Tupelo (*Nyssa aquatica*)	Virginia creeper (*Parthenocissus quinquifolia*)
	American holly (*Ilex opaca*)	Peppervine (*Ampelopsis arborea*)
	Yaupon (*Ilex vomitoria*)	Flatwoods plum (*Prunus umbellata*)
	Red mulberry (*Morus rubra*)	Poison ivy (*Rhus radicans*)
	Red ash (*Fraxinus pennsylvanicus*)	
	Southern magnolia (*Magnolia grandiflora*)	
	Great-leaved magnolia (*Magnolia macrophylla*)	
	Flowering dogwood (*Cornus florida*)	
Cypress swamp	Bald cypress (*Taxodium distichum*)	Southern arrow-wood (*Viburnum dentatum*)
	Tupelo (*Nyssa aquatica*)	Flatwoods plum (*Prunus umbellata*)
	Red ash (*Fraxinus pennsylvanicus*)	Hawthorn (*Crataegus marshallii*)
	Red maple (*Acer rubrum*)	Virginia willow (*Itea virginica*)
	Flowering dogwood (*Cornus florida*)	Anise (*Illicium floridanum*)
	Pines (*Pinus* spp.)	Titi or swamp cyrilla (*Cyrilla racemiflora*)
	American holly (*Ilex opaca*)	Horse sugar (*Symplocos tinctoria*)
	Beech (*Fagus grandifolia*)	Lizard tail (*Saururus cernuus*)

254 CHARACTERISTICS OF THE ESTUARINE SYSTEM TODAY

Vegetation Group	Major Trees	Understory Species
Slightly higher levels in the swamps	Post oak (*Quercus stellata*)	Farkle berry (*Vaccinium arboreum*)
	Cow oak (*Quercus prinus*)	Southern arrow-wood (*Viburnum dentatum*)
	Sweetgum (*Liquidamber styraciflua*)	Flatwoods plum (*Prunus umbellata*)
		Witch hazel (*Hamamelis virginiana*)
		Beautyberry (*Callicarpa americana*)
		Hawthorn (*Crataegus* spp.)
Immature pine forest	Loblolly pine (*Pinus taeda*)	Grasses
Shrub and immature pines	Loblolly pine (*Pinus taeda*)	Wax myrtle (*Myrica cerifera*)
		Blackberry or dewberry (*Rubus* spp.)
Shrub and old field		Wax myrtle (*Myrica cerifera*)
		Blackberry and dewberry (*Rubus* spp.)
		Consumption weed or groundsel bush, buckbush (*Baccharis halimifolia*)
		Pine saplings (*Pinus taeda*)
		Deer grass (*Rhexia mariana*)
		Persimmon (*Diospyros virginiana*)
		Sweetgum (*Liquidamber styraciflua*)
		Tall grasses
Roadside ditches and fences		Climbing fern (*Lygodium japonicum*)*
		Supplejack or rattan vine (*Berchemia scandens*)
		Greenbriar (*Smilax rotundifolia*)
		Catbriar (*Smilax glauca*)
		Summer grape (*Vitis aestivalis*)
		Muscadine (*Vitis rotundifolia*)
		Japanese honeysuckle (*Lonicera japonica*)*
		Grasses, rushes, and sedges
		Pokeweed (*Phytolacca americana*)

THE TERRESTRIAL COMMUNITIES 255

Vegetation Group	Major Trees	Understory Species
		Blackberry and dewberry (*Rubus* spp.)
		Butterfly pea (*Centrosema virginiana*)
		Wisteria (*Wisteria macrostachya*)*
		Silk tree or mimosa (*Albizzia julibrissin*)*
		Poison ivy (*Rhus radicans*)
		Dwarf sumac (*Rhus copallina*)
		Poison sumac (*Rhus vernix*)
		Peppervine (*Ampelopsis arborea*)
		Virginia creeper (*Parthenocissus quinquifolia*)
		Passion flower (*Passiflora incarnata*)
		Trumpet creeper (*Campsis radicans*)
		Evening trumpet flower (*Gelsemium sempervirens*)
		Verbena (*Verbena brasiliensis*)
		Lantana (*Lantana camara*)
		Nightshade (*Solanum americanum*)
		Horse nettle (*Solanum carolinense*)
		Buttonbush (*Cephalanthus occidentalis*)
		Buttonweed (*Diodia teres* and *D. tetragona*)
		Elderberry (*Sambucus canadensis*)*
		Dandelion (*Taraxacum* sp.)
		Bitterweed or yellowdicks (*Helenium amarum*)
Cleared areas in the forest		Arrowhead sida (*Sida rhombifolia*)
		Wooly croton (*Croton capitatus*)
		Buttonweed (*Diodia teres* and *D. tetragona*)

Vegetation Group	Major Trees	Understory Species
		Loosestrife (*Lythrum alatum* = *L. lanceolatum*)
		Several grasses
River and canal		Arrowhead (*Sagittaria* spp.)
		Yellow pondlily or cowlily (*Nuphar lutea* as *N. advena*)
		Waterlily (*Nymphaea* sp.)
		Water hyacinth (*Eichhornia crassipes*)*
		Pickerelweed (*Pontederia cordata*)
		Sedges and rushes

From Rylander (1969)
*Indicates a nonnative species

suburban developments. Continued rapid urban growth in the area will continue to modify this part of the Pontchartrain basin. More natural areas on the north shore need to be set aside as state or national forests, state parks, or wildlife management areas to help preserve and restore these dwindling resources. Existing preserves with remnant longleaf pine stands include Big Branch Marsh National Wildlife Refuge, Fontainebleau State Park, Northlake Nature Center, and three Nature Conservancy preserves (Abita Creek Flatwoods, Lake Ramsay, and Talisheek Pine Wetlands).

Postscript: Success?

The Lakes of Pontchartrain and their tributaries provide many valuable resources to the 1.5 million people who now live within the Lake Pontchartrain basin, including recreation, fisheries, and transportation. The populace has also had significant impacts on the lakes. As with many water bodies around the world, Lake Pontchartrain and its sister lakes have suffered environmental abuse and degradation. Their waters have been fouled, their wetlands destroyed, their surrounding forests cut, their shorelines littered, their beaches closed. They have been used and abused. However, various groups such as the Lake Pontchartrain Basin Foundation have worked to improve the condition of the basin, with considerable success. Continuation of these efforts may one day restore Lake Pontchartrain to a condition worthy of such a natural treasure. On the other hand, some areas (especially on the north shore of Lake Pontchartrain) are experiencing extremely rapid population growth (the fastest in the state since the year 2000), with all of the usual problems of urbanization, including increased destruction of natural habitats, increased surface runoff, and increased water pollution. The 24-mi. (39-km) long causeway and the Interstate 10 bridge provide automobile access across the lake from New Orleans and have made the north shore a somewhat convenient commuter haven for those wanting to escape the urban lifestyle. However, the massive relocation of residents from New Orleans to the north shore, especially in the aftermath of Hurricane Katrina, has generated many of the same urban problems on that side of the lake.

Houck et al. (1989) estimated that cleaning the major lakes and rivers of the Lake Pontchartrain basin so that they could be fully used by the year 2000 would provide an economic benefit of over $756 million, based upon recreational swimming, public recreation facilities, incremental tourist spending, increase in real estate values, and tax revenues generated. In addition, less tangible benefits would include improved quality of life and health for basin residents and an improved reputation for the area and state. Attempts to put such dollar values on environmental benefits result from a modern-day necessity to only value things in economic terms. But in reality, the true value of a clean environment and its many benefits cannot be measured in economic terms. Their true value is infinite. As the population increases, the potential aesthetic value of the lakes also increases.

The Pontchartrain basin was once a marvelous system of clear waters and old growth, virgin cypress swamps, with mature forests of massive 2000-year-old cypress trees. Such an environment must have been truly remarkable to the Native Americans and the first French explorers who saw ivory-billed woodpeckers, Carolina parakeets, American bison, and black bear in these swamps and adjacent habitats. The natural habitats that still exist today are only a remnant of the original natural environment. This should make them even more precious to us. We need to do what we can to preserve and restore as much of this remaining natural environment as possible.

Groups such as the Lake Pontchartrain Basin Foundation, the Sierra Club, and the Gulf Restoration Network have fought to restore this treasured resource and protect it from further abuse. Fortunately a small band of concerned citizens kept the faith that environmental abuse was not inevitable and worked tirelessly to convince citizens and civic leaders that the lakes could be restored. The battle cry of "Save Our Lake" eventually became the glowing symbol of victory that convinced many former cynics that success is possible. At the turn of the century, some optimistic voices began to speak of recovery and the possibility of beaches again being open for swimming. The Lake Pontchartrain Basin Foundation declared the lake "recovered" in February 2002, but the job is still not completed and our efforts must continue indefinitely.

There has been substantial progress in recent years, and the lake environment has greatly improved. But many unresolved environmental problems in the basin remain to be addressed. The task of restoring Lake Pontchartrain must continue and be supported by more and more committed individuals if it is to be successful. Lopez (2003) suggested that serious water quality impairment had not yet peaked, and overall water quality may still be declining. Hurricane Katrina in 2005 was a serious set-back to the restoration effort. Although the impact of the hurricane and the excessive pollution carried into the lake with the flood waters was substantial, their potential long-term effects are unknown. The natural flushing process continually removes pollutants from the lake, even from such catastrophic events. However, the environmental problems could become more acute as the human population grows, with additional urban and suburban expansion. But such problems can be solved if we are committed. We owe it to ourselves and to future generations.

Environmental problems are certainly not unique to the Pontchartrain basin, nor to Louisiana, but are universal problems of humanity. Throughout the world, waters have been used and abused. Rather than appreciating the value and necessity of clean waters, humans have fouled them with sewage, trash, hazardous chemicals, and excessive sediments. A large percentage of the world's waterways are considered so polluted as to be unsuited for their designated uses. The problem is most severe in overpopulated, developing countries but also occurs in most supposedly advanced societies. Proper treatment of human wastes and other environmental pollutants can be expensive, but it is not nearly as expensive as environmental abuse. We pay for treating our wastes one way or another: either by proper treatment and disposal methods that protect our environment or by increased diseases and associated medical expenses, diminished health and life expectancy, fewer food and water sources, lost recreational opportunities, and reduced aesthetics. The true value of the Lakes of Pontchartrain is indeed infinite. We should be willing to pay whatever it takes to protect them. We owe it to ourselves and to future generations.

I encourage all who read this book to study the Lakes of Pontchartrain, learn about their ecology and their infinite value to us all, and treasure and protect this wonderful natural resource.

References Cited

Abadie, S. W., and M. A. Poirrier. 2000. Increased density of large *Rangia* clams in Lake Pontchartrain after the cessation of shell dredging. Journal of Shellfish Research 19(1): 481–485.
Abadie, S. W., and M. A. Poirrier. 2001. Recent trends in water clarity and clam abundance. P. 165 *in* Shea Penland, Andrew Beall, and Jeff Waters, ed. Environmental atlas of the Lake Pontchartrain basin. Lake Pontchartrain Basin Foundation, New Orleans.
Alperin, Lynn M. 1983. History of the Gulf Intracoastal Waterway. Navigation History, National Waterways Study 83-9. U.S. Army Engineer Water Resources Support Center.
Anderson, A. C., A. Abdelghani, J. Stumpf, and J. C. Rice. 1990. Bacteriological criteria for recreational waters along the Tangipahoa River. DEQ Contract no. 24022-901-01. Tulane University School of Public Health and Tropical Medicine, New Orleans.
Anderson, Gary. 1985. Species profiles. Life histories and environmental requirements of coastal fishes and invertebrates (Gulf of Mexico): grass shrimp. U.S. Fish and Wildlife Service Biological Report 82(11.35).
Argyrou, M. E., T. S. Bianchi, and C. D. Lambert. 1997. Transport and fate of dissolved organic carbon in the Lake Pontchartrain estuary, Louisiana, U.S.A. Biogeochemistry 38: 207–226.
Association of Levee Boards of Louisiana, 1990. The system that works to serve our state. Association of Levee Boards of Louisiana, Baton Rouge.
Bacon, Edward. 1867. Among the cotton thieves. Free Press Steam Book and Job Printing House, Detroit, Mich. Reprint, 1962, Committee for the Preservation of the Port Hudson Battlefield.
Bahr, L. M., Jr., J. P. Sikora, and W. B. Sikora. 1980. Macrobenthic survey of Lake Pontchartrain. Pp. 659–710 *in* J. H. Stone, ed. Environmental analysis of Lake Pontchartrain, Louisiana, its surrounding wetlands, and selected land uses. Vols. 1 and 2. Publication no. LSU-CEL-80-08. Center for Wetland Resources, Louisiana State University, Baton Rouge.
Baldwin, Andrew H., and Irving A. Mendelssohn. 1998. Response of two oligohaline marsh communities to lethal and nonlethal disturbance. Oecolgia 116: 543–555.

262 REFERENCES CITED

Banbury, M. M., A. B. Rheams, S. E. Lyons, S. Flanagan, and M. C. Greene. 1997. Lessons on the lake: an educator's guide to the Pontchartrain basin. Lake Pontchartrain Basin Foundation, Metairie, La.

Barbé, D. E., S. Carnelos, and J. A. McCorquodale. 2001. Climatic effect on water quality evaluation. Journal of Environmental Science and Health A: Toxic/Hazardous Substances and Environmental Engineering 36(10): 1919–1933.

Barrett, Barney. 1970. Water measurements of coastal Louisiana. Louisiana Wildlife and Fisheries Commission, Baton Rouge.

Barrett, Barney. 1976. Grain size analyses of bottom sediments in Lakes Maurepas and Pontchartrain. Pp. 145–159 *in* Johnnie W. Tarver and L. B. Savoie, ed. An inventory and study of the Lake Pontchartrain–Lake Maurepas estuarine complex. Louisiana Wildlife and Fisheries Commission, Technical Bulletin no. 19. Phase IV: Sedimentology.

Barry, John M. 1997. Rising tide: the great Mississippi flood of 1927 and how it changed America. Simon & Schuster, New York.

Bartram, William. 1791. Travels through North and South Carolina, Georgia, East and West Florida, the Cherokee Country, the extensive territories of the Muscogulges, or Creek Confederacy, and the Country of the Chactaws; containing an account of the soil and natural productions of those regions, together with observations on the manners of the Indians. Reprint, 1928, Dover, New York.

Bassett, John S., and Sidney Bradshaw, ed. 1922. Major Howell Tatum's journal while acting topographical engineer (1814) to General Jackson. Smith College Studies on History. Vol. VII, October 1921 to April 1922. Department of History of Smith College, Northampton, Mass.

Beall, Andrew, Chris Zganjar, Karen Westphal, and Shea Penland. 2001. Shoreline types of the Lake Pontchartrain basin: summary. P. 56 *in* Shea Penland, Andrew Beall, and Jeff Waters, ed. Environmental atlas of the Lake Pontchartrain basin. Lake Pontchartrain Basin Foundation, New Orleans.

Bean, T. H. 1884. On the occurrence of the striped bass in the lower Mississippi valley. Proceedings of the U.S. National Museum 7: 242–244.

Beavers, R. C., M. C. Webb, T. R. Lamb, and J. R. Greene. 1985. Archaeological survey of the upper Tangipahoa River, Tangipahoa Parish, Louisiana. Research Report no. 11, Archaeological and Cultural Research Program, University of New Orleans.

Benavides, Alonso de. 1630. The memorial of Fray Alonso de Benavides, 1630. Mrs. Edward E. Ayer, trans. 1965. Horn and Wallace, Albuquerque, N.M.

Bernard, Shane K. 2002. M'sieu Ned's rat? Reconsidering the origin of nutria in Louisiana: the E. A. McIlhenny Collection, Avery Island, Louisiana. Louisiana History 43(3): 281–293.

Bezou, Henry C. 1973. Metairie: a tongue of land to pasture. Pelican, Gretna, La.

Bianchi, T. S., and M. E. Argyrou. 1997. Temporal and spatial dynamics of particulate organic carbon in the Lake Pontchartrain estuary, southeast Louisiana, U.S.A. Estuarine, Coastal, and Shelf Science 45: 557–569.

Bishop, Nathaniel H. 1879. Four months in a sneak-box. Lee and Shephard, Boston. Photoprint, 1976, Gale Research Co., Detroit.

Boesch, D. F., and R. E. Turner. 1984. Dependence of fishery species on salt marshes: the role of food and refuge. Estuaries 7: 460–468.

Boesch, Donald F., M. N. Josselyn, A. J. Mehta, J. T. Morris, W. K. Nuttle, C. A. Simenstead, and D. J. P. Swift. 1994. Scientific assessment of coastal wetland loss, restoration, and management in Louisiana. Journal of Coastal Research, Special Issue no. 20.

Bolton, H. E., ed. 1916. Spanish exploration in the Southwest, 1542–1706. Charles Scribner's Sons, New York.

Bordenave, Justin F. 1940. Wanted: one seawall. Jefferson Parish Yearly Review. Police Jury of Jefferson Parish, pp. 156–162.

Bouma, Arnold H., ed. 1976. Shell dredging and its influence on Gulf coast environments. Gulf Publishing Co., Houston, Tex.

Boundy, Jeff, and Curtis Kennedy. 2006. Trapping results for the alligator snapping turtle (*Macrochelys temminckii*) in southeastern Louisiana, with comments on exploitation. Chelonian Conservation and Biology 5(1): 3–9.

Bowman, P. E. 1973. Food habits of the lesser scaup (*Aythya affinis*) in Lake Pontchartrain. M.S. thesis, Southeastern Louisiana University, Hammond.

Brantley, C. G. 1998. Recent history and status of the brown pelican in Lake Pontchartrain. Abstract of unpublished paper presented at Basics of the Basin Symposium, New Orleans. Symposium program, pp. 21–23.

Brantley, C. G., and S. G. Platt. 1992. Experimental evaluation of nutria herbivory on baldcypress. Proceedings of the Louisiana Academy of Sciences 55: 21–25.

Brantley, C. G., and S. G. Platt. 2001. Canebrake conservation in the southeastern United States. Wildlife Society Bulletin 29(4): 1175–1181.

Brantley, C. G., J. W. Day Jr., R. R. Lane, E. Hyfield, J. N. Day, and Jae-Young Ko. 2008. Primary production, nutrient dynamics, and accretion of a coastal freshwater forested wetland assimilation system in Louisiana. Ecological Engineering 34: 7–22.

Brasseaux, Carl A. 1979. A comparative view of French Louisiana, 1699 and 1762: the journals of Pierre Le Moyne d'Iberville and Jean-Jacques-Blaise d'Abaddie. The USL History Series no. 13. Center for Louisiana Studies, University of Southwestern Louisiana, Lafayette.

Brewer, J. Stephen, and James B. Grace. 1990. Plant community structure in an oligohaline tidal marsh. Vegetatio 90: 93–107.

Britsch, Del, and J. B. Dunbar. 1996. Land loss in coastal Louisiana, New Orleans. Technical Report GL-90-2, Map 4 of 7. U.S. Army Corps of Engineers, New Orleans District, New Orleans.

Britsch, Louis D., and Joseph B. Dunbar. 1993. Land loss rates: Louisiana coastal plain. Journal of Coastal Research 9(2): 324–338.

Brooks, Robert A. 1969. Sedimentary geochemistry and clay mineralogy of Lake Pontchartrain and Lake Maurepas, Louisiana. M.S. thesis, Louisiana State University, Baton Rouge.

Brown, Kenneth M., and P. D. Banks. 2001. The conservation of unionid mussels in Louisiana rivers: diversity, assemblage composition and substrate use. Aquatic Conservation: Marine and Freshwater Ecosystems 11(3): 189–198.

Brown, Kenneth M., and J. P. Curole. 1997. Longitudinal changes in the mussels of the Amite River: endangered species, effects of gravel mining, and shell morphology. Pp. 236–246 *in* K. S. Cummings, A. C. Buchanan, C. A. Mayer, and T. J. Naimo, ed. Conservation and management of freshwater mussels. II. Initiatives for the future. Proceedings of a UMRCC symposium, 16–18 October 1995, St. Louis, Missouri. Upper Mississippi River Conservation Committee, Rock Island, Ill.

Brown, Samuel R. 1817. The western gazeteer, or emigrant's directory. Reprint, 1971, Arno Press, New York.

Burk-Kleinpeter, Inc. 1997. Lincoln Beach public access evaluation: existing site conditions. Report to the Board of Commissioners of the Orleans Levee District, December 1997.

Burns, J. W., Jr., M. A. Poirrier, and K. P. Preston. 1995. The status of *Potamogeton perfoliatus* (Potamogetonaceae) in Lake Pontchartrain, Louisiana. SIDA Contributions to Botany 16(4): 757–763.

Bushnell, David I., Jr. 1909. The Choctaw of Bayou Lacomb, St. Tammany Parish, Louisiana. Smithsonian Institution Bureau of American Ethnology, Bulletin no. 48.

Butler, Ruth L., trans. and ed. 1934. Journal of Paul du Ru. Caxton Club, Chicago.

Byrd, Kathleen M. 1976. The brackish water clam (*Rangia cuneata*): a prehistoric "staff of life" or a minor food resource. Louisiana Archaeology 3: 23–31.

Byrne, C. J., and I. R. DeLeon. 1987. Contributions of heavy metals from municipal runoff to the sediments of Lake Pontchartrain, Louisiana. Chemosphere 16(10–12): 2579–2584.

Cabelli, V. J., A. P. Dufour, L. J. McCabe, and M. A. Levin. 1982. Swimming-associated gastroenteritis and water quality. American Journal of Epidemiology 115(4): 606–616.

Campanella, Catherine. 2007. Images of America: Lake Pontchartrain. Arcadia, Charleston, S.C.

Caruso, John A. 1966. The Mississippi valley frontier: the age of French exploration and settlement. Bobbs-Merrill Co., Indianapolis.

Casey, Powell A. 1983. Encyclopedia of forts, posts, named camps, and other military installations in Louisiana, 1700–1981. Claitor's Publishing Division, Baton Rouge.

Cashner, Robert C., F. P. Gelwick, and W. J. Matthews. 1994. Spatial and temporal variation in the distribution of fishes of the LaBranche wetlands area of the Lake Pontchartrain estuary, Louisiana. Northeast Gulf Science 13(2): 107–120.

Castellanos, Henry C. 1895. New Orleans as it was. Episodes of Louisiana Life. L. Graham & Son, Ltd., New Orleans. Reprint, 1978, *in* George F. Reinecke, ed. Louisiana Bicentennial Reprint Series. Louisiana State University Press, Baton Rouge.

Cathcart, J. L. 1819. Journal. *In* Walter Prichard, F. B. Kniffen, and C. A. Brown, ed. 1945. Southern Louisiana and southern Alabama in 1819: the journal of James Leander Cathcart. Louisiana Historical Quarterly 28(3): 735–921.

Chabreck, Robert H., P. D. Keyser, D. A. Dell, and R. G. Linscombe. 1989. Movement patterns of muskrats in a Louisiana coastal marsh. Proceedings of the Annual Conference of Southeastern Association of Fish and Wildlife Agencies 43: 437–443.

Charlevoix, Pierre-François-Xavier de. 1722. The history and the journal. *In* Charles E. O'Neill, ed. 1977. Charlevoix's Louisiana: selections from the history and the journal. Louisiana State

University Press, Baton Rouge. Also published in French, B. F. 1851. Historical collections of Louisiana.... Part III. D. Appleton & Co., New York. Reprint, 1976, Vol. 3, pp. 119–126. AMS Press, Inc., New York.

Childers, G. W., K. Bancroft, and R. W. Hastings. 1985. A baseline study of the water quality and selected faunal communities in Lake Maurepas, its major tributaries, and Pass Manchac. Final report submitted to Louisiana Department of Natural Resources, Coastal Zone Management Division.

Cho, Hyun-jung, and Michael Poirrier. 2001. Spillway, hurricane, and drought effects on SAV (grassbeds) and recent resurgence of submersed aquatic vegetation. Pp. 126–127 *in* Shea Penland, Andrew Beall, and Jeff Waters, ed. Environmental atlas of the Lake Pontchartrain basin. Lake Pontchartrain Basin Foundation, New Orleans.

Cho, Hyun-jung, and Michael A. Poirrier. 2005. Response of submersed aquatic vegetation (SAV) in Lake Pontchartrain, Louisiana to the 1997–2001 El Niño Southern Oscillation shifts. Estuaries 28(2): 215–225.

Cipra, David L. 1997. Lighthouses, lightships, and the Gulf of Mexico. Cypress Communications, Alexandria, Va.

Cline, Isaac M. 1945. Storms, floods and sunshine: a book of memoirs. Pelican, New Orleans.

CNN News. 2005. Katrina: state of emergency. Andrews McMeel, Kansas City, Mo.

Coastal Environments, Inc. 1983. An assessment of prehistoric cultural resources within the coastal zone of Tangipahoa Parish. Report submitted to the Tangipahoa Parish Tourist Commission.

Coastal Environments, Inc. 1984a. Environmental characteristics of the Pontchartrain-Maurepas basin and identification of management issues. Coastal Management Division, Louisiana Department of Natural Resources, Baton Rouge.

Coastal Environments, Inc. 1984b. Environmental characteristics of the Pontchartrain-Maurepas basin and identification of management issues: an atlas. Coastal Management Division, Louisiana Department of Natural Resources, Baton Rouge.

Colten, Craig E. 2003. Cypress in New Orleans: revisiting the observations of Le Page du Pratz. Louisiana History 44(4): 463–477.

Colten, Craig E. 2005. An unnatural metropolis: wresting New Orleans from nature. Louisiana State University Press, Baton Rouge.

Conatser, W. E. 1992. Petroleum industry activity in the Lake Pontchartrain basin. Abstract of unpublished paper presented at Basics of the Basin Symposium, New Orleans.

Condrey, Richard, and Deborah Fuller. 1992. The U.S. Gulf shrimp fishery. Pp. 89–119 *in* Michael H. Glantz, ed. Climate variability, climate change and fisheries. Cambridge University Press, Cambridge, U.K.

Conner, William H., G. W. Cramer, and J. W. Day. 1980. Vegetation of the north shore marshes and west shore swamps of Lake Pontchartrain, Louisiana. Proceedings of the Louisiana Academy of Sciences 43: 139–145.

Conner, William H., J. R. Toliver, and F. H. Sklar. 1986. Natural regeneration of baldcypress (*Taxodium distichum* (L.) Rich.) in a Louisiana swamp. Forest Ecology and Management 14: 305–317.

Connor, Jr., Paul, Dinah Maygarden, and Shea Penland. 2001a. Bathymetric map of Lake Pontchartrain. P. 63 *in* Shea Penland, Andrew Beall, and Jeff Waters, ed. Environmental atlas of the Lake Pontchartrain basin. Lake Pontchartrain Basin Foundation, New Orleans.

Connor, Jr., Paul, Dinah Maygarden, Shea Penland, and Jack Kindinger. 2001b. Lake Pontchartrain dredge pit bathymetry. Pp. 149–152 *in* Shea Penland, Andrew Beall, and Jeff Waters, ed. Environmental atlas of the Lake Pontchartrain basin. Lake Pontchartrain Basin Foundation, New Orleans.

Conrad, Glenn R., ed. 1971. The historical journal of the establishment of the French in Louisiana (by Jean-Baptiste de La Harpe, c. 1723). Virginia Koenig and Joan Cain, trans. USL History Series no. 3, University of Southwestern Louisiana, Lafayette.

Corbeille, R. L. 1962. New Orleans barrier islands. Gulf Coast Association of Geological Societies Transactions 12: 223–229.

Counts, C. L. 1986. The zoogeography and history of the invasion of the United States by *Corbicula fluminea* (Bivalvia: Corbiculidae). American Malacological Bulletin, Special Ed. 2: 7–39.

Counts, C. L. 1991. *Corbicula* (Bivalvia: Corbiculidae). Tryonia: Miscellaneous Publications of the Department of Malacology, no. 21. The Academy of Natural Sciences of Philadelphia.

Cowdrey, Albert E. 1977. Land's end: a history of the New Orleans District, U.S. Army Corps of Engineers, and its lifelong battle with the lower Mississippi and other rivers wending their way to the sea. U.S. Army Corps of Engineers, New Orleans District.

Coxe, Daniel. 1722. A description of the English Province of Carolana, by the Spaniards called Florida, and by the French La Louisiane. London. Copied in B. F. French, 1850. Historical collections of Louisiana. . . . Part II. Daniels and Smith, Philadelphia. Reprint, 1976, Vol. 2, pp. 221–276. AMS Press, Inc., New York.

Cramer, G. W., and J. W. Day Jr. 1980. Productivity of the swamps and marshes surrounding Lake Pontchartrain, Louisiana. Pp. 593–645 *in* J. H. Stone, ed. Environmental analysis of Lake Pontchartrain, Louisiana, its surrounding wetlands, and selected land uses. Vols. 1 and 2. Publication no. LSU-CEL-80-08. Center for Wetland Resources, Louisiana State University, Baton Rouge.

Cramer, G. W., J. W. Day Jr., and W. H. Conner. 1981. Productivity of four marsh sites surrounding Lake Pontchartrain, Louisiana. American Midland Naturalist 106: 65–72.

Crowell, Sears, and R. M. Darnell. 1955. Occurrence and ecology of the hydroid *Bimeria franciscana* in Lake Pontchartrain, Louisiana. Ecology 36(3): 516–518.

Cry, George W. 1978. Surface waters of the lower Mississippi River region. Geoscience and Man 19: 65–73.

Cummins, Gary. 1980. Archeological overview of the lower Mississippi delta, southern Louisiana. Southeast/Southwest Team, Denver Service Center, National Park Service.

Cuzon du Rest, R. P. 1963. Distribution of the zooplankton in the salt marshes of southeastern Louisiana. Publication of the Institute of Marine Science, University of Texas 9: 132–155.

Dalrymple, Margaret Fisher, ed. 1978. The merchant of Manchac: the letters of John Fitzpatrick, 1768–1790. Louisiana State University Press, Baton Rouge.

Darby, W. 1816. Geographical description of the state of Louisiana. John Melish, Philadelphia, Pa.

Dardis, Deborah A. 1980. A preliminary study of the bacterial flora from selected streams and rivers in Tangipahoa Parish. M.S. thesis, Southeastern Louisiana University, Hammond.

Darnell, Rezneat M. 1958. Food habits of fishes and larger invertebrates of Lake Pontchartrain, Louisiana, an estuarine community. Publication of the Institute of Marine Science, University of Texas 5: 353–416.

Darnell, Rezneat M. 1959. Studies on the life history of the blue crab (*Callinectes sapidus*) in Louisiana waters. Transactions of the American Fisheries Society 88: 294–304.

Darnell, Rezneat M. 1961. Trophic spectrum of an estuarine community based on studies of Lake Pontchartrain, Louisiana. Ecology 42(3): 555–568.

Darnell, Rezneat M. 1962. Ecological history of Lake Pontchartrain, an estuarine community. American Midland Naturalist 68(2): 434–444.

Darnell, Rezneat M. 1967. Organic detritus in relation to the estuarine ecosystem. Pp. 376–382 *in* G. H. Lauff, ed. Estuaries. Publication no. 83, American Association for the Advancement of Science, Washington, D.C.

Darnell, Rezneat M. 1992. Ecological history, catastrophism, and human impacts on the Mississippi/Alabama continental shelf and associated waters: a review. Gulf Research Reports 8(4): 375–386.

Darnell, Rezneat M., and Austin B. Williams. 1956. A note on the occurrence of the pink shrimp *Penaeus duorarum* in Louisiana waters. Ecology 37(4): 844–846.

Davis, Dave D. 1984. Protohistoric cultural interaction along the northern Gulf coast. Pp. 216–231 *in* Dave D. Davis, ed. Perspectives on Gulf coast prehistory. University of Press of Florida, Gainseville.

Davis, Donald W. 1978. Wetlands trapping in Louisiana. Geoscience and Man 19: 81–92.

Davis, Frank. c. 1978. The fisherman's guide to Lake Pontchartrain. 1st ed. Frank Davis & Associates.

Davis, Frank. 1983. The fisherman's guide to Lake Pontchartrain. Pelican, Gretna, La.

Davis, Frank. 1988. The Frank Davis fishing guide to Lake Pontchartrain and Lake Borgne. Pelican, Gretna, La.

Davis, James T., B. J. Fontenot, C. E. Hoenke, A. M. Williams, and J. S. Hughes. 1970. Ecological factors affecting anadromous fishes of Lake Pontchartrain and its tributaries. Fisheries Bulletin no. 9, Louisiana Wildlife and Fisheries Commission.

Day, John W., Jr., Charles A. S. Hall, W. Michael Kemp, and Alejandro Yanez-Arancibia.1989. Estuarine ecology. Wiley, New York.

Day, John W., Jr., Robert R. Lane, and Rodney F. Mach. 1999. Water chemistry dynamics in Lake Pontchartrain, Louisiana, during the 1997 opening of the Bonnet Carré Spillway. Pp. 89–100 *in* L. P. Rozas, J. A. Nyman, C. E. Proffitt, N. N. Rabalais, D. J. Reed, and R. E. Turner, ed. Recent research in coastal Louisiana: natural system function and response to human influences. Louisiana Sea Grant Program, Baton Rouge.

Delanglez, Jean. 1945. El Rio del Espiritu Santo: an essay on the cartography of the Gulf coast and the adjacent territory during the sixteenth and seventeenth centuries. Monograph Series no. 21, U.S. Catholic Historical Society, New York.

DeLaune, R. D., and R. P. Gambrell. 1996. Role of sedimentation in isolating metal contaminants in wetland environments. Journal of Environmental Science and Health A: Toxic/Hazardous Substances and Environmental Engineering A31(9): 2349–2362.

DeLeon, I. R., J. B. Ferrario, and C. J. Byrne. 1988. Bioaccumulation of polynuclear aromatic hydrocarbons by the clam, *Rangia cuneata*, in the vicinity of a creosote spill. Bulletin of Environmental Contamination and Toxicology 41(6): 872–879.

Demaree, D. 1932. Submerging experiments with *Taxodium*. Ecology 13(3): 258–262.

Devall, Margaret S., L. B. Thien, E. Ellgaard, and G. Flowers. 2006. Lead transport into Bayou Trepagnier wetlands in Louisiana, USA. Journal of Environmental Quality 35: 758–765.

De Vorsey, Louis, Jr. 1982. The impact of the La Salle expedition of 1682 on European cartography. Pp. 60–78 *in* Patricia K. Galloway, ed. La Salle and his legacy: Frenchmen and Indians in the lower Mississippi valley. University Press of Mississippi, Jackson.

Din, Gilbert C. 1988. The Canary Islanders of Louisiana. Louisiana State University Press, Baton Rouge.

Dobie, J. L. 1971. Reproduction and growth in the alligator snapping turtle, *Macroclemmys temmincki* (Troost). Copeia 1971: 645–658.

Dortch, Q., M. L. Parsons, N. N. Rabalais, and R. E. Turner. 1999. What is the threat of harmful algal blooms in Louisiana coastal waters? Pp. 134–144 *in* L. P. Rozas, J. A. Nyman, C. E. Proffitt, N. N. Rabalais, D. J. Reed, and R. E. Turner, ed. Recent research in coastal Louisiana: natural system function and response to human influences. Louisiana Sea Grant Program, Baton Rouge.

Douglas, Neil H. 1974. Freshwater fishes of Louisiana. Claitor's Publishing Division, Baton Rouge.

Dow, David D., and R. Eugene Turner. 1980. Structure and function of the phytoplankton community in Lake Pontchartrain, Louisiana. Pp. 321–436 *in* J. H. Stone, ed. Environmental analysis of Lake Pontchartrain, Louisiana, its surrounding wetlands, and selected land uses. Vols. 1 and 2. Publication no. LSU-CEL-80-08. Center for Wetland Resources, Louisiana State University, Baton Rouge.

Dranguet, Charles A., Jr., and Roman J. Heleniak. 1985. Backdoor to the Gulf: the Pass Manchac region, 1699–1863. Regional Dimensions 3: 1–25.

Dranguet, Charles A., Jr., and Roman J. Heleniak. 1987. Ruddock and Frenier: swamp communities in the heart of the cypress forest, 1836 to 1915. Paper presented at Forests, Habitats, and Resources: A Conference in World Environmental History, April 30, Duke University, Durham, N.C.

Duffy, K. C., and D. M. Baltz. 1998. Comparison of fish assemblages associated with native and exotic submerged macrophytes in the Lake Pontchartrain estuary, USA. Journal of Experimental Marine Biology and Ecology 223(2): 199–221.

Duffy, McFadden. 1975. King of the coast. Louisiana Conservationist 27(July–August): 4–9.

Dugas, Ronald J., J. W. Tarver, and L. S. Nutwell. 1974. The mollusk communities of Lakes Pontchartrain and Maurepas, Louisiana. Technical Bulletin no. 10, Louisiana Wildlife and Fisheries Commission.

Duhe, Brian J. 1976. Preliminary evidence of seasonal fishing activity at Bayou Jasmine. Louisiana Archaeology 3: 33–73.

Dundee, H. A., and D. A. Rossman. 1989. The amphibians and reptiles of Louisiana. Louisiana State University Press, Baton Rouge.

Dunn, William E. 1917. Spanish and French rivalry in the Gulf region of the United States, 1678–1702. University of Texas Bulletin no. 1705, University of Texas Press, Austin. Reprint, 1971, University of Texas Press and Books for Libraries Press, Freeport, N.Y.

Ellis, Frederick S. 1981. St. Tammany Parish: L'Autre Coté du Lac. Pelican, Gretna, La.

Englande, Andrew J., Guang Jin, and Carlton Dufrechou. 2002. Microbial contamination in Lake Pontchartrain basin and best management practices on microbial contamination reduction. Journal of Environmental Science and Health A: Toxic/Hazardous Substances and Environmental Engineering A37: 1765–1779.

Fabel, Robin. 1983. The letters of R: the lower Mississippi in the early 1770s. Louisiana History 24(4): 402–427.

Fabel, Robin F. A. 2000. Colonial challenges: Britons, Native Americans, and Caribs, 1759–1775. University Press of Florida, Gainesville.

Fairbanks, L. D. 1963. Biodemographic studies of the clam, *Rangia cuneata* Gray. Tulane Studies in Zoology 10(1): 3–47.

Fannaly, Marion T. 1980. Macroplankton movement through the tidal passes of Lake Pontchartrain. Pp. 1031–1067 *in* J. H. Stone, ed. Environmental analysis of Lake Pontchartrain, Louisiana, its surrounding wetlands, and selected land uses. Vols. 1 and 2. Publication no. LSU-CEL-80-08. Center for Wetland Resources, Louisiana State University, Baton Rouge.

Favrot, H. Mortimer. 1943. Colonial forts of Louisiana. Louisiana Historical Quarterly 26(3): 722–754.

Ferrario, J. B., G. C. Lawler, I. R. DeLeon, and J. L. Laseter. 1985. Volatile organic pollutants in biota and sediments of Lake Pontchartrain. Bulletin of Environmental Contamination and Toxicology 34: 246–255.

Filipich, Judy A., and Lee Taylor. 1971. Lakefront New Orleans: planning and development, 1926–1971. Urban Studies Institute, Louisiana State University in New Orleans.

Fischetti, Mark. 2001. Drowning New Orleans. Scientific American 285(4): 76–85.

Fitzpatrick, John W., Martjan Lammertink, M. David Luneau Jr., Tim W. Gallagher, Bobby R. Harrison, Gene M. Sparling, Kenneth V. Rosenberg, Ronald W. Rohrbaugh, Elliott C. H. Swarthout, Peter H. Wrege, Sara Barker Swarthout, Marc S. Dantzker, Russell A. Charif, Timothy R. Barksdale, J. V. Remsen Jr., Scott D. Simon, and Douglas Zollner. 2005. Ivory-billed woodpecker (*Campephilus principalis*) persists in continental North America. Science 308(5727): 1460–1462.

Fleeger, J. W., W. B. Sikora, and J. P. Sikora. 1983. Spatial and long-term temporal variation of meiobenthic-hyperbenthic copepods in Lake Pontchartrain, Louisiana. Estuarine, Coastal, and Shelf Science 16(4): 441–453.

Flowers, George C., and Wayne C. Isphording. 1990. Environmental sedimentology of the Pontchartrain estuary. Transactions of the Gulf Coast Association of Geological Societies 40: 237–250.

Flowers, George C., J. N. Suhayda, J. W. Clymire, G. L. McPherson, L. V. Koplitz, and M. A. Poirrier. 1998. Impact of industrial effluent diversion on Bayou Trepagnier, Louisiana. Environmental and Engineering Geoscience 4(1): 77–91.

Ford, J. A., and G. I. Quimby Jr. 1945. The Tchefuncte culture, an early occupation of the lower Mississippi valley. Memoir no. 2, Society for American Archaeology, Menasha, Wis.

Forman, B. R., Jr. 1900. The amusements of New Orleans. Ch. 19 *in* Henry Rightor, ed. Standard history of New Orleans, Louisiana, giving a description of the natural advantages, natural history ... settlement, Indians, Creoles, municipal and military history, mercantile and commercial interests, banking, transportation, struggles against high water, the press, educational ... etc. Lewis, Chicago.

Fossier, A. E. 1951. History of yellow fever in New Orleans. Louisiana Historical Quarterly 34(3): 205–215.

Francis, J. C., and M. A. Poirrier. 1999. Recent trends in water clarity of Lake Pontchartrain. Gulf Coast Research Reports 11: 1–5.

Francis, J. C., M. A. Poirrier, D. E. Barbe, V. Wijesundera, and M. M. Mulino. 1994. Historic trends in the Secchi disk transparency of Lake Pontchartrain. Gulf Research Reports 9(1): 1–16.

Frazier, David E. 1967. Recent deltaic deposits of the Mississippi River: their development and chronology. Transactions of the Gulf Coast Association of Geological Societies 17: 287–311.

Freiberg, Edna B. 1980. Bayou St. John in colonial Louisiana, 1699–1803. Harvey Press, New Orleans.

French, B. F. 1850. Historical collections of Louisiana, embracing translations of many rare and valuable documents relating to the natural, civil, and political history of that state, compiled with historical and biographical notes, and an introduction. Part II. Daniels and Smith, Philadelphia. Reprint, 1976, Vol. 2, AMS Press, Inc., New York.

French, B. F. 1852. History of the discovery of the Mississippi River. *In* Historical collections of Louisiana.... Part IV. Redfield, Clinton Hall, New York. Reprint, 1976, Vol. 4, pp. vii–xl, AMS Press, Inc., New York.

French, B. F. 1869. Historical collections of Louisiana and Florida including translations of original manuscripts relating to their discovery and settlement, with numerous historical and biographical notes. New Series. J. Sabin & Sons, New York. Reprint, 1976, Vol. 1, AMS Press, Inc., New York.

French, B. F. 1875. Historical collections of Louisiana and Florida.... Second series. Historical memoirs and narratives, 1327–1702. Albert Mason, New York. Reprint, 1976, Vol. 2, AMS Press, Inc., New York.

French, Mike. 1995. Sources and impacts of pollution in Lake Pontchartrain. A report presented to the Louisiana State Mineral Board, Lake Pontchartrain Study Committee. Prepared by Technology Assessment Division, Louisiana Department of Natural Resources, Baton Rouge.

Froomer, N. L. 1982. The influence of water salinity on paludal erosion processes. Journal of Geology 90(2): 179–186.

Fuentes, Gustavo N., and Robert C. Cashner. 2002. Rio Grande cichlid established in the Lake Pontchartrain drainage, Louisiana. Southwestern Naturalist 47: 456–459.

Gagliano, Sherwood M. 1963. A survey of preceramic occupations in portions of south Louisiana and south Mississippi. Florida Anthropologist 16: 105–132.

Gagliano, Sherwood M. 1969. Big Oak and Little Oak Islands: prehistoric Indian sites in Orleans Parish, Louisiana. Coastal Studies Institute, Louisiana State University, Baton Rouge.

Gagliano, Sherwood M., and R. T. Saucier. 1963. Poverty Point sites in southeastern Louisiana. American Antiquity 28(3): 320–327.

Gallagher, Tim. 2005. The grail bird: hot on the trail of the ivory-billed woodpecker. Houghton Mifflin, Boston.

Gannett News. 2006. Katrina: Devastation, survival, restoration—a unique look through the eyes of 40 photojournalists. Pediment, Vancouver, Wa.

Garrison, Charles R. 1999. Statistical summary of surface-water quality in Louisiana: Lake Pontchartrain–Lake Maurepas basin, 1943–1995. Water Resources Technical Report no. 55G, Louisiana Department of Transportation and Development, Baton Rouge.

Gary, Don L., and Donald W. Davis. 1978. Louisiana's coastal marsh: camps and recreation. 1. Proceedings of the Louisiana Academy of Sciences 41: 13–15.

Gary, Don L., and Donald W. Davis. 1979. Recreational dwellings in the Louisiana coastal marsh. Sea Grant Publication no. LSU-T-79-002, Louisiana State University, Center for Wetland Resources, Baton Rouge.

Gaston, Gary R. 1999. Bayous of the northern Gulf of Mexico: distribution and trophic ecology of invertebrates. Pp. 919–947 *in* D. P. Batzer, R. Rader, and S. A. Wissinger, ed. Invertebrates in freshwater wetlands of North America: ecology and management. John Wiley and Sons, New York.

Gathright, Isabel Singer. 1992. Bernard Marigny: a forgotten patriot. Southeast Louisiana Historical Papers 15: 1–10.

Gayarre, Charles. 1854. History of Louisiana: the French domination. Vol. 1. Reprint, 1965, Pelican, New Orleans.

Georgiou, Ioannis, and Alex McCorquodale. 2001. Inner Harbor Navigation Canal. P. 158 *in* Shea Penland, Andrew Beall, and Jeff Waters, ed. Environmental atlas of the Lake Pontchartrain basin. Lake Pontchartrain Basin Foundation, New Orleans.

Giardino, Marco J. 1984. Documentary evidence for the location of historic Indian villages in the Mississippi delta. Pp. 232–257 *in* Dave D. Davis, ed. Perspectives on Gulf coast prehistory. University Press of Florida, Gainseville.

Gilbert, Janice Dee. 1989. John LeBreton and Russell Glockner, Mandeville: Fishing and harvesting soft shell crabs. Pp. 128–130 *in* Louisiana Folklife Program. Folklife in the Florida Parishes. Louisiana Division of the Arts, Office of Cultural Development, Department of Culture, Recreation, and Tourism, and Center for Regional Studies, Southeastern Louisiana University, Hammond.

Giraud, Marcel. 1974. A history of French Louisiana. Vol. 1, The reign of Louis XIV, 1698–1715. Joseph C. Lambert, trans. Louisiana State University Press, Baton Rouge.

Giraud, Marcel. 1993. A history of French Louisiana. Vol. 2, Years of transition, 1715–1717. Brian Pearce, trans. Louisiana State University Press, Baton Rouge.

Gomez, Gay M. 2001. Perspective, power, and priorities: New Orleans and the Mississippi River flood of 1927. Pp. 109–120 *in* Craig Colten, ed. Transforming New Orleans and its environs: centuries of change. University of Pittsburgh Press, Pittsburgh, Pa.

Gordon, Harry. 1766. Harry Gordon diary. Illinois State Historical Library Collections, XI, p. 306. Reprint, 1961, Journal of Captain Harry Gordon. *In* Newton D. Mereness, ed. Travels in the American colonies. Antiquarian Society, New York.

Gornitz, V. 1995. Sea-level rise: A review of recent past and near future trends. Earth Surface Processes and Landforms 20: 7–20.

Gornitz, V., S. Lebedeff, and J. Hansen. 1982. Global sea level trend in the past century. Science 215: 1611–1614.

Graham, F., Jr. 1991. Martin madness: to establish a bird sanctuary in Louisiana. Audubon 93(3): 12, 14.

Groene, Bertram. 1985. A brief survey of the principal naval actions on the Mississippi Sound–Lakes Borgne, Pontchartrain, and Maurepas, 1861–1865. Regional Dimensions 3: 26–46.

Groene, Bertram. 1986. An overview of fifty years of steam boating from 1850 to 1900. Regional Dimensions 4(2): 21–44.

Gunning, Gerald E., and R. D. Suttkus. 1990. Decline of the Alabama shad, *Alosa alabamae*, in the Pearl River, Louisiana-Mississippi, 1963–1988. Proceedings of the Southeastern Fishes Council 21: 3–4.

Gunter, Gordon. 1953. The relationship of the Bonnet Carré Spillway to oyster beds in Mississippi Sound and the "Louisiana Marsh," with a report on the 1950 opening. Publication of the Institute of Marine Science, University of Texas 3(1): 17–71.

Gunter, Gordon. 1979. The annual flows of the Mississippi River. Gulf Research Reports 6(3): 283–290.

Haag, William G. 1978. A prehistory of the lower Mississippi River valley. Geoscience and Man 19: 1–8.

Hall, Thomas F., and William T. Penfound. 1939. A phytosociological study of a cypress-gum swamp in southeastern Louisiana. American Midland Naturalist 21(2): 378–395.

Hallenbeck, Cleve. 1940. Alvar Nuñez Cabeza de Vaca: the journey and route of the first European to cross the continent of North America, 1534–1536. Reprint, 1971, Kennikat Press, Port Washington, N.Y.

Hamilton, Peter J. 1904. Was Mobile Bay the Bay of Spiritu Santo? Alabama Historical Society Transactions, 1899–1903. Vol. 4, reprint no. 3: 73–93.

Handley, Lawrence, Steve Hartley, James Johnston, Calvin O'Neil, DeWitt Braud, and John Snead. 2001. Lake Pontchartrain basin: land use/land cover. P. 71 *in* Shea Penland, Andrew Beall, and Jeff Waters, ed. Environmental atlas of the Lake Pontchartrain basin. Lake Pontchartrain Basin Foundation, New Orleans.

Haralampides, Katie, and Alex McCorquodale. 2001. Bonnet Carré Spillway and Pearl River salinity impact models. P. 156 in Shea Penland, Andrew Beall, and Jeff Waters, ed. Environmental atlas of the Lake Pontchartrain basin. Lake Pontchartrain Basin Foundation, New Orleans.

Harrison, Robert W., and W. W. Kollmorgen. 1947. Drainage reclamation in the coastal marshlands of the Mississippi River delta. Louisiana Historical Quarterly 30(2): 654–709.

Hartfield, P. D. 1989. Mussel survey of the Amite River, Louisiana, May 9–13, 1988. Appendix D.5 *in* Amite River Flood Control Study environmental report. State project no. 575-99-30. Prepared by Espey, Huston & Associates. Metairie, La.

Hastings, Robert W. 1987. Fishes of the Manchac Wildlife Management Area, Louisiana. Proceedings of the Louisiana Academy of Sciences 50: 21–26.

Hastings, Robert W. 2002. Comparative distribution and abundance of catfishes (Ictaluridae and Ariidae) in an oligohaline upper estuary. Proceedings of the Louisiana Academy of Sciences 64: 1–13.

Hastings, Robert W., D. A. Turner, and R. G. Thomas. 1987. The fish fauna of Lake Maurepas, an oligohaline part of the Lake Pontchartrain estuary. Northeast Gulf Science 9(2): 89–98.

Hawes, Suzanne R., and Harriet M. Perry. 1978. Effects of 1973 floodwaters on plankton populations in Louisiana and Mississippi. Gulf Research Reports 6(2): 109–124.

Heard, Richard W. 1979. Notes on the genus *Probythinella* Thiele, 1928 (Gastropoda: Hydrobiidae) in the coastal waters of the northern Gulf of Mexico and the taxonomic status of *Vioscalba louisianae* Morrison, 1965. Gulf Research Reports 6(3): 309–312.

Heard, Richard W. 1982. Guide to common tidal marsh invertebrates of the northeastern Gulf of Mexico. Mississippi-Alabama Sea Grant Consortium, MASGP-79-004.

Heleniak, Roman J., and Charles A. Dranguet. 1987. Changing patterns of human activity in the western basin of Lake Pontchartrain. Pp. 749–758 *in* Estuarine and coastal management: tools of the trade. Proceedings of the Tenth National Conference of the Coastal Society, October 12–15, 1986, New Orleans.

Hickman, Nollie W. 1966. The yellow pine industries in St. Tammany, Tangipahoa, and Washington Parishes, 1840–1915. Louisiana Studies 5(2): 75–88.

Higginbotham, Jay, trans. and ed. 1969. The journal of Sauvole: historical journal of the establishment of the French in Louisiana. Colonial Books, Mobile, Ala.

Higginbotham, N., K. Bancroft, and G. W. Childers. 1991. Evaluation of microbiological water quality of the Tickfaw River: a designated natural and scenic stream in southeastern Louisiana. Proceedings of the Louisiana Academy of Sciences 54: 46–54.

Hill, Geoffry E., D. J. Mennill, B. W. Rolek, T. L. Hicks, and K. A. Swiston. 2006. Evidence suggesting that ivory-billed woodpeckers (*Campephilus principalis*) exist in Florida. Avian Conservation and Ecology 1(3): 2. Available via http://www.ace-eco.org/vol1/iss3/art2/.

Hobbs, Horton H. 1989. An illustrated checklist of the American crayfishes (Decapoda: Astacidae, Cambaridae, and Parastacidae). Smithsonian Institution Press, Washington, D.C.

Holmes, Jack D. L. 1968. Naval stores in colonial Louisiana and the Floridas. Louisiana Studies 7(4): 295–309.

Holmes, Jack D. L. 1982. Andres de Pez and Spanish reaction to French expansion into the Gulf of Mexico. Pp. 106–128 *in* Patricia K. Galloway, ed. La Salle and his legacy: Frenchmen and Indians in the lower Mississippi valley. University Press of Mississippi, Jackson.

Houck, Oliver A., Fritz Wagner, and John B. Elstrott. 1989. To restore Lake Pontchartrain: a report to the Greater New Orleans Expressway Commission on the sources, remedies, and economic impacts of pollution in the Lake Pontchartrain basin. Greater New Orleans Expressway Commission, New Orleans.

Huber, Leonard V. 1970. Lakeview lore. Commemorating the opening of the First National Bank of Commerce, Harrison Avenue Office, New Orleans.

Hurston, Zora Neale. 1935. Mules and men. J. B. Lipincott Co., Philadelphia.

Hutchins, Thomas. 1784. An historical narrative and topographical description of Louisiana and West Florida. Introduction and index by Joseph G. Tregle Jr. Reprint, 1968, University Press of Florida, Gainesville.

Iberville, Pierre LeMoyne (d'Iberville).1699a. Narrative of the expedition of M. d'Iberville to Louisiana, translated from a copy of the original letter addressed to M. Le Comte de Pontchartrain, deposited in the archives of the Marine Department, Paris. Pp. 19–31 *in* B. F. French, ed. 1869. Historical collections of Louisiana and Florida including translations of original manuscripts relating to their discovery and settlement, with numerous historical and biographical notes. New Series. J. Sabin & Sons, New York. Reprint, 1976, Vol. 1, AMS Press, Inc., New York.

Iberville, Pierre LeMoyne (d'Iberville). 1699b. The journal of the Badine: the first voyage to the Mississippi. Pp. 19–105 *in* R. G. McWilliams, trans. and ed. 1981. Iberville's gulf journals. University of Alabama Press, Tuscaloosa.

Iberville, Pierre LeMoyne (d'Iberville). 1700. The journal of the Renommée: the second voyage to the Mississippi. Pp. 106–156 *in* R. G. McWilliams, trans. and ed. 1981. Iberville's gulf journals. University of Alabama Press, Tuscaloosa.

Iberville, Pierre LeMoyne (d'Iberville). 1702. The journal of the Renommée: the third voyage to the Mississippi. Pp. 157–179 *in* R. G. McWilliams, trans. and ed. 1981. Iberville's gulf journals. University of Alabama Press, Tuscaloosa.

Irion, Jack B., R. Draughon Jr., and D. V. Beard. 1994. Underwater cultural resources survey of the south entrance channel, Pass Manchac, Louisiana. Cultural Resources Series Report DACW29-92-D0011, U.S. Army Corps of Engineers New Orleans District.

Jackson, Jack. 1995. Flags along the coast. Charting the Gulf of Mexico, 1519–1759: a reappraisal. Book Club of Texas, Wind River Press, Austin.

Jacobs, Harry. 1936. Jefferson Parish within the favored flood-exempt New Orleans area. Jefferson Parish Yearbook, 1936, pp. 23–29.

Janes, Linda Sue. 1987. An analysis of the sanitary water quality of the Tangipahoa River and a survey of selected Tangipahoa Parish streams. M.S. thesis, Southeastern Louisiana University, Hammond.

Jeng, H. A. C., A. J. Englande, R. M. Bakeer, and H. B. Bradford. 2005. Impact of urban stormwater runoff on estuarine environmental quality. Estuarine Coastal and Shelf Science 63(4): 513–526.

Jin, Guang, A. J. Englande, H. Bradford, J. Waters, and G. C. Austin. 1999. Welcome back to the beach. Water Environment and Technology 11(9): 32–39.

Jin, Guang, A. J. Englande Jr., and A. Liu. 2003. A preliminary study on coastal water quality monitoring and modeling. Journal of Environmental Science and Health A: Toxic/Hazardous Substances and Environmental Engineering A38: 493–509.

Jin, Guang, J. England, H. Bradford, and H. W. Jeng. 2004. Comparison of *E. coli*, enterococci, and fecal coliform as indicators for brackish water quality assessment. Water Environment Research 76(3): 245–255.

Johnson, Cecil. 1942. British West Florida, 1763–1783. Yale University Press, New Haven, Conn. Reprint, 1971, Shoe String Press, Inc., North Haven, Conn.

Jordan de Reina, Juan. 1686. Log of the voyage of the frigate *Nuestra Senora de la Concepcion* sent by the viceroy of New Spain in search of the Bay of Espiritu Santo. *In* Irving A. Leonard, trans. and ed. 1936. The Spanish re-exploration of the Gulf coast in 1686. Mississippi Valley Historical Review 22(1): 547–557.

Joseph, E. B. 1957. A study of the systematics and life history of the gulf pipefish, *Syngnathus scovelli* (Evermann and Kendall). Ph.D. diss., Florida State University, Tallahassee.

Junot, J. A., M. A. Poirrier, and T. M. Soniat. 1983. Effects of saltwater intrusion from the Inner Harbor Navigation Canal on the benthos of Lake Pontchartrain, Louisiana. Gulf Research Reports 7(3): 247–254.

Kalff, Jacob. 2002. Limnology: inland water ecosystems. Prentice Hall, Upper Saddle River, N.J.

Keller, C. E., J. A. Spendelow, and R. D. Greer. 1984. Atlas of wading bird and seabird colonies in coastal Louisiana, Mississippi, and Alabama, 1983. U.S. Fish and Wildlife Service FWS/OBS-84/13.

Kelly, Mortimer F., III. 1975. Fort St. John. Southeast Louisiana Historical Association Papers 2: 54–65.

Kemp, John R. 1996. Introduction. Pp. 1–33 *in* Julia Sims. Manchac swamp: Louisiana's undiscovered wilderness. Louisiana State University Press, Baton Rouge.

Kemp, John R. 1997. New Orleans: an illustrated history. American Historical Press, Sun Valley, Calif.

Kemp, John R., and S. H. Colvin. 1981. St. Tammany, 1885–1945: a photographic essay. St. Tammany Historical Society Gazette, Mandeville, La.

Kemp, John R., and L. O. King. 1975. Louisiana images, 1880–1920: a photographic essay by George Francois Mugnier. Louisiana State University Press, Baton Rouge.

Kidder, Tristram R. 1996. Perspectives on the geoarchaeology of the lower Mississippi valley. Engineering Geology 45: 305–323.

Kidder, Tristram R. 1998. The rat that ate Louisiana: aspects of historical ecology in the Mississippi River delta. Pp. 141–168 *in* William Balee, ed. Advances in historical ecology. Columbia University Press, New York.

Kidder, Tristram R. 2001. Making the city inevitable. Pp. 9–21 *in* Craig Colten, ed. Transforming New Orleans and its environs: centuries of change. University of Pittsburgh Press, Pittsburgh, Pa.

King, Grace. 1893. Jean Baptiste le Moyne, Sieur de Bienville. Dodd, Mead and Co., New York.

Klerks, Paul L., and Sandra A. Lentz. 1998. Resistance to lead and zinc in the western mosquitofish, *Gambusia affinis*, inhabiting contaminated Bayou Trepagnier. Ecotoxicology 7(1): 11–17.

Kloeppel, James E. 1987. Danger beneath the waves: a history of the Confederate submarine *H. L. Hunley*. Adele Enterprises, College Park, Ga.

Knabb, Richard D., J. R. Rhome, and D. P. Brown. 2006a. Tropical cyclone report: Hurricane Katrina, August 23–30, 2005. National Hurricane Center. http://www.nhc.noaa.gov/pdf/TCR-AL122005_Katrina.pdf.

Knabb, Richard D., J. R. Rhome, and D. P. Brown. 2006b. Tropical Cyclone Report: Hurricane Rita, 18–26 September 2005. National Hurricane Center. http://www.nhc.noaa.gov/pdf/TCR-AL182005_Rita.pdf.

Kniffen, Fred B. 1935. Bayou Manchac: a physiographic interpretation. Geographical Review 25: 462–466.

Kniffen, Fred B. 1990. The lower Mississippi valley: European settlement, utilization and modification. Geoscience and Man 27: 3–34.

Kniffen, Fred B., Hiram F. Gregory, and George A. Stokes. 1987. The historic Indian tribes of Louisiana: from 1542 to the present. Louisiana State University Press, Baton Rouge.

Knight, Charles L., and R. W. Hastings. 1994. Fishes of the Tangipahoa River system, Mississippi and Louisiana. Tulane Studies in Zoology and Botany 29: 141–150.

Kopman, Henry H. 1900. The nature of bird life at New Orleans. Ch. 14 *in* Henry Rightor, ed. Standard history of New Orleans, Louisiana. Lewis, Chicago.

Ktsanes, Virginia K., Ann C. Anderson, and John E. Diem. 1981. Health effects of swimming in Lake Pontchartrain at New Orleans. Project Summary. U.S. Environmental Protection Agency, Health Effects Research Laboratory, Cincinnati, Ohio (EPA-600/S1-81-027).

Kunkel, Paul A. 1951. The Indians of Louisiana, about 1700: their customs and manner of living. Louisiana Historical Quarterly 34(3): 175–203.

Kysar, Douglas A., and T. O. McGarity. 2006. Did NEPA drown New Orleans? The levees, the blame game, and the hazards of hindsight. Duke Law Journal 56: 179–235.

LaHarpe, Jean-Baptiste Benard de. c. 1723. The historical journal of the establishment of the French in Louisiana. Virginia Koenig and Joan Cain, trans. Glenn R. Conrad, ed. 1971. University of Southwestern Louisiana History Series no. 3, USL Center for Louisiana Studies, Lafayette. Also published in French, B. F. 1851. Historical collections of Louisiana. . . . Part III. D. Appleton & Co., New York. Reprint, 1976, Vol. 3, pp. 9–118, AMS Press, Inc., New York.

Lake Pontchartrain Basin Foundation (LPBF). 1990. Foundation formed to save our lake. Around the Lake 1(1): 1.

Lake Pontchartrain Basin Foundation (LPBF). 1991a. Mineral Board update. Around the Lake 2(1): 2.

Lake Pontchartrain Basin Foundation (LPBF). 1991b. Foundation questions Bonnet Carré freshwater diversion project. Around the Lake 2(2): 1–2.

Lake Pontchartrain Basin Foundation (LPBF). 1992a. Executive director's report. Around the Lake 3(1): 2.

Lake Pontchartrain Basin Foundation (LPBF). 1992b. LPBF adds environmental director. Around the Lake 3(1): 6.

Lake Pontchartrain Basin Foundation (LPBF). 1993a. Lake Pontchartrain cleanup efforts moving forward with help from Senator Johnston. Around the Lake 4(1): 1.

Lake Pontchartrain Basin Foundation (LPBF). 1993b. Johnston dedicates funds for lake. Around the Lake 4(3): 1, 10.

Lake Pontchartrain Basin Foundation (LPBF). 1993c. Report to the people of the Lake Pontchartrain basin. Summary: The Lake Pontchartrain Basin Draft Comprehensive Management Plan Phase II.

Lake Pontchartrain Basin Foundation (LPBF). 1995a. Wildlife preserve is dedicated. Around the Lake 6(1): 1, 3, 4.

Lake Pontchartrain Basin Foundation (LPBF). 1995b. Spillway leaks linked to algae and fish kills. Around the Lake 6(3): 1.

Lake Pontchartrain Basin Foundation (LPBF). 1995c. Lake Pontchartrain Basin Foundation Comprehensive Management Plan, Phase III, Save our lake.

Lake Pontchartrain Basin Foundation (LPBF). 1996. Bonnet Carré diversion killed by Governor Foster. Around the Lake 7(3): 1, 11–12.

Lake Pontchartrain Basin Foundation (LPBF). 1997a. Big Branch keeps on growing. Around the Lake 7(4): 3.

Lake Pontchartrain Basin Foundation (LPBF). 1997b. Corps opens the Bonnet Carré Spillway. Around the Lake 8(1): 1, 11.

Lake Pontchartrain Basin Foundation (LPBF). 1997c. Spillway opening causes worst algae bloom in history. Around the Lake 8(2): 1, 5.

Lake Pontchartrain Basin Foundation (LPBF). 2000a. Mad about manatees. Around the Lake 9(3): 1.

Lake Pontchartrain Basin Foundation (LPBF). 2000b. Testing the waters: water quality monitoring in Lake Pontchartrain. Around the Lake 10(2): 5.

Lake Pontchartrain Basin Foundation (LPBF). 2001a. Artificial reef program launched in Lake Pontchartrain. Around the Lake 11(1): 5.

Lake Pontchartrain Basin Foundation (LPBF). 2001b. Go jump in the lake? Now we're one step closer. Around the Lake 11(2): 1, 3.

Lake Pontchartrain Basin Foundation (LPBF). 2001c. Testing the waters: water quality monitoring in Lake Pontchartrain.

Lake Pontchartrain Basin Foundation (LPBF). 2001d. New "reel" estate in Lake Pontchartrain: plans for constructing additional artificial reefs are now underway. Around the Lake 11(3): 5.

Lake Pontchartrain Basin Foundation (LPBF). 2006a. Comprehensive Habitat Management Plan for the Lake Pontchartrain Basin.

Lake Pontchartrain Basin Foundation (LPBF). 2006b. Congress deauthorizes MRGO. Basin Bulletin 1(6), Special Edition, June 9.

Lambousy, Greg. 1999. Lost drawings identify the *Pioneer*. Louisiana Cultural Vistas (Fall): 8–10.

Lane, R. R., J. W. Day, G. P. Kemp, and D. K. Demcheck. 2001. The 1994 experimental opening of the Bonnet Carré Spillway to divert Mississippi River water into Lake Pontchartrain, Louisiana. Ecological Engineering 17(4): 411–422.

Laurent, Lubin F. 1982. A history of St. John the Baptist Parish. L'Observateur, Reserve, La. (Originally published in 1922–1923 in serial form, 53 chapters).

Ledoux, Amy. 1993. MR-GO: Economic blessing or ecological disaster? City Business, October 11, 19–20A.

Lee, D. S., C. R. Gilbert, C. H. Hocutt, R. E. Jenkins, D. E. McAllister, and J. R. Stauffer Jr. 1980. Atlas of North American freshwater fishes. Publication no. 1980-12, North Carolina Museum of Natural History, Raleigh.

Leonard, Irving A., trans. and ed. 1936. The Spanish re-exploration of the Gulf coast in 1686. Mississippi Valley Historical Review 22(1 March): 547–557.

Leonard, Irving A., trans. 1939. Spanish approach to Pensacola, 1689–1693. Reprint, 1967, Arno Press, New York.

Le Page du Pratz, Antoine Simon. 1774. The history of Louisiana, or of the western parts of Virginia and Carolina: containing a description of the countries that lie on both sides of the River Mississippi: with an account of the settlements, inhabitants, soil, climate, and products. Facsimile reproduction, 1975, Louisiana State University Press, Baton Rouge.

Levine, Steven J. 1980. Gut contents of forty-four Lake Pontchartrain, Louisiana, fish species. Pp. 899–1029 *in* J. H. Stone, ed. Environmental analysis of Lake Pontchartrain, Louisiana, its surrounding wetlands, and selected land uses. Vols. 1 and 2. Publication no. LSU-CEL-80-08. Center for Wetland Resources, Louisiana State University, Baton Rouge.

Lewis, Peirce F. 1976. New Orleans: the making of an urban landscape. Ballinger, Cambridge, Massachusetts.

Llewellyn, Daniel W., and G. Shaffer. 1993. Marsh restoration in the presence of intense herbivory: the role of *Justicia lanceolata*. Wetlands 13(3): 176–184.

Lopez, John A. 2003. Chronology and analysis of environmental impacts within the Pontchartrain basin of the Mississippi delta plain, 1718–2002. Ph.D. diss., University of New Orleans.

Louisiana Coastal Wetlands Conservation and Restoration Task Force. 1993. Louisiana Coastal Wetlands Restoration Plan: main report and environmental impact statement. Louisiana Department of Natural Resources, Coastal Restoration Division.

Louisiana Coastal Wetlands Conservation and Restoration Task Force. 1997. The 1997 evaluation report to the U.S. Congress on the effectiveness of Louisiana coastal wetland restoration projects. Louisiana Department of Natural Resources, Coastal Restoration Division.

Louisiana Natural Heritage Program. 1988. The natural communities of Louisiana. Louisiana Department of Wildlife and Fisheries, Baton Rouge.

Lowery, George H., Jr. 1974a. The mammals of Louisiana and its adjacent waters. Louisiana State University Press, Baton Rouge.

Lowery, George H. Jr., 1974b. Louisiana birds, 3rd ed. Louisiana State University Press, Baton Rouge.

Lowery, Woodbury. 1959. The Spanish settlements within the present limits of the United States, 1513–1561. Russell & Russell, New York.

MacCash, Doug. 2001. Mystery ship: its past is murky but its future is clear: museum's Civil War-era submarine is being restored. The Times-Picayune (New Orleans), April 18, Living, p. 1; and Civil War-era submarine being restored. The Advocate (Baton Rouge), April 23, p. 5B.

Mancil, E. M. 1972. An historical geography of industrial cypress lumbering. Ph.D. diss., Louisiana State University, Baton Rouge.

Mancil, E. M. 1980. Pullboat logging. Journal of Forest History 24(3): 135–141.

Marcantonio, F., G. C. Flowers, L. Thien, and E. G. Ellgaard. 1998. Lead isotopes in tree rings: chronology of pollution in Bayou Trepagnier. Environmental Science and Technology 32: 2371–2376.

Marcantonio, F., G. C. Flowers, and N. Templin. 2000. Lead contamination in a wetland watershed: isotopes as fingerprints of pollution. Environmental Geology 39: 1070–1076.

Marchand, Sidney. 1931. The story of Ascension Parish, La. Sidney A. Marchand, Donaldsonville, La.

Martin, Richard P., and Gary D. Lester. 1990. Atlas and census of wading bird and seabird nesting colonies in Louisiana, 1990. Louisiana Department of Wildlife and Fisheries, Louisiana Natural Heritage Program, Baton Rouge.

Mayer, G. N. 1986. The submerged aquatic vegetation of the Lake Pontchartrain estuarine system, Louisiana. M.S. thesis, University of New Orleans.

Maygarden, Benjamin D., J. Yakubik, E. Weiss, C. Peyronnin, and K. R. Jones. 1999. National Register evaluation of New Orleans drainage system, Orleans Parish, Louisiana. Cultural Resources Series Report no. COELMN/PO-98/09, U.S. Army Corps of Engineers New Orleans District.

Maygarden, Dinah F. 1996. LaBranche: lessons of a wetland paradise: an educator's guide. The Audubon Institute, New Orleans.

Maygarden, Dinah F., G. M. Frierson, and A. B. Rheams. 2000. A guide to the wetlands of the Lake Pontchartrain basin. The Lake Pontchartrain Basin Foundation, Metairie, La., and The Coastal Research Laboratory in the Geology Department of the University of New Orleans.

McCann, Elizabeth. 1941. Penicaut and his chronicle of early Louisiana. Mid-America: An Historical Review 23(4): 288–304.

McCorquodale, Alex, Donald Barbé, Youchao Wang, and Suzanne Carnelos. 2001a. Freshwater inflows to the Lake Pontchartrain system. P. 65 *in* Shea Penland, Andrew Beall, and Jeff Waters, ed. Environmental atlas of the Lake Pontchartrain basin. Lake Pontchartrain Basin Foundation, New Orleans.

McCorquodale, Alex, Ioannis Georgiou, and Katie Haralampides. 2001b. Bottom dissolved oxygen and salinity in Lake Pontchartrain. P. 160 *in* Shea Penland, Andrew Beall, and Jeff Waters, ed. Environmental atlas of the Lake Pontchartrain basin. Lake Pontchartrain Basin Foundation, New Orleans.

McDermott, John F. 1976. Captain Philip Pittman's "The present state of the European settlements on the Mississippi: with a geographical description of the river." Facsimile ed. Memphis State University Press, Memphis, Tenn.

McElroy, Mark G., Timothy Morrison, and Ron Gouguet. 1990. Age, growth, and maturity of channel catfish in two southeast Louisiana lakes. Proceedings of the Annual Conference of Southeastern Association of Fish and Wildlife Agencies 44: 13–19.

McFall, Jo Ann, Shelley R. Antoine, and Ildefonso R. DeLeon. 1985a. Organics in the water column of Lake Pontchartrain, New Orleans, Louisiana, USA. Chemosphere 14(9): 1253–1266.

McFall, Jo Ann, Shelley R. Antoine, and Ildefonso R. DeLeon. 1985b. Base-neutral extractable organic pollutants in biota and sediments from Lake Pontchartrain. Chemosphere 14(10): 1561–1569.

McIlhenny, E. A. 1935. The alligator's life history. Christopher, Boston.

McIlwain, T. D. 1968. Distribution of the striped bass, *Roccus saxatilis* (Walbaum), in Mississippi waters. Proceedings of the 21st Annual Conference of Southeastern Association of Game and Fish Commissions 21: 254–257.

McNease, Larry, David Richard, and Ted Joanen. 1992. Reintroduction and colony expansion of the brown pelican in Louisiana. Proceedings of the Annual Conference of Southeastern Association of Fish and Wildlife Agencies 46: 223–229.

McQuaid, John, and Mark Schleifstein. 2002. Washing away. Times-Picayune (New Orleans), Section J, 1–14.

McWilliams, R. G., trans. and ed. 1953. Fleur de lys and calumet: being the Penicaut narrative of French adventure in Louisiana. Louisiana State University Press, Baton Rouge.

McWilliams, R. G. 1969. Iberville at the Birdfoot Subdelta: final discovery of the Mississippi River. Pp. 127–140 in J. M. McDermott, ed. Frenchmen and French ways in the Mississippi valley. University of Illinois Press, Urbana.

McWilliams, R. G., trans. and ed. 1981. Iberville's gulf journals. University of Alabama Press, Tuscaloosa.

Melancon, George E. 1995. Evaluation of wintering lesser scaup concentrations in relation to food abundance on Lake Pontchartrain and Lake Borgne, Louisiana. M.S. thesis, Louisiana State University, Baton Rouge.

Miller, Andrew C., B. S. Payne, and D. W. Aldridge. 1986. Characterization of a bivalve community in the Tangipahoa River, Mississippi. The Nautilus 100(1): 18–23.

Montz, G. N. 1978. The submerged vegetation of Lake Pontchartrain, Louisiana. Castanea 43(2): 115–128.

Montz, G. N., and A. Cherubini. 1973. An ecological study of a baldcypress swamp in St. Charles Parish, Louisiana. Castanea 38(4): 378–386.

Morrison, Joseph P. E. 1965. New brackish water mollusks from Louisiana. Proceedings of the Biological Society of Washington 78: 217–224.

Mulholland, R. 1985. Habitat suitability index models: lesser scaup (wintering). U.S. Fish and Wildlife Service Biological Report 82(10.91).

Myers, Randell S., G. P. Shaffer, and D. W. Llewellyn. 1995. Baldcypress restoration in southeast Louisiana: the relative effects of herbivory, flooding, competition, and macronutrients. Wetlands 15(2): 141–148.

Nature Conservancy, The. 2004. Conservation Area Plan for the Lake Pontchartrain Estuary. Northshore Field Office, Covington, La.

Neuman, Robert W. 1976. Archaeological techniques in the Louisiana coastal region. Louisiana Archaeology 3: 1–21.

Neuman, Robert W. 1984. Archaeology of the Louisiana coastal zone, 1970 to the present. Pp. 156–164 in Dave D. Davis, ed. Perspectives on Gulf coast prehistory. University Press of Florida, Gainesville.

Neuman, Robert W., and Nancy W. Hawkins. 1993. Louisiana prehistory. 2nd ed. Louisiana Department of Culture, Recreation, and Tourism, Baton Rouge.

Newsom, John D., T. Joanen, and R. J. Howard. 1987. Habitat suitability index models: American alligator. U.S. Fish and Wildlife Service, Biological Report 82(10.136).

Nichols, C. Howard. 1990. Mandeville on the lake: a sesquicentennial album. St. Tammany Historical Society, Mandeville, La.

Norman, Donald, and R. D. Purrington. 1970. The demise of the brown pelican in Louisiana. Louisiana Ornithological News no. 55.

NPDES Storm Water Permit. 1993. Part 2, permit application, Vol. A, for Jefferson Parish, Louisiana. Prepared May 1993 by Montgomery Watson, Inc., Metairie, La.

Oberdorster, E., M. Martin, C. F. Ide, and J. A. McLachlan. 1999. Benthic community structure and biomarker induction in grass shrimp in an estuarine system. Archives of Environmental Contamination and Toxicology 37: 512–518.

O'Connell, Martin T., R. C. Cashner, and C. S. Schieble. 2004. Fish assemblage stability over fifty years in the Lake Pontchartrain estuary: comparisons among habitats using canonical correspondence analysis. Estuaries 27(5): 807–817.

Odum, William E., and E. J. Heald. 1975. The detritus-based food web of an estuarine mangrove community. Pp. 265–286 in L. E. Cronin, ed. Estuarine research. Vol. 1, Chemistry, biology and the estuarine system. Academic Press, New York.

Odum, William E., J. C. Zieman, and E. J. Heald. 1973. The importance of vascular plant detritus to estuaries. Pp. 91–114 in R. H. Chabreck, ed. Proceedings of the coastal marsh and estuary management symposium. Louisiana State University, Baton Rouge.

Officer, C. B. 1976. Physical oceanography of estuaries (and associated coastal waters). John Wiley and Sons, New York.

Ogg, Frederic A. 1904. The opening of the Mississippi: a struggle for supremacy in the American interior. Macmillan, New York.

O'Neil, Ted. 1949. The muskrat in the Louisiana coastal marshes. Louisiana Department of Wildlife and Fisheries, New Orleans.

O'Neill, Charles E., ed. 1977. Charlevoix's Louisiana: selections from the history and the journal. Louisiana State University Press, Baton Rouge.

Otvos, Ervin G., Jr. 1978a. Calcareous benthic foraminiferal fauna in a very low salinity setting, Lake Pontchartrain, Louisiana. Journal of Foraminiferal Research 8(3): 262–269.

Otvos, Ervin G., Jr. 1978b. New Orleans–South Hancock Holocene barrier trends and origins of Lake Pontchartrain. Transactions of the Gulf Coast Association of Geological Societies 28: 337–355.

Overton, Edward B., M. H. Schurtz, K. M. St. Pé, and C. Byrne. 1986. Distribution of trace organics, heavy metals, and conventional pollutants in Lake Pontchartrain, Louisiana. Pp. 247–270 in M. L. Sohn, ed. Organic marine geochemistry. American Chemical Society, Washington, D.C.

Paerl, Hans W., Robin L. Dennis, and David R. Whitall. 2002. Atmospheric deposition of nitrogen: implications for nutrient over-enrichment of coastal waters. Estuaries 25(4b): 677–693.

Palmisano, A. W., Ted Joanen, and L. L. McNease. 1973. An analysis of Louisiana's 1972 experimental alligator harvest program. Proceedings of the 27th Annual Conference of the Southeastern Association of Game and Fish Commissions 27: 184–206.

Pardue, J. H., W. M. Moe, D. McInnis, L. J. Thibodeaux, K. T. Valsaraj, E. Maciasz, I. Van Heerden, N. Korevec, and Q. Z. Yuan. 2005. Chemical and microbiological parameters in New

Orleans floodwater following Hurricane Katrina. Environmental Science and Technology 39(22): 8591–8599.

Parkerson, Codman. 1969. Those strange Louisiana names. No publisher identified.

Pattillo, Mark E., T. E. Czapla, D. M. Nelson, and M. E. Monaco. 1997. Distribution and abundance of fishes and invertebrates in Gulf of Mexico estuaries. Vol. II, Species life history summaries. ELMR Report no. 11. NOAA/NOS Strategic Environmental Assessments Division, Silver Spring, Md.

Pearson, Charles E., G. J. Castille, D. Davis, T. E. Redard, and A. R. Saltus. 1989. A history of waterborne commerce and transportation within the U.S. Army Corps of Engineers New Orleans District and an inventory of known underwater cultural resources. Cultural Resources Series Report COELMN/PD-88/11, U.S. Army Corps of Engineers New Orleans District.

Pearson, Charles E., W. D. Reeves, and A. R. Saltus Jr. 1993. Remote-sensing survey of the Bayou Labranche wetlands restoration borrow area, St. Charles Parish, Louisiana. Cultural Resources Series Report COELMN/PO-93/06, U.S. Army Corps of Engineers New Orleans District. Coastal Environments, Inc., Baton Rouge, La.

Penfound, William T., and E. S. Hathaway. 1938. Plant communities in the marshlands of southeastern Louisiana. Ecological Monographs 8: 1–56.

Penfound, William T., and J. A. Howard. 1940. A phytosociological study of an evergreen oak forest in the vicinity of New Orleans, Louisiana. American Midland Naturalist 23(1): 165–174.

Penfound, William T., and A. G. Watkins. 1937. Phytosociological studies in the pinelands of southeastern Louisiana. American Midland Naturalist 18(4): 661–682.

Penicaut, Andre. 1722. Penicaut's narrative. Published as McWilliams, R. G., trans. and ed. 1953. Fleur de lys and calumet: Being the Penicaut narrative of French adventure in Louisiana. Louisiana State University Press, Baton Rouge. Also published as Annals: Penicaut (1698–1721). Pp. 33–162 in B. F. French, ed. 1869. Historical collections of Louisiana and Florida including translations of original manuscripts relating to their discovery and settlement, with numerous historical and biographical notes. New Series. J. Sabin & Sons, New York. Reprint, 1976, Vol. 1, AMS Press, Inc., New York.

Penland, S., H. H. Roberts, S. J. Williams, A. H. Sallenger Jr., Donald R. Cahoon, and C. G. Groat. 1990. Coastal land loss in Louisiana. Transactions of the Gulf Coast Association of Geological Societies 40: 685–699.

Penland, Shea, Andrew Beall, and Jeff Waters, ed. 2001a. Environmental atlas of the Lake Pontchartrain basin. Lake Pontchartrain Basin Foundation, New Orleans.

Penland, Shea, Andrew Beall, Del Britsch, and Jeffress Williams. 2001b. Pontchartrain basin land loss. Pp. 130–132 in Shea Penland, Andrew Beall, and Jeff Waters, ed. Environmental atlas of the Lake Pontchartrain basin. Lake Pontchartrain Basin Foundation, New Orleans.

Penland, Shea, Dinah Maygarden, and Andrew Beall. 2001c. Status and trends of the Lake Pontchartrain basin. Pp. 8–19 in Shea Penland, Andrew Beall, and Jeff Waters, ed. Environmental atlas of the Lake Pontchartrain basin. Lake Pontchartrain Basin Foundation, New Orleans.

Penland, Shea, Philip McCarty, Andrew Beall, and Dinah Maygarden. 2001d. Regional description of the Lake Pontchartrain basin. Pp. 3–6 in Shea Penland, Andrew Beall, and Jeff

Waters, ed. Environmental atlas of the Lake Pontchartrain basin. Lake Pontchartrain Basin Foundation, New Orleans.

Penn, George H., Jr. 1950. The genus *Cambarellus* in Louisiana (Decapoda, Astacidae). American Midland Naturalist 44(2): 421–426.

Penn, George H., Jr. 1952. The genus *Orconectes* in Louisiana (Decapoda, Astacidae). American Midland Naturalist 47(3): 743–748.

Penn, George H., Jr. 1956. The genus *Procambarus* in Louisiana. American Midland Naturalist 56(2): 406–422.

Penn, George H., Jr. 1959. An illustrated key to the crawfishes of Louisiana with a summary of their distribution within the state (Decapoda, Astacidae). Tulane Studies in Zoology 7(1): 3–20.

Penn, George H., Jr., and Guy Marlow. 1959. The genus *Cambarus* in Louisiana. American Midland Naturalist 61(1): 191–203.

Perret, W. S., B. B. Barrett, W. R. Latapie, J. F. Pollard, W. R. Mock, G. B. Adkins, W. J. Gaidry, and C. J. White. 1971. Cooperative Gulf of Mexico estuarine inventory and study, Louisiana. Phase I. Area description. Louisiana Wildlife and Fisheries Commission, New Orleans.

Peters, Allyson, and Andrew Beall. 2001. Climate history. Pp. 29–35 *in* Shea Penland, Andrew Beall, and Jeff Waters, ed. Environmental atlas of the Lake Pontchartrain basin. Lake Pontchartrain Basin Foundation, New Orleans.

Phillips, P. Lee. 1975. Notes on the life and works of Bernard Romans. University Press of Florida, Gainseville. (A facsimile reproduction of the 1924 edition.).

Pittman, Philip. 1770. The present state of the European settlements on the Mississippi. London, J. Nourse. Republished as Captain Philip Pittman's "The present state of the European settlements on the Mississippi: with a geographical description of the river." Facsimile edition, 1976. Memphis State University Press, Memphis, Tenn.

Platt, Steven G. 1988. A checklist of the flora of the Manchac Wildlife Management Area, St. John the Baptist Parish, Louisiana. Proceedings of the Louisiana Academy of Sciences 51: 15–20.

Platt, Steven G., and C. G. Brantley. 1997. Canebrakes: an ecological and historical perspective. Castanea 62(1): 8–21.

Platt, Steven G., C. G. Brantley, and L. W. Fontenot. 1989. Herpetofauna of the Manchac Wildlife Management Area, St. John the Baptist Parish, Louisiana. Proceedings of the Louisiana Academy of Sciences 52: 22–28.

Platt, Steven G., C. G. Brantley, and R. W. Hastings. 1990. Food habits of juvenile American alligators in Louisiana. Northeast Gulf Science 11(2): 123–130.

Platt, Steven G., R. W. Hastings, and C. G. Brantley. 1997. Nesting ecology of the American alligator in southeastern Louisiana. Proceedings of the Annual Conference of the Southeastern Association of Fish and Wildlife Agencies 49: 632–642.

Platt, Steven G., C. G. Brantley, and T. R. Rainwater. 2001. Canebrake fauna: wildlife diversity in a critically endangered ecosystem. Journal of the Elisha Mitchell Scientific Society 11(1): 1–19.

Poirrier, Michael A. 1976. A taxonomic study of the *Spongilla alba, S. cenota, S. wagneri* species group (Porifera: Spongillidae) with ecological observations of *S. alba*. Pp. 203–213 *in* F. W. Harrison and R. R. Cowden, ed. Aspects of sponge biology. Academic Press, New York.

Poirrier, Michael A. 1978a. Epifaunal invertebrates as monitors of water quality in Lake Pontchartrain. Pp. 105–111 *in* Proceedings of the Third Coastal Marsh and Estuary Management Symposium.

Poirrier, Michael A. 1978b. Studies of salinity stratification in southern Lake Pontchartrain near the Inner Harbor Navigation Canal. Proceedings of the Louisiana Academy of Sciences 41: 26–35.

Poirrier, Michael A., and M. M. Mulino. 1975. The effects of the 1973 opening of the Bonnet Carré Spillway upon the epifaunal invertebrates in southern Lake Pontchartrain. Proceedings of the Louisiana Academy of Sciences 38: 36–40.

Poirrier, Michael A., and M. M. Mulino. 1977. The impacts of the 1975 Bonnet Carré Spillway opening on epifaunal invertebrates in southern Lake Pontchartrain. Journal of the Elisha Mitchell Scientific Society 93(1): 11–18.

Poirrier, Michael A., and M. R. Partridge. 1979. The barnacle, *Balanus subalbidus*, as a salinity bioindicator in the oligohaline estuarine zone. Estuaries 2(3): 204–206.

Poirrier, Michael A., J. S. Rogers, M. M. Mulino, and E. S. Eisenberg. 1975. Epifaunal invertebrates as indicators of water quality in southern Lake Pontchartrain. Louisiana Water Research Institute, Technical Report no. 5, Louisiana State University, Baton Rouge.

Poirrier, Michael A., T. M. Soniat, Y. A. King, and L. E. Smith. 1984. An evaluation of the southern Lake Pontchartrain benthos community. Report submitted to Louisiana Department of Environmental Quality, Office of Water Resources, Water Pollution Control Division (Interagency Agreement no. 64003-84-05).

Poirrier, Michael A., Boris Maglic, John C. Francis, Carol D. Franze, and Hyun-Jung Cho. 1999. Effects of the 1997 Bonnet Carré Spillway opening on Lake Pontchartrain submersed aquatic vegetation. Pp. 123–133 *in* L. P. Rozas, J. A. Nyman, C. E. Proffitt, N. N. Rabalais, D. J. Reed, and R. E. Turner, ed. Recent research in coastal Louisiana: natural system function and response to human influences. Louisiana Sea Grant Program, Baton Rouge.

Poirrier, Michael A., Z. Rodriguez del Rey, and E. A. Spalding. 2006. Status of benthic invertebrates in Lake Pontchartrain with emphasis on the effects of hurricane Katrina. Abstract of paper presented at Basics of the Basin Symposium, New Orleans. Symposium program, pp. 42–44.

Poplin, Eric C., P. C. Armstrong, C. J. Poplin, and R. C. Goodwin. 1988. Phase 2 of the cultural resources inventory of the Bonnet Carré Spillway, St. Charles Parish, Louisiana: final report. Cultural Resources Series Report COELMN/PD-88/04, U.S. Army Corps of Engineers New Orleans District.

Portnoy, John W. 1977. Nesting colonies of seabirds and wading birds: coastal Louisiana, Mississippi, and Alabama. U.S. Fish and Wildlife Service, FWS/OBS-77/07.

Power, Tyrone. 1836. Impressions of America during the years 1833, 1834, and 1835. Carey, Lea & Blanchard, Philadelphia.

Presley, S. M., T. R. Rainwater, G. P. Austin, S. G. Platt, J. C. Zak, G. P. Cobb, E. J. Marsland, K. Tian, B. H. Zhang, T. A. Anderson, S. B. Cox, M. T. Abel, B. D. Leftwich, J. R. Huddleston, R. M. Jeter, and R. J. Kendall. 2006. Assessment of pathogens and toxicants in New Orleans, La., following hurricane Katrina. Environmental Science and Technology 40(2): 468–474.

Price, Keith C., and Robin J. Kuckyr. 1974. Environmental impact of shell dredging in Lake Pontchartrain. Gulf South Research Institute, New Iberia, La.

Prichard, W., F. B. Kniffen, and C. A. Brown, ed. 1945. Southern Louisiana and southern Alabama in 1819: the journal of James Leander Cathcart. Louisiana Historical Quarterly 28(3): 735–921. (See Cathcart, 1819.)

Pritchard, D. W. 1967. What is an estuary: physical viewpoint. Pp. 3–5 *in* G. H. Lauff, ed. Estuaries. Publication no. 83, American Association for the Advancement of Science, Washington, D.C.

Ragan, Mark K. 1999. Union and Confederate submarine warfare in the Civil War. Savas, Mason City, Iowa.

Ramsey, Karen E., and Shea Penland. 1989. Sea-level rise and subsidence in Louisiana and the Gulf of Mexico. Transactions of the Gulf Coast Association of Geological Societies 39: 491–500.

Ramsey, Karen, Andrew Beall, Marcus Howard, Anna Strimas, Allyson Peters, and Shea Penland. 2001. Mean sea level rise in Lake Pontchartrain. P. 46 *in* Shea Penland, Andrew Beall, and Jeff Waters, ed. Environmental atlas of the Lake Pontchartrain basin. Lake Pontchartrain Basin Foundation, New Orleans.

Read, William A. 1927. Louisiana place-names of Indian origin. Louisiana State University and Agricultural and Mechanical College Bulletin 19(2).

Read, William A. 1928. More Indian place-names in Louisiana. Louisiana Historical Quarterly 11(3): 445–462.

Read, William A. 1931. Louisiana-French. Louisiana State University Studies no. 5. Louisiana State University Press, Baton Rouge.

Redfield, A. C., B. H. Ketchum, and F. A. Richards. 1963. The influence of organisms on the composition of sea-water. Chapter 2 *in* M. N. Hill, ed. The sea: ideas and observations on progress in the study of the seas. Vol. 2. Interscience, New York.

Reed, C. F. 1977. History and distribution of Eurasian watermilfoil in the United States and Canada. Phytologia 36: 417–436.

Roberts, D. W. 1981. Structure and function of nearshore and open lake benthic communities in Lake Pontchartrain, Louisiana. M.S. thesis, University of New Orleans.

Roberts, Kenneth J., and Mark E. Thompson. 1982. Economic elements of commercial crabbing in Lake Pontchartrain and Lake Borgne. Louisiana Sea Grant Publication no. LSU-TL-82-001.

Roberts, W. Adolphe. 1946. Lake Pontchartrain. Bobbs-Merrill, Indianapolis.

Robin, C. C. 1807. Voyage to Louisiana, 1803–1805. Reprint, 1966, translated by Stuart O. Landry Jr., Pelican, New Orleans.

Romans, Bernard. 1774. A concise natural history of East and West Florida. Cited in Phillips, P. Lee. 1975. Notes on the life and works of Bernard Romans. University Press of Florida, Gainseville. (A facsimile reproduction of the 1924 edition.).

Ross, Stephen T. 2001. The inland fishes of Mississippi. University Press of Mississippi, Jackson.

Rouquette, Dominique. 1938. The Choctaws. Survey of Federal Archives in Louisiana.

Rowett, C. L. 1957. A Quaternary molluscan assemblage from Orleans Parish, Louisiana. Gulf Coast Association of Geological Societies Transactions 7: 153–164.

Rule, John C. 1969. Jerome Phelypeaux, Comte de Pontchartrain, and the establishment of Louisiana, 1696–1715. Pp. 179–197 *in* John F. McDermott, ed. Frenchmen and French ways in the Mississippi valley. University of Illinois Press, Urbana. Reprint, 1989 *in* R. B. Holtman and G. R. Conrad. French Louisiana: a commemoration of the French Revolution bicentennial. Center for Louisiana Studies, University of Southwestern Louisiana, Lafayette (pp. 19–32).

Russell, R. J. 1936. Physiography of lower Mississippi River delta. Louisiana Geological Survey, Geological Bulletin 8: 3–199.

Rylander, M. K. 1969. An ecological and floristic study of the vegetation of the Delta Regional Primate Research Center, Covington, St. Tammany Parish, Louisiana. Proceedings of the Louisiana Academy of Sciences 32: 83–111.

Saltus, Allen R. 1987. Submerged cultural resources investigation of the western portion of the Maurepas basin. Center for Regional Studies, Southeastern Louisiana University, Hammond.

Saltus, Allen R. 1988. Submerged cultural resources investigation of various waterways of Lake Pontchartrain's north shore. Center for Regional Studies, Southeastern Louisiana University, Hammond.

Saltus, Allen R. 1991. Watercraft remains in the central Gulf coast riverine environment. Southeast Louisiana Historical Papers 14: 25–38.

Saucier, Roger T. 1963. Recent geomorphic history of the Pontchartrain basin. Coastal Studies Institute, Report no. 9. Louisiana State University Press, Baton Rouge.

Saucier, Roger T. 1994. Geomorphology and Quaternary geologic history of the lower Mississippi valley. Vol. 1. U.S. Army Engineer Waterways Experiment Station, Vicksburg, Miss.

Schurtz, Michael H., and Kerry M. St. Pé. 1984. Water quality investigation of environmental conditions in Lake Pontchartrain: report on interim findings. Louisiana Department of Environmental Quality, Water Pollution Control Division.

Shallat, Todd. 2001. In the wake of Hurricane Betsy. Pp. 121–137 *in* Craig Colten, ed. Transforming New Orleans and its environs: centuries of change. University of Pittsburgh Press, Pittsburgh, Pa.

Sharitz, Rebecca R., and W. J. Mitsch. 1993. Southern floodplain forests. Pp. 311–372 *in* W. H. Martin, S. G. Boyce, and A. C. Echternacht, ed. Biodiversity of the southeastern United States, lowland terrestrial communities. John Wiley & Sons, New York.

Shea, John G. 1903. Discovery and exploration of the Mississippi valley with the original narratives of Marquette, Allouez, Membré, Hennepin, and Anastase Douay. Joseph McDonough, Albany, N.Y.

Shenkel, J. Richard. 1974. Big Oak and Little Oak Islands: excavations and interpretations. Louisiana Archaeology 1: 37–65.

Shenkel, J. Richard. 1981. Pontchartrain Tchefuncte site differentiation. Louisiana Archaeology 8: 21–35.

Shenkel, J. Richard. 1984. Early woodland in coastal Louisiana. Pp. 41–71 *in* Dave D. Davis, ed. Perspectives on Gulf coast prehistory. University Press of Florida, Gainesville.

Shenkel, J. Richard, and J. L. Gibson. 1974. Big Oak Island: an historical perspective of changing site function. Louisiana Studies 8(2): 173–186.

Siguenza y Gongora, Don Carlos de. 1693. Description of the Bay of Santa Maria de Galve (formerly Pensacola), Mobile Bay, and Palizada River on the northern coast of the Gulf of

Mexico. Document 10, pp. 152–192 *in* Irving A. Leonard, trans. 1939. Spanish approach to Pensacola, 1689–1693. Reprint, 1967, Arno Press, New York.

Sikora, W. B., and B. Kjerfve. 1985. Factors influencing the salinity regime of Lake Pontchartrain, Louisiana, a shallow coastal lagoon: analysis of a long-term data set. Estuaries 8: 170–180.

Sikora, Walter B., and Jean P. Sikora. 1982. Ecological characterization of the benthic community of Lake Pontchartrain, Louisiana. Publication no. LSU-CEL-82-05. Prepared for U.S. Army Engineer District, New Orleans (Contract no. DACW29-79-C-0099). Coastal Ecology Laboratory, Center for Wetland Resources, Louisiana State University, Baton Rouge.

Sikora, Walter B., Jean P. Sikora, and Anny M. Prior. 1981. Environmental effects of hydraulic dredging for clam shells in Lake Pontchartrain, Louisiana. Publication no. LSU-CEL-81-18. Prepared for U.S. Army Engineer District, New Orleans (Contract no. DACW29-79-C-0099). Coastal Ecology Laboratory, Center for Wetland Resources, Louisiana State University, Baton Rouge.

Sinclair, Henri de Ville Du, trans. 1974. Journal of the frigate *Le Marin* (September 5th, 1698–July 2nd, 1699): a chapter from *Memoirs and Documents* by Pierre Margry. Blossman Printing Co., Ocean Springs, Miss.

Smith, Latimore. 1999. Historic vegetation types of the Florida parishes. Louisiana Natural Heritage Program, Louisiana Department of Wildlife and Fisheries, Baton Rouge.

Solem, Alan. 1961. Hydrobiid snails from Lake Pontchartrain, Louisiana. Nautilus 74(4): 157–160.

Souther, Rebecca Faye, and G. P. Shaffer. 2000. The effects of submergence and light on two age classes of the baldcypress (*Taxodium distichum* (L.) Richard) seedlings. Wetlands 20(4): 697–706.

Springer, J. W. 1973. The prehistory and cultural geography of coastal Louisiana. Ph.D. diss., Yale University, New Haven, Conn.

Stahle, D. W., M. K. Cleaveland, and J. G. Hehr. 1988. North Carolina climate changes reconstructed from tree rings: A.D. 372 to 1985. Science 240: 1517–1519.

Stall, Buddy. 1997. Buddy Stall's historical spotlight: ozone belt north of Lake Pontchartrain? Around the Lake 7(4): 10.

Stanley Consultants, Inc. 1980. Lake Pontchartrain Basin Water Quality Management Plan. Phase II. Prepared for Louisiana Department of Natural Resources, Office of Environmental Affairs, Division of Water Pollution.

Stapor, Frank W., and G. W. Stone. 2004. A new depositional model for the buried 4000 yr BP New Orleans barrier: implications for sea-level fluctuations and onshore transport from a nearshore shelf source. Marine Geology 204: 215–234.

Starr, S. Frederick, ed. 2001. Inventing New Orleans: writings of Lafcadio Hearn. University Press of Mississippi, Jackson.

Steinmayer, R. A. 1939. Bottom sediments of Lake Pontchartrain, Louisiana. Bulletin of the American Association of Petroleum Geologists 23(1): 1–23.

Sterling, David L. 1951. New Orleans: an account by John Pintard. Louisiana Historical Quarterly 34(3): 217–233.

Stern, D. H., and M. S. Stern. 1969. Physical, chemical, bacterial, and plankton dynamics of Lake Pontchartrain, Louisiana. Technical Report no. 4. Louisiana Water Resources Research Institute, Louisiana State University, Baton Rouge.

Stickney, Robert R. 1984. Estuarine ecology of the southeastern United States and Gulf of Mexico. Texas A&M University Press, College Station.

Stoeckel, Donald M., R. N. Bushon, D. K. Demcheck, S. C. Skrobialowski, C. M. Kephart, E. E. Bertke, B. E. Mailot, S. V. Mize, and R. B. Fendick Jr. 2005. Bacteriological water quality in the Lake Pontchartrain basin, Louisiana, following Hurricanes Katrina and Rita, September 2005. Data Series no. 143. U.S. Geological Survey.

Stoessel, Ronald K. 1980. Nutrient and carbon geochemistry in Lake Pontchartrain, Louisiana. Pp. 217–319 *in* J. H. Stone, ed. Environmental analysis of Lake Pontchartrain, Louisiana, its surrounding wetlands, and selected land uses. Vols. 1 and 2. Publication no. LSU-CEL-80-08. Center for Wetland Resources, Louisiana State University, Baton Rouge.

Stone, J. H., ed. 1980. Environmental analysis of Lake Pontchartrain, Louisiana, its surrounding wetlands, and selected land uses. Vols. 1 and 2. Publication no. LSU-CEL-80-08. Center for Wetland Resources, Louisiana State University, Baton Rouge. Prepared for USACOE, NOD, Contract no. DACW29-77-C-02.

Stone, J. H., N. A. Drummond, L. L. Cook, E. C. Theriot, and D. M. Lindstedt. 1980. The distribution and abundance of plankton of Lake Pontchartrain, Louisiana, 1978. Pp. 437–590 *in* J. H. Stone, ed. Environmental analysis of Lake Pontchartrain, Louisiana, its surrounding wetlands, and selected land uses. Vols. 1 and 2. Publication no. LSU-CEL-80-08. Center for Wetland Resources, Louisiana State University, Baton Rouge.

Stone, J. H., L. M. Bahr Jr., J. W. Day Jr., and R. M. Darnell. 1982. Ecological effects of urbanization on Lake Pontchartrain, Louisiana, between 1953 and 1978, with implications for management. Pp. 243–252 *in* B. Bornkamm, J. A. Lee, and M. R. D. Seaward, ed. Urban ecology. The Second European Ecological Symposium, Berlin, September 8–12, 1980. Blackwell Scientific, Oxford, U.K.

Strahan, Jerry E. 1994. Andrew Jackson Higgins and the boats that won World War II. Louisiana State University Press, Baton Rouge.

Surrey, N. M. M. 1916. The commerce of Louisiana during the French regime, 1699–1763. Columbia University Press, New York.

Suttkus, Royal D., and Robert C. Cashner. 1981. A new species of cyprinodontid fish, genus *Fundulus* (*Zygonectes*), from Lake Pontchartrain tributaries in Louisiana and Mississippi. Bulletin of the Alabama Museum of Natural History 6: 1–17.

Suttkus, Royal D., R. M. Darnell, and J. H. Darnell. 1954. Biological study of Lake Pontchartrain. *In* Annual report, 1953–1954. Zoology Department, Tulane University, New Orleans.

Swanton, J. R. 1911. Indian tribes of the lower Mississippi valley and adjacent coast of the Gulf of Mexico. Bulletin no. 43. Bureau of American Ethnology, Smithsonian Institution, Washington, D.C.

Swanton, John R. 1946. The Indians of the southeastern United States. Bulletin no. 137. Bureau of American Ethnology, Smithsonian Institution, Washington, D.C.

Swanton, John R. 1952 (1953). Indian tribes of North America. Bulletin no. 145. Bureau of American Ethnology, Smithsonian Institution, Washington, D.C.

Swenson, E. M. 1980a. General hydrography of Lake Pontchartrain, Louisiana. Pp. 57–155 *in* J. H. Stone, ed. Environmental analysis of Lake Pontchartrain, Louisiana, its surrounding wetlands, and selected land uses. Vols. 1 and 2. Publication no. LSU-CEL-80-08. Center for Wetland Resources, Louisiana State University, Baton Rouge.

Swenson, E. M. 1980b. General hydrography of the tidal passes of Lake Pontchartrain, Louisiana. Pp. 157–215 *in* J. H. Stone, ed. Environmental analysis of Lake Pontchartrain, Louisiana, its surrounding wetlands, and selected land uses. Vols. 1 and 2. Publication no. LSU-CEL-80-08. Center for Wetland Resources, Louisiana State University, Baton Rouge.

Swenson, E. M. 1981. Physical effects of the 1979 opening of the Bonnet Carré Spillway. Proceedings of the Louisiana Academy of Sciences 44: 121–131.

Swenson, E. M., and W. Chuang. 1983. Tidal and subtidal water volume exchange in an estuarine system. Estuarine, Coastal, and Shelf Science 16: 229–240.

Tarver, Johnnie W. 1972. Occurrence, distribution, and density of *Rangia cuneata* in Lakes Pontchartrain and Maurepas, Louisiana. Technical Bulletin no. 1. Louisiana Wildlife and Fisheries Commission.

Tarver, Johnnie W. 1974. Bonnet Carré '73: catastrophe or natural phenomenon? Louisiana Conservationist 26(1–2): 24–27.

Tarver, Johnnie W., and R. J. Dugas. 1973. A study of the clam, *Rangia cuneata*, in Lake Pontchartrain and Lake Maurepas. Technical Bulletin no. 5. Louisiana Wildlife and Fisheries Commission.

Tarver, Johnnie W., and L. B. Savoie. 1976. An inventory and study of the Lake Pontchartrain–Lake Maurepas estuarine complex. Technical Bulletin no. 19. Louisiana Wildlife and Fisheries Commission.

Tavaszi, Maria, and B. Maygarden. 1994. Historical research and archeological reconnaissance of the Mandeville seawall replacement, St. Tammany Parish, Louisiana: Final report. Cultural Resources Series Report Number COELMN/PD-93/15, U.S. Army Corps of Engineers New Orleans District.

Taylor, Katherine L., and James B. Grace. 1995. The effects of vertebrate herbivory on plant community structure in the coastal marshes of the Pearl River, Louisiana, USA. Wetlands 15(1): 68–73.

Templet, Paul H., and K. J. Meyer-Arendt. 1988. Louisiana wetland loss: a regional water management approach to the problem. Environmental Management 12(2): 181–192.

Theriot, Ronald J. 1991. Frenier and other lost towns of St. John the Baptist Parish. Unpublished paper, St. John the Baptist Parish Public Library.

Thomas, Alfred B. 1939. Spanish activities in the lower Mississippi valley, 1513–1698. Louisiana Historical Quarterly 22(4): 933–942.

Thomas, R. Dale, and C. M. Allen. 1993. Atlas of the vascular flora of Louisiana. Vol. I, Ferns and fern allies, conifers, and monocotyledons. Louisiana Department of Wildlife and Fisheries, Natural Heritage Program, Baton Rouge.

Thomas, R. Dale, and C. M. Allen. 1996. Atlas of the vascular flora of Louisiana. Vol. II, Dicotyledons: Acanthaceae–Euphorbiaceae. Louisiana Department of Wildlife and Fisheries, Natural Heritage Program, Baton Rouge.

Thomas, R. Dale, and C. M. Allen. 1998. Atlas of the vascular flora of Louisiana. Vol. III, Dicotyledons: Fabaceae–Zygophyllaceae. Louisiana Department of Wildlife and Fisheries, Natural Heritage Program, Baton Rouge.

Thomas, Robert A. 1996. The good, the bad, and the ugly: Louisiana's exotic species. CoastWise (Coalition to Restore Coastal Louisiana) 6(2): 8–13.

Thompson, B. A., and J. A. Stone. 1980. Selected commercial fish and shellfish data from Lake Pontchartrain, Louisiana, during 1963–1975, some influencing factors, and possible trends. Pp. 1069–1134 in J. H. Stone, ed. Environmental analysis of Lake Pontchartrain, Louisiana, its surrounding wetlands, and selected land uses. Vol. 2. Publication no. LSU-CEL-80-08. Center for Wetland Resources, Louisiana State University, Baton Rouge.

Thompson, B. A., and J. S. Verret. 1980. Nekton of Lake Pontchartrain, Louisiana, and its surrounding wetlands. Pp. 711–864 in J. H. Stone, ed. Environmental analysis of Lake Pontchartrain, Louisiana, its surrounding wetlands, and selected land uses. Vol. 2. Publication no. LSU-CEL-80-08. Center for Wetland Resources, Louisiana State University, Baton Rouge.

Thompson, R. 1973. Albert Baldwin Wood: the man who made water run uphill. New Orleans Magazine 7(1): 40–43, 74–79.

Törnqvist, T. E., T. R. Kidder, W. J. Autin, K. van der Borg, A. F. M. de Jong, C. J. W. Klerks, E. M. A. Snijders, J. E. A. Storms, R. L. van Dam, and M. C. Wiemann. 1996. A revised chronology for Mississippi River subdeltas. Science 273: 1693–1696.

Townsend, Mary A. 1881. Xariffa's poems. 3rd ed. J. B. Lippincott, Philadelphia.

Trautman, Frederic, ed. and trans. 1990. Travels on the lower Mississippi, 1879–1880: a memoir by Ernst von Hesse-Wartegg. University of Missouri Press, Columbia.

Turner, R. E. 1976. Geographic variation in salt marsh macrophyte production: a review. Contributions to Marine Science 20: 47–68.

Turner, R. E. 1997. Wetland loss in the northern Gulf of Mexico: multiple working hypotheses. Estuaries 20(1): 1–13.

Turner, R. E. 2001. Nitrogen loading into Lake Pontchartrain. P. 167 in Shea Penland, Andrew Beall, and Jeff Waters, ed. Environmental atlas of the Lake Pontchartrain basin. Lake Pontchartrain Basin Foundation, New Orleans.

Turner, R. E., R. M. Darnell, and J. Bond. 1980. Changes in the submerged macrophytes of Lake Pontchartrain (Louisiana): 1954–1973. Northeast Gulf Science 4: 44–49.

Turner, R. E., Q. Dortch, D. Justić, and E. M. Swenson. 2002. Nitrogen loading into an urban estuary: Lake Pontchartrain (Louisiana, U.S.A.). Hydrobiologia 487: 137–152.

Twain, Mark. 1883. City sights. Ch. 44 in Life on the Mississippi. Osgood, Boston.

Twilley, R. R., E. J. Barron, H. L. Gholz, M. A. Harwell, R. L. Miller, D. J. Reed, J. B. Rose, E. H. Siemann, R. G. Wetzel, and R. J. Zimmerman. 2001. Confronting climate change in the Gulf coast region: prospects for sustaining our ecological heritage. Union of Concerned Scientists, Cambridge, Mass., and Ecological Society of America, Washington, D.C.

Tyler, Stephen. 1996. Bayou of the lost: the legacy of the LaBranche Wetlands. Videotape produced by the Coalition to Restore Coastal Louisiana in association with WYES-TV, New Orleans.

Upham, Warren. 1902. Growth of the Mississippi delta. American Geologist 30: 103–111.

U.S. Army Corps of Engineers. 1974. Flood of '73: post-flood report. Vols. 1 and 2.

U.S. Army Corps of Engineers. 1984. Mississippi and Louisiana estuarine areas: freshwater diversion to Lake Pontchartrain basin and Mississippi Sound. Feasibility study, Vol. 1, Main report, environmental impact statement, April 1984.

U.S. Army Corps of Engineers. 1987. Clam shell dredging in Lakes Pontchartrain and Maurepas, Louisiana. Final environmental impact statement and appendixes, Vol. 1, November 1987.

U.S. Army Corps of Engineers. 1988. Lake Pontchartrain, Louisiana, and vicinity, Hurricane Protection Project, mitigation study: draft mitigation report/supplement II to the environmental impact statement.

U.S. Army Corps of Engineers. 1992. North Pass–Pass Manchac, Louisiana: draft detailed project report and draft environmental assessment.

U.S. Army Corps of Engineers. 1998a. Water resources development in Louisiana.

U.S. Army Corps of Engineers. 1998b. Southeastern Louisiana Flood Control Project. The SELA Report no. 1, Winter 1998.

U.S. Fish and Wildlife Service and National Marine Fisheries Service. 2003. Endangered and threatened wildlife and plants: designation of critical habitat for the Gulf sturgeon. Federal Register 68(53): 13370–13495.

Usner, Daniel H., Jr. 1989. American Indians in colonial New Orleans. Pp. 296–306 *in* Peter H. Wood, Gregory A. Waselkov, and M. Thomas Hatley, ed. Powhatan's mantle: Indians in the colonial Southeast. University of Nebraska Press, Lincoln. Reprint, 1996, *in* Gilbert C. Din, ed. The Louisiana Purchase bicentennial series in Louisiana history. Vol. II, The Spanish presence in Louisiana, 1763–1803. Center for Louisiana Studies, University of Southwestern Louisiana, Lafayette, pp. 296–306.

Usner, Daniel H., Jr. 1998. American Indians in the lower Mississippi valley: social and economic history. University of Nebraska Press, Lincoln.

Van Deusen, Paul C., G. A. Reams, M. S. Devall, G. L. Rochon, and T. R. Dell. 1993. Study turns up ancient cypress trees. Forests and People (3rd quarter): 24–27.

Van Heerden, Ivor, and Mike Bryan. 2006. The storm. What went wrong and why during Hurricane Katrina: the inside story from one Louisiana scientist. Viking, New York.

Van Metre, Peter C., A. J. Horowitz, B. J. Mahler, W. T. Forman, C. C. Fuller, M. R. Burkhardt, K. A. Elrick, E. T. Furlong, S. C. Skrobialowski, J. J. Smith, J. T. Wilson, and S. D. Zaugg. 2006. Effects of Hurricanes Katrina and Rita on the chemistry of bottom sediments in Lake Pontchartrain, Louisiana, USA. Environmental Science and Technology 40(22): 6894–6902.

Vidrine, M. F. 1993. The historical distribution of freshwater mussels in Louisiana. Gail Q. Vidrine Collectibles, Eunice, La.

Viosca, Percy. 1927. Flood control in the Mississippi valley in its relation to Louisiana fisheries. Transactions of the American Fisheries Society 57: 49–64.

Viosca, Percy. 1933. Louisiana out-of-doors: a handbook and guide. Published by the author, New Orleans.

Viosca, Percy. 1938. Effect of Bonnet Carré Spillway on fisheries. Louisiana Conservation Review 6: 51–53.

Waldon, Michael G., and C. Frederick Bryan. 1999. Annual salinity and nutrient budget of Lake Pontchartrain and impact of the proposed Bonnet Carré diversion. Pp. 79–88 *in* L. P. Rozas, J. A. Nyman, C. E. Proffitt, N. N. Rabalais, D. J. Reed, and R. E. Turner, ed. Recent research in coastal Louisiana: natural system function and response to human influences. Louisiana Sea Grant Program, Baton Rouge.

Waldon, Michael G., and E. D. Smythe. 1994. Patterns of fecal coliform contamination in the Tangipahoa River. Proceedings of the Louisiana Academy of Sciences 57: 21–26.

Walker, Norman. 1885. Out-door life in Louisiana. Outing 5(5): 333–339.

Wall, D. P., and S. P. Darwin. 1999. Vegetation and elevational gradients within a bottomland hardwood forest of southeastern Louisiana. American Midland Naturalist 142(1): 17–30.

Ware, Stewart, C. Frost, and P. D. Doerr. 1993. Southern mixed hardwood forest: the former longleaf pine forest. Pp. 447–493 *in* W. H. Martin, S. G. Boyce, and A. C. Echternacht, ed. Biodiversity of the southeastern United States: lowland terrestrial communities. John Wiley & Sons, New York.

Watson, M. B., C. J. Killebrew, M. H. Schurtz, and J. L. Landry. 1981. A preliminary survey of Blind River, Louisiana. Pp. 303–319 *in* L. A. Krumholz, ed. The Warmwater Streams Symposium: a national symposium of fisheries aspects of warmwater streams. Southern Division, American Fisheries Society, Knoxville, Tenn.

Weber, David J. 1992. The Spanish frontier in North America. Yale University Press, New Haven, Conn.

Weddle, Robert S. 1985. Spanish sea: the Gulf of Mexico in North American discovery, 1500–1685. Texas A&M University Press, College Station.

Weddle, Robert S. 1987. La Salle, the Mississippi, and the Gulf. Texas A&M University Press, College Station.

Weddle, Robert S. 1991. The French thorn: rival explorers in the Spanish Sea, 1682–1762. Texas A&M University Press, College Station.

White, D. A. 1983. Plant communities of the lower Pearl River basin, Louisiana. American Midland Naturalist 110(2): 381–396.

Whittington, G. P. 1927. Dr. John Sibley of Natchitoches, 1757–1837. Louisiana Historical Quarterly 10(4): 463–512.

Widmer, Mary Lou. 1989. New Orleans in the thirties. Pelican, Gretna, La.

Widmer, Mary Lou. 1990. New Orleans in the forties. Pelican, Gretna, La.

Widmer, Mary Lou. 1991. New Orleans in the fifties. Pelican, Gretna, La.

Widmer, Mary Lou. 1993. New Orleans in the twenties. Pelican, Gretna, La.

Widmer, Mary Lou. 2000. New Orleans in the sixties. Pelican, Gretna, La.

Williams, Luis, K. Grandine, K. Hymel, T. Fenn, and W. P. Athens. 1996. Cultural resources survey and testing of the Mandeville Hurricane Protection Project, Mandeville, St. Tammany Parish, Louisiana: final report. U.S. Army Corps of Engineers, Cultural Resource Series COELMN/PD-96/04.

Wolfe, James A., D. K. Bradshaw, and R. H. Chabreck. 1987. Alligator feeding habits: new data and a review. Northeast Gulf Science 9(1): 1–8.

Xu, Y. J., and K. S. Wu. 2006. Seasonality and interannual variability of freshwater inflow to a large oligohaline estuary in the northern Gulf of Mexico. Estuarine, Coastal, and Shelf Science 68(3–4): 619–626.

Yamazaki, Gordon, and Shea Penland. 2001. Recent hurricanes producing significant basin damage. P. 36 *in* Shea Penland, Andrew Beall, and Jeff Waters, ed. Environmental atlas of the Lake Pontchartrain basin. Lake Pontchartrain Basin Foundation, New Orleans.

Zacharie, James S. 1885. New Orleans guide, with descriptions of the routes to New Orleans, sights of the city arranged alphabetically ... also, outlines of the history of Louisiana. The New Orleans News Co.

Zganjar, Chris, George Frierson, Karen Westphal, Philip McCarty, Susan Bridges, and Shea Penland. 2001. Shoreline changes of Lake Maurepas, Lake Pontchartrain, and Lake Borgne. Pp. 133–140 *in* Shea Penland, Andrew Beall, and Jeff Waters, ed. Environmental atlas of the Lake Pontchartrain basin. Lake Pontchartrain Basin Foundation, New Orleans.

Zumwalt, T. H. 1963. West Indian and gulf hurricanes and their effects on our operating properties. Louisiana Studies 2(1): 3–36.

General Index

A

Abita Creek Flatwoods, 256
Abita Springs, 72, 115
agricultural runoff, 103, 136, 154, 155
agriculture, 11, 13, 82, 93, 104, 106, 107, 125, 133, 187, 250
Airline Highway, 88
algal blooms, 133, 142, 144, 188, 234
alligators, 11, 12, 39, 47, 63, 64, 69, 97, 112, 226, 227
American Revolution, 41, 43, 45
ammonia, 186, 187, 188
anaerobic, 186, 233
anoxic, 84, 142, 163, 184, 186, 233
Archaeological Periods
   Archaic, or Meso-Indian, 11
   Coles Creek, 13
   Historic, 14
   Marksville, 13
   Mississippian, or Plaquemine, 13
   Paleo-Indian, 11
   Poverty Point, 11
   Tchefuncte, or Tchula, 12
Archaeological Sites
   Bayou Jasmine, 12
   Big Oak Island, 12
   Fontainebleau, 12
   Garcia, 12
   Hoover, 13
   LaBranche-Trepagnier, 13
   Linsley, 12
   Little Oak Island, 12
   Manchac, 13
   Tangipahoa, 13
Armingeon, Neil, 153
arsenic, 148
artificial reefs, 212
asbestos, 148
Ascanthia, 14, 30, 31

B

Back to the Beach, 153
Bacon, Lieutenant-Colonel Edward, 63
Bacteria, 129, 130, 131, 133, 135, 136, 143, 147, 156, 184, 186, 187, 188, 196, 204, 233, 234, 235, 236
   cyanobacteria/bluegreen algae, 142, 187, 197, 232, 233, 238
   fecal coliform, 129, 130, 131, 135, 136, 138, 156, 188
   fecal streptococci, 129, 136
   sulfur, 233

Bahia del Espiritu Santo, 22, 24, 26
Balize delta, 9, 124
barium, 145, 148
Barroto, Juan Enriques, 25, 26, 27, 29
Bartram, William, 16, 44
Basics of the Basin, 153
Baton Rouge, 6, 15, 45, 65, 107, 110, 146, 157, 188
Baton Rouge Fault, 6
Bay of Pines, 5
Bayous, 135, 171, 247
   Alligator, 173, 175
   Bayou Barbary, 31
   Bayou Bienvenue, 47, 50, 75, 175
   Bayou Black, 173, 175
   Bayou Bonfouca, 46, 48, 55, 60, 71, 82, 147, 148, 174, 177, 222, 247
   Bayou Castiglione, 172, 175
   Bayou Castine, 15, 35, 40, 45, 156, 174, 177
   Bayou Chinchuba, 174, 177
   Bayou Choupic, 34
   Bayou Couchon, 172, 175
   Bayou De Sair, 64
   Bayou deSert, 64, 175
   Bayou Dupre, 50
   Bayou Jasmine, 12, 175
   Bayou LaBranche, 13, 14, 15, 32, 34, 74, 125, 173, 225, 226, 248
   Bayou Lacombe, 18, 40, 45, 46, 48, 55, 89, 174, 177, 247
   Bayou Laurier, 173, 175
   Bayou Le Bar (Labarre), 173, 175
   Bayou Liberty, 40, 149
   Bayou Manchac, 14, 15, 16, 24, 25, 27, 31, 33, 36, 37, 40, 41, 42, 43, 44, 48, 50, 68, 86, 124, 140, 178
   Bayou Philippon, 50
   Bayou Piquant, 33, 173
   Bayou Sauvage, 47, 50, 92, 155, 175, 181, 191, 194, 243
   Bayou St. John, 14, 15, 17, 18, 30, 33, 34, 35, 37, 38, 39, 40, 41, 42, 43, 45, 46, 47, 48, 49, 50, 52, 53, 55, 56, 57, 65, 74, 76, 77, 83, 84, 85, 90, 102, 119, 130, 156, 173, 175, 248
   Bayou Tchoupitoulas, 173, 175
   Bayou Tigouyou, 35, 44, 175
   Bayou Trepagnier, 33, 35, 44, 146, 147, 226
   Black, 172, 173, 175
   Cane, 34, 89, 174, 222
   Choupicatcha, 14, 34
   Desert, 64, 173, 175
   Double, 173, 175
   Indian, 173, 175
   Irish, 172, 175
   Little Bayou Couchon, 172, 175
   Metairie, 9
   Owl, 70
   Shell Bank, 12, 173, 175
   Turtle, 172, 175
beaches, 166, 168, 169, 171, 210
bear oil (bear fat), 16, 17, 37, 42
Beauregard, Major P. G. T., 44, 51
benthic organisms, 91, 139, 196, 200, 205, 206, 211, 212
benzopyrene, 147, 148
Bienville, Jean Baptiste le Moyne, Sieur de, 31, 32, 33, 34, 35, 37, 38
Big Oak Island, 12
Big Point, 119, 145, 174
Biloxi, Mississippi, 55
biodiversity, 103, 105, 113, 127, 189
biological oxygen demand, 139, 152, 184
biological productivity, 144, 189
Bisente, Juan (Juan Vicente), 27, 28, 29
Bishop, Nathaniel H., 68, 69
Boats (ships)
   Bienville, 62
   Bon, 29
   California, 53
   Camelia, 67, 77
   canoe, 17, 25, 30
   Carolina Galley, 35
   Carondelet, 62
   Hunley, 66

GENERAL INDEX **297**

La Badine, 15
Le Marin, 15, 29, 30
Maid of Orleans, 53
Neptune, 53
New Camelia, 67
New London, 62, 63, 65
Oregon, 62
Pioneer, 65, 66
pirogue, 18
Pontchartrain, 54
Santo Cristo de Maracaibo, 29
Southdown, 77
St. James, 53
steamship, 49
submarine, 65
Susquehanna, 77
Valentine, 65
West Florida, 45
Zephyr, 67
Bonnabel, Antonio (Antoine), 45
Bonnet Carré Spillway, 30, 32, 86, 88, 90, 94, 103, 116, 133, 140, 141, 144, 146, 155, 173, 175, 177, 178, 179, 181, 188, 194, 197, 199, 208, 215, 232, 247
borrow pits, 122, 138
Boudreau, Jean-Baptiste (Graveline), 39
brackish marsh, 165, 194, 217, 221, 228
Breakwater Drive, 181
Breton Sound, 27, 29, 32, 36, 92, 122, 127, 171
brick-making, 55
British, 16, 21, 40, 41, 42, 43, 45, 50
British West Florida, 16, 48
Brote, Susan and Conrad, 115
Browne, Lieutenant Governor Montfort, 40
Bucktown, 53, 68, 89, 94, 173
Burnside, 144
Burton, William, 70
Butler, General Benjamin F., 14, 29, 33, 34, 62, 107

C

Cabo de Lodo (Mud Cape), 26, 27, 29

calcium, 185, 186
calcium carbonate, 184, 185
Camp Williams, 63
Campbell, Captain James, 41
camps, 77, 133, 156
canals
  Bonnabel, 173, 175, 176
  Carondelet, 45, 46, 47, 83, 130
  Duncan, 173, 175
  Elmwood, 173
  Industrial (*see* canals: Inner Harbor Navigation)
  Inner Harbor Navigation, 83, 84, 85, 90, 92, 93, 94, 96, 119, 126, 127, 147, 148, 163, 171, 172, 175, 180, 184, 200, 205
  Lafayette Relief Outfall (*see* canals: Peoples Avenue)
  London Avenue (London Avenue Relief Outfall), 76, 96, 173, 175
  Metairie Relief Outfall (*see* canals: Seventeenth Street)
  New Basin (New Canal), 52, 53, 55, 65, 68, 75, 76, 82, 83, 84, 90, 92, 119
  New Orleans Navigation (*see* canals: New Basin)
  Orleans (Orleans Relief Outfall), 76, 173, 175
  Parish Line, 173
  Peoples Avenue (Peoples Avenue Relief Outfall), 76, 173
  Ruddock, 64, 173
  Seventeenth (17th) Street, 68, 76, 96, 131, 148, 173, 175
  St. Charles Parish Line, 175
  Suburban, 173, 175
  Upper Drainage (*see* canals: Seventeenth Street)
  Upper Line Tail Race (*see* canals: Seventeenth Street)
  Walker, 173
carbon, 184, 185, 234
carbon dioxide, 184, 185
Carondelet, Governor Don Francisco Luis

Hector, Baron de, 43, 45, 46, 47, 62, 83, 130
causeway, 88, 90, 91, 204, 206, 257
Chandeleur Islands, 27
Chandeleur Sound, 27, 29, 32, 36, 207
Charlevoix, Pierre-François-Xavier de, 38, 39
Chata-Ima, 55
Chef Menteur Highway, 88, 90, 165
Chef Menteur Pass, 5, 32, 50, 62, 71, 93, 94, 119, 125, 147, 164, 171, 172, 175, 180, 194, 200
Chinchuba, 55, 171, 174, 177, 245, 247
chlorinated hydrocarbons, 143
cholera, 18, 52, 133
chromium, 146, 148
Citizens for a Clean Tangipahoa (CFACT), 138, 154
Civil War, 17, 51, 53, 57, 60, 62, 64, 65, 67, 69, 130
Clark, Colonel Thomas, 63
clay, 7, 138, 179
climate, 82, 177
Cochran, Steve, 153
coffee grounds, 63, 171, 234
commercial fisheries, 208
Comprehensive Management Plan, 154, 155
consumers, 233, 234, 235, 236, 237, 238
copper, 143, 148
Cortes map, 23, 24
Covington, 48, 49, 50, 55, 62, 72, 74, 118, 178
crabbing, 53, 89, 102, 152
creosote, 71, 147, 148
crevasse, 56, 86, 143, 178
cyanide, 131, 147

D

dairy farm, 135, 136, 152, 155, 156
Daspit, Armand P., 115
DDT, 113, 135, 147, 203
dead zone, 127
delta, 3, 5, 6, 7, 8, 9, 10, 12, 13, 21, 25, 26, 38, 101, 104, 124, 140, 226
demersal, 201, 203, 204, 205, 210, 212
Denham Springs, 107

DeSair, 56
detritivore, 207, 209, 236, 237
detritus, 7, 63, 171, 185, 224, 232, 233, 234, 235, 236, 237, 238, 239
diatoms, 185, 186, 196, 197, 204, 210, 231, 232, 233, 235, 239
diazinon, 135
dieldrin, 135, 143, 147
disease, 18, 43, 67
dissolved oxygen, 93, 114, 127, 130, 184
dissolved solids, 131
drainage, 25, 46, 63, 68, 74, 75, 82, 93, 94, 101, 103, 111, 122, 129, 130, 132, 144, 156, 162, 171, 175, 191, 247
dredge hole, 84, 163, 183, 202
dredge spoil, 140
dredging, 68, 83, 84, 89, 92, 101, 103, 107, 125, 138, 139, 140, 145, 152, 153, 156, 163, 179, 180, 203, 205, 215
Dufrechou, Carlton, 153

E

Ecological Communities, 106, 191, 192
Eden Isles, 82, 93, 119, 125, 174
Elkins, Harvey, 53
Elkinsburg, 53
endangered species, 103, 111, 112
English Turn, 32, 35
environmental abuse, 5, 102, 103, 107, 188, 257, 258, 259
epidemic, 67
erosion, 6, 51, 60, 71, 79, 82, 84, 88, 92, 103, 105, 117, 119, 120, 121, 122, 123, 124, 127, 128, 140, 145, 171, 179, 186, 224
Espiritu Santo Bay, 22, 25, 26
euryhaline, 183, 196, 197, 207
eutrophication, 133, 136
exotic species, 73, 113, 115, 117, 243, 251

F

farming, 49, 82, 145
Faubourg Marigny, 54
Faubourg Ste. Marie, 52

faulting, 6
fish, 11, 12, 17, 20, 31, 34, 39, 47, 69, 97, 116, 133, 135, 142, 143, 147, 148, 188, 189, 190, 197, 198, 200, 201, 202, 203, 208, 209, 211, 212, 215, 225, 226, 229, 231, 232, 233, 235, 236, 237, 238, 245
fish kill, 133, 142, 188, 197
fishing, 12, 16, 17, 44, 49, 53, 54, 69, 71, 84, 86, 88, 89, 102, 135, 137, 138, 152, 202, 208
Five-Mile Bridge, 88
Florida Parishes, 40, 106, 110, 135, 137
Fontainebleau Beach, 156
Fontainebleau Plantation, 54
food chains/webs, 231, 238
forests, 103, 105, 109, 192, 193, 240
    Bottomland Hardwood, 111, 194, 195, 251
    Cypress-Tupelo Swamp, 71, 155, 194, 222, 240, 242, 247
    Hardwood Slope, 251
    Longleaf Pine Flatwoods/Savannahs, 107
    Mixed Hardwood-Loblolly, 251
    Pine Flatwoods, 251
    Pine Savannahs, 101, 251
    Shortleaf Pine/Oak-Hickory, 251
    Slash Pine/Post Oak, 251
    Upland Longleaf Pine, 106, 107, 251
    Wooded Seeps and Bayhead Swamps, 251
forts
    Fort Beauregard, 51
    Fort Biloxi (Fort Maurepas), 32, 35
    Fort Boulaye (Fort Mississippi), 33, 34, 35
    Fort Bute, 41, 43, 45
    Fort Macomb, 50, 62
    Fort Maurepas (Fort Biloxi), 32
    Fort Petite Coquilles, 50, 51
    Fort Pike, 17, 50, 51, 57, 62, 69, 165, 181
    Fort Proctor, 51
    Fort San Gabriel de Manchac, 41
    Fort St. John, 43, 46, 53
    Fort St. Philip, 50
    Fort Stevens, 64, 73
    Fort Wood, 50
    Martello Castle, 50, 51
    redoubt, 30, 43, 44, 50, 73
    Spanish Fort, 43, 50, 52, 53, 65, 67, 69, 74, 75, 84, 85, 118
    Tower Dupre, 50
    Tower Philippon, 50
fossils, 8, 121
Foster, Governor Mike, 153
Fraser, Lieutenant Alexander, 16, 41
French, 3, 5, 15, 16, 21, 23, 25, 26, 27, 29, 30, 31, 32, 34, 37, 38, 40, 41, 43, 45, 46, 48, 130
French and Indian War, 36, 40
French explorers, 11, 17, 33, 35, 248, 258
French Settlement, 53
Frenier, 12, 56, 70, 71, 74, 88, 89, 94, 95, 124, 165, 170, 171, 173, 181
Frenier Beach, 71
fresh marsh, 165, 194, 217, 221, 222
freshwater diversion, 103, 143, 152, 153
Freshwater Lakes and Ponds, 192, 249
Freshwater Tributaries, 193, 247

G

Gage Island, 41
Galvez, Governor Bernardo de, 43, 45
Galveztown, 43, 45
Gamarra, Francisco de, 26
Garay, Francisco de, 21
garden mulch, 106
Garyville, 144
Gentilly, 9, 45, 175
Geological Periods
    Late Quaternary, 6
    Pleistocene Epoch, 6, 7, 124, 191, 250
    Recent (Holocene) Epoch, 6, 7, 8, 124
    Tertiary, 124
Geology, 6
geomorphic regions, 191
global warming, 98, 123
Goose Point, 34, 44, 96, 123, 145, 174, 179, 209, 214
Gordon, Harry, 42, 43
Grand Lagoon, 119, 174

grassbeds, 139, 140, 145, 202, 204, 214, 215, 216, 238
Greater New Orleans Expressway (Causeway) Commission, 152
Green Point, 44, 54, 123, 174
groins, 79, 86, 212
Gulf of Mexico, 3, 6, 7, 22, 23, 24, 25, 28, 32, 68, 112, 123, 124, 148, 163, 182, 183, 188, 211

H

Hainkel, State Senator John, 152
Hammond Highway, 88, 89
hard substrate, 91, 206, 208, 211, 212, 213
Hayne Boulevard, 102
Hearn, Lafcadio, 52, 69
heavy metals, 130, 131, 145, 146, 147, 188
hepatitis, 133
herbivore, 235
Hesse-Wartegg, Ernst von, 68, 71
Higgins, Andrew Jackson, 90
Higgins Industries, 90
Higgins landing barges, 90
Houck Report, 152
Howze Beach, 93, 119, 125, 174
Hubert, Marc-Antoine, 37
Hunley, Captain Horace Lawson, 65, 66
hunting, 12, 14, 16, 17, 30, 44, 49, 71, 86, 88, 89, 128, 227
hurricane protection, 93, 94, 95, 163, 241
Hurricanes and Tropical Storms
　Hurricane Andrew, 50, 90, 97, 127
　Hurricane Betsy, 92, 94, 127
　Hurricane Bob, 127
　Hurricane Camille, 94, 95, 127
　Hurricane Georges, 94, 95, 127, 134
　Hurricane Ivan, 96
　Hurricane Juan, 25, 27, 29, 95, 127
　Hurricane Katrina, 57, 92, 94, 96, 97, 98, 123, 125, 127, 131, 132, 134, 149, 157, 205, 257, 258
　Hurricane Rita, 96, 97, 127, 131, 132
　Tropical Storm Beryl, 127, 227
　Tropical Storm Florence, 127
　Tropical Storm Frances, 65, 127
Hutchins, Thomas, 42, 43, 45
hydrogen ion concentration (pH), 185
hydrogen sulfide, 186, 233
hypoxic, 127, 184, 205

I

Iberville (Pierre le Moyne, Sieur d'Iberville), 3, 14, 15, 17, 18, 21, 25, 27, 29, 30, 31, 32, 33, 34, 35, 42, 43, 44, 45, 50, 67, 165
industrial cypress logging, 105
intermediate marsh, 194, 217, 220, 223
Interstate-10, 172, 174
Intracoastal Waterway, 12, 83, 92, 171
Iriarte, Antonio de, 26
iron, 66, 74, 147, 186
Isle of Orleans, 40, 48

J

Jackson, General Andrew, 50
Johnston, Senator J. Bennett, 155
Johnstone, George, 41
Jones Island, 41, 50, 63

K

Kenner, 64, 88, 89, 92, 107, 130, 134, 164, 175, 181
Kennerville, 56, 63, 74
Kjeldahl nitrogen, 131

L

La Salle, René-Robert Cavelier de, 14, 15, 22, 23, 25, 26, 29, 30
LaBranche, 13, 14, 15, 32, 33, 34, 56, 74, 82, 88, 95, 96, 114, 119, 123, 125, 163, 171, 173, 175, 194, 225, 226, 242, 247, 248
LaBranche Wetlands, 82, 88, 95, 96, 114, 119, 123, 125, 163, 194, 242
Lacustrine Communities, 247
Laguna de Pez, 27
LaHarpe, Jean-Baptiste Benard de, 14, 22, 26, 29, 32, 35

GENERAL INDEX 301

Lake Maurepas Society, 154
Lake Pontchartrain Basin Foundation, 57, 139, 142, 152, 153, 155, 157, 188, 257, 258
Lake Pontchartrain Basin Maritime Museum and Research Center, 54
Lake Pontchartrain Basin Water Quality Management Plan, 151
Lake Pontchartrain Swimming Task Force, 156
Lake Pontchartrain Task Force, 151
Lake Vista, 84
Lakefront Airport, 85, 163, 172
Lakefront Land Reclamation Project, 83, 163
Lakes
　Blind, 3
　Lago de Lodo (Muddy Lake), 26, 27, 28, 29, 32
　Lake Borgne, 3, 9, 12, 22, 26, 27, 29, 40, 50, 51, 69, 75, 76, 112, 116, 118, 119, 121, 122, 123, 162, 163, 164, 165, 166, 171, 175, 176, 179, 181, 183, 191, 194, 196, 197, 198, 199, 200, 202, 203, 206, 207, 208, 212, 213, 220, 221, 227, 228, 244, 247
　Lake Chef Menteur, 5
　Lake Maurepas, 3, 7, 10, 16, 25, 27, 31, 33, 43, 44, 48, 55, 60, 64, 70, 121, 122, 140, 144, 145, 151, 154, 155, 162, 163, 164, 165, 166, 171, 177, 179, 183, 185, 186, 187, 190, 191, 194, 196, 200, 201, 209, 210, 211, 212, 220, 242, 246, 247
　Lake Ramsay, 256
　Lake St. Catherine, 3, 5, 164, 166, 194, 209
　Lake St. Louis, 3
　St. John's, 52
Lakeshore Estates, 93, 125
Laketown, 134, 156
Lakeview, 52, 82
Lambert, Robert J., 153
land bridge, 96, 123, 191, 194, 222
land loss, 10, 97, 118, 119, 122, 123, 124, 127
land reclamation, 93, 122, 125
LaPlace, 15, 56, 86, 88, 89
Laveau, Marie, 52

Law, John, 38
lead, 37, 131, 146, 148, 154, 241
Leche, Governor Richard W., 89
Lessons of the Lake, 153
LeSueur, Pierre-Charles, 33
levee, 7, 12, 37, 38, 44, 79, 83, 84, 86, 89, 93, 95, 103, 163, 224, 242, 243
Lewisburg, 44, 55, 63, 174
lighthouse, 32, 51, 57, 58, 60, 68, 69, 74, 88, 121
Lighthouse Point, 165
lime, 41, 46, 47, 205
Lincoln Beach, 86, 156, 172, 181, 202, 214
litter, 103, 149, 150, 208
Little Lagoon, 175, 222
Little Oak Island, 12
Little Woods, 77, 81, 83, 86, 124, 133, 163, 172, 183
logging, 7, 71, 83, 101, 105, 122, 224, 241, 242
Long Point, 181
Lopez, John, 86, 101, 119, 141, 153, 188, 212, 258
Lotham Cypress Company, 70
Louisiana Coastal Wetlands Conservation and Restoration Task Force, 10, 118, 122, 125, 217
Louisiana Cypress Lumber Company, 71
Louisiana Department of Natural Resources, 151
Louisiana Natural Heritage Program, 107, 194, 202, 217, 220, 221, 240, 249, 251
Louisiana Purchase, 46, 48
lumber, 39, 41, 47, 52, 55, 62, 69, 74, 75, 105, 241, 242
Luna y Arellano, Don Tristan de, 24
Lyon Villa, 243

M

Macomb, Major General Alexander, 50
Madisonville, 8, 48, 49, 50, 53, 54, 55, 57, 62, 69, 71, 74, 82, 83, 125, 147, 148, 165, 181
Madisonville Creosote Works, 148
Madisonville rice fields, 82, 125, 148
Maison Blanche, 52
Malbanchia, 23, 30

GENERAL INDEX

Malheureux Point, 165
Manchac, 31, 33, 37, 41, 42, 43, 44, 45, 56, 63, 64, 70, 71, 72, 73, 89, 93, 117, 144, 165, 173, 181, 218, 242, 245, 246
Mandeville, 44, 54, 55, 63, 67, 69, 72, 74, 79, 81, 88, 95, 107, 119, 124, 165, 171, 174, 181, 194
Mar Pequena, 24, 25
Marigny de Mandeville, Bernard Xavier de, 54
Marigny estate, 89
marine preserve/sanctuary, 209
marine species, 111, 127, 189, 190, 196, 198, 200, 207, 248
marsh, 7, 8, 64, 65, 69, 92, 97, 98, 105, 115, 123, 124, 125, 126, 127, 128, 155, 165, 167, 171, 177, 184, 186, 194, 199, 203, 215, 217, 220, 221, 222, 223, 224, 225, 227, 228, 229, 230, 231, 232, 233, 234, 241, 242, 243, 244, 245, 249
Martineau, Harriet, 51
Matagorda Bay, 22, 25, 26
Maurepas, Jerome Phelypeaux de, 3
Maurepas Swamp, 155, 181
McClintock, James, 65, 66
McIlhenny, Edward Avery, 112, 114, 115
megalops, 207
mercury, 143, 148, 149
Metairie, 34, 89, 92, 107, 115, 130, 164, 169, 170, 175, 176, 181
Metairie Ridge, 47, 63
Metairie-Gentilly Ridge, 9
Michoud Assembly Facility, 92
Milne, Alexander, 51
Milneburg, 51, 52, 54, 67, 68, 74, 77, 80, 85, 133, 173
Mississippi Bubble, 38
Mississippi River Gulf Outlet (MRGO), 12, 92, 103, 123, 171, 183, 207
Mississippi Sound, 3, 26, 29, 30, 32, 36, 39, 143, 144, 162, 166, 183, 198, 199, 212
Mobile, Alabama, 35, 37, 40, 42, 43, 53, 55, 62, 65, 66, 69, 74
Mobile Bay, 22, 24, 26

N

Napton, 56
Narvaez, Panfilo de, 24
Nassau Bay, 36
Native Americans (Indians), 5, 11, 16, 18, 21, 104, 258
   Acolapissa, 14, 15, 17, 19, 35
   Alabama, 45
   Ananis (Biloxi), 15
   Annocchy, 14
   Bayogoula, 14, 30, 33
   Biloxi (Bylocchy), 14, 15, 16, 19
   Chatots, 15
   Cherokee, 14
   Chickasaw, 14, 35
   Choctaw, 5, 14, 16, 17, 18, 20, 31, 40, 45, 55
   Colapissa, 14
   Creek, 17
   Houma, 14, 19
   Mobilian, 31
   Mouloubis, 15
   Mugulasha, 14, 18, 30
   Natchitoches Indians, 15
   Okelousa, 14
   Quinipissa, 14, 15, 19
   Tangipahoa (Taensapoa), 13, 14, 15, 16, 44
   Tunicas, 15, 16
nekton, 239
New Basin, 53, 92
New Lake End, 75
New Negro Beach, 86
New Orleans, 3, 7, 15, 16, 17, 18, 25, 29, 33, 37, 38, 39, 40, 41, 42, 43, 45, 46, 47, 49, 50, 51, 52, 53, 54, 55, 56, 57, 62, 63, 65, 67, 68, 69, 70, 71, 72, 73, 74, 75, 76, 77, 79, 81, 82, 83, 84, 85, 86, 88, 89, 90, 91, 92, 93, 94, 95, 96, 97, 98, 101, 105, 107, 114, 116, 121, 124, 125, 129, 130, 131, 132, 134, 140, 149, 152, 154, 155, 164, 165, 171, 172, 174, 175, 177, 178, 181, 194, 247, 257
New Orleans Barrier Island, 8
New Orleans Drainage Plan, 75
New Orleans East, 12, 92, 155, 243

New Orleans Health Department, 129
New Orleans Lakefront Airport, 85
New Orleans Levee Board, 83
New Orleans Municipal Yacht Harbor, 134
New Orleans Pontchartrain Bridge Company, 60, 88
New Orleans Refining Company, 146
New Orleans Sewerage and Water Board, 82
nickel, 147, 148
nitrates and nitrites, 131
Norco, 146
North Pass, 5, 10, 41, 44, 93, 181
North Shore, 93, 118, 123, 125, 174, 209
Northlake Nature Center, 89, 256
Northshore Beach, 93, 125, 156, 167, 174
nutrients, 107, 133, 136, 140, 142, 143, 144, 151, 163, 187, 189, 217, 232, 234

O

Oak Harbor, 93, 125
Ocean Springs, Mississippi, 32
oil and gas drilling, 103, 105, 145, 146, 148, 224
oil and grease, 131, 188
Old Lake End, 74
Old Spanish Trail, 48
oligohaline, 183, 199, 207, 216, 221
Open Water Estuarine Community, 192
outboard motors, 134
Ozone Belt, 67

P

Palustrine Communities, 240
Parishes
   Ascension, 47
   Florida Parishes, 40, 106, 110, 135, 137
   Jefferson, 51, 53, 68, 88, 92, 116, 129, 131, 132, 171, 181
   Livingston, 31, 110
   Orleans, 8, 9, 47, 92, 98, 119, 131, 175, 181, 209
   St. Bernard, 86, 92, 96, 115, 228
   St. Charles, 70, 88
   St. John the Baptist, 71, 88
   St. Tammany, 91, 92, 93, 98, 110, 111, 252
   Tangipahoa, 93, 110, 135
Parks
   Bogue Falaya, 156
   Bonnabel Boat Launch, 181
   City, 52, 53, 82, 84, 85, 90
   Fairview Riverside State, 181
   Fontainebleau State, 12, 89, 256
   Linear, 89, 169
   Pontchartrain Beach Amusement, 84, 85
   Pontchartrain Center, 181
   Spanish Fort, 84
   Tchefuncte State (see Parks: Fontainebleau State)
   West End Lake Shore, 181
   West End, 77
Pass á Guyon, 32
Pass Manchac, 5, 10, 13, 16, 17, 31, 33, 34, 40, 41, 48, 50, 53, 56, 57, 63, 64, 70, 73, 121, 145, 153, 164, 166, 173, 174, 176, 180, 183, 197, 200, 224
Penicaut, 17, 29, 31, 34, 35, 37
Penicaut Narrative, 29
Pensacola, Florida, 24, 40, 42, 43, 45, 55, 96
Pensacola Bay, 24, 26
pentachlorophenol, 135, 147
Pez, Andres de, 26, 27
phenol, 147
phosphates, 133, 142, 187, 189, 232
phosphorus, 131, 151, 187, 188
photosynthesis, 139, 145, 184, 185, 204, 217, 231, 232
phytoplankton, 116, 187, 197, 231, 232, 234, 235, 238
Pickles, Captain William, 45
Pike, Zebulon, 50
Pine Island Beach Trend, 8, 9
Pineda, Alvarez de, 22, 24, 25
pitch, 40, 41, 46, 47
Pittman, Captain Philip, 31, 41, 42
plankton, 185, 197, 198, 199, 200, 233, 234, 235, 239
Pleistocene Terrace, 6, 7, 191

304 GENERAL INDEX

Point, The, 181
Point du Chien, 174, 214
Point Platte, 119, 168, 174, 214
Pointe aux Herbes (Grass Point), 34, 60
Pointe-aux-Coquilles, 34
polio, 133
polychlorinated biphenyls (PCBs), 143
polycyclic aromatic hydrocarbons, 146, 147
Ponchatoula, 8, 13, 56, 62, 63, 64, 69, 71, 89, 118
Ponchatoula Beach, 89
Pontchartrain, Louis Phelypeaux, Comte de, 3, 27
Pontchartrain Beach, 57, 84, 85, 86, 90, 129, 153, 156, 181, 202
Pontchartrain Embayment, 7, 8, 10
Pontchartrain Hotel, 53
Pontchartrain Restoration Act, 156
population, 5, 11, 19, 43, 45, 46, 49, 55, 70, 75, 77, 82, 83, 91, 92, 97, 98, 101, 102, 104, 130, 132, 133, 134, 135, 157, 250, 257, 258, 259
Port Louis, 8, 174
Port Manchac, 93
Port Pontchartrain, 51, 54, 57, 69
Port Vincent, 69
portage, 15, 30, 32, 33, 34, 38, 41, 107
prairie, 33, 65, 68, 74, 125, 165, 250
Prairie Terrace Complex, 6
Pratz, Antoine Simon Le Page du, 3, 15, 29, 32, 34, 37, 39, 40, 105
primary producer, 231, 233, 235
Proctorsville, 51
pullboat, 70, 71
pumping station, 76, 94, 116, 130, 131, 132, 175, 176

R

Rabbit Island, 57
Railroads
   Alabama Great Southern, 71
   Illinois Central, 56, 88, 175
   Jefferson and Lake Pontchartrain Railway, 52, 53
   Louisville and Nashville, 69
   New Orleans and Carrollton, 52
   New Orleans and Northeastern Railway, 70
   New Orleans City and Lake Railway, 75
   New Orleans, Jackson, and Great Northern, 55
   New Orleans, Mobile, and Texas, 69
   Pontchartrain, 51, 68, 69, 74, 89
   Queen and Crescent Route, 74
rainfall, 156, 176, 178, 180, 187
Ravine du Sueur, 33, 44
Read, Captain Abner, 62
recreation, 77, 93, 103, 156, 257, 258
Redfield ratio, 187
redoubt, 30, 43, 44, 50, 73
Reina, Juan Jordan de, 25, 29
resin, 40, 47, 106
restoration, 5, 10, 60, 79, 101, 103, 107, 113, 143, 153, 154, 155, 202, 258
rice fields, 82, 125, 148
Richard King Mellon Foundation, 155
ridges, 13, 97, 101, 194, 243
Rigolets, 3, 12, 17, 32, 34, 39, 40, 41, 50, 51, 57, 62, 68, 69, 71, 74, 79, 83, 94, 95, 118, 147, 164, 166, 171, 172, 174, 175, 176, 177, 180, 181, 194, 200, 202, 222
Rigolets Estates, 125
Rivas, Martin de, 26
Rivers, 7, 129, 135, 171
   Amite, 10, 15, 16, 31, 33, 40, 41, 42, 43, 44, 45, 47, 48, 60, 102, 111, 148, 177, 178, 247, 248, 249
   Black, 148, 174
   Blind, 70, 144, 149, 177, 178, 242, 247, 248
   Bogue Falaya, 49, 138
   Colbert, 23
   Comite, 47, 126, 177
   Iberville, 31, 33, 42, 43, 44
   Little, 172, 175
   Mississippi, 3, 5, 6, 7, 8, 9, 10, 12, 13, 14, 15, 16, 18, 21, 22, 23, 24, 25, 26, 27, 29, 30, 32, 33,

GENERAL INDEX   305

34, 35, 36, 37, 38, 39, 40, 41, 42, 43,
44, 47, 50, 56, 62, 68, 71, 75, 83, 86, 87,
92, 95, 97, 101, 103, 104, 112, 116, 123, 124,
130, 135, 140, 141, 142, 143, 144, 145, 146,
153, 163, 164, 171, 176, 177, 178, 179, 183,
188, 191, 199, 207, 209, 232, 234, 247,
248
Natalbany, 10, 48
New, 47, 126, 178
Pascagoula, 14, 32
Pearl, 8, 14, 15, 18, 32, 35, 40, 47, 57, 72, 109,
111, 112, 116, 149, 171, 175, 176, 177, 181, 191,
194, 221, 223, 242, 244, 247, 248, 249
Rio de la Palizada, 23, 25, 26
Rio del Espiritu Santo, 22, 23, 24
Riviere d'Orleans, 34
Tangipahoa, 13, 15, 16, 40, 89, 111, 112, 116,
120, 135, 136, 137, 140, 149, 156, 167, 171,
174, 177, 190, 213, 241, 247, 249
Tchefuncte, 12, 40, 48, 54, 55, 57, 62, 67, 74,
82, 111, 148, 149, 165, 171, 177, 181, 194, 197,
214, 222, 247
Tickfaw, 55, 64, 137, 138, 148, 154, 165, 171,
177, 247
Robert S. Maestri Bridge, 88
Robin, C. C., 46
Roemer, Governor Buddy, 153
Romero, Antonio, 25, 26, 27, 29
Rouquette, Adrien, 55
Rouquette, Dominique, 55
Roxana Petroleum Company, 146
Ruddock, 56, 70, 71, 89, 94, 119, 120, 173, 181
Ruddock, C. H., 70
Ruddock Cypress Company, 70

S

sagamité bread, 17, 34
sailing, 54, 75, 102
Saint Malo, 69
saline marsh, 217, 221
salinity, 9, 84, 92, 106, 122, 126, 127, 143, 145,
163, 165, 178, 182, 183, 184, 189, 190, 196,
197, 198, 200, 201, 205, 206, 207, 209, 212,
214, 215, 217, 220, 221, 222, 242
salinity stratification, 184, 205
salmonella, 133
salt wedge, 126, 183
saltwater intrusion, 103, 105, 126, 127, 154, 155,
194, 224, 241
sand, 7, 8, 41, 44, 46, 51, 52, 55, 56, 74, 75, 79,
88, 89, 90, 103, 111, 138, 171, 179, 201, 202,
203, 235, 247
sand and gravel mining, 138
Sand Island, 41
Sauvole, M. de, 29, 31, 32
Save Our Lake, 152, 258
scrub, 221, 240, 241, 244, 245
sea level, 6, 7, 10, 12, 37, 82, 86, 94, 95, 97, 98,
123, 124, 140, 141, 175, 242, 244
seawall, 77, 79, 84, 85, 88, 90, 119, 121
Secchi disk depth, 179
sedimentation, 6, 7, 8, 124
sediments, 6, 7, 9, 38, 124, 125, 131, 138, 140,
143, 144, 145, 146, 147, 163, 164, 179, 182,
186, 187, 204, 205, 206, 212, 213, 217, 234,
242, 259
seiches, 181
Seven Years War, 40
sewage, 49, 68, 77, 101, 102, 103, 129, 130, 131,
132, 133, 134, 135, 152, 154, 155, 156, 188, 259
Shell Beach, 51, 166, 181
shell dredging, 103, 138, 139, 140, 145, 153, 156,
179, 180, 203, 205, 215
shell middens, 13, 101
Shell Petroleum Corporation, 146
Ship Island, 14, 30
ship-building, 82
shipyards, 53
shoreline areas, 203, 210, 211
shoreline/coastal erosion, 6, 51, 60, 71, 79,
82, 84, 88, 92, 103, 105, 117, 119, 120, 121,
122, 123, 124, 127, 128, 140, 145, 171, 179,
186, 224
shrimping, 102, 209

Siguenza y Gongora, Don Carlos de, 26, 27
silt, 7, 124, 138, 171, 179, 214, 247
siltation, 112, 138
Slidell, 8, 55, 70, 71, 72, 74, 82, 83, 90, 91, 93, 107, 118, 125, 147, 165, 178, 194, 221
smallpox, 18
smuggling, 42, 62
Soft Bottom Benthic Community, 192
solid waste, 103, 149
Soto, Hernando de, 22, 24, 25
Southern Shipbuilding Corporation, 148
Southern Yacht Club, 53, 74, 90
Spanish, 16, 21, 22, 23, 24, 25, 26, 27, 29, 40, 41, 42, 43, 45, 46, 48
Spanish moss, 20, 51, 56, 63, 240, 243
Spanish West Florida, 45, 48
Sparkling River Committee, 154
special management area, 151
Springfield, 48, 55, 69, 118
St. Bernard Cypress Company, 70
St. Francisville, 48
St. John's Eve, 52
St. John's Rowing Club, 74
stenohaline, 207
Stone Report, 151
storm tides, 70, 124
Strader Cypress Company, 70
subsidence, 6, 10, 71, 82, 105, 121, 122, 123, 124, 125, 127, 143, 164, 194, 223, 224
sulfates, 186
sulfides, 186
sulfur, 186, 233
Superdome, 53, 92
suspended solids, 131, 139, 152
swimming, 43, 53, 65, 69, 86, 102, 129, 131, 135, 137, 152, 156, 157, 181, 188, 196, 200, 210, 228, 235, 258

T

Talisheek Pine Wetlands, 256
tannins, 44

tar, 40, 41, 42, 46, 47, 62, 71
Tchefuncte Boat Launch, 156
Tchoutchouma, 15
temperature, 177, 182, 184, 189
Three Rivers Basin Foundation, 154
Tickfaw River Basin Group, 154
tides, 56, 68, 70, 124, 180, 181, 182, 197
Tigonillou portage, 32, 33
timber cutting, 49
To Restore Lake Pontchartrain, 103, 152
transportation routes, 5
trapping, 115, 226, 227, 228
trawls, 201, 208
Treasure Chest Casino, 134
Treasure Island, 93, 125, 175
Treaty of Ildefonso, 46
Treaty of Paris, 40
tributaries, 5, 49, 102, 116, 133, 135, 136, 137, 146, 148, 151, 154, 157, 181, 195, 202, 220, 232, 247, 257
tributyltin, 148
turbidity, 107, 138, 139, 143, 145, 179, 187, 205, 215, 232, 233
turpentine, 40, 46, 47, 55, 62
turtle, 12, 111, 226
Turtle Cove, 128
Turtle Cove Environmental Research Station, 153, 223, 224
Twain, Mark, 74
Twin Spans, 91
2,4-D, 135
typhoid fever, 133

U

Universities
　Louisiana State, 51, 96, 145, 151, 154
　Southeastern Louisiana, 154
　Tulane, 65, 154
　University of New Orleans, 57, 154
urban runoff, 75, 76, 102, 103, 130, 155, 182, 187, 188
urbanization, 5, 102, 133, 187, 257

V

vanadium, 148
Venetian Isles, 93, 125
Vieux Carré, 52, 54
viruses, 129, 133, 136
voodoo, 52
voyageurs, 35, 37

W

Wagram, 56
War of 1812, 50
Washington Hotel, 51
water clarity, 139, 140, 151, 156, 215
water quality, 86, 93, 102, 103, 107, 112, 129, 133, 135, 137, 138, 143, 150, 152, 154, 155, 156, 157, 181, 188, 202, 204, 205, 208, 215, 241, 258
Watson, Baxter, 65
Watson-Williams Bridge, 88
Wehner, Frances Joseph, 65
West End, 52, 53, 57, 67, 68, 74, 75, 77, 83, 84, 88, 92, 102, 119, 124, 173, 181
West Florida Republic, 48
wetland loss, 105, 117, 118, 119, 121, 122, 125, 155
wetlands, 10, 83, 92, 93, 96, 98, 103, 105, 114, 117, 119, 122, 123, 124, 125, 127, 128, 132, 133, 140, 143, 144, 151, 153, 165, 181, 185, 191, 194, 195, 211, 217, 227, 229, 240, 242, 249, 251, 257
Wharton, 49, 50
Wildlife Management Areas
    Biloxi, 181
    Joyce, 181
    Manchac, 114, 123, 127, 181, 223, 225, 226, 242, 245
    Maurepas Swamp, 155, 181
    Pearl River, 181
Wildlife Refuges
    Bayou Sauvage National, 92, 155, 181, 243
    Big Branch Marsh National, 155, 181, 256
wing nets/butterfly nets, 208
Wisner, Edward, 82

Wolfe, Louisiana Supreme Court Justice J. M., 53, 227
Wood, A. Baldwin, 82
Wood, Eleazer Derby, 50
Wooden Boat Festival, 54
World War I, 60, 82, 83, 84, 89, 90, 102
World War II, 60, 84, 89, 90, 102

Y

yellow fever, 18, 35, 52, 67

Z

Zephyr roller coaster, 85
zinc, 131, 143, 146, 147, 148
zoea larvae, 190, 199, 207

Taxonomic Index

ANIMALS

Amphibians
    Acris crepitans - northern cricket frog, 226
    Bufo valliceps - Gulf coast toad, 226
    Eleutherodactylus recordi - greenhouse frog, 117
    Gastrophryne carolinensis - eastern narrow-mouthed toad, 226
    Hyla cinerea - green treefrog, 226
    Rana catesbeiana - bullfrog, 226
    Rana gryllio - pig frog, 226
    Rana sevosa - gopher frog, 111, 112
    Rana sphenocephala - southern leopard frog, 226
Annelida
    Hirudinea - leeches, 225
    Hobsonia (= *Hypaniola*) *florida* - polychaete, 206, 225
    Mediomastus californiensis - polychaete, 206
    Oligochaet worms, 225
    Polydora websteri - polychaete, 213
Arthropods
    Crustacea

Amphipods
    Cerapus benthophilus, 206
    Corophium lacustre, 206, 213, 239
    Corophium louisianum, 225
    Gammarus mucronatus, 225
    Gammarus spp., 239
    Grandidierella bonnieroides, 206, 225
    Monoculoides edwardsii, 206
Barnacles
    Balanus subalbidus, 213
Cladocerans
    Bosmina coregoni, 199
    Bosmina longirostris, 198
    Diaphanosoma brachyurum, 199
    Moina micrura, 199
Conchostraca - clam shrimps, 225
Copepods, 199, 235
    Acartia tonsa, 189, 191, 198, 199, 206, 235
    Canuella sp., 198
    Cyclops sp., 199
    Diaptomus sp., 199
    Ergasilus sp., 199
    Eurytemora affinis, 198, 199
    Halicyclops fosteri, 206
    Halicyclops sp., 198

TAXONOMIC INDEX

Mesocyclops sp., 199
Oithona brevicornis, 198
Paracalanus crassirostris, 198
Pseudobradya sp., 206
Scottolana canadensis, 206

Decapods
  Alpheus estuariensis - pistol shrimp, 213
  Callianassa jamaicense - mud shrimp, 207
  Callinectes sapidus - blue crab, 189, 201, 204, 207, 208, 212, 215, 227, 234, 236, 237, 238, 239
  Cambaridae - freshwater crayfish, 227, 249
  crayfish, 225, 226, 227, 249
  Farfantepenaeus aztecus - brown shrimp, 189, 201, 207, 208, 215, 234
  Litopenaeus setiferus - white shrimp, 189, 201, 207, 208, 234, 236
  Macrobrachium ohione - river shrimp, 207, 233
  Menippe adina - Gulf stone crab, 212
  Palaemonetes intermedius - grass shrimp, 215, 216
  Palaemonetes kadiakenis - grass shrimp, 215, 216, 225
  Palaemonetes paludosus - grass shrimp, 216
  Palaemonetes pugio - grass shrimp, 215, 216, 225
  Palaemonetes spp. - grass shrimp, 207, 215, 239
  Palaemonetes vulgaris - grass shrimp, 216
  Procambarus clarkii - red swamp crayfish, 225, 249
  Rhithropanopeus harrisii - mud crab, 189, 190, 199, 206, 214, 237

Isopods
  Cyathura polita, 206, 225, 239
  Edotea montosa, 206
  Sphaeroma terebrans, 214

Mysids
  Mysidopsis almyra - opossum shrimp, 206, 235, 239
  Taphromysis louisianae - mysid, 225

Tanaids
  Hargeria rapax, 213

Insects
  Ablabesmyia - chironomid, 206
  Aedes aegypti - mosquito, 67
  Anopheles sp. - mosquito, 68
  Apis mellifera - honey bee, 117
  Ceratopogonidae - biting midges, 225
  Chaoborus sp. - phantom midge, 199
  Coleoptera - water beetles, 227
  damselflies - Zygoptera, 225
  Dendroctonus frontalis - southern pine beetle, 106
  dragonflies - Anisoptera, 225
  Hemiptera - water bugs, 227
  midges, 225
  Romalea guttata - eastern lubber grasshopper, 229
  Solenopsis invicta - fire ant, 116

Birds
  Actitis macularia - spotted sandpiper, 211
  Agelaius phoeniceus - redwinged blackbird, 225
  Aix sponsa - wood duck, 229, 246
  Anas americana - American wigeon, 203, 229
  Anas clypeata - northern shoveler, 203, 229
  Anas crecca - green-winged teal, 203, 229
  Anas discors - blue-winged teal, 203, 229
  Anas fulvigula - mottled duck, 203, 229
  Anas platyrhynchos - mallard, 203, 229
  Anas strepera - gadwall, 203, 229
  Anhinga anhinga - anhinga, 246

TAXONOMIC INDEX

Ardea herodias - great blue heron, 228, 246
Aythya affinis - lesser scaup, 203, 204
Aythya collaris - ring-necked duck, 203, 229
Branta canadensis - Canada goose, 17
Bubo virginianus - great horned owl, 229
Bubulcus ibis - cattle egret, 229, 246
Bucephala albeola - bufflehead, 203
Buteo jamaicensis - red-tailed hawk, 229
Buteo lineatus - red-shouldered hawk, 229
Butorides virescens - green heron, 229
Calidris mauri - western sandpiper, 211
Calidris melanotos - pectoral sandpiper, 211
Calidris minutilla - least sandpiper, 211
Calidris pusilla - semipalmated sandpiper, 211
Campephilus principalis - ivory-billed woodpecker, 106, 107, 258
Cardinalis cardinalis - northern cardinal, 229
Casmerodius alba - great egret, 229, 246
Ceryle alcyon - belted kingfisher, 229
Charadrius vociferus - killdeer, 211
Chen caerulescens - snow or blue goose, 17
Circus cyaneus - Northern harriers or marsh hawks, 229
Conuropsis carolinensis - Carolina parakeet, 107, 258
Corvus ossifragus - fish crow, 229
Cyanocitta cristata - blue jay, 229
Dendroica coronata - yellow-rumped warbler, 229
Dryocopus pileatus - pileated woodpecker, 229, 246
duck, 17, 68, 127
Ectopistes migratorius - passenger pigeon, 107
Egretta thula - snowy egret, 229, 246
Egretta tricolor - tricolored heron, 229
Eudocimus albus - white ibis, 229, 246
Florida caerulea - little blue heron, 228, 246
Fulica americana - American coot, 229
Gallinula chloropus - common moorhen, 229
Haliaeetus leucocephalus - bald eagle, 112, 113, 203
Himantopus mexicanus - black-necked stilt, 211
Hirundo rustica - Barn swallow, 204
Larus atricilla - laughing gull, 203
Larus delawarensis - ring-billed gull, 203
Limnodromus griseus - short-billed dowitcher, 211
Limnodromus scolopaceus - long-billed dowitcher, 211
Melanerpes carolinus - red-bellied woodpecker, 229
Meleagris gallopavo - wild turkey, 17, 30, 31, 34, 89, 112
Melospiza georgiana - swamp sparrow, 229
Mergus serrator - red-breasted merganser, 203
Mimus polyglottos - northern mockingbird, 229
Nyctanassa violacea - yellow-crowned night-heron, 229, 246
Nycticorax nycticorax - black-crowned night-heron, 229, 246
Pandion haliaetus - osprey, 112
Parula americana - northern parula, 229, 246
Parus bicolor - tufted titmouse, 229
Parus carolinensis - Carolina chickadee, 229
Pelecanus occidentalis - brown pelican, 111, 112, 113, 203
Phalacrocorax auritus - double-crested cormorant, 113, 203

TAXONOMIC INDEX **311**

Picoides borealis - red-cockaded woodpecker, 112
Plegadis chihi - white-faced ibis, 229, 246
Plegadis falcinellus - glossy ibis, 229, 246
Pluvialis squatarola - black-bellied plover, 211
Polioptila caerulea - blue-gray gnatcatcher, 229
Porgne subis - purple martin, 204
Porphyrio martinica - purple gallinule, 229
Porzana carolina - sora, 229
Protonotarius citrini - prothonotary warbler, 229, 246
Quiscalus major - boat-tailed grackle, 228
Quiscalus quiscla - common grackle, 228
Rallus elegans - king rail, 229
Rallus limicola - Virginia rail, 229
Rallus longirostris - clapper rail, 229
Regulus calendula - ruby-crowned kinglet, 229
Rynchops niger - black skimmer, 203
Sterna antillarum - least tern, 203
Sterna caspia - Caspian tern, 203
Sterna maxima - royal tern, 203
Strix varia - barred owl, 229
Tachycineta bicolor - tree swallow, 204
Thryothorus ludovicianus - Carolina wren, 229
Tringa flavipes - lesser yellowlegs, 211
Tringa melanoleuca - greater yellowlegs, 211
Turdus migratorius - American robin, 229
Vireo griseus - white-eyed vireo, 229
Vireo olivaceous - red-eyed vireo, 229
Zonotrichia albicollis - white-throated sparrow, 229

Bryozoa (Ectoprocta)
  Membranipora sp., 213
  Victorella pavida, 213

Cnidarians
  Chrysaora (=*Dactylometra*) *quinquecirrha* - sea nettle jellyfish, 200
  Cordylophora caspia - hydroid, 213
  Garveia (=*Bimeria*) *franciscana* - hydroid, 213

Ctenophores
  Mnemiopsis mccradyi - comb jellyfish, 200

Fishes
  Acipenser oxyrinchus desotoi - Gulf sturgeon, 109, 111, 112, 201
  Alosa alabamae - Alabama shad, 112, 202
  Alosa chrysochloris - skipjack herring, 201
  Amia calva - bowfin, 12, 34, 148, 149
  Anchoa mitchilli - bay anchovy, 189, 201, 203, 210, 211, 226, 235, 236, 238
  Anguilla rostrata - American eel, 210
  Aplodinotus grunniens - freshwater drum, 12, 148, 149, 201, 202, 204, 237, 238
  Archosargus probatocephalus - sheepshead, 12, 201, 202, 210, 212, 225, 226, 237, 238
  Ariopsis [= *Arius*] *felis* - hardhead catfish, sea catfish, 201, 203, 210, 234, 236, 237, 238
  Atractosteus spatula - alligator gar, 12, 201, 238
  Bagre marinus - gafftopsail catfish, 202, 210
  Bairdiella chrysoura - silver perch, 201, 210, 235, 238
  Brevoortia patronus - Gulf menhaden, 201, 203, 210, 211, 226, 232, 234, 236, 237, 238
  Caranx hippos - jack crevalle, 202
  Carassius auratus - goldfish, 116
  Carcharhinus leucas - bull shark, 201
  Catostomidae, 248
  Centrarchidae, 248
  Cichlasoma cyanoguttatum - Rio Grande cichlid, 116

Cynoscion nebulosus - spotted seatrout, 189, 201, 202, 215, 235, 237, 238
Cynoscion arenarius - sand seatrout, 201, 202, 235
Cyprinidae, 248
Cyprinodon variegatus - sheepshead minnow, 201, 210, 225, 226
Cyprinodontidae, 225
Cyprinus carpio - Eurasian carp, 39, 115
Dasyatis sabina - Atlantic stingray, 210
Dorosoma cepedianum - gizzard shad, 201, 236, 237
Dorosoma petenense - threadfin shad, 201, 232, 235, 238
Elassoma zonatum - banded pygmy sunfish, 245
Elops saurus - ladyfish, 201
Fundulidae, 225, 227, 248
Fundulus euryzonus - broadstripe topminnow, 248
Fundulus grandis - Gulf killifish, 210, 211
Fundulus pulvereus - bayou killifish, 226
Gambusia affinis - western mosquitofish, 146, 225
Gobiesox strumosus - skilletfish, 210, 214
Gobiosoma bosc - naked goby, 210, 211, 214, 215
Heterandria formosa - least killifish, 211, 226
Ictaluridae, 248
Ictalurus furcatus - blue catfish, 201, 202, 210, 235, 236, 237, 238
Ictalurus punctatus - channel catfish, 201, 202, 210, 236, 237
Ictalurus sp. - catfish, 12, 211
Ictiobus cyprinellus - bigmouth buffalo, 148, 149
Ictiobus sp. - buffalo fish, 12
Lagodon rhomboides - pinfish, 201, 211, 233, 236, 237, 238
Leiostomus xanthurus - spot, 34, 201, 203, 210, 233, 236, 237

Lepisosteus oculatus - spotted gar, 211, 226, 238
Lepisosteus osseus - longnose gar, 12
Lepomis macrochirus - bluegill, 211
Lepomis megalotis - longear sunfish, 211
Lepomis microlophus - redear sunfish, 149
Lepomis miniatus - red-spotted sunfish, 226
Lepomis sp. - sunfish, 12
Lucania parva - rainwater killifish, 211, 215, 226
Megalops atlantica - tarpon, 39, 84, 202
Menidia beryllina - inland silverside, 201, 210, 211, 226, 237
Microgobius gulosus - clown goby, 215
Micropogonias undulatus - Atlantic croaker, 201, 202, 203, 210, 234, 235, 236, 237, 238
Micropterus punctulatus - spotted bass, 148, 149
Micropterus salmoides - largemouth bass, 116, 148, 149, 202, 211, 238
Micropterus sp. - freshwater bass, 12
Morone mississippiensis - yellow bass, 201, 235, 238
Morone saxatilis - striped bass, 112, 202
Mugil cephalus - striped mullet, 201, 210, 226, 232, 233, 234, 236, 237, 238
Myrophis punctatus - speckled worm eel, 210
Paralichthys lethostigma - southern flounder, 202, 210
Percidae, 248
Pimephales promelas - fathead minnow, 116
Poecilia latipinna - sailfin molly, 211, 225, 226
Poeciliidae, 225, 227
Pogonias cromis - black drum, saltwater drum, 201, 202, 204, 212, 237, 238
Polyodon spathula - paddlefish, 201
Pomoxis annularis - white crappie, 148

TAXONOMIC INDEX **313**

Pylodictus olivaris - flathead catfish, 149, 202, 210
Sciaenidae, 238
Sciaenops ocellatus - red drum, 201, 202, 238
Syngnathus louisianae - chain pipefish, 210
Syngnathus scovelli - Gulf pipefish, 201, 210, 211, 215
Trinectes maculatus - hogchoker, 201, 210, 211, 236, 237

Mammals
Bison bison - American bison, buffalo, 17, 30, 31, 35, 109, 228, 258
Canis familiaris - dog, 12
Castor canadensis - beaver, 12, 35, 112, 246
Dasypus novemcinctus - armadillo, 228
Didelphis virginiana - Virginia opossum, 12, 13, 30, 206, 228, 235
Glaucomys volans - flying squirrels, 245
Lutra canadensis - river otter, 12, 228, 246
Lynx rufus - bobcat, 246
Mustela frenata - long-tailed weasel, 228
Mustela vison - mink, 228, 246
Myocastor coypus - nutria, 97, 105, 114, 115, 224, 227, 228, 246
Odocoileus virginianus - white-tailed deer, 12, 17, 19, 35, 41, 89, 97, 228, 229, 246
Ondatra zibethicus - muskrat, 12, 13, 89, 114, 115, 227, 228
Oryzomys palustris - marsh rice rat, 228
Procyon lotor - raccoon, 12, 13, 228
Puma concolor - puma, cougar, mountain lion, 106, 109
Sciurus carolinensis - gray squirrel, 12, 19, 245
Sciurus niger - fox squirrel, 12, 19
Sus scrofa - pig, 18, 226
Sylvilagus aquaticus - swamp rabbit, 12, 19, 228, 246
Sylvilagus floridanus - eastern cottontail, 12, 19
Trichechus manatus - West Indian manatee, 111, 202
Tursiops truncatus - bottlenose dolphin, 201
Ursus americanus luteolus - Louisiana black bear, 16, 17, 19, 30, 37, 42, 106, 109, 111, 258

Mollusca
Bivalves
Corbicula fluminea - Asian clam, 116, 248
Crassostrea virginica - American oyster, 206, 212
Dreissena polymorpha - zebra mussel, 116
Elliptio crassidens - elephant ear, 248
Glebula rotundata - round pearlshell, 249
Ischadium recurvum - hooked mussel, 213
Lampsilis ornate - southern pocketbook, 248
Lampsilis straminea or *L. claibornensis* - southern fatmucket, 248
Lampsilis teres - yellow sandshell, 248
Leptodea fragilis - fragile papershell, 248
Macoma mitchilli - Mitchill's macoma clam, 206
Mulinia pontchartrainensis - dwarf surf clam, 205, 206
Mytilopsis [=*Congeria*] *leucophaeta* - dark false mussel, 9, 206, 213, 237
Plectomerus dombeyanus - bankclimber, 249
Potamilus inflatus - Inflated heelsplitter mussel, 111, 249
Potamilus purpureus - bleufer, 248
Quadrula quadrula - mapleleaf, 248
Quadrula refulgens - purple pimpleback, 248
Rangia cuneata - Rangia clam, 9, 11, 12,

147, 169, 189, 190, 203, 204, 205, 206, 225, 236, 237
Rangianella (=*Mulinia pontchartrainensis*), 206
Teredo navalis - teredo, or shipworm, 71, 214
Unionidae - freshwater mussels, 17, 35, 91, 248, 249
Villosa lienosa - little spectaclecase, 248
Cephalopods
Loligo pealii - squid, 200
Lolliguncula brevis - squid, 200
Gastropods
hydrobiid snails, 9, 225
Physella gyrina - snail, 225
physid snails, 225
Planorbella or *Helisoma* - snail, 225
Probythinella protera - Hydrobiid snail, 9, 205, 206
Texadina barretti - Hydrobiid snail, 205
Texadina sphinctostoma - Hydrobiid snail, 9, 205, 206
Nematodes, 206, 225, 233, 237
Reptiles
Agkistrodon piscivorus - cottonmouth, 226
Alligator mississippiensis - American alligator, 12, 13, 20, 69, 74, 112, 117, 201, 226, 227, 238
Anolis carolinensis - green anole, 227
Caretta caretta - Loggerhead sea turtle, 111
Chelydra serpentina - common snapping turtle, 12, 226
Coluber constrictor - black-masked racer, 227
Elaphe obsoleta - Texas rat snake, 227
Eumeces fasciatus - five-lined skink, 227
Eumeces laticeps - broad-headed skink, 227

Farancia abacura - mud snake, 226
Gopherus polyphemus - gopher tortoise, 18, 111
Graptemys oculifera - Ringed map turtle, 111
Hemidactylus turcicus - Mediterranean gecko, 117
Kinosternon subrubrum - eastern mud turtle, 226
Lampropeltis getulus - speckled kingsnake, 227
Lepidochelys kempii - Kemp's ridley sea turtle, 111
Macrochelys temmincki - alligator snapping turtle, 226
Nerodia cyclopion - western green water snake, 226
Nerodia erythrogaster - yellow-bellied water snake, 226
Nerodia fasciata - broad-banded water snake, 226
Nerodia rhombifera - diamond-backed water snake, 226
Opheodrys aestivus - rough green snake, 226
Pseudemys floridana - Florida cooter, 215
Regina rigida - delta crayfish snake, 226
Scincella lateralis - ground skink, 227
Sternotherus odoratus - stinkpot, 226
Terrapene carolina - box turtle, 18
Thamnophis proximus - Gulf coast ribbon snake, 226
Trachemys scripta - red-eared slider, 226
Rotifers
Brachionus angularis, 198, 199
Brachionus calyciflorus, 198
Brachionus deitersi, 199
Brachionus havanaensis, 198
Brachionus plicatilis, 198, 199
Conochilus sp., 199
Filinia longiseta, 198
Filinia pejleri, 199

Keratella cochlearis, 199
Keratella gracilenta, 198
Keratella valga, 198
Pedalia fennica, 198
Polyarthra trigla, 198
Sinantherina semibullata, 198
Synchaeta bicornis, 198
Synchaeta cecilia, 198
Synchaeta littoralis, 198
Synchaeta spp., 199
Sponges
   Spongilla alba, 213
   Trochospongilla leidii, 213

BACTERIA

cyanobacteria/bluegreen algae, 142, 187, 197, 231, 232, 233, 238
   Anabaena circinalis, 142, 197
   Anabaena sp., 187, 232, 238
   Lyngbya sp., 197
   Microcystis aeruginosa, 142, 197, 238
   Oscillatoria sp., 197
Enterococcus, 131, 136, 138, 156, 188
Escherichia coli, 131, 135, 156, 188
fecal coliform bacteria, 129, 130, 131, 135, 136, 138, 156, 188
fecal streptococcus, 129, 136
Streptococcus bovis, 136
sulfur bacteria, 233

PLANTS

Angiosperms
   Dicots
      Acacia farnesiana - acacia, 47
      Acer negundo - box elder, 47
      Acer rubrum - red maple, 224, 240, 251, 252, 253
      Acer rubrum var. *drummondii* - swamp red maple, 224, 240, 251
      Albizzia julibrissin - silk tree or mimosa, 251, 255
      Alternanthera philoxeroides - alligator weed, 114, 198, 220, 225, 251
      Amorpha fruticosa - dull-leaf indigo or lead plant, 241
      Ampelopsis arborea - peppervine, 244, 252, 253, 255
      Asimina triloba - pawpaw, 243
      Baccharis halimifolia - groundsel bush, 222, 241, 254
      Bacopa monnieri - coastal water hyssop, 221
      Berchemia scandens - supplejack or rattan vine, 244, 254
      Betula nigra - river birch, 244
      Cabomba caroliniana - fanwort, 214, 224, 248, 249
      Callicarpa americana - beautyberry, 243, 252, 254
      Campsis radicans - trumpet creeper, 245, 255
      Carpinus caroliniana - American hornbeam, 244
      Carya aquatica - water hickory, 244, 251
      Carya illinoensis - pecan, 47, 242, 250
      Carya spp. - hickory, 18, 19, 244
      Carya tomentosa - Mockernut hickory, 252
      Castanea pumila - chinquapin, 20, 251
      Cephalanthus occidentalis - buttonbush, 223, 240, 255
      Ceratophyllum demersum - coontail, 214, 224, 248, 249
      Chaemaecyparis thyoides - white cedar, 34
      Convolvulus repens - marsh bindweed, 223

316 TAXONOMIC INDEX

Cornus drummondii - roughleaf dogwood, 244
Cornus foemina - swamp dogwood, 240
Cyrilla racemiflora - swamp cyrilla or titi, 240, 253
Daubentonia drummondii - rattlebox, 223, 244
Daucus carota - Queen Anne's lace, 117
Desmodium nudiflorum - bare-stem ticktrefoil, 253
Desmodium paniculatum - panicled ticktrefoil, 253
Diodia teres - poor joe, 255
Diodia tetragona (see *Diodia virginiana*)
Diodia virginiana - Virginia buttonweed, 222, 255
Diospyros virginiana - persimmon, 47, 244, 254
Forestiera acuminata - swamp privet, 240
Fraxinus americana - white ash, 244
Fraxinus caroliniana - Carolina ash, 224, 244
Fraxinus excelsior - European ash, 44
Fraxinus pennsylvanica - green ash, 240
Fraxinus profunda - pumpkin ash, 240
Fraxinus tomentosa (see *Fraxinus profunda*)
Gelsemium sempervirens - yellow jessamine, 243, 252, 255
Gleditisia triacanthos - honey-locust, 244
Gleditsia aquatica - water locust, 240
Hibiscus lasiocarpus - marsh mallow, 219, 223
Hydrocotyle spp. - pennywort, 225
Ilex decidua - possumhaw, or deciduous holly, 244
Ilex opaca - American holly, 244, 252, 253
Ilex vomitoria - yaupon, 243, 252, 253
Ipomoea sagittata - marsh morning glory, 222
Itea virginica - Virginia willow, 240, 253
Iva frutescens - marsh elder, 223, 241
Juglans nigra - black walnut, 20, 44
Juglans squamosa (see *Carya* spp.)
Kosteletzkya virginica - saltmarsh mallow, 219, 223
Leucothoe racemosa - sweetbells or leucothoe, 240
Ligustrum japonicum - Japanese privet, 114
Ligustrum sinense - Chinese privet, 114, 251
Liquidamber styraciflua - sweet gum, 44, 47, 224, 242, 250, 252, 254
Liriodendron tulipifera - yellow poplar, 44, 47, 251
Lonicera japonica - Japanese honeysuckle, 114, 251, 254
Ludwigia peploides - floating waterprimrose, 215, 225
Lythrum lanceolatum - winged loosestrife, 256
Lythrum lineare - wand loosestrife, 222
Magnolia grandiflora - magnolia, 44, 242, 250, 253
Magnolia virginiana - sweetbay, 244, 251, 252
Melia azedarach - Chinaberry tree, 251
Micranthemum umbrosum - shade mudflower, 243
Mikania scandens - climbing hempvine, 244
Morella [=*Myrica*] *cerifera* - wax myrtle, 39, 223, 241
Morus alba - white mulberry, 251, 252
Morus rubra - red mulberry, 44, 252, 253
Myriophyllum spicatum - Eurasian watermilfoil, 114, 214, 225, 248

TAXONOMIC INDEX 317

Nuphar lutea advena - yellow waterlily or spatterdock, 214, 224, 248, 256
Nymphaea odorata - white waterlily, 214, 224, 248
Nymphaea sp. - waterlily, 256
Nyssa aquatica - water tupelo, 19, 224, 240, 253
Nyssa sylvatica - black tupelo, black gum, 224, 251, 252
Nyssa sylvatica var. biflora - swamp tupelo, swamp black gum, 251
Persea borbonia - red-bay, 44, 245
Persea palustris - swamp-bay, 244
Phaseolus diversifolius - wild bean, 18
Phyla nodiflora - turkey tangle fogfruit, 222
Planera aquatica - waterelm, 240, 244
Platanus occidentalis - American sycamore, 242, 251
Pluchea camphorata - camphor-weed, 220
Polygonum punctatum - dotted smartweed, 221
Polygonum spp. - smartweed, 220, 221, 245
Populus deltoides - cottonwood, 242
Populus heterophylla - swamp cottonwood, 244
Proserpinaca palustris - marsh mermaid weed, 243
Prunus serotina - wild cherry, 47
Ptilimnium capillaceum - mock bishopsweed, 222
Pueraria montana - kudzu, 114
Quercus aquatica (see *Quercus nigra*)
Quercus falcata - southern red oak, 19, 250
Quercus laurifolia - laurel oak, 240
Quercus lyrata - overcup oak, 47, 244
Quercus marilandica - blackjack oak, 250, 253
Quercus michauxii - basket oak, 244

Quercus nigra - water oak, 18, 47, 243, 251
Quercus pagoda - cherrybark oak, 251
Quercus stellata - post oak, 251, 253, 254
Quercus texana (see *Quercus falcata*)
Quercus tinctoria (see *Quercus nigra*)
Quercus virginiana - live oak, 47, 224, 242, 251, 253
Rhus radicans - poison ivy, 224, 252, 253, 255
Rubus trivialis - dewberry, 224
Rubus spp., 252, 254, 255
Rumex crispus - yellow dock, 19
Salix nigra - black willow, 30, 47, 240, 251
Sambucus canadensis - elderberry, 243, 251, 255
Sassafras albidum - sassafras, 18, 44
Saururus cernuus - lizard's tail, 221, 243, 253
Sesbania herbacea - sicklepod or coffeeweed, 223
Solidago mexicana - seaside goldenrod, 224
Toxicodendron pubescens - Atlantic poison oak, 245
Toxicodendron radicans - eastern poison ivy, 243
Ulmus americana - American elm, 243, 250
Ulmus rubra - slippery elm, 244
Utricularia macrorhiza - common bladderwort, 243
Utricularia spp. - bladderworts, 225
Vigna luteola - deerpea or hairypod cowpea, 218, 220
Vitis spp. - grape, 244
Wisteria macrostachya - wisteria, 251, 255
Monocots
Arundinaria gigantea - Giant cane, switch cane, 19, 47, 126, 242

TAXONOMIC INDEX

Cladium jamaicense - sawgrass, 220, 243
Colocasia esculenta - wild taro, 117, 220
Crinum americanum - swamp lily, 220
Cyperus odoratus - fragrant flatsedge, 220
Distichlis spicata - salt grass, 221
Echinochloa crus-galli - barnyard grass, 222
Echinochloa walteri - walter millet, 220
Eichhornia crassipes - water hyacinth, 73, 114, 198, 225, 248, 249, 251
Eleocharis fallax - creeping spikerush, 222
Eleocharis parvula - dwarf spikerush, 214, 221
Eleocharis spp. - spikesedge or spikerush, 220, 245
Hymenocallis caroliniana - spider lily, 220, 243
Imperata cylindrica - cogon grass, 114
Iris virginica - Louisiana iris or southern blue flag, 218, 220
Juncus roemerianus - black rush, 220
Lemna minor - duckweed, 198, 225
Leptochloa fusca (= *Leptochloa fascicularis*) - bearded sprangletop, 220
Limnobium spongia - frogbit, 214, 225
Najas guadalupensis - southern naiad or bushy pondweed, 214, 224, 248
Oplismenus setarius - oak forest grass or shortleaf basketgrass, 243
Panicum dichotimiflorum - fall panicum, 223
Panicum hemitomon - maiden cane or paille fine, 128, 220
Panicum spp. - panic grasses, 221
Panicum virgatum - switch grass, 220, 245
Paspalum fluitans - water paspalum, 215, 225
Paspalum vaginatum - seashore paspalum, 220
Peltandra virginica - arrow arum, 220
Phalaris angusta - Timothy canary grass, 117
Phragmites australis - common reed, roseau cane, 220
Pistia stratiotes - water lettuce, 114, 198, 249
Pontederia cordata - pickerelweed, 220, 243, 256
Potamogeton perfoliatus - clasping pondweed, 214, 224
Ruppia maritima - widgeon grass, 214, 215, 221
Sabal minor - dwarf palmetto, 18, 47, 223, 241
Sagittaria lancifolia (= *S. falcata*) - bulltongue, lance-leaf arrowhead, or paddleweed, 218, 220, 242
Scirpus americanus (= *S. olneyi*) - common three-cornered grass, 220
Scirpus californicus - giant bulrush, 220
Scirpus maritimus - leafy three-square, 223
Scirpus robustus - salt marsh bulrush, 221
Scirpus tabernaemontani (= *S. validus*) - softstem bulrush, 222
Serenoa repens - saw palmetto, 18
Smilax laurifolia - laurel greenbriar, 18
Smilax spp. - greenbriar, 245
Smilax walteri - coral greenbrier, 243
Spartina alterniflora - saltmarsh cordgrass, 220
Spartina cynosuroides - big cordgrass, 220
Spartina patens - marshhay cordgrass, 167, 220, 234, 243
Spirodela polyrrhiza - duckweed, 198

TAXONOMIC INDEX

Tillandsia usneoides - Spanish moss, 56
Typha augustifolia - narrowleaf cattail, 221
Typha latifolia - broadleaf cattail, 221
Vallisneria americana - water celery or eelgrass, 214
Wolffia columbiana - watermeal, 198
Wolffiella floridana - bogmat, 198, 225
Xanthosoma sagittifolium - elephant ear, 220
Zannichellia palustris - horned pondweed, 214, 224
Zizania aquatica - annual wild rice, 220, 225
Zizaniopsis miliacea - southern wild rice or giant cutgrass, 220

Gymnosperms
Juniperus virginiana - red cedar, 34
Pinus echinata - shortleaf pine, 250, 253
Pinus elliotti - slash pine, 7, 250
Pinus palustris - longleaf pine, 7, 47, 83, 106, 250
Pinus taeda - loblolly pine, 48, 83, 106, 250, 252, 253, 254
Taxodium ascendens - pond cypress, 250
Taxodium distichum - bald cypress, 20, 47, 83, 105, 224, 240, 253

Pteridophytes and Bryophytes
Azolla caroliniana - water fern, 225, 249
Isoetes louisianensis - Louisiana quillwort, 111
Lygodium japonicum - Japanese climbing fern, 114, 251, 254
Osmunda regalis - royal fern, 221, 245
Riccia fluitans - floating liverwort, 225
Salvinia minima - water spangle, 114, 198, 225, 249
Thelypteris palustris - marsh fern, 221, 245

PROTISTA

Charophyceae
  Chara vulgaris - muskgrass, 214
Chlorophyceae (green algae)
  Ankistrodesmus, 197
  Chlamydomonas, 197
  Cladophora, 142, 210, 211, 215
  Eudorina elegans, 198
  Gonium pectorale, 198
  green algae, 142, 197, 231, 232, 233, 238
  Oedogonium, 210, 211
  Pandorina morum, 198
  Phacotus, 197
  Platydorina caudata, 198
  Rhizoclonium, 210, 211
  Sphaerocystis, 197
  Spirogyra, 210
  Volvox tertius, 198
Chrysophyceae (diatoms)
  Biddulphia, 210
  Chaetoceros, 197
  Coscinodiscus, 197
  Cymbella, 210
  diatoms, 185, 186, 196, 197, 204, 210, 231, 232, 233, 235, 239
  Navicula, 210
  Pinnularia, 210
  Terpsinoe, 210
Cryptomonads
  Cryptomonas, 197
Dinoflagellates
  Ceratium furca, 197
  Ceratium fusus, 197
  Peridinium divergens, 197
Foraminifera, 185, 237
  Ammonia beccarii, 207
  Ammotium salsum, 207

www.ingramcontent.com/pod-product-compliance
Lightning Source LLC
Chambersburg PA
CBHW030334240426
43661CB00052B/1626